D1294718

WHITE COLLAR CRIME

IN A NUTSHELL®

FIFTH EDITION

by

ELLEN S. PODGOR
Gary R. Trombley Family White-Collar
Research Professor
Professor of Law
Stetson University College of Law

JEROLD H. ISRAEL
Alene and Allan F. Smith
Professor of Law Emeritus,
University of Michigan Law School
Ed Rood Eminent Scholar Emeritus,
University of Florida,
Fredric G. Levin College of Law

WEST
ACADEMIC
PUBLISHING

Nutshell Series, In a Nutshell and the Nutshell Logo are trademarks registered in the U.S. Patent and Trademark Office.

COPYRIGHT © 1993 WEST PUBLISHING CO.
© West, a Thomson business, 1997, 2004
© 2009 Thomson Reuters
© 2015 LEG, Inc. d/b/a West Academic

      444 Cedar Street, Suite 700
      St. Paul, MN 55101
      1-877-888-1330

West, West Academic Publishing, and West Academic are trademarks of West Publishing Corporation, used under license.

Printed in the United States of America

ISBN: 978-0-314-29153-0

Dedicated to our parents:

Yetta & Benjamin Podgor

Florence & Harry Israel

PREFACE

White collar crime is a relatively new concept, having first achieved recognition in 1939. Despite its short life, white collar crime has quickly grown to its present status of being a major focus of the Department of Justice. This nutshell is intended to provide to students a general overview of this growing area. It is hoped that this book will assist in providing a structure to a basically unstructured body of law.

Because of the general focus of this book, it is not recommended as a source for deciding a specific legal issue. Cases were selected for this book to be illustrative, rather than comprehensive of each area being discussed. Specific crimes were selected to provide a sampling of the wide array of crimes encompassed within this enormous body of law. This book focuses on white collar crime in the federal criminal context, and does not delve into developments at the state and local level. References to one gender includes the other unless the context otherwise indicates.

The second edition added the expertise of Jerold Israel, resulting in its substantial expansion of the coverage of procedural issues that impact white collar crime. The third, fourth, and fifth editions update materials by adding new cases and statutory developments that occurred since the prior editions.

It is important to note that the study of white collar crime is a continuing study, with ever changing rules and precedent. Many of the issues within white collar crime, as noted throughout this book, have yet to be resolved.

Following the fourth edition, the authors of this book, along with Peter J. Henning and Nancy J. King authored the Hornbook on White Collar Crime (2013). Throughout this new edition there are references to the Hornbook and they appear using the letters WCH. Thanks go to those who assisted with this updated fifth edition, specifically Paul Borman, Peter J. Henning, and Nancy J. King.

If you have any questions, you can email us at: israelj@umich.edu and epodgor@law.stetson.edu.

ELLEN S. PODGOR
JEROLD H. ISRAEL

May 2015

OUTLINE

PART 2. SPECIFIC OFFENSES

PART 4. PUNISHMENT

TABLE OF CASES

References are to Pages

WHITE COLLAR CRIME
CRIME
IN A NUTSHELL®

FIFTH EDITION

PART 1
GENERAL PRINCIPLES

CHAPTER 1

SCOPE OF WHITE COLLAR CRIME

§ 1.01   INTRODUCTION

Sociologist Edwin Sutherland is noted for having coined the phrase "White Collar Crime." The term appeared in a speech he gave to the American Sociological Society in 1939. In his speech, Sutherland openly attacked criminologists whose theories considered crime to be a result of poverty or psychopathic and sociopathic conditions. His criticism was in part based upon their failure to consider white collar criminals. Sutherland saw improper business practices of individuals in powerful positions as criminal offenses and not simply civil wrongs. He saw this as a significant issue for society's consideration.

In his book *White Collar Crime*, Sutherland defined the term white collar crime as "crime committed by a person of respectability and high social status in the course of his occupation." His definition concentrated on the offender's social status and occupation, although his focus tended to be more narrowly confined to crimes committed by large corporate enterprises.

Although white collar crime has been subject to varying definitions, a definition that focuses on the offense rather than the offender is prevalent today. In the 1983 Annual Report of the Attorney General, white collar crimes were defined as:

... illegal acts that use deceit and concealment—rather than the application or threat of physical force or violence—to obtain money, property, or service; to avoid the payment or loss of money; or to secure a business or professional advantage. White collar criminals occupy positions of responsibility and trust in government, industry, the professions and civic organizations.

Even when one adopts an offense approach in defining white collar crime, the scope of the term remains uncertain in that there is no list of included and excluded offenses.

Although there are no set categories of offenses that make up white collar crime, there are several federal statutes that continually appear in this context. Some of these federal offenses are not limited solely to white collar crime, but have been used to prosecute street and property crimes as well. These statutes are often used for white collar criminality due to the broad interpretation given to them by the courts. For example, many white collar offenses are prosecuted as mail fraud (18 U.S.C. § 1341), wire fraud (18 U.S.C. § 1343), conspiracy (18 U.S.C. § 371), racketeering (18 U.S.C. §§ 1961–1963), bribery (18 U.S.C. § 201), false statements (18 U.S.C. § 1001), obstruction of justice (18 U.S.C. §§ 1501–1521) and tax crimes (26 U.S.C. §§ 7201–7217). There are other statutes that are used almost exclusively for white collar offenses. For example, criminal acts involving bank fraud (18 U.S.C.

§ 1344) and false claims (18 U.S.C. § 287) usually fit the white collar crime category.

These lists of offenses are by no means exhaustive. White collar crime includes corporate offenses and most offenses involving public corruption. Many white collar crime prosecutions have employed statutes relating to securities fraud and antitrust violations. Encompassed by the term in recent years are criminal acts prohibited by environmental, health, and computer laws.

Although white collar crime is a relatively new concept, it has grown extensively during its short life. Key areas within white collar crime that the Department of Justice has recently focused on are financial institution fraud, defense procurement fraud, health care fraud, computer crime, and international bribery. The Department of Justice has also continued its efforts in combating antitrust violations, public corruption, and money laundering. Some U.S. Attorneys' offices have had an increased focus on insider trading and environmental crimes.

White collar crime, although not a legal concept, is a useful term for administrative purposes. It offers a designation for an area of legal specialization within law firms and prosecution offices.

§ 1.02   SCOPE OF FEDERAL CRIMINAL LAW

Clearly a prosecutor needs a statutory base for prosecuting white collar criminal conduct. In the realm of the federal criminal law system, this conduct can be based on a vast array of statutory offenses. In recent years there has been a growth of statutes added to the federal criminal code that specifically pertain to white collar criminal conduct. This has been noticeable in provisions added to combat financial frauds.

It is necessary that Congress, in enacting these statutes, remain within the bounds of the Constitution. Article I, Section 8 of the United States Constitution sets forth the congressional powers, including provisions that grant Congress postal, taxing, and commerce powers.

Federal criminal law's use of Congress' postal power is best evidenced by the mail fraud statute. (18 U.S.C. § 1341). This pervasive statute has been extensively used in the realm of white collar crime.

The taxing power granted Congress serves as the jurisdictional base for many tax offenses. (26 U.S.C. §§ 7601–7607). Before 1970 it also served to criminalize many drug offenses. Drug statutes today usually employ the commerce powers.

The most widely used jurisdictional base for criminalizing federal offenses is the commerce power. The Constitution of the United States gives Congress the power "to regulate Commerce with Foreign Nations, and among the several States, and with the Indian Tribes." "Congress may regulate the use of the channels of interstate commerce," "regulate and protect the instrumentalities of interstate commerce, or persons or things in interstate commerce, even though the threat may come only from intrastate activities," and "regulate those activities having a substantial relation to interstate commerce, i.e., those activities that substantially affect interstate commerce." *U.S. v. Lopez*, 514 U.S. 549 (1995).

Many federal statutes used in the prosecution of white collar crime employ the commerce clause as the jurisdictional basis. For example, wire fraud (18 U.S.C. § 1343) requires interstate commerce. A racketeering prosecution requires an "enterprise which is engaged in, or the activities of which affect, interstate or foreign commerce." (18 U.S.C. § 1962). Likewise, the Hobbs Act requires that the robbery or extortion affect commerce.

The conduct itself, under certain federal criminal statutes, can be purely local and yet be prosecuted as a federal offense. These local activities are part of a class of activities that Congress determines warrants congressional intervention because of their impact on commerce. In *Perez v. U.S.*, 402 U.S. 146 (1971) the Supreme Court affirmed a conviction under the Consumer Credit Protection Act. (18 U.S.C. § 891 et seq.). The Court found that although petitioner's loan sharking may have been intrastate, he was a member of a class that engaged in "extortionate credit transactions" that affected commerce. The Court found that "loan sharking in its national setting is one way organized crime holds its guns to the heads of the poor and the rich alike and syphons funds from numerous localities to finance its national operations."

Most federal criminal statutes using the commerce clause as its jurisdictional base predicate the action on direct transportation in interstate commerce or conduct that actually affects interstate commerce. In *U.S. v. Lopez* the Supreme Court held that the Gun-Free School Zone Act, prohibiting possession of a weapon in the vicinity of a school, exceeded Congress' Commerce Clause authority in that it involved intrastate activity not involved in commerce and not economic activity. Likewise, in *U.S. v. Morrison*, 529 U.S. 598 (2000), the Court held that a provision of the Violence Against Women Act of 1994 failed to contain a jurisdictional element premised on the commerce clause. The Court stated, "[t]he regulation of punishment of intrastate violence that is not directed at the instrumentalities, channels, or goods involved in interstate commerce has always been the province of the States." See WCH § 1.7.

§ 1.03   STATE AND/OR FEDERAL PROSECUTION

Less than two percent of the criminal prosecutions brought in the United States are in the federal system. Prosecutions against white collar crimes are, likewise, not limited to the federal system in that many state statutes focus on conduct that meets accepted definitions of white collar crime. The same white collar criminal offenses often can be prosecuted by both the federal and state systems. For example, the RICO statute uses nine state crimes as predicates for a racketeering charge.

(18 U.S.C. § 1961). These predicate acts can be prosecuted as state crimes.

When criminal conduct fits the definition of both the federal and state jurisdictions a joint decision is often made as to which body will proceed with the prosecution. Factors considered in choosing the jurisdiction may include the available investigative and prosecutorial resources, the jurisdiction with the law that best supports the government, the location with the maximum possible penalty and the place where the criminality best fits the policy priorities of that jurisdiction. Efficiency factors such as the jurisdiction with greater expertise and experience, the better ability to handle the case within their caseload and present location of the suspects can play a part in determining who will proceed with the action. In many instances the conduct is subject to state prosecution but has been ignored by the state prosecutor or local police for political reasons. The use of the federal system in these instances offers a neutral forum for proceeding. In some instances the state attorney general, as well as a local state prosecutor may be investigating and proceeding against alleged illegal conduct.

Under the dual sovereignty rule, there is no restriction to both the state and federal jurisdiction prosecuting the defendant for what is basically the same conduct. Because the state and federal governments are separate entities each may determine its own offenses. *U.S. v. Lanza*, 260 U.S. 377 (1922). Some states, however, by statute or case law prohibit a state prosecution following a federal trial. Additionally, some federal statutes prohibit a federal prosecution when the same act or acts previously resulted in a conviction or acquittal on the merits under state law. For example, the federal statute that criminalizes certain acts involving the interstate or foreign shipments by carrier, expressly prohibits a federal prosecution under the statute where there has been a conviction or acquittal on the merits under the laws of any state. (18 U.S.C. § 659).

Often the issue of dual prosecution is resolved by examination of the policies of the respective government prosecutors. For example, the Department of Justice has a policy against duplicative federal and state prosecutions. Known as the *Petite* policy, it "precludes the initiation or continuation of a federal prosecution, following a prior state or federal prosecution based on substantially the same act(s) or transaction(s), unless:" the matter involves a "substantial federal interest," the prior prosecution left the interest "demonstrably unvindicated," and the "defendant(s)' conduct constitutes a federal offense" with admissible evidence "sufficient to obtain and sustain a conviction." The prosecution must also "be approved by the appropriate Assistant Attorney General." Where the government fails to abide by the *Petite* policy, cases have found that there is no legal basis for overturning the defendant's conviction. *Haley v. U.S.*, 394 F.Supp. 1022 (W.D.Mo. 1975).

Besides overlapping prosecutions within the federal and state system, white collar offenses often find themselves the subject of parallel proceedings in regulatory bodies and civil courts. Procedural questions related to collateral estoppel, staying of proceedings, effect upon fifth amendment rights, and use of grand jury materials are questions that have merited resolution in this context (see chap. 18).

§ 1.04   FEDERAL INFLUENCE IN INTERNATIONAL PROSECUTIONS

Federal prosecutions may also be premised upon conduct occurring outside the United States. In some instances the federal statute will specifically contain a provision providing for extraterritoriality. (18 U.S.C. § 1512). Other instances require courts to ascertain whether an extraterritorial application should be permitted. *U.S. v. Bowman*, 260 U.S. 94 (1922). In *Morrison v. National Australia Bank LTD*, 561 U.S. 247 (2010), the Court held in a civil action that § 10(b) of the Securities Exchange Act's silence on extraterritoriality limited the statute's application to the territorial jurisdiction of the United States. See WCH § 1.7(D).

Several courts have allowed white collar prosecutions where the conduct occurred outside the United States. For example, in *U.S. v. Nippon Paper Industries Co., Ltd.*, 109 F.3d 1 (1st Cir.1997), the First Circuit held that as with civil antitrust actions involving extraterritorial conduct, criminal antitrust actions could be predicated "on wholly foreign conduct which has an intended and substantial effect in the United States."

Further, some federal statutes are specifically focused on conduct occurring outside the United States. For example, the Foreign Corrupt Practices Act (FCPA) was implemented to combat bribery of foreign officials by United States companies (see § 7.01).

In *U.S. v. Castle*, 925 F.2d 831 (5th Cir.1991), the Fifth Circuit held that since "foreign officials" were excluded from prosecution under the FCPA, the United States government could not prosecute foreign officials "under 18 U.S.C. § 371, for conspiracy to violate the FCPA." The court noted the "legislative policy to leave unpunished a well-defined group of persons [foreign officials] who were necessary parties to the acts constituting a violation of the substantive law." "Most likely Congress made this choice because United States businesses were perceived to be the aggressors and the efforts expended in resolving the diplomatic, jurisdictional, and enforcement difficulties that would arise upon the prosecution of foreign officials was not worth the minimal deterrent value of such prosecutions." The court also noted that "many foreign nations already prohibited the receipt of a bribe by an official."

§ 1.05 APPLICATION OF GENERAL PRINCIPLES OF CRIMINAL LAW

White collar crimes, like other crimes, are subject to general principles of criminal law. These principles emanate from the United States

Constitution, federal and state statutes, and court interpretations. They are affected in some instances by the procedures provided by administrative regulations and rulings. Although there is no specific principle that is altered when applied in the white collar crime setting, there are certain statutory principles and criminal defenses that routinely appear and others that are seldom dominating forces. For example, one occasionally sees an entrapment defense in a white collar crime case. It is rare, however, to see an insanity defense.

General principles relative to actus reus, mens rea, and causation are placed in the perspective of the specific federal statute as it is examined within this book. For example, discussed in the context of a specific statute are common defense arguments in white collar cases, such as reliance on a lawyer's advice or lack of knowledge of an illegality. Whether the accused was willfully blind to the criminal conduct is an issue that can also arise in a white collar case. For example, a CEO may argue that he or she did not know the criminal conduct was occurring within the company. In *Global Tech Appliances, Inc. v. SEB S.A.*, 131 S.Ct. 2060 (2011), the Court held that mere recklessness or negligence were insufficient for willful blindness. The Court stated that willful blindness required a showing that (1) "the defendant must subjectively believe that there is a high probability that a fact exists;" and (2) "the defendant must take deliberate actions to avoid learning of that fact."

Many of the statutes used in white collar cases include attempts to commit the offense within the statutory terms. Additionally, conspiracy is discussed (18 U.S.C. § 371) as both a separate federal offense premised on a conspiracy to defraud the United States and as it relates to other statutes as a conspiracy to commit any offense against the United States. Punishment of white collar offenders and the role of federal sentencing guidelines, provides unique considerations that merit separate examination.

In addition to the general adoption of criminal law principles relative to white collar offenses, it is also important to note that federal law includes general provisions regarding principals and accessories. In 18 U.S.C. § 2 a principal is defined as one who "commits an offense against the United States or aids, abets, counsels, commands, induces or procures its commission." A second provision of this same statute incorporates the agency theory that one is a principal if they willfully cause an act to be done that if performed by that person or another would be a criminal offense.

Accessories after the fact are the subject of a separate federal statute. 18 U.S.C. § 3 criminalizes and defines accessories after the fact and also provides a lesser penalty for the accessory then would be received by the principal. The application of these provisions appears to be no different in the context of white collar crimes then with other types of crime.

§ 1.06   DEFENSES

Defenses available to white collar defendants are, likewise, no different from those available to the nonwhite collar defendants. Limitations to responsibility premised upon infancy, insanity, or intoxication have equal applicability in white collar crime cases as in other types of crime. Principles relating to duress and necessity remain unmodified when applied to white collar offenses. Defenses such as alibi, self defense, or defense of property, although available, seldom constitute an issue in the white collar case.

More prominent in white collar cases is the entrapment defense. Entrapment arises from individual instances of the government enticing a defendant to commit acts of criminality as well as elaborate government sting operations that attempt to net central figures and groups of individuals engaged in criminal activity.

For the last several decades, differing views have appeared in the law as to whether entrapment should be judged from an objective or subjective perspective. The objective view concentrated on the government conduct while the subjective view looked to the defendant's predisposition to commit the offense. The majority view today adopts a test that is predominantly a subjective approach. This view has been adhered to in federal courts.

"Where the Government has induced an individual to break the law and the defense of entrapment is at issue, . . ., the prosecution must prove beyond reasonable doubt that the defendant was disposed to commit the criminal act prior to first being approached by Government agents." *Jacobson v. U.S.*, 503 U.S. 540 (1992). Government officials may not originate a criminal design, "implant in the mind of an innocent person the disposition to commit the alleged offense and induce its commission in order that they may prosecute." *Sorrells v. U.S.*, 287 U.S. 435 (1932).

Entrapment first requires a showing of government inducement. A private party, unrelated to the government, who induces the defendant does not provide a basis for invoking an entrapment defense. Where defendants were convicted of conspiracy for knowingly transporting stolen shirts in interstate commerce, an entrapment defense was properly denied where the alleged entrapment was by a shirt manufacturer who used private investigators to locate the individuals suspected of taking the shirts. The Fifth Circuit held that "entrapment does not extend to inducement by private citizens." *U.S. v. Maddox*, 492 F.2d 104 (5th Cir.1974).

In addition to government inducement, entrapment requires a lack of predisposition by the defendant to engage in criminal conduct. Recently, in reversing a conviction for an alleged violation of the Child Protection Act (18 U.S.C. § 2252), the Supreme Court in *Jacobson v. U.S.* stated that "[w]hen the Government's quest for convictions leads to the apprehension of an otherwise law-abiding citizen who, if left to his own devices, likely would have never run afoul of the law, the courts should intervene."

There is no requirement in federal criminal law that a defendant admit all the elements of the crime in order to proceed with an entrapment defense. Where the facts support an entrapment defense, an instruction on entrapment should be submitted to the jury, despite inconsistent defenses being offered by the defendant. *Mathews v. U.S.*, 485 U.S. 58 (1988).

In *Mathews*, an employee of the Small Business Administration (SBA) was convicted of accepting a gratuity in exchange for an official act. (18 U.S.C. § 201(g)). The defendant was alleged to have accepted loans in return for cooperation in SBA matters. The district court refused defendant's request for an entrapment jury instruction finding that the instruction should not be given where the defendant failed to admit the elements of the offense. The Supreme Court reversed and remanded this case, noting the permissibility of inconsistent defenses but also finding it necessary for the lower court to consider whether there was sufficient evidence to support the giving of an entrapment instruction.

The use, although unsuccessfully, of the entrapment defense in the context of white collar crime prosecutions is seen in examining cases resulting from Operation Abscam. One such case is *U.S. v. Williams*, 705 F.2d 603 (2d Cir.1983).

In *Williams*, Senator Harrison Williams was convicted of charges, including bribery, as part of Operation Abscam. His defense was based alternatively upon no crime being committed and entrapment. On appeal the Second Circuit rejected defendant's argument that there was insufficient evidence to support the jury's conclusion that the defendant was predisposed to commit the crime. The Senator had argued that he initially rejected the criminal conduct and that it was performed as a result of the government's persistence "in persuading [him] to commit the crimes that [he was] not ready and willing to commit." Although the court in *Williams* found strong evidence of government persuasion, it likewise found that the totality of the evidence provided a sufficient basis for the jury's finding that the defendant was " 'ready and willing' to commit the crimes charged as soon as the opportunity was first presented."

In *Williams* the defendant also argued that the "government's agents in developing the case against them exceeded an outer limit of fairness mandated by the Due Process Clause." Outrageous government conduct differs from an entrapment defense in that the focus of a claim is on the government's improper conduct as opposed to whether the defendant is predisposed to commit the offense. In examining a claim of outrageous government conduct one looks at the government conduct to decide whether there is a constitutional due process violation. In *Williams* the Second Circuit rejected this claim as it had in other Abscam cases. Despite the enormity of the inducement offered Senator Williams, the court did not consider it "unconstitutional when offered to a person with the experience and sophistication of a United States Senator."

CHAPTER 2

CORPORATE CRIMINAL LIABILITY

§ 2.01 OVERVIEW OF CORPORATE CRIMINAL LIABILITY

The initial common law view was that a corporation could not be held criminally liable, although the individual members of the corporation could. Lacking a mind, the corporation could not form the mens rea necessary for criminality. Not having physical attributes, there was no actus reus. Additionally, even if convicted of an offense, the corporation could not be imprisoned for the crime.

The development toward corporate criminal liability emerged in response to corporate violations involving acts of omission with respect to regulatory nuisance type offenses. Since these strict liability offenses did not require a mens rea, lacked an affirmative act, and had punishment in the form of fines, the acceptance of corporate criminal liability for these crimes was in keeping with accepted doctrine.

The barriers to corporate criminal liability further disintegrated by the extension of criminality to acts of misfeasance. Although still applicable only to the strict liability offenses, courts found no rationale for differentiating between acts of nonfeasance and those of misfeasance.

Eventually, corporate criminal liability expanded beyond the strict liability arena and grew to encompass crimes with an intent element. Pivotal in this development of corporate criminal liability was the Supreme Court's ruling in *New York Central & Hudson River Railroad Co. v. U.S.*, 212 U.S. 481 (1909).

In *New York Central*, the railroad company and its assistant traffic manager were convicted for violations of the Elkins Act. The Elkins Act prohibited a person or corporation from granting or receiving rebates with respect to the transportation of property in interstate commerce by common carrier. The act was not limited to conduct amounting to an omission, but included affirmative acts by "any director or officer thereof, or any receiver, trustee, lessee, agent or person acting for or employed by such corporation." Defendants were accused of paying rebates to companies shipping sugar as well as to the consignees of the sugar. The corporate defendant questioned the constitutionality of subjecting a corporation to criminal prosecution, alleging a violation of the Due Process Clause. The corporation argued that punishing a corporation would in effect be punishing innocent stockholders. Since the corporation's board of directors and stockholders could not authorize an illegal act, the corporation could not be found criminally liable. The corporation also argued that the statute deprived the corporation of the due process right to a presumption of innocence.

In affirming the applicability of the Elkins Act to a corporation, the Supreme Court authorized prosecutions against corporations for certain specific intent crimes. The Court employed a tort theory of liability and applied it in this criminal context, finding that acts of an agent, done for the benefit of the principal and within the scope of the employment, are imputed to the principal. To effectuate a public policy, the Court determined it was proper, with respect to the Elkins Act, that the corporation could be "held responsible for and charged with the knowledge and purposes of their agents, acting within the authority conferred upon them."

Although *New York Central* provides a firm basis in the law for finding a corporation guilty of an offense with an intent element, there has been significant criticism of corporate criminal liability. Critics question whether there is any deterrent effect in punishing a corporation and whether the innocent shareholders and eventual consumers will, in fact, bear the ultimate cost. Despite this criticism, it is apparent that corporate criminal liability is an accepted and growing body of law. In *Citizens United v. Federal Election Commission*, 558 U.S. 310 (2010), the Court in a case focused on campaign finance law and election law, held that "political speech does not lose First Amendment protection 'simply because its source is a corporation.'"

Legislatures do not always limit corporate criminal liability to property offenses. Crimes "against the person" have been successfully prosecuted. For example, in *Granite Construction Co. v. Superior Court of Fresno County*, 149 Cal.App.3d 465 (Cal.App.1983), a California

Appellate Court permitted a corporation to be prosecuted for manslaughter. The court chose to uphold the legislative language found in the California Penal Code, which defined "person" to include corporations. The court noted that "[i]f corporations are liable for crimes of specific intent, then they should be equally liable for crimes of negligence or recklessness."

Although corporate criminal liability has been extended to a vast array of criminal offenses, some jurisdictions have refused to extend liability to corporations for acts, like manslaughter, that are against the person. The statutory language defining the crime, as relating to human beings only, has been the determining factor for rejecting corporate criminal liability. Most courts, however, interpret the term "person" to include corporations. For example, in *State v. Richard Knutson, Inc.*, 537 N.W.2d 203 (Wis.Ct.App.1995), the Wisconsin Court of Appeals found that a corporation could be prosecuted for negligent homicide by vehicle in that it was "within the class of perpetrators covered by the statute."

Corporate criminal liability has played a significant role in the prosecution of environmental crimes (see chap. 14). Corporations can also be prosecuted for workplace deaths resulting from a willful disregard of an Occupational Health and Safety Administration (OSHA) standard. A full appreciation of corporate criminal liability must also take into account the federal sentencing guidelines. (see § 24.07).

§ 2.02   STANDARDS OF IMPUTING CORPORATE CRIMINAL LIABILITY

The criminal liability of a corporation is predicated upon acts or omissions of its agents. Two standards have developed as to when liability should be imputed to the corporation. These can best be expressed by reference to the Model Penal Code and the common law doctrine of respondeat superior.

Section 2.07 of the Model Penal Code offers a somewhat restrictive approach to corporate criminal liability. Corporate liability under the Model Penal Code can only be found in one of three ways: (1) for violations (minor offenses not classified as crimes that are punishable by fine only) or offenses defined by statute outside the criminal code where the legislature has clearly imposed liability on the corporation "and the conduct is performed by an agent acting in behalf of the corporation within the scope of his office or employment;" (2) where there is an omission of a specific duty of affirmative performance imposed on corporations by law; or (3) where the offense was authorized, performed, or recklessly tolerated by the board of directors or by a high managerial agent acting in behalf of the corporation within the scope of employment.

Although this code provision restricts liability to three categories, it does not limit the criminal liability exclusively to corporations. Rather, it extends its realm to unincorporated associations. An association can be liable when there is a "specific duty of affirmative performance imposed on associations by law," or the offense is defined by statute outside the criminal code and the legislature has clearly imposed liability on the association, "and the conduct is performed by an agent of the association acting in behalf of the association within the scope of his office or employment." The exception to finding liability in this circumstance, for both the corporation and unincorporated association, is where the legislature has designated an accountable agent or has specified the circumstances of accountability. In these latter instances the legislature's designation will control.

While the Model Penal Code restricts corporate criminal liability to three categories and provides deference only to clear legislative language for liability, it also assumes the imputation of liability to the corporation where the offense is a strict liability prohibition. Absent a clear legislative intent to reject strict liability to the corporation, offenses of this nature will be assumed to apply to corporations.

The Model Penal Code addresses individual liability for the conduct of corporate agents acting on behalf of the corporation (see § 2.05). It also provides a defense to the corporation where, absent a contrary legislative purpose, there is proof "by a preponderance of the evidence that the high managerial agent having supervisory responsibility over the subject matter of the offense employed due diligence to prevent its commission."

States that have incorporated a Model Penal Code-type provision within their statutes have experienced controversies on a variety of issues. For example, in *State v. Shepherd Construction Co.*, 281 S.E.2d 151 (Ga.1981), the corporate defendant was charged with a violation of a Georgia statute that prohibited conspiracies "in restraint of free and open competition in transactions with the State." The corporation argued that the statutory provision under which they were charged only provided for imprisonment. Since a corporation was incapable of being imprisoned, the defendant argued, the legislature did not intend to include corporations.

The Georgia Supreme Court, in rejecting this argument in the *Shepherd* case, noted that the state code defined "person" to include corporations and also provided courts with the power to suspend a prison sentence and impose a fine of up to ten thousand dollars. By reading the conspiracy statute in light of existing definition sections of the state code, the court determined that it was in keeping with legislative intent to prosecute corporations for violations of this statute.

A forceful dissent in *Shepherd* by Justice Smith objected to the majority's finding of a legislative intent based upon these facts. Although supportive of corporate criminal liability, this dissent stated, "the determination that corporations are to be held accountable is for the legislature."

The Model Penal Code's application of corporate criminal liability when the offense is committed, authorized, or recklessly tolerated by "a high managerial agent acting in behalf of the corporation within the scope of his office or employment," raises questions as to (1) who is a "high managerial agent," and (2) when is that individual acting in behalf of the corporation. Although "high managerial agent" is defined in the Model Penal Code, the definition is far from being a bright line determinant. The definition provides that the agent is one "having duties of such responsibility that his conduct may fairly be assumed to represent the policy of the corporation or association."

One court refused to find a corporation liable for the acts of its managers and employees where there was no finding of complicity by the officers or directors of the corporation. In order to assess liability against the corporation, it was necessary to have evidence of criminal intent. Evidence of intent is apparent when the crime results from direct authorization of the board of directors. Where, however, the criminal act is committed by an employee and no authorization or knowledge by the corporation is presented, the criminal intent element of the statute is not met. Despite the fact that the manager handled the operations of the automobile dealership, the court found that the corporation was not subject to liability in that the president had no real knowledge and control of the day-to-day business operations. The dealership in this case was owned by a corporation that was the subsidiary of another corporation which in turn was owned by the president. *State v. Chapman Dodge Center, Inc.*, 428 So.2d 413 (La.1983).

Another court found corporate criminal liability for conduct involving a rebate scheme in an automobile dealership where the individual directly accused of having committed the criminal acts was a salesperson and fleet manager. The Minnesota Supreme Court, finding corporate criminal liability, noted that the individual "was acting in furtherance of the corporation's business interests." The corporation, and not the individual, would be receiving the benefit of the rebate. This coupled with participation by a corporate officer and acknowledgement of the problem by the president, provided sufficient evidence to support finding the corporation criminally liable. *State v. Christy Pontiac-GMC, Inc.*, 354 N.W.2d 17 (Minn.1984).

Federal courts apply the common law rule of respondeat superior in assessing whether it is proper to impute the acts of an agent to the corporation. In contrast to the Model Penal Code, which concentrates on whether the individual who committed the acts is a "high managerial agent," a court employing respondeat superior would only examine whether the agent was acting within the scope of his or her authority and on behalf of the corporation. The doctrine of respondeat superior therefore does not limit corporate criminal liability to the upper echelon of the corporation, but rather permits liability to be found when the criminal actions are the result of any employee acting within the scope of employment in behalf of the corporation.

In *Commonwealth v. Beneficial Finance Co.*, 275 N.E.2d 33 (Mass.1971), the Massachusetts Supreme Court was presented with the question of whether the Model Penal Code or a trial court's jury instructions correctly reflected the law in that jurisdiction. The corporate defendants argued that acts of a "high managerial agent" were required for imposing criminal liability on the corporation. In contrast, the Commonwealth argued for the trial court's standard that stated, "[i]t isn't the name of the office that counts, but it's the position in which the corporation placed that person with relation to its business, with regard to the powers and duties and responsibilities and authority which it gave to him which counts." The court's instructions concentrated on whether the "acts and the intent of the individuals were the acts and intent of the corporation."

The Massachusetts Supreme Court adopted the trial court's view that a standard similar to the rule of respondeat superior should be employed. "The Commonwealth must prove that the individual for whose conduct it seeks to charge the corporation criminally was placed in a position by the corporation where he had enough power, duty, responsibility and authority to act for and in behalf of the corporation to handle the particular business or operation or project of the corporation in which he was engaged at the time that he committed the criminal act, with power of decision as to what he would or would not do while acting for the corporation, and that he was acting for and in behalf of the corporation in the accomplishment of that particular business or operation or project, and that he committed a criminal act while so acting." This approach to corporate criminal liability seemed more appropriate to the court in light of the evidentiary deficiencies of the Model Penal Code approach.

Use of both the Model Penal Code and respondeat superior standards raise the issue as to when an agent is acting on behalf of a corporation. According to the Fifth Circuit, corporate criminal liability requires that the conduct be for the benefit of the corporation. It does not, however, mandate that the corporation actually receive a benefit. In *Standard Oil Co. of Texas v. U.S.*, 307 F.2d 120 (5th Cir.1962), the Fifth Circuit reversed convictions where the statute required the conduct to be a knowing violation. Since the individuals from whom the government was imputing knowledge to the corporation were acting to further their own criminal enterprise and not the corporations, the court found it improper to hold the corporation liable. The court stated, "[u]nder a statute requiring that there be 'a specific wrongful intent,' . . . the corporation does not acquire that knowledge or possess the requisite 'state of mind essential for responsibility' through the activities of unfaithful servants whose conduct was undertaken to advance the interests of parties other than their corporate employer." Other jurisdictions have ruled in accord with this Fifth Circuit view.

The issue of when an agent is acting on behalf of a corporation is further complicated when the agent acts directly against orders given by the corporation. Courts have liberally interpreted the phrase "acting on behalf of a corporation," finding liability despite the action being contrary to a corporation's instructions. Where the offense is a regulatory nuisance offense, such as a prohibition against throwing garbage from a ship into navigable waters, the corporation can be held liable despite the fact that personnel were told not to engage in these acts. *The President Coolidge (Dollar Steamship Co. v. U.S.)*, 101 F.2d 638 (9th Cir.1939).

In *U.S. v. Hilton Hotels Corp.*, 467 F.2d 1000 (9th Cir.1972), the Ninth Circuit concluded "that as a general rule a corporation is liable under the Sherman Act for the acts of its agents in the scope of their employment, even though contrary to general corporate policy and express instructions to the agent." The *Hilton* case involved a purchasing agent who participated in a boycott by threatening a supplier with loss of the hotel's business if the supplier refused to pay a fee to an association organized to attract conventions to the city. The agent's conduct was in direct opposition to corporate policy and instructions. The court, in imputing liability to the corporation, noted that agents are pressured to maximize profits for a corporation and that violations of the Sherman Act result in profit to the corporation and not the individual. The court also stressed the difficulty the government would have in identifying the particular agent responsible for the violation. The court believed that punishment of the agent would not likely be a deterrent, while punishment of the corporation would be an effective deterrent.

§ 2.03   COLLECTIVE KNOWLEDGE

Where corporate criminal liability was once applicable only to strict liability offenses, as noted in the *New York Central* case, it now can apply to offenses with an intent element. As a result of this extension, the issue has arisen as to what level of culpability is required for corporate liability. Where an individual agent possesses sufficient intent, the issue becomes whether that agent's knowledge can be imputed to the corporation. As noted, the resolution of this question may depend upon whether the jurisdiction applies a respondeat superior rule or adopts a Model Penal Code approach. In the context of respondeat superior, courts have also considered where no one corporate agent possesses the necessary intent, but rather the intent is formed as a result of collective knowledge.

In *U.S. v. Bank of New England, N.A.*, 821 F.2d 844 (1st Cir.1987) the First Circuit examined the propriety of jury instructions that permitted the imputation of knowledge to the corporation by use of collective knowledge. The Bank of New England was convicted of thirty-one violations of the Currency Transaction Reporting Act in failing to report transactions in excess of ten thousand dollars by a customer who used multiple checks that were each under ten thousand dollars. The customer had presented these checks to a single bank teller. One of several arguments raised on appeal contested the trial court's instructions to the jury on "willfulness," which here requires knowledge of the reporting requirements.

The trial court had instructed the jury that it could "look at the bank as an institution." Its knowledge, the district court stated, "is the sum of the knowledge of all of the employees." In finding these instructions proper, the First Circuit noted that a collective knowledge instruction is appropriate when applied in the context of corporate criminal liability. The court stated, "[c]orporations compartmentalize knowledge, subdividing the elements of specific duties and operations into smaller components." One department or individual may be unaware of the operations of another unit of the corporation. The court noted that "[s]ince the Bank had the compartmentalized structure common to all large corporations, the court's collective knowledge instruction was not only proper but necessary."

§ 2.04　CHARGING CORPORATIONS

Prosecutors have enormous, although not "unfettered," discretion in deciding who to charge and for what crimes. They cannot exceed the scope of the law, but often in white collar cases they can select to proceed criminally, civilly, or decline prosecution. A President's Corporate Fraud Task Force was established in 2002 "in response to a number of high-profile acts of fraud and dishonesty" within corporations. In 2009 it was renamed the Financial Fraud Enforcement Task Force with a focus on financial institution fraud. See WCH § 2.1(F).

The Department of Justice provides policy as to when it is appropriate to charge a corporation, although the policy has fluctuated under different Attorney Generals' administration. The policy statements provide U.S. Attorneys with a list of factors to be considered in deciding whether to proceed with a criminal prosecution. For example, "pervasiveness of wrongdoing," "the corporation's past history," and "cooperation and voluntary disclosure" are some of the factors to be examined in deciding whether to prosecute a corporation. See WCH § 2.4(A). A corporation's compliance program is a consideration in both charging and sentencing a corporation. See chap. 24.7.

Charging a corporation can have enormous consequences. For example, the government charged Arthur Andersen, LL.P, a then-major accounting firm, with obstructing justice for its alleged destruction of documents related to the Enron Corporation. Although the Supreme Court reversed the conviction, the company went out of business and did not revive when the conviction was reversed. *U.S. v. Andersen, LLP.*, 544 U.S. 696 (2005) (see chap. 6).

In an effort to avoid prosecution and the consequences of a criminal charge, corporations often cooperate with the government. Often they conduct internal investigations to ascertain criminal conduct within the entity. They typically will then reach a non-prosecution or deferred prosecution agreement that may include a substantial fine and allow for monitoring by the government. The monitor may provide oversight to assure that the company has an effective compliance program and that there are no further violations of law.

Deferred prosecution agreements proved controversial when the corporation was asked to waive its attorney-client privilege, not pay attorney fees for employees or provide information of employee misconduct to the government. In *U.S. v. Stein*, 541 F.3d 130 (2d Cir.2008), the Second Circuit considered whether government pressure had influenced a company, KPMG, from paying the attorney fees of indicted employees. The court highlighted the complexity of this white collar case and noted that the "[d]efendants were indicted based on a fairly novel theory of criminal liability; they faced substantial penalties; [and] the relevant facts [were] scattered throughout over 22 million documents." This complexity, as well as the number of documents, would result in an exceptional legal expense which made reimbursement important. The court found "that KPMG's adoption and enforcement of a policy under which it conditioned, capped and ultimately ceased advancing legal fees to defendants followed as a direct consequence of the government's overwhelming influence, and that KPMG's conduct therefore amounted to state action." The Second Circuit upheld the dismissal of some of the indictments, finding that it was a Sixth Amendment violation for the government to interfere "with defendants' relationship with counsel and their ability to mount a defense." See chap. 22.9.

Current DOJ policy provides that "prosecutors should not take into account whether a corporation is advancing or reimbursing attorneys' fees or providing counsel to employees, officers, or directors under investigation or indictment." See WCH § 2.4(A). Likewise, waiving the attorney-client privilege and work product protections are not a prerequisite for being viewed as cooperative with the government.

§ 2.05   DEAD CORPORATIONS

Dissolved corporations can be the subject of a criminal prosecution when a state provides for the continuation of the entity after dissolution. In *Melrose Distillers, Inc. v. U.S.*, 359 U.S. 271 (1959), the Supreme Court permitted a criminal action against a corporation that had dissolved. The Court predicated its decision on the fact that the applicable state statutes of Maryland and Delaware continued the corporations to make them "existing" corporations for the purposes of section eight of the Sherman Act. The Court stated, "[i]n this situation there is no more reason for allowing them to escape criminal penalties than damages in civil suits." The *Melrose* case has been used by courts to extend liability to defunct corporations when the specific statute involved contains a survival clause or permits the corporation to exist for a purpose.

Cases have also applied criminal liability to corporations despite a merger. For example, a bank was found criminally liable for failing to file currency transaction reports despite its merger with another bank. The court stated that the bank could not escape punishment by merging with another bank and assuming that bank's "corporate persona." *U.S. v. Alamo Bank of Texas*, 880 F.2d 828 (5th Cir.1989).

§ 2.06   NON-CORPORATE ENTITY LIABILITY

Courts have not limited entity liability exclusively to the corporate body. In *U.S. v. A & P Trucking Co.*, 358 U.S. 121 (1958), the Supreme Court reversed the dismissal of informations charging a partnership with violations of Interstate Commerce Commission regulations and the Motor Carrier Act. The Court noted that the Motor Carrier Act defined "person" to include partnerships. The Interstate Commerce Commission regulation used the term "whoever," which the Court considered defined by the "Rules of Construction" definition of "person." (1 U.S.C. § 1). The Court stated that "it certainly makes no difference whether the carrier which commits the infraction is organized as a corporation, a joint stock company, a partnership, or an individual proprietorship. The mischief is the same, and we think that Congress intended to make the consequences of infraction the same." Thus, despite language of "knowingly and willfully" in the regulations, the Court held that partnerships can be prosecuted for violations of these statutes.

Partnership liability can include a law partnership for crimes of fraud even though only one partner might "be involved in the alleged crimes." A New York state court held that "[n]ot only do law partners, as any partners, benefit financially from the fruits of one partner's fraudulent conduct committed in the name of the firm, but there is a strong public interest in regulating the ethics of the legal profession." *People v. Lessoff & Berger*, 608 N.Y.S.2d 54 (N.Y. Sup. Ct. 1994).

§ 2.07   OVERVIEW OF PERSONAL LIABILITY OF CORPORATE AGENTS

While corporate criminal liability evolved over time, historically corporate agents have always been held personally liable for their criminal conduct. The fact that an agent may be acting on behalf of a corporation does not release the agent from being held criminally accountable. In recent years high-level executives, including the CEOs of major corporations have been prosecuted for their role in fraud occurring within the corporation. (e.g., Jeffrey Skilling—the former CEO of Enron; Bernard Ebbers—former CEO of Worldcom; John Rigas—former CEO of Adelphia Communications Corporation).

This principle of personal liability of a corporate agent was reinforced in the Supreme Court case of *U.S. v. Wise*, 370 U.S. 405 (1962), where the government contested on direct appeal a district court's dismissal of an indictment against a corporate officer for violations of the Sherman Act. The District Court's rationale was that the Sherman Act was inapplicable to corporate officers who act in their representative capacity. In reversing this lower court decision, the Supreme Court noted that the Sherman Act's inclusion of corporations in its definition of "persons" did not serve to exclude prosecutions against individuals who have a responsible share in the criminal conduct.

The Model Penal Code (§ 2.07(6)) imposes individual liability on the corporate agent for conduct performed on behalf of the corporation "to the same extent as if it were performed in his own name or behalf." Where there is an affirmative duty to act, the agent "having primary responsibility for the discharge of the duty is legally accountable for a reckless omission to perform the required act to the same extent as if the duty were imposed by law directly upon himself."

Where the criminal conduct is performed directly by the agent of the corporation, courts have had little difficulty in imposing liability. Even when the agent is not an officer, director, or manager, liability has been found for the criminal acts committed. There have been occasional instances in which it is argued that a subordinate should not be held liable for the criminal act in that the individual was acting under the orders of a superior. In *U.S. v. Gold*, 743 F.2d 800 (11th Cir.1984), the Eleventh Circuit found "that 'following orders' can only be a defense where a defendant has no idea that his conduct is criminal." There is, however, no consistent body of law endorsing the position taken in the *Gold* case.

When the offense involves an element of criminal intent, courts generally require that the corporate agent have personally performed, had knowledge of the acts, or have had direction or control over the conduct. For example, in *Bourgeois v. Commonwealth*, 227 S.E.2d 714 (Va.1976), the Virginia Supreme Court ruled that despite the fact that the individual charged with the crime was the president of the corporation, it was necessary for the state to present evidence that this individual controlled the circumstances of the illegal acts. Absent evidence of participation in the criminal conduct or knowledge imputed from the business procedures of the corporation or the personnel, the Court found that there was no basis for imputing knowledge of wrongdoing to the president.

§ 2.08   RESPONSIBLE CORPORATE OFFICER

Responsible corporate officers have been held criminally liable by a statute with a "knowing" element, despite the fact that they had no actual knowledge of the criminal conduct. *U.S. v. Johnson & Towers, Inc.*, 741 F.2d 662 (3rd Cir.1984). Willful blindness to the criminal conduct can be used to support the element of knowledge. The mere fact that one is in the position of official responsibility does not, however, constitute knowledge. *U.S. v. MacDonald & Watson Waste Oil Co.*, 933 F.2d 35 (1st Cir.1991). However, where knowledge is an element of the offense, it often can be inferred from circumstantial evidence. This evidence may include the position and responsibilities of the corporate officer. *U.S. v. Iverson*, 162 F.3d 1015 (9th Cir.1998).

When the offense is a strict liability offense, there is no need to concentrate on the level of knowledge held by the indicted corporate agent. The offense is imputed via the "responsible corporate officer" doctrine. This doctrine originates from the Supreme Court decision in *U.S. v. Dotterweich*, 320 U.S. 277 (1943).

Dotterweich, along with the Buffalo Pharmacal Company, Inc., was charged with violating the Federal Food, Drug and Cosmetic Act. As president and general manager of the corporation, he was accused of violations involving the shipping in interstate commerce of adulterated and misbranded drugs. The drugs had been purchased from the manufacturer, repacked under the Buffalo Pharmacal Company name, and shipped in interstate commerce. Only Dotterweich was convicted after a jury trial.

Justice Frankfurter, writing for the majority, found that Dotterweich was a "person" punishable for violations of the Federal Food, Drug, and Cosmetic Act. The Court recognized the offense as a strict liability crime, thus eliminating any requirement for the government to show knowledge on the part of Dotterweich. Liability, the court found, rests upon whether the individual has a "responsible share in the furtherance of the transaction." The Court declined in this opinion to define the term "responsible share," leaving the definition to "the good sense of prosecutors, the wise guidance of trial judges, and the ultimate judgment of juries."

In a dissent written by Justice Murphy, and joined by three members of the court, it was noted that guilt was being "imputed to the respondent solely on the basis of his authority and responsibility as president and general manager of the corporation." The dissent objected to this imputation of criminality, absent clear statutory authority, and found it "inconsistent with established canons of criminal law to rest liability on an act in which the accused did not participate and of which he had no personal knowledge."

The Supreme Court elaborated on the *Dotterweich* case thirty-two years later in the case of *U.S. v. Park*, 421 U.S. 658 (1975). Park, the chief executive officer of a national retail food chain, was charged with violations of the Federal Food, Drug, and Cosmetic Act. His office was located in Philadelphia, Pennsylvania while the warehouse contaminated with rodents, from which there were interstate food shipments, was located in Baltimore, Maryland. Park had been advised that steps were being taken to remedy the conditions in the warehouse. In finding defendant Park criminally liable, the Supreme Court reiterated its holding in *Dotterweich*. The Court emphasized that those who have a "responsible relationship" have a duty under the Act not only "to seek out and remedy violations" but also a duty "to implement measures that will insure that violations will not occur." A defendant is afforded the defense, and has the burden of proof if offered, of showing that he or she is " 'powerless' to prevent or correct the violation." The government is only required to show "that the defendant had, by reason of his position in the corporation, responsibility and authority either to prevent in the first instance, or promptly to correct, the violation complained of, and that he failed to do so."

The Court in *Park* examined the trial court's instructions and determined that taken as a whole they properly reflected this legal standard. The instructions did not permit a finding of guilt strictly upon Park's position in the corporation. Rather, the instructions "advised the jury that to find guilt it must find respondent 'had a responsible relation to the situation,' and 'by virtue of his position . . . had . . . authority and responsibility' to deal with the situation."

Three members of the Court dissenting in *Park* agreed with what it termed "the language of negligence" of the majority. The dissent, however, felt that the instructions used in the case had failed to adhere to the standard set by the Court. Whether strict liability has been abandoned for a negligence standard in applying the "responsible officer" doctrine is a subject of legal debate.

Corporate executives and employees indicted for alleged acts committed in their corporate capacity have sought reimbursement from the corporation for their attorney fees and other expenses. Likewise, if the corporate executive or employee is convicted, reimbursement has been sought for fines assessed against them. Courts have resolved issues premised upon indemnification in a variety of contexts with varying results. Executives seeking indemnification have proceeded using statutory authority, corporate policy, or an implied or express agreement between the corporation and the executive. Indemnification or payment of current expenses has been sought directly from the corporation, or alternatively pursuant to a Directors and Officers Liability Insurance Policy. See *U.S. v. Stein* § 2.04.

Corporate directors can be civilly obligated to institute adequate corporate compliance measures to preclude criminal activity. *In re Caremark International Inc. Derivative Litigation*, 698 A.2d 959 (Ct. Chancery Del.1996). The Sarbanes Oxley Act of 2002, a legislative response to corporate improprieties, modifies the criminal law by adding new crimes, new reporting requirements, and increasing criminal penalties. (see chaps. 4, 5, 6, 24). The Act is aimed at promoting "greater corporate integrity."

PART 2
SPECIFIC OFFENSES

CHAPTER 3
CONSPIRACY

§ 3.01 INTRODUCTION

Throughout the United States Code there are specific conspiracy statutes. Some of these statutes appear within the criminal code. [i.e., conspiracy against rights of citizens (18 U.S.C. § 241)]. Other conspiracy statutes exist outside Title 18. [i.e., conspiracy in restraint of trade (15 U.S.C. § 1); conspiracy to monopolize trade (15 U.S.C. § 2)]. In some instances conspiracy provisions are incorporated within the terms of a statute. [i.e., racketeering conspiracies (18 U.S.C. § 1962 (d)); conspiracy in bribery in sporting contests (18 U.S.C. § 224)]. The one general federal conspiracy statute, 18 U.S.C. § 371, criminalizes conspiracies to commit any offense against the United States as well as conspiracies to defraud the United States or its agencies.

Judge Learned Hand referred to conspiracy as "that darling of the modern prosecutor's nursery." *Harrison v. U.S.*, 7 F.2d 259 (2d Cir.1925). This is especially true when placed in the context of white collar crime. Although individual acts of white collar crime are abundant, an overwhelming number of white collar criminal acts are group related. Conspiracy charges have sometimes resulted in megatrials that involve many defendants and lengthy trials.

Conspiracy is an inchoate crime. One of the essential aims of conspiracy is to protect against concerted criminal activity. Conspiracy is punished as a crime to attack the special dangers resulting from group activity. ("In union there is strength").

Conspiracy charges offer prosecutors several advantages. As an inchoate crime, it provides a legal basis for stopping the effects of criminality prior to it reaching full fruition. A federal conspiracy charge under 18 U.S.C. § 371 can be filed when there is an agreement and an overt act. It is unnecessary to wait until the criminal conduct is complete to proceed with conspiracy charges.

The conspiracy offense also offers prosecutors procedural advantages. For example, a charge of conspiracy permits joinder of the co-conspirators for trial. From a practical perspective this enhances the likelihood of conviction in that the evidence to the jury will not be limited to the acts of one individual. Guilt by association can be fostered when the prosecutor presents, in the same trial, evidence of criminal conduct by those associated with the defendant.

Another procedural advantage to the prosecutor in charging conspiracy is found in the broader selection offered in choosing the forum where the case will be heard. The venue of conspiracy charges is in the location where the conspiracy was formed or where any of the overt acts took place. With several defendants and possibly several overt acts, prosecutorial discretion with respect to venue is enhanced by charging conspiracy under section 371.

The conspiracy statute also can have evidentiary advantages for the prosecutor. Hearsay evidence is not permitted at trial unless it meets an exception to the hearsay rule. Federal evidence rules provide as one of the exceptions to hearsay "a statement by a co-conspirator of a party during the course and in furtherance of the conspiracy." (Federal Rules of Evidence, Rule 801(d)(2)(E)). Thus, in a conspiracy trial, statements of a co-conspirator made during the conspiracy may possibly be admitted despite the fact that the statement is hearsay. Relevant evidence also may be expanded by the presence of multiple co-conspirators and possibly several overt acts. Since many conspiracies are proved through circumstantial evidence, the increase in admissible evidence can benefit the prosecutor.

Prosecutors also have an advantage should the evidence at trial be deficient on one of several objects of a conspiracy. A general verdict on a multiple object conspiracy is proper even though the evidence on one of the objects of the conspiracy may be inadequate to support a conviction. When the inadequacy relates to inadequate evidence as opposed to being a "legal error," due process does not require setting aside the verdict. *Griffin v. U.S.*, 502 U.S. 46 (1991).

The main federal conspiracy statute, 18 U.S.C. § 371, requires proof of the following elements: (1) an agreement, (2) an unlawful object, (3) knowledge and intent, and (4) an overt act. The statute provides for a penalty of up to five years imprisonment and a fine. If the unlawful object of the conspiracy is a misdemeanor then the punishment is limited to the maximum punishment provided for that misdemeanor. There is no double jeopardy violation when a defendant is prosecuted for both the substantive crime and conspiracy to commit that crime under section 371. Conspiracy to commit a crime is a separate and distinct offense from the crime itself. *U.S. v. Felix*, 503 U.S. 378 (1992).

§ 3.02   AGREEMENT

At the heart of the crime of conspiracy is the agreement. The agreement does not have to be written, oral, or explicit. It can be inferred from the "facts and circumstances of the case." *Iannelli v. U.S.*, 420 U.S. 770 (1975). If the minds of the parties meet and an understanding is reached to achieve a common purpose, there is an agreement. Mere knowledge, without agreement, does not meet this element of the offense.

Incumbent to forming an agreement is, however, some knowledge. The conspirators must know of the conspiracy's purpose and must knowingly participate in it. Conspirators do not have to agree to every step of the conspiracy. An overall agreement to carry out the objectives of the conspiracy suffices.

Although it is necessary to have evidence beyond a reasonable doubt that the conspirators agreed on the "essential nature of the plan," it is not necessary to prove that all conspirators had knowledge of all the plan's details or even of the participation of all others in the conspiracy. *Blumenthal v. U.S.*, 332 U.S. 539 (1947). For example, a conspiracy conviction was affirmed despite the fact that the defendant convicted of conspiracy to violate the money laundering statute (18 U.S.C. § 1956) believed the money was from narcotics trafficking and the co-conspirator believed the money came from gambling. Because the conspirators agreed on the essential scheme, to launder money, the agreement element of the conspiracy was satisfied. *U.S. v. Stavroulakis*, 952 F.2d 686 (2d Cir.1992). The agreement must be to achieve an unlawful objective. (see § 3.04).

A defense to a conspiracy charge may be premised upon a defendant's withdrawal from the conspiracy. The defendant arguing withdrawal must prove an affirmative act of withdrawal. This can be shown through action communicated to co-conspirators that disavows or defeats the purpose of the conspiracy. In *Smith v. U.S.*, 133 S.Ct. 714 (2013), the Court held that "[a] defendant who withdraws outside the relevant statute-of-limitations period has a complete defense to prosecution."

§ 3.03 PLURALITY

Conspiracy requires two or more parties forming the agreement. This plurality requirement does not necessitate that the government charge all members of the conspiracy. It is common to see a conspiracy case proceed against one defendant with unindicted co-conspirators mentioned in the charging document.

With plurality required, the issue arises as to whether there are in fact two or more persons to the agreement when one defendant is acquitted and another is convicted. For many years case law relative to conspiracy prohibited inconsistent verdicts. Thus, if one defendant of a two person conspiracy was acquitted, then the other defendant's conviction could not stand. Further, if all but one of the defendants of a multiple party conspiracy were acquitted, then the remaining defendant would have to be acquitted. Since the essence of a conspiracy is the agreement between two or more individuals, the elimination by acquittal of all those with whom the defendant could have conspired precluded a conspiracy conviction for the remaining defendant.

The rule prohibiting inconsistent verdicts did not apply where one defendant was tried and convicted and the other defendant was not charged with the crime. It likewise did not apply to the situation where two defendants were convicted but one was acquitted. As long as an agreement could be shown, there was no inconsistency in the verdicts. Additionally, some courts refused to extend the rule prohibiting inconsistent verdicts to situations where the defendants were tried separately. These courts only allowed for the reversal of inconsistent verdicts where the verdicts resulted from the same trial.

Many courts have now departed from the rule of prohibiting inconsistent verdicts. Reference is often made to the case of *U.S. v. Powell*, 469 U.S. 57 (1984) which held that inconsistency alone is not a basis for reversing a conviction. In *Powell* the

Supreme Court found it acceptable to have a defendant's conviction for the crime of using the telephone to facilitate the offense when there is an acquittal of the offense itself. (The charges were conspiracy to possess cocaine and possession of cocaine). *Powell*, however, did not directly address the issue of inconsistency in conspiracy verdicts between co-conspirators.

In *U.S. v. Bucuvalas*, 909 F.2d 593 (1st Cir.1990), the First Circuit found that jury verdicts acquitting one alleged conspirator and convicting the sole other alleged conspirator at the same trial on the same count did not require a reversal of the appellant's conviction. The court noted that justice is met in that the appellate tribunal reviews the evidence to determine its sufficiency to support the jury's decision. In applying *Powell* to inconsistent verdicts between two alleged conspirators, the court found the "rule of consistency" no longer viable. Not all courts, however, apply *Powell* to inconsistent verdicts between alleged conspirators. Some courts see the rule of consistency between co-conspirators in a conspiracy case as an exception to *Powell*.

The requirement of plurality also raises issues of whether two parties are forming an agreement when both parties are corporations or the agreement is between a corporation and its employees. Courts have found that two corporations can form a conspiracy where the indictment involves two corporations and an individual associated with each. Plurality, likewise, exists if the conspiracy involves a corporation and one of its officers with a third party. Plurality, however, has been found not to exist when a single agent acts for both corporations. *U.S. v. Santa Rita Store Co.*, 113 P. 620 (N.M.1911).

Intracorporate conspiracies have been rejected when only one human actor is involved. In *U.S. v. Stevens*, 909 F.2d 431 (11th Cir.1990), the Eleventh Circuit reversed a conspiracy conviction where the defendant, accused of conspiring with a corporation, had been convicted of conspiracy to defraud the government pursuant to 18 U.S.C. § 371. In *Stevens* the defendant was the sole stockholder of the corporation and acted as its sole agent. The court acknowledged that outside the context of antitrust violations, corporations can be criminally liable under section 371 for conspiracies involving its officers or employees. Where, however, the conspiracy involves only one human actor, as in *Stevens*, than the crime of conspiracy is improper.

The existence of plurality also can become an issue when the offense, by its very nature, requires two individuals. For example, crimes of bribery, adultery, incest or bigamy necessitate a minimum of two individuals to achieve the substantive offense. Historically, Wharton's Rule prohibited conspiracy prosecutions "when the crime is of such a nature as to necessarily require the participation of two persons for its commission."

Wharton's Rule has been significantly limited over time. If more than the minimum number of offenders participate in the offense, the rule has been found inapplicable. Further, Wharton's Rule cannot be used if the statute only criminalizes the conduct of one of the parties to the crime. The Model Penal Code does not endorse Wharton's Rule.

The Supreme Court held in *Iannelli v. U.S.*, 420 U.S. 770 (1975), that in federal court, Wharton's Rule only acts "as a judicial presumption, to be applied in the absence of legislative intent to the contrary." According to this case, Wharton's Rule requires not only that the parties to the agreement be the only parties to participate in the commission of the offense, but also that "the immediate consequences of the crime rest on the parties themselves rather than on society at large." In *Iannelli*, Wharton's Rule was held not to apply to an alleged gambling conspiracy, in that the offense, a violation of 18 U.S.C. § 1955, differed from the traditional Wharton Rule offenses. Further, the court found that the harm emanating from large gambling activities was not limited to the parties but rather sought to include the participation of additional individuals who, in the case of bettors, were not a party to the conspiracy or to the substantive offense.

Plurality will not be found where a statute specifically protects one party to the offense. Where a party is legislatively protected, it is improper for the government to charge conspiracy. Clearly victims of a crime should not be prosecuted for conspiracy for their unwilling participation in a crime.

Plurality is seriously jeopardized when one of the parties to the conspiracy is a government agent.

Courts have found that there is no agreement unless there is "at least one bona fide co-conspirator." *U.S. v. Schmidt*, 947 F.2d 362 (9th Cir.1991). If the only person that the defendant conspires with is a government agent, there is no true agreement nor a meeting of the minds. If, however, the agreement includes a government agent coupled with other individuals, then a conspiracy can exist.

§ 3.04 UNLAWFUL OBJECT OF CONSPIRACY

18 U.S.C. § 371 can be subdivided as follows: (1) conspiracies to commit any **offense** against the United States, or (2) conspiracies to **defraud** the United States or its agencies. The offense and defraud clauses of this statute offer alternative methods of charging under section 371.

Under the **offense** provision, the conspiracy has as its object the violation of other civil and criminal statutes. For example, a conspiracy to commit mail fraud (18 U.S.C. § 1341) and conspiracy to obstruct justice (18 U.S.C. § 1503) would be violations of 18 U.S.C. § 371.

In contrast the **defraud** provision focuses not on specific offense activity, but rather on conduct that defrauds the United States. A conspiracy to defraud the United States requires a showing that the accused either cheated the government out of property or money, or interfered with or obstructed a lawful government function by "deceit, craft or trickery, or at least by means that are dishonest."

Hammerschmidt v. U.S., 265 U.S. 182 (1924). It is not incumbent that there be an actual financial or property loss where there is an obstruction or impairment of a lawful function of a department of the government. Thus, even though the charges against the defendant did not allege that the government suffered any monetary loss, the defraud clause was applicable where a release of a cotton crop report to select market speculators obstructed or impaired the lawful delivery of the information by the government. *Haas v. Henkel*, 216 U.S. 462 (1910).

The scope of the scheme to defraud in section 371 is broad in that the very language of the statute states a defrauding of the United States "in any manner or for any purpose." Courts, however, are bound to scrutinize criminal conspiracy charges carefully to make certain that its wide net does not "ensnare the innocent as well as the culpable." *Dennis v. U.S.*, 384 U.S. 855 (1966). Lenity is to be used in resolving ambiguities as to the scope of the defraud clause. *Tanner v. U.S.*, 483 U.S. 107 (1987).

The relationship between the offense and defraud clause of section 371 has been the subject of controversy. One view is that although the government can prosecute a defendant under both the offense and defraud clauses of section 371, only one conviction and one punishment is possible. *U.S. v. Bilzerian*, 926 F.2d 1285 (2d Cir.1991).

In *U.S. v. Minarik*, 875 F.2d 1186 (6th Cir.1989), however, the Sixth Circuit held that the government should be limited to the offense clause of section

371, as opposed to using the defraud clause, in those instances where Congress specifically enacted a statute that covers the wrongful conduct. The court noted that to hold otherwise would allow prosecutors to circumvent a misdemeanor penalty. By charging the offense as the felony of conspiracy to defraud the United States, the government could effectively obtain a felony punishment where the specific offense is only a misdemeanor.

Other newer decisions in the Sixth Circuit limit *Minarik* to the facts presented in the case. Where the alleged conduct violates more than one specific offense, fits within the defraud clause, and the indictment provides adequate notice to the defendant of the alleged charges, the court does not require that the conspiracy be charged under the offense clause rather than the defraud clause of the conspiracy statute. *U.S. v. Kraig*, 99 F.3d 1361 (6th Cir.1996).

Even though the "object of the conspiracy" may be "impossible to achieve," as when the government intercedes and defeats the conspiracy object, a conspiracy can still exist as "conspiracy law does not contain" an "'automatic termination' rule." *U.S. v. Jimenez Recio*, 537 U.S. 270 (2003).

§ 3.05   KNOWLEDGE AND INTENT

Conspiracy requires both knowledge and specific intent. As previously noted, the defendant must agree to the conspiracy. This requires knowledge of the conspiracy's existence, as well as knowledge of the objective of the conspiracy. It does not, however, require knowledge by the accused of all the details of the conspiracy (see § 3.02).

In addition to knowledge, the defendant must also intend to participate in the conspiracy. The degree of mens rea required for the conspiracy is dependent upon the level of intent required for the underlying specific offense. Conspiracy to commit a specific offense only exists when there is sufficient evidence of at least the degree of criminal intent required for the substantive offense. *Ingram v. U.S.*, 360 U.S. 672 (1959).

Although knowledge and intent are required, in almost all instances it is not necessary that there be knowledge of a jurisdictional element. "The concept of criminal intent does not extend so far as to require that the actor understand not only the nature of his act but also its consequence for the choice of a judicial forum." *U.S. v. Feola*, 420 U.S. 671 (1975). Only in the rare circumstance where the parties need to have knowledge to establish the existence of federal jurisdiction, will it be required that there be knowledge of the federal jurisdiction for the conspiracy offense. In almost all instances, knowledge by the defendant of the existence of federal jurisdiction is not required for the substantive offense, and therefore, will not be required for a conspiracy.

§ 3.06   OVERT ACT

Many state jurisdictions and some specific federal conspiracy statutes find the actus reus of a conspiracy charge to be solely the agreement. For example, both the RICO statute (*Salinas v. U.S.*, 522 U.S. 52 (1997)) and the money laundering statute (*Whitfield v. U.S.*, 543 U.S. 209 (2005)) do not require proof of an overt act. Section 371, however, requires both an agreement and an overt act in furtherance of the agreement. The overt act does not have to be a criminal act. Further, it does not have to be performed by the individual accused of the crime of conspiracy. As long as one member of the conspiracy committed an overt act in furtherance of the conspiracy, the element is met.

The overt act must take place during the conspiracy. For purposes of the statute of limitations for a conspiracy prosecution, the time does not commence to run until the commission of the last overt act in furtherance of the conspiracy as alleged in the charging document. It is incumbent that the government prove an overt act within the statute of limitations.

§ 3.07   SINGLE OR MULTIPLE CONSPIRACIES

Whether the parties are properly joined in one conspiracy and whether the acts of the parties constitute a single or multiple conspiracy, are issues raised in some conspiracy cases. The substantive, procedural, and evidentiary advantages afforded a prosecutor in charging conspiracy can be further enhanced by including in one prosecution multiple defendants and multiple acts. As a result, the government often finds itself arguing that the parties formed one general conspiracy as opposed to several smaller conspiracies, and that the acts of these parties are part of a single conspiracy as opposed to multiple conspiracies.

Although it is necessary to have one overall agreement between the parties to charge conspiracy, it is not necessary to have every participant of the conspiracy know the other individuals involved or know the specific details of every aspect of the conspiracy. When there are more than two members of a conspiracy, the question arises whether in fact all are part of the same conspiracy or perhaps some are involved in one conspiracy and others involved in a different conspiracy.

This issue arose in the case of *Kotteakos v. U.S.*, 328 U.S. 750 (1946) where defendants were convicted of a conspiracy to obtain loans under the National Housing Act. One individual, Brown, conspired with many of the defendants and served as the "common and key figure in all the transactions proven." In many cases, however, the defendants did not have any relationship with each other except Brown's connection with each transaction. The Supreme Court rejected this connection as sufficient for a single conspiracy.

The *Kotteakos* court analogized these facts to the hub of a wheel with its spokes. In this case Brown served as the hub of the wheel. The spokes were the individual defendants, who in this case had no relationship to each other. Except for Brown, the individual conspirators were not interested in anything but their own loan. The conspiracies were therefore separate and disconnected with no one overriding plan. Absent a single comprehensive plan, there was no single conspiracy. Rather the defendants were involved in multiple conspiracies with Brown.

The "wheel and spoke" conspiracy has been distinguished from the "chain" conspiracy. In a "chain" conspiracy, the court looks to whether the parties serve as links in a chain. In *Blumenthal v. U.S.*, 332 U.S. 539 (1947), the Supreme Court found that the parties had agreed to sell liquor at prices exceeding the ceiling set by regulations of the Office of Price Administration. The Court found that the agreements were steps in the formulation of one larger general conspiracy. By reason of all having knowledge of the plan's general scope and common end, the disposing of the whiskey, they could be drawn together in a single conspiracy.

A single agreement with multiple criminal objectives is one conspiracy, as opposed to several separate conspiracies. It is improper to charge several counts of conspiracy when only one agreement is involved. *Braverman v. U.S.*, 317 U.S. 49 (1942). This is not, however, true when there is a single agreement to violate different conspiracy statutes. *Albernaz v. U.S.*, 450 U.S. 333 (1981).

§ 3.08 PINKERTON RULE

In *Pinkerton v. U.S.*, 328 U.S. 640 (1946), the Supreme Court held that a conspirator can be liable for the substantive offenses of a co-conspirator that are in furtherance of the conspiracy. Defendant Pinkerton's convictions for violations of the Internal

Revenue Code and conspiracy were affirmed despite the fact that there was no evidence that he had directly participated in or had knowledge of the substantive offenses. The evidence showed that defendant's brother committed these substantive offenses while the defendant was in prison. The jury, however, found that these substantive offenses were committed in furtherance of the conspiracy.

Pinkerton requires that to find a conspirator liable for the substantive offense of a co-conspirator, the substantive offense (1) must be within the scope and in furtherance of the conspiracy, (2) be committed by one or more members of the conspiracy, and (3) the individual accused of the substantive offense must be a member of the conspiracy at the time the specific offense was committed. It is within the province of a jury to apply this rule to the facts.

In some instances *Pinkerton* is applied when the substantive crime is a primary goal of the alleged conspiracy. *U.S. v. Alvarez*, 755 F.2d 830 (11th Cir.1985). Other cases employ the *Pinkerton* Rule where the substantive crime "facilitates the achievement of one of the primary goals" of the conspiracy.

In *Pinkerton*, the Supreme Court noted that its holding did not encompass cases where the substantive offenses were not reasonably foreseen as a necessary or natural consequence of the unlawful agreement. Some courts have used this language to find liability where the substantive offenses were not the objective of the conspiracy, but were reasonably foreseeable by the conspirators. *U.S. v. Tilton*, 610 F.2d 302 (5th Cir.1980). Reasonably foreseeable, but originally unintended, substantive offenses may be limited to where the conspirator "played more than a 'minor' role in the conspiracy, or had actual knowledge of at least some of the circumstances and events culminating in the reasonably foreseeable but originally unintended substantive crime." *U.S. v. Alvarez*, 755 F.2d 830 (11th Cir.1985).

§ 3.09 ANTITRUST CONSPIRACIES

Section One of the Sherman Act addresses conspiracies intended to produce an unreasonable restraint of trade or commerce. It requires plurality as well as an interstate nexus. In contrast, section two of the Sherman Act can be met absent plurality in that it prohibits "every person" from monopolizing any part of trade or commerce. Issues raised in prosecutions under section one have included whether plurality exists when there is an intra-enterprise or intra-corporate conspiracy. Alleged violators of section one have also contested the level of intent necessary for the prosecution.

Historically intra-enterprise conspiracies were subject to the Sherman Act. As early as 1947, the Supreme Court rejected arguments that a Sherman Act conspiracy could not be premised upon affiliated corporations. *U.S. v. Yellow Cab Co.*, 332 U.S. 218 (1947). This position was significantly altered by the United States in 1984 when the Court issued its decision in *Copperweld Corp. v. Independence Tube Corp.*, 467 U.S. 752 (1984).

In *Copperweld*, the Supreme Court held that a parent corporation and its wholly owned subsidiary were incapable of conspiring with each other for purposes of section one of the Sherman Act. Officers and employees of the same company lack the necessary plurality of actors needed for a section one conspiracy. The Court found that section one did not reach conduct that was "wholly unilateral."

The Court did not, however, resolve whether this prohibition should be extended to intra-enterprise conspiracies where the parent corporation is accused of conspiring with an affiliated corporation that it does not completely own. A Louisiana court interpreting a state antitrust statute declined to adopt the *Copperweld* position, noting that it departed from the Supreme Court's own precedent and from a prevailing decision of the Louisiana Court. *Louisiana Power and Light Co. v. United Gas Pipe Line Co.*, 493 So.2d 1149 (La.1986).

Plurality does not exist when the parties are part of the same corporation. Unlike the general conspiracy provision found in section 371, section one of the Sherman Act does not permit intracorporate conspiracies. "A corporation cannot conspire with itself any more than a private individual can, and it is the general rule that the acts of the agent are the acts of the corporation." *Nelson Radio & Supply Co. v. Motorola, Inc.*, 200 F.2d 911 (5th Cir.1952).

When the defendant is accused of a violation of section one of the Sherman Act, and the conduct is not per se illegal, it is necessary for the government to prove intent. In *U.S. v. United States Gypsum Co.*, 438 U.S. 422 (1978), the Supreme Court held that a mens rea is the rule rather than the exception in criminal law. The trial court in *Gypsum* had erred in instructing the jury that "if the effect of the exchanges of pricing information was to raise, fix, maintain, and stabilize prices, then the parties to them are presumed, *as a matter of law*, to have intended that result." The Court found that "action undertaken with knowledge of its probable consequences and having the requisite anticompetitive effects can be a sufficient predicate for a finding of criminal liability under the antitrust laws."

If the offense is a per se violation, courts have found that there is no requirement to show that the accused intended to restrain trade. Showing that the defendant knowingly engaged in conduct that violated the law suffices. *U.S. v. Cargo Service Stations, Inc.*, 657 F.2d 676 (5th Cir.1981). Agreements to fix prices are unlawful per se under the Sherman Act. *U.S. v. Socony-Vacuum Oil Co., Inc.*, 310 U.S. 150 (1940).

CHAPTER 4

MAIL, WIRE, AND BANK FRAUD

§ 4.01   INTRODUCTION

The mail fraud statute was one of 327 sections of the 1872 recodification of the Postal Act. Its initial emphasis was on the misuse of the postal system by way of a counterfeit scheme.

In its infancy there was a disparity of interpretation of this criminal offense with some courts reading the mail fraud statute to include any scheme that misused the postal system while others endorsed a more literal reading. Congress clarified the scope of the offense by providing in 1889 a detailed mail fraud statute that listed all imaginable counterfeit schemes that the framers of the Act could envision. Included within the array of schemes outlawed by this congressional revision were schemes dealing with "green articles," "counterfeit money fraud," and "paper goods."

Durland v. U.S., 161 U.S. 306 (1896) set the tone for future mail fraud cases by interpreting this new act broadly. Mail fraud would include "everything designed to defraud by representations as to the past or present, or suggestions and promises as to the future." *Durland's* holding was followed by a 1909 congressional revision that added to the mail fraud statute the language "or for obtaining money or property by means of false or fraudulent pretenses, representations, or promises."

Today, the crime of mail fraud is located in section 1341 of Title 18 of the United States Code. It requires proof of four elements: (1) a scheme devised or intending to defraud or for obtaining money or property by fraudulent means, (2) intent, (3) materiality, and (4) use or causing to use the mails (or private carrier) in furtherance of the fraudulent scheme. Unlike its predecessor, the present day offense does not require that the mails be an essential aspect of the scheme to defraud. A mailing that is "incident to an essential part of the scheme" (*Pereira v. U.S.*, 347 U.S. 1 (1954)) or "a step in the plot" (*Badders v. U.S.*, 240 U.S. 391 (1916)) suffices.

Due to the breadth of the statute, as well as its simplicity of proof, mail fraud is extensively used by federal prosecutors. Chief Justice Burger termed mail fraud the "stopgap" provision in his dissenting opinion in *U.S. v. Maze*, 414 U.S. 395 (1974), finding that the offense served the purpose of providing criminality to new frauds until particularized legislation could be passed. In reality, however, mail fraud often serves as the charged offense despite the existence of a specific statute that criminalizes the conduct.

The felony of mail fraud carries a penalty of not more than twenty years imprisonment and a fine. Where the mail fraud affects a financial institution, the allowed penalty is increased to imprisonment of not more than thirty years and a fine of up to one million dollars. Following Hurricane Katrina, Congress passed a statute that also allowed a maximum penalty of thirty years when the fraud related to "a presidentially declared major disaster or emergency." As part of the Sarbanes-Oxley Act of 2002, Congress passed 18 U.S.C. § 1349 which allows for attempts and conspiracy under the fraud statutes.

Many fraud statutes are modeled after the mail fraud statute. These include the wire fraud (§ 4.08), bank fraud (§ 4.09), and health care fraud (§ 4.10) statutes. In 1988, Congress passed 18 U.S.C. § 1031, the Major Fraud Act, a statute with a one million dollar threshold for frauds relating to items such as federal grants, contracts, loans, and moneys provided through the Troubled Asset Relief program. WCH § 4.12.

§ 4.02   SCHEME TO DEFRAUD, INTENT & MATERIALITY

The scheme to defraud element of the crime of mail fraud encompasses a myriad of frauds. The ever expanding list includes credit card fraud, divorce mill fraud, franchise fraud, insurance fraud, securities fraud, medical drug fraud and fraud premised upon political malfeasance. Rarely is conduct excluded from the bounds of this element. Today, schemes to defraud are premised on "money or property" or "the right to honest services." See § 4.03. Property includes intangible property. See § 4.04.

The scheme to defraud element is not limited by the common law definition of fraud. Conduct characterized by the deprivation of something of value by "trick, deceit, chicane, or overreaching" are encompassed within the terms of the statute. *Hammerschmidt v. U.S.*, 265 U.S. 182 (1924). Use of extortion, however, does not equate with conduct included within a scheme to defraud. Thus, in *Fasulo v. U.S.*, 272 U.S. 620 (1926), the Supreme Court rejected the use of mail fraud for demands of money by threat and coercion through fear and force. The Court found that a scheme premised upon threats of murder and bodily harm was not a "scheme to defraud."

Implicit within the scheme to defraud element is that the defendant have a fraudulent intent. Courts have varied on the degree of fraudulent intent necessary to support a mail fraud conviction. Some require proof of a specific intent to defraud while others have been satisfied when the defendant acts recklessly or with willful blindness. There is, however, no requirement to show an intent "to inflict economic harm on or injure the property rights of another," although such proof can assist is showing an intent to defraud. *U.S. v. Welch*, 327 F.3d 1081 (10th Cir.2003). Irrespective of the standard employed, courts often allow the mens rea to be inferred from the evidence.

An intent to deceive does not, however, always coincide with an intent to defraud. For example, in *U.S. v. Regent Office Supply Co.*, 421 F.2d 1174 (2d Cir.1970), the Second Circuit rejected the use of mail fraud premised upon use of false pretenses in the preliminary stages of a sales solicitation. The defendant in *Regent* stipulated that its agents used false pretenses and representations in obtaining access to customers of stationary supplies. Argued, however, was that the price and quality of the merchandise to be sold were being honestly portrayed to the customers. The Second Circuit found that false representations which are "not directed to the quality, adequacy or price of goods to be sold, or otherwise to the nature of the bargain," do not form a scheme to defraud. Although actual defrauding is not required for conviction, the government does have to show that "some actual harm or injury was contemplated by the schemer."

The statute has been held not to require "proof of a scheme calculated to deceive a person of ordinary prudence" as mail fraud "does not 'differentiate between schemes that will ensnare the ordinary prudent investor and those that attract only those with lesser mental acuity." *U.S. v. Svete*, 556 F.3d 1157 (11th Cir.2009).

In *U.S. v. D'Amato*, 39 F.3d 1249 (2d Cir.1994), the Second Circuit reversed mail fraud convictions finding insufficient evidence of intent on either a "right to control theory" or a "false pretenses theory." Rejecting the government's use of "right to control theory," the court stated that "[w]here a third party acting upon instructions from a corporate agent is charged with depriving shareholders of their right to control, the government must prove that the third party knew that the concealment would involve" "(i) information available to shareholders as provided by the state of incorporation's laws providing access to corporate books and records," "(ii) information that, if withheld or inaccurate would result in rendering information that is public materially misleading," or "(iii) information that would materially aid shareholders in enforcing management's fiduciary obligations under state law." The court also rejected a "false pretenses" theory, declining the "government's invitation to infer fraudulent intent on the part of an attorney who accepts a retainer agreement and is subsequently not called upon to perform services that the government or trier of fact deems worth the fee paid."

Materiality is an essential element of the federal mail fraud, wire fraud and bank fraud statutes. In *Neder v. U.S.*, 527 U.S. 1 (1999), the Court remanded a case to determine whether it was harmless error for the trial court to fail to instruct the jury on materiality as an element of the fraud statute. In finding materiality an element of these federal fraud statutes, the Court noted that "the common law could not have conceived of 'fraud' without proof of materiality."

§ 4.03   INTANGIBLE RIGHTS

Schemes to defraud premised upon the deprivation of intangible rights surfaced in the 1940s and developed in the 1970s and 1980s. Public officials were charged with the crime of mail fraud for depriving the citizenry of the right to good government and honest services. During this period, mail fraud was not limited to cases where a victim suffered monetary or property loss but included breaches of an owed fiduciary duty. Routinely encompassed within the words "any scheme or artifice to defraud" were political malfeasance that deprived citizens of intangible rights. In addition to political malfeasances, the charge of mail fraud was also used in instances when an employee was alleged to have deprived an employer of honest and faithful services. *U.S. v. George*, 477 F.2d 508 (7th Cir.1973).

McNally v. U.S., 483 U.S. 350 (1987) abruptly halted the use of an intangible rights theory. The Supreme Court reversed mail fraud convictions of three defendants who were convicted for participating in a scheme to defraud the citizens and government of Kentucky of their intangible right to have the Commonwealth's affairs conducted honestly.

Defendant Hunt, then chairperson of the state democratic party had been given de facto control over selecting the insurance agencies from which the state would purchase its policies. Hunt, together with codefendants McNally and Gray, were accused of a scheme that extracted commissions from Kentucky's worker's compensation insurance business into agencies in which the defendants had an interest.

Both the government's charge and the jury's instructions in the *McNally* case did not include language of a deprivation of the Commonwealth's money or property. The essence of the action was the fiduciary duty owed by a public official to the public and the misuse of a public office for private gain.

In reversing the convictions, Justice White stated that while the mail fraud statute protected property rights, it did not encompass the intangible right of the citizenry to good government. Absent congressional clarification, allegations of a deprivation of money or property would be required to meet the scheme to defraud element of the mail fraud statute.

Justice Stevens, joined in parts by Justice O'Connor, offered a heavily footnoted dissent in the *McNally* case. He rejected the narrow construction provided by the majority in defining the term "defraud" as contradicting the construction that the federal courts had consistently given the statute, as well as the meaning provided the term in § 371, the prohibition of conspiracies to "defraud the United States."

In 1988, Congress accepted Justice White's invitation in the *McNally* decision for congressional clarification by enacting 18 U.S.C. § 1346. This provision, applicable to several fraud statutes, defines the term "scheme or artifice to defraud" to include "a scheme or artifice to deprive another of the intangible right of honest services." Section 1346 has been used in prosecutions of both public officials and those in the private sector. *U.S. v. Williams*, 441 F.3d 716 (9th Cir.2006).

Cases repeatedly challenged section 1346. The Supreme Court accepted three cases with section 1346 honest services issues. The Court vacated and remanded all three cases, with an in-depth discussion of 1346 provided in one of the cases, *Skilling v. U.S.*, 561 U.S. 358 (2010).

Jeffrey Skilling, former CEO of Enron, was convicted of charges that included honest services fraud. He challenged the constitutionality of section 1346 and also unsuccessfully argued that the venue of the trial should have been moved in light of pre-trial publicity. Although the Court did not invalidate the statute, it did limit section 1346 to cases involving bribes and kickbacks. The Court stated that the "vast majority" of the honest-services cases "involved offenders who, in violation of a fiduciary duty, participated in bribery or kickback schemes." The Court stated that "Congress' reversal of *McNally* and reinstatement of the honest-services doctrine . . . can and should be salvaged by confining its scope to the core pre-McNally applications."

Justices Scalia and Thomas offered a concurring opinion that was joined in part by Justice Kennedy. They accused the Court of rewriting the statute in finding that § 1346 criminalized only bribery and kickbacks. WCH § 4.5(B).

Cases post-*Skilling* looked at whether the conviction was premised on bribery or kickbacks, often looking at the indictment and jury instructions to make this determination. Some cases were reversed, others affirmed and in some instances errors were determined to be harmless. For example, the former governor of Alabama had honest services counts premised on bribery affirmed, but two counts based upon self-dealing were reversed. *U.S. v. Siegelman*, 640 F.3d 1159 (11th Cir. 2011).

§ 4.04   INTANGIBLE PROPERTY

Within months of the *McNally v. U.S.*, 483 U.S. 350 (1987) decision, the Supreme Court accepted and decided the case of *Carpenter v. U.S.*, 484 U.S. 19 (1987). While *McNally* foreclosed the use of mail fraud premised upon intangible **rights** (absent the congressional redefinition in § 1346 and later interpretation in *Skilling*), *Carpenter* opened new doors by permitting schemes to defraud based upon intangible **property**.

In *Carpenter*, defendant Winans, a reporter for the Wall Street Journal, authored a highly regarded column that offered information on selected stocks and takeovers. The Wall Street Journal had an official policy and practice that before publication, the contents of the "Heard on the Street" column were the confidential information of the newspaper. Defendant Winans revealed this confidential information to co-conspirators Felis and Brant, stockbrokers, who used the advance information to buy and sell stocks based upon the probable impact of the newspaper articles on the market.

Although the contents of the newspaper articles were not altered to increase the potential profits of the conspirators, Felis and Winans were convicted for mail fraud, wire fraud and securities violations. Defendant Carpenter, a roommate of Winans, was convicted for aiding and abetting.

The Supreme Court unanimously affirmed the mail fraud and wire fraud convictions. Justice White, the author of the opinion, commenced his legal analysis of the case by reaffirming the *McNally* requirement of a deprivation of money or property for upholding mail and wire fraud convictions. He noted that although mail fraud is limited in its scope to the protection of property rights, there is no requirement that these property rights be tangible. The fiduciary obligation owed by Winans to the Wall Street Journal and the breach of that duty by exploiting the confidential business information for a personal benefit, resulted in a scheme to defraud of intangible property.

Carpenter therefore serves to reinforce *McNally's* holding requiring that a charge of mail fraud include a deprivation of "money or property" as opposed to intangible **rights**. It also, however, extends its reach to include both tangible and intangible **property**.

State and municipal licenses have been found not to constitute property. In *Cleveland v. U.S.*, 531 U.S. 12 (2000), the Supreme Court held that Louisiana's video poker licenses in the hands of the licensor were not property for purposes of the mail fraud statute.

The property does not, however, have to be property of someone in the United States. Uncollected excise taxes of Canada on liquor imported into its country was considered property for purposes of the wire fraud statute. In *Pasquantino v. U.S.*, 544 U.S. 349 (2005), the

Supreme Court held that tax evasion that deprived Canada of money was a deprivation of "something of value" and met the property element of the statute.

§ 4.05　USE OF THE MAILS "IN FURTHERANCE"

Besides the crime of mail fraud requiring a scheme to defraud, intent, and materiality, it is also necessary that the mails be used in furtherance of the fraudulent scheme. This second element of the offense of mail fraud requires (a) a mailing, (b) by the defendant or caused to be mailed by the defendant, (c) in furtherance of a scheme to defraud. Some courts focus on the use of the mails in determining venue and require that the mailing have passed through the district prosecuting. *U.S. v. Wood*, 364 F.3d 704 (6th Cir.2004). Other circuits concentrate on where a fraud occurred in determining venue. *U.S. v. Brennan*, 183 F.3d 139 (2d Cir.1999).

Historically, the use of the United States Postal System was the jurisdictional object that brought the fraudulent conduct within the bounds of a federal statute. The statute, however, was amended in 1994 to include the language "or deposits or caused to be deposited any matter or thing whatever to be sent or delivered by any private or commercial interstate carrier." Items sent using Federal Express, UPS, or similar carriers may now be subject to prosecution under the mail fraud statute.

It is unnecessary, however, for the defendant to have personally sent a letter. Use of an agent can suffice. In *Pereira v. U.S.*, 347 U.S. 1 (1954), the Supreme Court set forth the test to decide whether the defendant had caused the mails to be used. The Court held that "[w]here one does an act with knowledge that the use of the mails will follow in the ordinary course of business, or where such use can reasonably be foreseen, even though not actually intended, then he 'causes' the mails to be used."

In addition to a mailing by the defendant, or caused to be mailed by the defendant, it is also necessary that there be a nexus between the scheme to defraud and the mailing. This is reflected in the requirement that the mailing be "in furtherance" of the scheme to defraud. This latter subpart has been the subject of several controversies presented to courts.

§ 4.06   LIMITATIONS TO "IN FURTHERANCE"

Historically, cases reflected four legal limitations to a mailing being in furtherance of a scheme to defraud. Mailings which conflicted with the scheme, were an imperative command of duty imposed by the state, occurred prior to commencement of the scheme, or occurred after fruition of the scheme, were found not to be in furtherance of the scheme to defraud.

In *U.S. v. Maze*, 414 U.S. 395 (1974), the defendant's conviction for mail fraud was reversed in that the mailings were "not sufficiently closely related to the respondent's scheme to bring his conduct within the statute." The defendant was alleged to have stolen his roommate's credit card and used the card for the purchase of food and lodging in his travels to various states. The four counts of mail fraud were based upon the merchant's mailing of the sales slips of purchase to the bank issuing the credit card.

In *Maze*, the Supreme Court rejected the use of mail fraud, finding that the mailing of the credit card slips conflicted with the defendant's purpose and that the mailing occurred after fruition of the scheme to defraud. As a result of *Maze*, mailings that aid in the detection of the fraud or are counterproductive to the scheme to defraud are considered as not within the legal limits of being "in furtherance" of the scheme to defraud.

In *Parr v. U.S.*, 363 U.S. 370 (1960), the Supreme Court rejected the use of mail fraud as not being in furtherance of the scheme to defraud because the mailings were an imperative duty to the state. Also alleged was that the mailings in *Parr* were after the scheme to defraud had reached fruition. The twenty count indictment for mail fraud and conspiracy to commit mail fraud in *Parr* was based upon defendant's alleged scheme to defraud a school district of money through misappropriation and embezzlement. The mailings included letters for the assessment and collection of school taxes. The Court rejected the use of mail fraud stating that mailings "under the imperative command of duty imposed by state law" are not criminal for the purposes of mail fraud "even though some of those who are so required to do the mailing for the District plan to steal."

Although some courts have found that the mailing of fraudulent tax returns are not barred from prosecution by the "legal duty" limitation, *Parr* has supported conviction reversals when the items being mailed were "not themselves false and fraudulent." In *U.S. v. Lake*, 472 F.3d 1247 (5th Cir.2007), the Tenth Circuit used the *Parr* case to support the reversal of convictions that were premised upon reports that were not false or fraudulent but "were filed because they had to be."

Mailings prior to commencement of the scheme or after fruition of the scheme, were recognized by courts as not in furtherance of the scheme to defraud. In *U.S. v. Beall*, 126 F.Supp. 363 (N.D.Cal.1954), the Northern District of California Court found mailings of a fund raising campaign for the Infantile Paralysis Foundation to be a part of a lawful fund raising effort. A later misappropriation of the money was therefore embezzlement and not mail fraud. In that the mailing was prior to any fraud, it was not in furtherance of the scheme to defraud.

Kann v. U.S., 323 U.S. 88 (1944) showed the Supreme Court's initial adoption of an after-the-fact mailing not being in furtherance of the scheme to defraud. Defendant Kann, president of a corporation that manufactured munitions, was indicted with fellow workers for allegedly divesting company funds on government contracts for their personal benefit. The mailings that formed the basis of the charges were checks cashed by defendants that were presented to the drawee banks for purposes of collection. The nexus between the mailing and the scheme to defraud was lacking in that the scheme was completed at the time of the mailing.

Like *Kann*, the mailings in *Parr* and *Maze* were also mailings to collect on funds. In all these cases, the scheme had reached fruition and thus the mailings were immaterial to defendants' continuation of the scheme to defraud. *Kann, Parr,* and *Maze* contained forceful dissents by justices of the Supreme Court.

A recognized exception to after-the-fact mailings being considered "in furtherance" of the scheme is where the mailings serve to "lull" the victims into the defendant's scheme. *U.S. v. Sampson*, 371 U.S. 75 (1962). In *U.S. v. Lane*, 474 U.S. 438 (1986), the Supreme Court rejected respondent's claim that there was insufficient evidence to support mail fraud convictions based upon insurance claims mailed after fruition of the scheme to defraud. In referring to *Sampson*, the *Lane* Court concluded that the after-the-scheme mailings met the "in furtherance" element in that they "were designed to lull the victims into a false sense of security."

§ 4.07   THE "IN FURTHERANCE" TEST

In 1989 the Supreme Court in *Schmuck v. U.S.*, 489 U.S. 705 (1989) enunciated a new test for determining whether a mailing was in furtherance of a scheme to defraud. The Court stated that a mailing is in furtherance if it "is part of the execution of the scheme as conceived by the perpetrator at the time."

In *Schmuck*, the defendant was convicted of twelve counts of mail fraud in a scheme of selling automobile dealers vehicles with rolled back odometers at prices artificially inflated as a result of the altered low-mileage. The mailings were twelve title applications submitted by the automobile dealers on behalf of their customers to the Wisconsin Department of Transportation.

The Supreme Court, in addition to rejecting defendant's argument that he was entitled to have the jury instructed on the lesser charge of odometer tampering, also rejected defendant's claim that the mailings were not in furtherance of the scheme to defraud.

Justice Blackmun, writing the opinion for the majority noted that the use of the mails need not be an essential element of the scheme. It is, likewise, irrelevant if it is later shown that the mailings were counterproductive to the scheme. Unlike *Kann, Parr,* and *Maze*, the mailings did not resemble post-fraud accounting. The Court found that the evidence in the *Schmuck* case supported a rational finding that the mailing was part of the execution as conceived by the defendant at the time. The title application was essential to the successful passage of title to the customers and thus to the continuity of the scheme. A failure in the passage of title would have jeopardized the defendant's "trust and goodwill with the retail dealers upon whose unwitting cooperation" the scheme depended.

A four person dissent criticized the majority in *Schmuck* for discarding precedent and for making mail fraud into a crime of "mail" and "fraud" as opposed to mailings that are in furtherance of the fraud. Whether the decision will create "problems for tomorrow," as predicted by the dissenters, remains to be seen. Likewise uncertain, is the viability of the four limitations to in furtherance previously recognized by courts.

§ 4.08 WIRE FRAUD

The wire fraud statute, 18 U.S.C. § 1343, was passed in 1952 and operates parallel to mail fraud. Like mail fraud, the emphasis of the crime is on the scheme to defraud as opposed to the means used in effectuating the deception. Wire fraud does, however, require a transmittal in interstate or foreign commerce by means of wire, radio, or television communication of writings, signs, signals, pictures or sounds.

Although there is a requirement of an interstate transmission, there is no requirement that the defendant know or foresee of the transmission going interstate. In *U.S. v. Bryant*, 766 F.2d 370 (8th Cir.1985), defendants sent two telegrams from Kansas City, Missouri to Bridgetown, Missouri. The telegrams, however, were routed through Middletown, Virginia. The Eighth Circuit affirmed the defendants' convictions for wire fraud finding that the defendant need not know or foresee that the communication would be interstate. The necessity for an interstate transmittal is merely a jurisdictional requirement to satisfy the constitutional limitation on congressional acts over intrastate activities pursuant to the Commerce Clause of the United States Constitution.

Like mail fraud, wire fraud requires that the government prove an intent to defraud. In *U.S. v. Czubinski*, 106 F.3d 1069 (1st Cir.1997), the First Circuit examined the convictions of an Internal Revenue Service representative for wire fraud, honest services fraud, and computer fraud. The court held that "[m]ere browsing of the records of people about whom one might have a particular interest, although reprehensible, is not enough to sustain a wire fraud conviction on a 'deprivation of intangible property' theory." See § 15.03.

§ 4.09　BANK FRAUD

In response to the increase in financial frauds, Congress in 1984 passed the bank fraud statute (18 U.S.C. § 1344). This statute criminalizes the conduct of one who "knowingly executes, or attempts to execute, a scheme or artifice (1) to defraud a financial institution, or (2) to obtain . . . property owned by, or under the custody or control of, a financial institution, by means of false or fraudulent pretenses, representations, or promises." Like mail fraud's provision relative to financial institutions, bank fraud today carries a penalty of up to thirty years imprisonment and a maximum fine of one million dollars.

The term "scheme to defraud" mirrors the term as seen in the mail and wire fraud statutes. In interpreting this element in the context of bank fraud, a court remarked that a scheme to defraud is incapable of precise definition. It requires case by case analysis to determine whether the scheme demonstrates a "departure from fundamental honesty, moral uprightness, or fair play and candid dealings in the general life of the community." *U.S. v. Goldblatt*, 813 F.2d 619 (3rd Cir.1987). In some cases, check kiting has been found to be a scheme to defraud that can be prosecuted as bank fraud. Courts have not, however, ruled consistently on whether the term "execute" should be interpreted to refer to the entire series of acts or whether multiple counts for each act can be charged.

In *Loughrin v. U.S.*, 134 S.Ct. 2384 (2014), the Supreme Court resolved a split in lower courts as to whether the government had to prove under subsection (2) of the statute that the defendant intended to defraud a bank. Finding that this statute differed from the mail fraud statute, the Court held that this was not required. The Court also rejected the defendant's federalism argument finding that "the test of § 1344(2) already limits its scope to deceptions that have some real connection to a federally insured bank, and thus implicate the pertinent federal interest."

§ 4.10　HEALTH CARE FRAUD

There are several different statutes that focus on health care fraud. Some of these are found in Title 42 of the United States Code. One statute, enacted in 1996 as part of the Health Insurance Portability and Accountability Act of 1996, and amended in 2010, is the health care fraud statute that is modeled after the mail fraud statute.

Like mail fraud, the health care fraud statute located in 18 U.S.C. § 1347 involves a scheme or article to defraud. It includes defrauding "(1) any health care benefit program; or (2) to obtain, by means of false or fraudulent pretenses, representations, or promises, any of the money or property owned by, or under the custody or control or, any health care benefit program." Unlike mail fraud, subsection (b) of the statute specifies that "a person need not have actual knowledge of this section or specific intent to commit a violation of this section."

Section 1347 carries fines and imprisonment of not more than ten years. But if the violation results in serious bodily injury it can be increased to twenty years, and if it results in death, then a term of years or life imprisonment.

§ 4.11   MAIL FRAUD AND OTHER CRIMES

Mail fraud is often used in place of or in conjunction with a statute that is specifically tailored to meet the prohibited conduct. It is rare that courts find it inappropriate to use mail fraud in these scenarios.

For example, in *U.S. v. Computer Sciences Corp.*, 689 F.2d 1181 (4th Cir.1982), the Fourth Circuit concluded that the district court had erred in dismissing mail and wire fraud charges being prosecuted in conjunction with a charge pursuant to the false claims statute (18 U.S.C. § 287). The court found no language in the statutes that revealed "mutual exclusivity insofar as the prosecution is concerned."

Mail fraud is used in cases where the crimes could be prosecuted under the Bankruptcy Act, Landum-Griffin Act, Jenkins Act, National Stolen Property Act, Truth in Lending Act and the Federal Trade Commission Act. Mail fraud is often an alternative to a securities violation. In *Edwards v. U.S.*, 312 U.S. 473 (1941) the Supreme Court rejected the argument that securities laws preempt the use of the mail fraud statute. The Court noted that "[t]he two can exist and be useful, side by side."

A rare instance of finding the use of mail fraud as overcharging by a prosecutor is seen in the case of *U.S. v. Henderson*, 386 F.Supp. 1048 (S.D.N.Y. 1974). This 1974 decision of the United States District Court of the Southern District of New York involved charges of attempted evasion of taxes and mail fraud for the mailing of the tax returns. The court rejected the joint charges as a "pyramiding of sentences" that was "utterly unrealistic." Use of mail fraud to reach the same conduct prohibited by the Internal Revenue Code was found to be "beyond the intent of Congress."

The *Henderson* court view has been rejected by the majority of courts deciding issues of a similar nature. The Department of Justice did, however, recently add a guideline requiring department approval prior to bringing a mail fraud prosecution that is premised upon mailed tax returns. This guideline provides that authorization for this type of prosecution will only be granted in exceptional circumstances.

CHAPTER 5

SECURITIES FRAUD

§ 5.01   INTRODUCTION

An overlap between civil and criminal law is apparent in examining cases involving securities fraud. An individual violating securities statutes can be subject to civil and administrative proceedings, criminal prosecution, or dual civil and criminal actions (see chap. 18). The Supreme Court, however, held in *Central Bank of Denver v. First Interstate Bank of Denver*, 511 U.S. 164 (1994), that a private plaintiff could not use 18 U.S.C. § 2, the aiding and abetting statute, as the basis of their suit under § 10(b) of the Securities Exchange Act. To sustain a criminal prosecution it is necessary that the accused acted willfully.

Securities violations are typically investigated by the Securities and Exchange Commission (SEC). Most often criminal prosecutions arise when the SEC refers the matter to the Department of Justice for criminal prosecution. (15 U.S.C. § 78u(d)). Selective enforcement of violations occurs both in the referring of matters to the Department of Justice and in their decision of whether to prosecute.

Although securities violations may arise under an array of federal acts, most often prosecutions under securities law emanate from the Securities Act of 1933 and the Securities Exchange Act of 1934.

These acts are found in Title 15 of the United States Code.

Section 24 of the Securities Act of 1933 (15 U.S.C. § 77x) provides criminality to willful violations of provisions under the Act or rules and regulations of the Commission. It also prohibits, in a registration statement filed under the Act, the making of any untrue statement of material fact or omitting to state any material fact required to be stated or necessary so as to keep a statement from being misleading. This felony offense authorizes a fine and imprisonment up to five years.

The Securities Exchange Act of 1934, likewise, provides criminality to willful violations of the civil provisions of the Act. A willful violation of a provision of this Act, or rule or regulation thereunder, can result in criminal penalties. Additionally, false or misleading statements of material facts made willfully and knowing in "any application, report, or document required to be filed" by the Act are subject to criminal prosecution with individuals eligible to receive fines up to five million dollars and imprisonment up to twenty years. This can be increased to twenty-five million dollars for organizations. The authorized term of imprisonment cannot be imposed if the defendants prove that they had no knowledge of the rule or regulation violated. The penalty provision also differs for a violation of 15 U.S.C. § 78dd–1, the statute pertaining to the prohibited foreign trade practices by issuers.

Prosecutions of securities fraud have concentrated on violations of section 17(a) of the

Securities Act of 1933 and section 10(b) of the Securities Exchange Act of 1934 and its accompanying Rule 10b–5. WCH § 5.4. Cases examining alleged 10(b) violations have considered whether there was a misstatement or omission of a material fact; whether the accused acted with applicable level of scienter; and whether the activity was in connection with the purchase or sale of a security. WCH § 5.4.

In recent years, prosecutions under these provisions have been the subject of significant publicity with increased government investigations into insider trading. Legislative response to insider trading is seen in the passage of two congressional acts. The Insider Trading Sanctions Act (ITSA) and the Insider Trading and Securities Fraud Enforcement Act (ITSFEA) include provisions that increase the penalties to individuals engaged in improper insider trading.

Other securities sections have also served as the basis of a criminal prosecution. For example, prosecutions have been brought under section 5 of the Securities Act of 1933 for failure to register the sale of securities. Failure to file reports or the filing of false reports are among the prosecutions brought under the Securities Exchange Act of 1934.

The Sarbanes Oxley Act of 2002 added a securities fraud statute and placed it in title 18 with other criminal offenses. The statute carries a penalty of up to twenty-five years. (18 U.S.C. § 1348) The Sarbanes Oxley Act also added a statute for failure of corporate officers to certify financial reports (18 U.S.C. § 1350) and a statute that allows prosecutions of attempts and conspiracies under the fraud statutes in title 18. (18 U.S.C. § 1349).

Securities fraud is not prosecuted exclusively under specific securities statutes. The government sometimes uses general criminal provisions such as mail fraud. Other general criminal statutes that have been employed include wire fraud, false statements, perjury, obstruction of justice, interstate transportation of stolen property, and conspiracy to commit an offense against the United States or to defraud the United States.

§ 5.02　MENS REA

Willfulness is necessary for a criminal prosecution under the Securities Act and Securities Exchange Act. This mens rea precludes prosecutions when the accused acted through mistake, excusable neglect, or inadvertence. Acts that are deliberate and intentional have been found sufficient to meet the willfulness requirement. Although willfulness does not necessitate that the defendant be aware of the applicable statute or rule, some circuits require that the prosecutor establish "a realization on the defendant's part that he was doing a wrongful act." *U.S. v. Peltz*, 433 F.2d 48 (2d Cir.1970).

Although most courts find mere negligent conduct insufficient, reckless indifference has been found to be an intentional misrepresentation. Courts have found it proper to charge a jury "that the specific intent to deceive may be found from a material misrepresentation of fact made with reckless disregard of the facts." *U.S. v. Boyer*, 694 F.2d 58 (3rd Cir.1982).

One who acts with willful blindness can also be found culpable. When a person standing in a position of authority takes a "hands off" position, it has been found proper for the court to give a "conscious avoidance" instruction. *U.S. v. Langford*, 946 F.2d 798 (11th Cir.1991). In *U.S. v. Ebbers*, 458 F.3d 110 (2d Cir.2006), the court found that a conscious-avoidance instruction was proper when the accused, the former CEO of Worldcom, Inc. testified that he signed documents that "he didn't bother to read in full," and tossed a "management budget variance report in the trash without reading it." Recently, defendants relying on *Global Tech Appliances, Inc. v. SEB, S.A.*, 131 S.Ct. 2060 (2011) have argued for a higher standard—"deliberate acts"—for a court to give a willful blindness instruction. See § 1.05.

Willfulness can be proved through circumstantial evidence. A jury may infer this intent from the evidence presented. The experience and intellect of the accused, as well as the cumulative effect of all the evidence presented, have been factors used in supporting a jury determination of willfulness. *U.S. v. White*, 124 F.2d 181 (2d Cir.1941).

Defendants have argued unsuccessfully that the government should be required to prove violations of GAAP, the Generally Accepted Accounting Principles that serve as the official standards of the American Institute of Certified Public Accountants.

Although a "good faith attempt to comply with GAAP or reliance upon an accountant's advice regarding GAAP may negate the government's claim of an intent to deceive," it cannot be used as a "shield [ ]in a case ... where the evidence showed that accounting methods known to be misleading—although perhaps at times fortuitously in compliance with particular GAAP rules—were used for the express purpose of intentionally misstating WorldCom's financial condition and artificially inflating its stock price." *U.S. v. Ebbers*, 458 F.3d 110 (2d Cir.2006).

A person can be found culpable for willfully violating a statute, rule, or regulation of the Securities Act of 1933 and Securities Exchange Act of 1934 absent knowledge of the existence of the applicable statute, rule, or regulation. Knowledge, however, is required under the Securities Exchange Act of 1934 when the criminal charge is premised upon a false or misleading statement of any material fact in any application, report, or document required to be filed under the Act. *U.S. v. Dixon*, 536 F.3d 1388 (2d Cir.1976). Thus, the government must prove that the accused acted both willfully and knowingly when proceeding under the second clause of section 32(a) of the Securities Exchange Act of 1934.

When a defendant, convicted under the Securities Exchange Act of 1934, has no knowledge of the violated rule or regulation, the court is precluded by statute from entering a sentence of imprisonment. The defendant, however, has the burden to demonstrate a lack of knowledge. Since the no knowledge proviso is directed toward sentencing, it has been found not to place an unconstitutional burden on the defendant to disprove an element of the offense. *U.S. v. Mandel*, 296 F.Supp. 1038 (S.D.N.Y.1969).

A defendant, who plead guilty to a violation of Rule 10b–5, was precluded from obtaining the benefits of the no knowledge proviso in *U.S. v. Lilley*, 291 F.Supp. 989 (S.D.Tex.1968). The court found that the "no knowledge" clause meant that the accused had no knowledge that their conduct was contrary to law. The court stated that it does not mean that the defendant did not know "the precise number or common name of the rule, the book and page where it was to be found, or the date upon which it was promulgated. It does not even mean proof of a lack of knowledge that their conduct was proscribed by rule rather than by statute." The court found that by pleading guilty to securities fraud, the "defendants admitted that they knew securities fraud was prohibited, which is the substance of Rule 10b–5. No more knowledge is required."

§ 5.03   INSIDER TRADING

There is an "expectation of the securities marketplace that all investors trading on impersonal exchanges have relatively equal access to material information." *Securities and Exchange Commission v. Texas Gulf Sulphur Co.*, 401 F.2d 833 (2d Cir.1968). Insider trading, although not specifically defined by any statute, arises when an insider, with material nonpublic information, trades in securities without first disclosing the material inside information to the public. Issues arise as who is an insider and when it is necessary to disclose nonpublic information. Issues can also arise as to whether the information is material.

There are two approaches to insider trading: "(1) a 'classical theory' involving corporate insiders, and (2) a 'misappropriation theory' involving 'persons who are not corporate insiders but to whom material non-public information has been entrusted in confidence and who breach a fiduciary duty to the source of the information to gain personal profit in the securities market.'" *U.S. v. O'Hagan*, 521 U.S. 642 (1997).

In addition to considering whether one is a corporate insider or one who misappropriates information under a fiduciary obligation, insider trading law has also been applied to instances where one of these parties "discloses the information to an outsider ("tippee") who then trades on the basis of the information before it is publicly disclosed." *U.S. v. Newman*, 664 F.2d 12 (2d Cir.2014).

Insider trading prosecutions have been at the forefront of white collar crime cases. Investment bankers, lawyers, arbitragers, and financial executives have been among the many that have been indicted and convicted for violations of securities laws. In many instances the individuals reached plea agreements that required government cooperation in further investigations. Significant publicity has surrounded many of the insider trading cases.

Insider trading cases are sometimes prosecuted under section 10(b) of the Securities Exchange Act of 1934 and its accompanying Rule 10b–5. The government has the burden of proving that the accused willfully employed a scheme to defraud, or misrepresented or failed to disclose a material fact, or engaged in a course of business which operated as a fraud, in connection with the purchase or sale of any security. *U.S. v. Koenig*, 388 F.Supp. 670 (S.D.N.Y.1974). Federal jurisdiction is attained by showing that the accused used a means or instrumentality of interstate commerce, the mails, or any facility of any national securities exchange. 10(b) has been found not to apply extraterritorially. *Morrison v. National Australia Bank Ltd.*, 561 U.S. 247 (2010). See WCH 8.2(A)(2).

In *Chiarella v. U.S.*, 445 U.S. 222 (1980), the Supreme Court reversed a criminal conviction that was predicated on a violation of Rule 10b–5. Petitioner Chiarella worked as a "markup man" for a financial printer engaged in the printing of announcements of corporate takeover bids. Although the documents delivered to the printer did not initially disclose the names of the target companies, petitioner deduced this information and purchased stock in the target companies prior to this information being disclosed to the public. Chiarella's profits from the purchase and sale of these stocks exceeded thirty thousand dollars.

Justice Powell, writing the opinion for the majority, examined the effect of silence on the part of a person holding nonpublic market information. The Court reaffirmed the position taken in the Securities and Exchange Commission case of *In the Matter of Cady, Roberts & Co.*, 40 S.E.C. 907 (1961), which held that a corporate insider must abstain from trading in the shares of the corporation unless the corporate insider has first disclosed all known material inside information. The obligation to disclose, however, rested upon one having the affirmative "duty to disclose arising from a relationship of trust and confidence between parties to a transaction."

Distinguishing petitioner's conduct from this precedent, the Court noted that Chiarella was not a corporate insider and that he had not received confidential information from the target company. The Court found error that the trial court "[i]n effect . . . instructed the jury that petitioner owed a duty to everyone; to all sellers, indeed, to the market as a whole." Not being an agent, fiduciary, or person in whom the sellers had placed their trust and confidence petitioner did not have a duty to disclose. To hold otherwise, the Court believed would create a "general duty between all participants in market transactions to forego actions based on material, nonpublic information."

The Court in *Chiarella* refused to speculate on what duty may be owed to anyone other than the seller, in that the issue had not been submitted to the jury. The dissenting opinions, however, addressed this second question finding that the jury instructions properly charged a violation of Section 10(b) and Rule 10b–5. Chief Justice Burger, in his dissenting opinion, expressed the view that Chiarella had "misappropriated—stole to put it bluntly—valuable nonpublic information entrusted to him in the utmost confidence."

The Court expounded upon the ramifications of the disclosure of information in the case of *Dirks v. Securities and Exchange Commission*, 463 U.S. 646 (1983). Dirks, a securities analyst, received inside information from a former officer of Equity Funding of America. This information, of alleged overstatement of assets by the company as a result of fraudulent corporate practices, was given to Dirks for the purpose of verification and disclosure to the public. Dirks received a censure from the SEC for disclosure of this inside information to clients and investors. The SEC took the position that a tippee "inherits" the duty to disclose the information or abstain whenever the tippee receives the information from an insider. By passing the information to traders the SEC found that Dirks had breached this fiduciary duty.

In reversing the SEC position that had been upheld by the lower courts, the Supreme Court in a 6–3 decision found that Dirks had no duty to abstain from using this information. Justice Powell, writing the majority opinion, found that "[t]he tippers received no monetary or personal benefit for revealing Equity Funding's secrets, nor was their purpose to make a gift of valuable information to

Dirks." Since the motivation was the exposure of the fraud, the Court found no breach of duty to shareholders by the insider. Absent a breach of duty by the insider, there was no derivative breach by Dirks.

In *U.S. v. Newman*, 664 F.2d 12 (2d Cir.2014), the Second Circuit held that to "sustain an insider trading conviction against a tippee, the Government must prove" the following elements: "(1) the corporate insider was entrusted with a fiduciary duty; (2) the corporate insider breached his fiduciary duty by (a) disclosing confidential information to a tippee (b) in exchange for a personal benefit; (3) the tippee knew of the tipper's breach, that is, he knew the information was confidential and divulged for personal benefit; and (4) the tippee still used that information to trade in a security or tip another individual for personal benefit." In vacating convictions the court stated that "the insider's disclosure of confidential information, standing alone, is not a breach." It must also be shown that the "tippee knows of the personal benefit received by the insider in exchange for the disclosure."

§ 5.04 DEVELOPMENT OF THE MISAPPROPRIATION THEORY

In both *Chiarella* and *Dirks* the Court concentrated on the duty owed to shareholders by an insider and by individuals receiving information from the insider. Absent a duty owed, the Court was not willing to extend insider trading liability. Some appellate courts, however, permitted the bounds of insider trading to be extended through the use of a misappropriation theory.

The doctrine of misappropriation arose in Chief Justice Burger's dissenting opinion in the *Chiarella* case. He expressed the view "that a person who has misappropriated nonpublic information has an absolute duty to disclose that information or to refrain from trading." In *U.S. v. Newman*, 664 F.2d 12 (2d Cir.1981), the Second Circuit accepted and applied this misappropriation theory. Newman was accused of participating in a scheme to misappropriate confidential information regarding upcoming tender offers. He, along with two co-conspirators, employees of two investment banking firms, were alleged to have gathered and traded on nonpublic information.

The prosecution's indictment in the *Newman* case focused on the issue unresolved in *Chiarella*, that being, duties owed to persons other than the sellers. The government's case specifically rested upon a duty allegedly owing to the defendant's employers and their employers' clients. The court in *Newman* reversed the district court's dismissal of the indictment, finding that Rule 10b–5 contained "no specific requirement that fraud be perpetrated upon the seller or buyer of securities." The court noted that in other areas of the law, deceitful misappropriation of confidential information by a fiduciary, was considered a crime. The court found that this same standard should be applied to conduct under the Securities Acts.

The tenuous status of the misappropriation theory was highlighted by the fact that the 1981 *Newman* case was not a unanimous decision. A concurring and dissenting opinion, written by Senior District Judge Dumbauld, noted that "[t]he culprits in the case at bar (as in *Chiarella*) owed no duty to the sellers of the target company securities which they purchased." Despite the deceptive and improper violation of a fiduciary duty to employers and customers of the employers, Judge Dumbauld stated that these parties had not at the time actually purchased or sold any target securities.

Later decisions in the second circuit, however, affirmed the use of the misappropriation theory in the context of an employee misappropriating confidential information. In *Securities and Exchange Commission v. Materia*, 745 F.2d 197 (2d Cir.1984), the Second Circuit affirmed an injunction and disgorgement of unlawfully obtained profits where an employee of a printing company misappropriated confidential information concerning tender offers and subsequently traded on the information. The court found that the misappropriation of material nonpublic information by an employee, perpetrated a fraud upon the employer that was prohibited by the antifraud provisions of the Securities Exchange Act of 1934.

In *U.S. v. Carpenter*, 791 F.2d 1024 (2d Cir.1986), the Second Circuit revisited the misappropriation theory in the context of convictions of a newspaper reporter, former newspaper clerk, and stockbroker for violations of section 10(b) of the Securities

Exchange Act of 1934 and Rule 10b–5. The Supreme Court accepted certiorari on this case but affirmed the securities violations by an equally divided court. Defendants' convictions for mail and wire fraud were unanimously affirmed in a landmark Supreme Court case that held that the "money or property" clause of the mail fraud statute included both tangible and intangible property (see chap. 4).

In affirming the district court's judgment of conviction on the securities fraud counts, the Second Circuit in *Carpenter* examined the misappropriation theory as applied to an insider trading scheme that misappropriated information from the Wall Street Journal prior to its publication. Although *Newman* and *Materia* involved corporate clients of the employer, the court found that the misappropriation theory "broadly proscribes the conversion by 'insiders' or *others* of material non-public information in connection with the purchase or sale of securities."

The Supreme Court directly addressed and endorsed the misappropriation theory in its decision in *U.S. v. O'Hagan*, 521 U.S. 642 (1997). Justice Ginsberg's majority opinion initially distinguishes the "classical theory" from the "misappropriation theory." "The classical theory targets a corporate insider's breach of duty to shareholders with whom the insider transacts; the misappropriation theory outlaws trading on the basis of nonpublic information by a corporate 'outsider' in breach of a duty owed not to a trading party, but to the source of the information." "In lieu of premising liability on a fiduciary relationship between company insider and purchaser or seller of the company's stock, the misappropriation theory premises liability on a fiduciary turned trader's deception of those who entrusted him with access to confidential information."

Finding "deception" through nondisclosure "central" to a misappropriation theory, the Court noted "if the fiduciary discloses to the source that he plans to trade on the nonpublic information, there is no 'deceptive device' and thus no § 10(b) violation— although the fiduciary turned trader may remain liable under state law for breach of a duty of loyalty." The Court also noted that the element "in connection with the purchase or sale of [a] security" is met "because the fiduciary's fraud is consummated, not when the fiduciary gains the confidential information, but when, without disclosure to his principal, he uses the information to purchase or sell securities." *U.S. v. O'Hagan*, 521 U.S. 642 (1997).

CHAPTER 6

OBSTRUCTION OF JUSTICE

§ 6.01 INTRODUCTION

Most of the obstruction of justice offenses are found in chapter 73 of Title 18. Here one finds a conglomerate of specific statutes that protect proceedings in the three branches of government in addition to the individuals connected with these proceedings. There has been a growth and restructuring of these offenses in recent years to increase the protection afforded witnesses, victims, and informants as well as provide smoother federal audits and examinations of financial institutions. There has also been several high-profile cases that included obstruction of justice charges. (e.g., Martha Stewart, I. Lewis "Scooter" Libby, Arthur Andersen, LL.P).

The breadth of protection provided by the obstruction of justice statutes in chapter 73 is seen by examining these specific offenses. Criminalized by specific statutes are obstructive conduct involving an assault on a process server (§ 1501), resistance to an extradition agent (§ 1502), influencing a juror through a writing (§ 1504), theft or alteration of a record or process (§ 1506), picketing, parading, using sound equipment, or demonstrating in or near a courthouse or "a building or residence occupied or used by such judge, juror, witness, or court officer" (§ 1507), "[r]ecording, listening to, or observing proceedings of grand or petit juries while [they are] deliberating or voting" (§ 1508), obstruction relating to court orders (§ 1509), and obstruction pertaining to state and local law enforcement (§ 1511).

Section 1503 has historically served as the focal point of the obstruction charges. Although its original protection was for officers, jurors, and witnesses, the passage of the Victim and Witness Protection Act in 1982 transferred the specific reference to witnesses in section 1503 into new provisions of this chapter. Despite the elimination in section 1503's language of obstruction against witnesses, the section remains a noteworthy provision in that it contains an omnibus clause that prohibits obstruction of the "due administration of justice."

The Victim and Witness Protection Act also modified section 1505. This section pertains to obstruction under the Antitrust Civil Process Act and proceedings before departments, agencies, and committees of the government. This section plays a crucial role in the prosecution of obstructions related to proceedings before Congress and federal agencies. In *U.S. v. Poindexter*, 951 F.2d 369 (D.C.Cir.1991), the District of Columbia held the term "corruptly," as used in section 1505, to be "too vague to provide constitutionally adequate notice that it prohibits lying to the Congress." The court stated that, "neither the legislative history nor the prior judicial interpretation of § 1505 supplies the constitutionally required notice that the statute on its face lacks."

In 1996 Congress modified this section by including in § 1515, the definitions section of the obstruction statutes, that the term "corruptly" as used in § 1505 "means acting with an improper purpose, personally or by influencing another, including making a false or misleading statement, or withholding, concealing, altering, or destroying a document or other information." 18 U.S.C. § 1515(b). Also added was a statement that the "chapter does not prohibit or punish the providing of lawful, bona fide, legal representation services in connection with or anticipation of an official proceeding." 18 U.S.C. § 1515(c).

Originally, section 1505 criminalized obstructive conduct directed against both witnesses and parties. As a result of the Victim and Witness Protection Act, witnesses and parties are now incorporated into the obstruction statutes. Untouched by the 1982 amendment, however, is the omnibus clause of section 1505 that protects "the due and proper administration of the law under which any pending proceeding is being had before any department or agency of the United States."

Two of the provisions created by the Victim and Witness Protection Act, sections 1512 and 1513, heighten the scrutiny provided to obstruction involving witnesses, victims, and informants. Section 1512 criminalizes conduct that uses intimidation, physical force, or threats, or conduct that involves corruptly persuading another person to withhold testimony, destroy objects of an official proceeding, evade legal process, or be absent from an official proceeding. This section includes conduct involving attempts to kill and actual killing of a person to prevent that individual from testifying, producing evidence, or communicating information about the commission of a crime or a violation of probation, parole, or release. As part of the Sarbanes Oxley Act, section 1512 was amended to include document destruction by the accused.

Section 1512 is applicable to incidents within the United States, as well as providing extraterritorial federal jurisdiction. Additionally, the government is given discretion to bring an action for violation of this section in either the district of the official proceeding, or alternatively, the location where the alleged offense occurred.

Where section 1512 concentrates on obstruction prior to a proceeding, section 1513 focuses on retaliation against witnesses, victims, and informants. Section 1513 prohibits conduct that causes or threatens to cause "bodily injury to another person" as retaliation for being a witness, providing evidence in an official proceeding, or giving information relating to an offense to a law enforcement officer. Section 1513 also applies to acts both inside and outside the United States. The Sarbanes Oxley Act of 2002 amended this section to include retaliation against whistleblowers who provide information to law enforcement.

Also added to the obstruction offenses by the Victim and Witness Protection Act of 1982 is a provision that permits a government attorney to bring a civil action to restrain harassment of a victim or witness. (§ 1514). This section provides for a temporary restraining order and issuance of protective order where "there are reasonable grounds to believe that harassment of an identified victim or witness in a Federal criminal case exists or that such an order is necessary to prevent and restrain an offense under section 1512 of this title, other than an offense consisting of misleading conduct, or under section 1513 of this title."

Another key provision for the government's prosecution of obstructive conduct is found in section 1510 of title 18. This section prohibits obstruction of criminal investigations by means of bribery. It criminalizes obstruction of criminal investigations by officers of financial institutions and obstruction by those involved in the business of insurance.

This recent focus on financial criminality is reflected not only in section 1510, but also by several other additions to the obstruction statutes. These are section 1516, a provision criminalizing obstruction of a federal audit and section 1517, making it a criminal offense to obstruct the examination of a financial institution. The focus on health care fraud is reflected in the addition of section 1518, a section relating to obstruction of criminal investigations of health care offenses.

The Sarbanes Oxley Act added section 1519 and 1520 to the obstruction statutes. Section 1519, which carries a penalty of up to twenty years imprisonment pertains to the "destruction alteration, or falsification of records in Federal investigations and bankruptcy." Section 1520, a statute with a maximum penalty of ten years, relates to "destruction of corporate audit records."

In *Yates v. U.S.*, 135 S.Ct. 1074 (2015), the Court rejected the use of the Sarbanes Oxley Act's § 1519 "tangible objects" provision for a fisherman who threw over fish after being told to bring them to shore. The Court stated, "we hold that a 'tangible object' within § 1519's compass is one used to record or preserve information."

Penalties for obstruction of justice vary dependent upon the specific statutory offense employed. For example, the basic sentence for a violation of § 1503, is up to ten years imprisonment, but can be increased with imprisonment of up to twenty years in the case of an attempted killing or where the offense is against a petit jury and a class A or B felony has been charged. An actual killing can result in a sentence of death. Where the offense "occurs in connection with a trial of a criminal case, and the act in violation of this section involves the threat of physical force or physical force, the maximum term of imprisonment which may be imposed for the offense shall be the higher of that otherwise provided by law or the maximum term that could have been imposed for any offense charged in such case."

In addition to obstruction of justice being a crime, it also serves as an enhancement under the federal sentencing guidelines. Obstruction conduct can increase the defendant's sentence. WCH § 6.1(C).

§ 6.02   OVERVIEW OF SECTION 1503

Section 1503 of Title 18 is a contempt statute emanating from the Act of March 2, 1831. Section one of the Act of 1831 pertained to contemptuous conduct occurring in the presence of the court. Section two of this act focused on conduct away from the court. This predecessor statute was eventually split into two distinct offenses with 18 U.S.C. § 401 being obstruction in the court's presence and 18 U.S.C. § 1503 being obstruction away from the court. *U.S. v. Essex*, 407 F.2d 214 (6th Cir.1969).

Section 1503 originally served as the focus of obstruction offenses for obstructive acts against witnesses, parties, jurors, or court officers. The Victim and Witness Protection Act removed witnesses and parties from the language of section 1503 making the specific emphasis of the statute on acts occurring against grand and petit jurors and judicial officers. The Victim and Witness Protection Act did not, however, modify the catch-all clause of section 1503 that prohibits obstruction of the "due administration of justice." Thus, today, section 1503 can be divided into two categories; (a) acts of obstruction to jurors or court officers, and (b) obstruction of the "due administration of justice."

Acts of obstruction against jurors or court officers includes **threats or force** that endeavor to "influence, intimidate, or impede any grand or petit juror" or court officer in the discharge of their duties or alternatively, acts of obstruction that **injure** jurors or court officers. "Jurors" has been interpreted to include prospective jurors, and federal district court judges have been found to be included within the category of "officer[s] in or of any court."

The most noteworthy aspect of section 1503 still remains the omnibus clause that covers conduct impeding the "due administration of justice." In order to sustain a conviction under the omnibus clause of section 1503 the government must show that the accused (1) "corruptly or by threats or force," (2) endeavored, (3) "to influence, obstruct, or impede, the due administration of justice." These elements are not always distinct entities, but are often intertwined, with the same evidence being sufficient to meet several aspects of the offense.

§ 6.03 CORRUPTLY OR BY THREATS OR FORCE—SECTION 1503

Section 1503 requires that the defendant engage in conduct "corruptly, or by threats or force, or by any threatening letter or communication." Courts have generally interpreted these provisions in the alternative finding it only necessary for the government to have evidence of either the accused acting "corruptly" or using some type of "threats or force."

Controversy has existed as to the level of proof required to meet the statutory requisite of "corruptly." Some courts find the term "corruptly" not to be an element of the offense that necessitates specific proof. It can be met by a showing of any attempt to influence a juror or court officer. For example in *U.S. v. Ogle*, 613 F.2d 233 (10th

Cir.1979) the Tenth Circuit agreed with the trial judge's position that "an endeavor to influence a juror in the performance of his or her duty or to influence, obstruct or impede the due administration of justice is per se unlawful and is tantamount to doing the act corruptly." The court in *Ogle* noted "that the term 'corruptly' does not superimpose a special and additional element on the offense such as a desire to undermine the moral character of a juror." Some courts admit that the term "corruptly" is capable of "different meanings in different connections," but then conclude that as used in section 1503 it includes "any endeavor to influence a witness or to impede and obstruct justice." *U.S. v. Cohen*, 202 F.Supp. 587 (D.Conn.1962).

In contrast, other courts have made "corruptly" a separate element that the government must specifically prove. "The offending conduct must be prompted, at least in part, by a 'corrupt motive'. . . . and if there is a fair doubt as to whether the defendants' conduct is embraced within the prohibition, the policy of lenity requires that the doubt be resolved in favor of the accused." *U.S. v. Brand*, 775 F.2d 1460 (11th Cir.1985). In this context, "corruptly" can require a showing that the accused acted "for an evil or wicked purpose." *U.S. v. Ryan*, 455 F.2d 728 (9th Cir.1971). In some instances the "evil or wicked purpose" is met by a showing that the accused acted intentionally or willfully.

In *U.S. v. Thomas*, 916 F.2d 647 (11th Cir.1990), the Eleventh Circuit combined some of the varying approaches used in defining the element of "corruptly." The court found "corruptly" to be "the specific intent of the crime," but noted that its meaning can vary with the prosecution. The court stated that, "[g]enerally, the government must show that the defendant knowingly and intentionally undertook an action from which an obstruction of justice was a reasonably foreseeable result. . . . Although the government is not required to prove that the defendant had the specific purpose of obstructing justice . . . it must establish that the conduct was prompted, at least in part, by a 'corrupt motive.' "

A wide assortment of activities have been found to meet the definition of "corruptly." For example "the destruction or concealment of documents can fall within the prohibition of the statute." *U.S. v. Rasheed*, 663 F.2d 843 (9th Cir.1981). Although acts of bribery are not required to meet this element of the offense, when there is evidence of bribery, courts have found that there is per se evidence of acting "corruptly." Fraudulent conduct by the accused also can form the basis of this element. As stated in *U.S. v. Polakoff*, 121 F.2d 333 (2d Cir.1941), "[i]t is as 'corrupt' to persuade a public officer by lies as by bribes."

In *Cole v. U.S.*, 329 F.2d 437 (9th Cir.1964), the Ninth Circuit discussed the relationship between advising someone to claim the constitutional privilege against self-incrimination and violating section 1503. Although exercising this constitutional right is lawful, where one "bribes, coerces, forces or threatens a witness to claim it, or advises with corrupt motive the witness to take it," it can be found to be an obstruction of justice. In affirming the defendant's conviction in *Cole*, the court noted that the jury had been instructed "that only *corrupt* methods were prohibited; that *corrupt* influence was the only influence proscribed;—that only any act committed *corruptly* was to be considered."

The question of whether a defendant endeavored to influence a witness "corruptly" has been held by one court to be a "mixed question of law and fact, if not one of fact alone." *U.S. v. Fayer*, 523 F.2d 661 (2d Cir.1975). Most courts hold that whether the endeavor was "corrupt" is a question for the jury to determine. *U.S. v. Fasolino*, 586 F.2d 939 (2d Cir.1978).

§ 6.04   ENDEAVORS—SECTION 1503

For the crime of obstruction of justice, an actual obstruction is not required. It is only necessary that the accused "endeavored" to obstruct justice. "[A]n endeavor within the statute . . . is very similar to a criminal solicitation statute . . . and does not require proof that would support a charge of attempt." *U.S. v. Fasolino*, 586 F.2d 939 (2d Cir.1978).

In *U.S. v. Silverman*, 745 F.2d 1386 (11th Cir.1984), the Eleventh Circuit stated that " '[e]ndeavor' . . . describes any effort or assay to accomplish the evil purpose the statute was enacted to prevent. . . . The government is not required to prove, however, that the defendant harbored the specific purpose of obstructing the due administration of justice; all the government has to establish is that the defendant should have reasonably foreseen that the natural and probable consequence of the success of his scheme would achieve precisely that result." Thus, one does not have to succeed in the endeavor for there to be a successful prosecution for obstruction of justice.

Discussion of whether the defendant endeavored to obstruct justice has occasionally come into play when there is an issue related to the obtaining or giving of a false statement to a court officer. Reversed by the Eleventh Circuit was a conviction where the false statement was not submitted to the prosecutor and it was shown that the false statement never in fact existed. *U.S. v. Brand*, 775 F.2d 1460 (11th Cir.1985). Where, however, the false statement actually existed, the government relied upon its existence, and there was evidence that it was likely that the statement would be produced in court and justice would be obstructed, it has been found sufficient to satisfy the "endeavor" element. The fact that the false statement was never actually used in court does not bring the conduct outside the purview of the statute. *U.S. v. Fields*, 838 F.2d 1571 (11th Cir.1988).

§ 6.05   TO INFLUENCE, OBSTRUCT OR IMPEDE THE DUE ADMINISTRATION OF JUSTICE—SECTION 1503

To meet the element of influencing, obstructing, or impeding the due administration of justice, there must be (1) a pending proceeding, (2) that the accused knew or had notice of, and (3) that the accused intended to influence, obstruct, or impede its administration. Here again, an actual obstruction, although helpful, is not required. The "conduct must be such, however, that its natural and probable effect would be the interference with the due administration of justice." *U.S. v. Thomas*, 916 F.2d 647 (11th Cir.1990).

Although a "pending proceeding" is required for application of the omnibus clause of section 1503, courts have liberally construed the term. The term "proceeding" is not limited to an actual court trial. Rather, conduct relating to grand jury proceedings and conduct occurring while a matter is proceeding on appeal have been found sufficient to support an obstruction of justice charge.

Some courts have interpreted "pending proceeding" to include acts occurring after at least a complaint has been filed with the magistrate or a grand jury impaneled. Thus, obstruction of FBI, IRS, or other government agency investigations would not by itself be sufficient to meet the "judicial proceeding" requirement.

Even though a grand jury has been impaneled, however, does not mean that the "pending proceeding" element has always been satisfied. Courts vary on the level of activity required by the grand jury to meet this element. Where an impaneled grand jury has issued no subpoenas, has not been apprised of the alleged criminal conduct, and there has been no showing that the defendant has knowledge of the federal grand jury proceeding, it has been found there was insufficient activity to meet the pending judicial proceeding element. In contrast, where subpoenas have been issued by the Assistant United States Attorney, even though the grand jury has no knowledge of the subpoena or criminal conduct, there was activity sufficient to form the basis of an obstruction charge. *U.S. v. Simmons*, 591 F.2d 206 (3d Cir.1979). If the subpoena, however, is merely to furnish documents for an agency investigation, as opposed to an actual grand jury investigation, it has been found insufficient to meet the requirement of a proceeding for purposes of section 1503.

Besides there being a pending judicial proceeding, it is incumbent that the accused have knowledge or notice of that fact. In *Pettibone v. U.S.*, 148 U.S. 197 (1893), a case involving a conspiracy to obstruct the due administration of justice, the Court stated that " ... a person is not sufficiently charged with obstruction or impeding the due administration of justice in a court unless it appears that he knew or had notice that justice was being administered in such court."

Cases after *Pettibone* have held that there is no requirement that there be direct evidence of knowledge. Information or a reasonably founded belief can be sufficient. Further, knowledge can be inferred from the evidence. Although knowledge is required, the government does not have to prove that the defendant knew that it was a federal proceeding. In *U.S. v. Aguilar*, 515 U.S. 593 (1995), the Supreme Court stated that "[t]he action taken by the accused must be with an intent to influence judicial or grand jury proceedings; it is not enough that there be an intent to influence some ancillary proceeding, such as an investigation independent of the court's or grand jury authority."

Knowledge or notice of the pending proceeding must be accompanied by an intent to impede its administration. *U.S. v. Guzzino*, 810 F.2d 687 (7th Cir.1987). Although a specific intent to impede the administration of justice is an essential element of the offense, direct evidence of this intent is not required. Circumstantial evidence may be used to infer the intent. The level of intent necessary may depend upon what definition a court gives to the term "corruptly." In *U.S. v. Quattrone*, 441 F.3d 153 (2d Cir.2006), the Second Circuit vacated convictions holding that "a defendant must know that his corrupt actions are 'likely to affect the . . . proceeding.'" Merely calling for the destruction of documents that are within an agency's proceeding is not equivalent to corrupt conduct by a defendant who does acts that are likely to affect the proceedings.

§ 6.06   NEXUS

Most courts find that perjury and false statements alone do not constitute an obstruction of justice. *U.S. v. Essex*, 407 F.2d 214 (6th Cir.1969). "To show an obstruction of justice based on false testimony, the government must establish a nexus between the false statements and the obstruction of the administration of justice." *U.S. v. Thomas*, 916 F.2d 647 (11th Cir.1990). Recently in *U.S. v. Bonds*, 2015 WL 1842752 (9th Cir. 2015), the Ninth Circuit en banc reversed the former baseball player's obstruction of justice conviction finding that "a rambling, non-responsive answer to a simple question" was not material.

In *U.S. v. Aguilar*, 515 U.S. 593 (1995), the Supreme Court reexamined the "nexis" required between the act and the judicial proceeding, finding that the "act must have a relationship in time, causation, or logic with the judicial proceedings." The Court rejected use of § 1503 where the evidence was limited to "uttering false statements to an investigating agent . . . who might or might not testify before a grand jury." The Court stated that, "what use will be made of false testimony given to an investigating agent who has not been subpoenaed or otherwise directed to appear before the grand jury is far more speculative." The Court in *Aguilar* found this could not "be said to have the 'natural and probable effect' of interfering with the due administration of justice."

The nexus requirement was also an issue in the case of Arthur Andersen, LL.P, Enron Corporation's auditor, who was accused of destroying documents pursuant to a company document retention policy. Charged with obstruction of justice under the then-18 U.S.C. § 1512, the company went to trial and was convicted. In reversing the conviction, the Supreme Court held the jury instructions improper in that they "failed to convey the requisite consciousness of wrongdoing." Additionally, the instructions were improper in that "they led the jury to believe that it did not have to find *any* nexus between the 'persuasion' to destroy documents and any particular proceeding." *Arthur Andersen, LLP v. U.S.*, 544 U.S. 696 (2005). Despite this reversal, the company did not survive.

§ 6.07   SECTION 1503 AS IT RELATES TO OTHER OBSTRUCTION STATUTES

Along with the passage of the Victim and Witness Protection Act also came a restructuring of some of the obstruction offenses found in chapter 73. Removed from section 1503 was specific language relating to witnesses and parties. This excluded language formed the basis for the offenses found in sections 1512 and 1513.

As a result of this reorganization, courts have found it necessary to resolve controversies pertaining to the use of the omnibus clause of section 1503 when sections 1512 and 1513 might more specifically criminalize the conduct. Some courts take the position that section 1503 can be charged alternatively or in conjunction with section 1512 when the conduct involves obstruction against a witness. *U.S. v. Lester,* 749 F.2d 1288 (9th Cir.1984). Others take the position that the general obstruction charge of section 1503 is overridden by the specific victim and witness protection provided in section 1512. There is an added complexity to this issue as a result of an additional modification made to the statute in 1988 by Congress that added the word "corruptly" to section 1512(b). *U.S. v. Masterpol,* 940 F.2d 760 (2d Cir.1991). Most circuits, however, reject the position taken by the Second Circuit finding that "[t]he fact that § 1512 more specifically addresses improper conduct involving a witness does not preclude application of § 1503." *U.S. v. Kenny,* 973 F.2d 339 (4th Cir.1992).

CHAPTER 7
BRIBERY AND EXTORTION

§ 7.01 INTRODUCTION

Official corruption is often prosecuted by charges premised upon the statutory offenses of Bribery of Public Officials and Witnesses (18 U.S.C. § 201), the Hobbs Act (18 U.S.C. § 1951) or the Travel Act (18 U.S.C. § 1952). The line between each of these three offenses is not always discernible and often a prosecutor has a choice in deciding what statute to use in prosecuting specific conduct. In *Evans v. U.S.*, 504 U.S. 255 (1992), Justice Thomas, joined by Chief Justice Rehnquist and Justice Scalia, cautioned in their dissent that "[b]y stretching the bounds of extortion to make it encompass bribery, the Court today blurs the traditional distinction between the crimes." Permitting Hobbs Act charges when the conduct is in essence bribery serves to provide federal jurisdiction for what otherwise might be a state crime. Courts have found that bribery and extortion are not mutually exclusive.

Federalism concerns have been raised by the use of federal corruption statutes in cases involving state and local officials. In *Sabri v. U.S.*, 541 U.S. 600 (2004), the Supreme Court rejected a federalism challenge to 18 U.S.C. § 666(a)(2), a statute that allows for the prosecution of state and local officials when an agency or organization has accepted benefits in any one year period in excess of ten thousand dollars as part of a federal program. (See

§ 7.04). The defendant, a real estate developer who was alleged to have offered bribes to a member of the Board of Commissioners of the Minneapolis Community Development Agency, challenged the statute as facially unconstitutional because it did not require a nexus between the alleged local corruption and the federal funds received by the agency. The Court found the statute constitutional even though the funds might not be traceable to the specific federal program. It was enough, the Court held, that the statute was conditioned "on a threshold amount of federal funds defining the federal interest."

There are also conflict of interest statutes designed to combat government corruption. For example, 18 U.S.C. § 208 prohibits certain acts that affect a personal financial interest. WCH § 7.6.

§ 7.02   OVERVIEW OF BRIBERY

The first federal bribery statute of general application was passed in 1853 and titled "An Act to Prevent Frauds Upon the Treasury of the United States." Although today there are many federal bribery offenses in the federal criminal law, the most prominent is section 201 of Title 18. This statute pertains to bribery (§ 201 (b)) and gratuities (§ 201 (c)).

Congress enacted section 201 in 1962 "as part of an effort to reformulate and rationalize all federal criminal statutes dealing with the integrity of government." *Dixson v. U.S.*, 465 U.S. 482 (1984). The statute focuses on criminalizing conduct of those who improperly seek preferential treatment from government officials and also those who improperly use their public office for their personal gain. The statute also covers bribes and gratuities given to witnesses for influencing their testimony or absenting themselves from a proceeding. Section 201 criminalizes the conduct of the person giving the bribe as well as the person who receives it.

Bribery (§ 201 (b)(1)) requires the government to show that (1) something of value was given, offered, or promised (2) to a federal public official (3) corruptly to influence an official act. Subsection two of this provision concerns those instances when the offender committing the bribery is the public official. The remaining two subsections of part (b) criminalize conduct of bribing a witness in a federal proceeding or seeking or accepting a bribe as such a witness.

Subsection (c) of section 201 pertains to gratuities. When one is the public official charged with demanding or accepting a gratuity, it is incumbent for there to be a showing that the public official personally sought or accepted something of value. A distinguishing factor separating bribery from gratuities is the level of intent. The gratuity statute does not require proof of a quid pro quo. Unlike bribery, it "may constitute merely a reward for some future act that the public official will take (and may have already determined to take), or for a past act that he has already taken." *U.S. v. Sun-Diamond Growers of California*, 526 U.S. 398 (1999).

The gratuities section does not apply to government offers of leniency in exchange for testimony from witnesses and co-defendants. In *U.S. v. Singleton*, 165 F.3d 1297 (10th Cir.1999), an en banc Tenth Circuit stated that "18 U.S.C. § 201(c)(2) does not apply to the United States or an Assistant United States Attorney functioning within the official scope of the office." The court did note that this does not "permit[ ] an agent of the government to step beyond the limits of his or her office to make an offer to a witness other than one traditionally exercised by the sovereign."

Bribery carries a maximum penalty of fifteen years imprisonment and a fine. Additionally it permits disqualification from public office. In contrast, the gratuities provision of this statute provides for a maximum imprisonment of two years.

§ 7.03   BRIBERY—THINGS OF VALUE

A liberal construction has been given to the requirement of the bribery payment being "anything of value." Actual commercial value is not necessary. It is the "value which the defendant subjectively attaches to the items received," which controls. Thus, loans and a promise of future employment to an official in financial straits can be value for purposes of the statute. *U.S. v. Gorman*, 807 F.2d 1299 (6th Cir.1986).

In *U.S. v. Williams*, 705 F.2d 603 (2d Cir.1983), Senator Harrison Williams was convicted of charges, including bribery, as a part of Operation Abscam. The Second Circuit found that defendant's acceptance of stock in corporations that he believed had value, was sufficient to support the "anything of value" element and the jury instruction, despite defendant's argument of the stock having no commercial value.

§ 7.04   BRIBERY—PUBLIC OFFICIAL

The public official element of the bribery statute includes both federal public officials and "persons who have been selected to be public officials." These terms are descriptively defined by the statute. Further, courts have expansively interpreted these definitions. WCH § 7.2(B).

In *Dixson v. U.S.*, 465 U.S. 482 (1984), petitioners were charged with bribery for their acceptance of kickbacks from contractors seeking work on a project arising as part of an urban renewal program. The City of Peoria, the recipient of two federal block grants from the Department of Housing and Urban Development, designated a social service organization as subgrantee in charge of administering the funds. Petitioners served in a supervisory capacity with this agency with certain fiscal and contracting authority. The issue before the Supreme Court was "whether officers of a private, nonprofit corporation administering and expending federal community development block grants are 'public officials' for purposes of the federal bribery statute."

The Supreme Court affirmed the convictions of the petitioners finding them to be "public officials." The Court was clear, however, to state that the "mere presence of some federal assistance" or being an employee of a local organization responsible for administering a federal grant does not make one a "public official." The Court found that to be a "public official," one "must possess some degree of official responsibility for carrying out a federal program or policy."

Those individuals who may not meet the "public official" element of this statute are not necessarily immune from federal prosecution. In 1984 Congress passed 18 U.S.C. § 666, an act that now extends federal criminality to agents of state and local organizations that receive ten thousand dollars or more in federal funds. Congress stated that the purpose of the act was "to augment the ability of the United States to vindicate significant acts of theft, fraud and bribery involving Federal monies which are disbursed to private organizations or State and local governments pursuant to a Federal program." Under section 666 it is not necessary for the government "to prove the bribe in question had any particular influence on federal funds." *Salinas v. U.S.*, 522 U.S. 52 (1997).

When the prosecution of the public official entails a member of the federal Congress, an issue that may arise is the effect of the Constitution's Speech and Debate Clause. Established to protect the independence of the legislature, this constitutional provision provides that "for any Speech or Debate in either House, they [Senators and Representatives] shall not be questioned in any other place."

In *U.S. v. Brewster*, 408 U.S. 501 (1972), the Supreme Court rejected the use of the Speech and Debate Clause in a case charging Senator Brewster with bribery under section 201. The Court stated that "a Member of Congress may be prosecuted under a criminal statute provided that the Government's case does not rely on legislative acts or the motivation for legislative acts." The taking of a bribe, the Court stated is not a legislative act and is not "part of or even incidental to the role of a legislator."

§ 7.05   BRIBERY—CORRUPTLY TO INFLUENCE OFFICIAL ACTS

When the charge pertains to bribery of a public official, it is incumbent that the government prove that the defendant acted corruptly to influence an official act. The statute defines "official act" as "any decision or action on any question, matter, cause, suit, proceeding or controversy, which may at any time be pending, or which may by law be brought before any public official, in such official's official capacity, or in such official's place of trust or profit." Despite the extensiveness of this definition, courts have not always found a defendant's conduct sufficient to meet this element.

In *U.S. v. Muntain*, 610 F.2d 964 (D.C.Cir.1979), the charges against the defendant included illegal gratuities pursuant to section 201. Muntain, employed as the Assistant to the Secretary for Labor Relations at the United States Department of Housing and Urban Development, was convicted after a jury trial based upon evidence of "his involvement in a private scheme to sell group insurance to labor unions as a negotiated benefit in union contracts." Defendant argued on appeal that his actions were not "official acts" in that they did not involve matters that would be brought before him in his official capacity. The District of Columbia Circuit Court of Appeals accepted this argument, finding that the promotion of group automobile insurance was not a matter that would be brought before Muntain in his capacity as the Secretary of Labor Relations at HUD. Thus, although the court found the conduct reprehensible, it did not find it sufficient to meet the element of influencing an official act.

The "official act" language is not limited to future acts. Rather, the legislature's use of the words "at any time" precludes a defendant from escaping "liability for bribe-solicitation by proving that he had successfully hidden the truth of past performance from the bribe-payer." Bribery does not require that the public official actually have the power to perform the act for which the money was received. The crux of the offense is that money is solicited or received on the representation that it is for the purpose of influencing an official act. *U.S. v. Arroyo*, 581 F.2d 649 (7th Cir.1978).

The bribe must be offered with a corrupt intent to influence any official act. It is immaterial to some courts whether the act could or would ever be performed. Thus, a defense of "playacting" would not negate the charge. A public official who gives false promises of assistance to individuals offering money, cannot avoid section 201's criminality claiming that the official's subjective intent was not corrupt. *U.S. v. Myers*, 692 F.2d 823 (2d Cir.1982).

Bribery does, however, require proof of an actual or intended quid pro quo. Thus, an individual who accepts money may not be liable under the bribery statute if the money was not accepted in exchange for being influenced to perform a specific official act. *U.S. v. Dean*, 629 F.3d 257 (D.C.2011). But in *U.S. v. Jefferson*, 674 F.3d 332 (4th Cir.2012), the Fourth Circuit permitted an instruction "that an official act need not be prescribed by statute, but rather may include acts that a congressman customarily performs, even if the act falls outside the formal legislative process." But this was allowed because it was given along with another instruction; thus keeping the jury from relying exclusively on the defendant's settled practice.

Arguments claiming insufficiency of the quid pro quo mandate are common to cases where the defendant believes that the charge of gratuity, as opposed to bribery, more aptly describes the conduct. Considering the difference in sentencing options for these two offenses, (bribery—15 years, gratuities—2 years) the issue is significant. In distinguishing the bribery offense from the gratuity offense, the Fourth Circuit in *U.S. v. Muldoon*, 931 F.2d 282 (4th Cir.1991), stated that "[b]ribery requires proof that the payor acted corruptly with the intent of influencing any official act, influencing a public official to defraud the government, or to do or omit an act in violation of his official duties." In contrast, the court found that proof of a gratuity "need not show that the payor intended to exact action by the recipient, although it must show that the payor gave the gratuity because of the act."

§ 7.06   INTERNATIONAL BRIBERY

The Foreign Corrupt Practices Act (FCPA) serves to combat bribery of foreign officials. The Act, originally passed in 1977, is incorporated into provisions of the Securities Exchange Act of 1934. Under the FCPA, certain corporations are subject to accounting requirements that include the keeping of records "in reasonable detail [to] accurately and fairly reflect the transactions and disposition of the assets of the issuer." (15 U.S.C. § 78m(b)(2)(A)). The crux of the FCPA provides for the prosecution of those who bribe foreign officials. (15 U.S.C. § 78dd–1 et. seq.) (see § 1.04). Significant fines have been levied against U.S. corporations in FCPA cases. For example, Siemens AG and three subsidiaries plead guilty to FCPA violations and agreed to pay a fine of $450 million. Often the fines are part of a deferred or non-prosecution agreement with the government. See § 2.04.

Other countries have joined in the fight against international bribery in passing the Convention on Combating Bribery of Foreign Public Officials in International Business Transactions. The United States in keeping with this international convention passed the International Anti-Bribery and Fair Competition Act of 1998.

§ 7.07   OVERVIEW OF HOBBS ACT

The Anti-Racketeering Act of 1934 was the predecessor extortion statute of the Hobbs Act. Congress modified this initial act in 1946 in reaction to a United States Supreme Court decision that restrictively applied the 1934 Act to exclude the payment of wages by a bona fide employer to a bona fide employee. *U.S. v. Local 807*, 315 U.S. 521 (1942). Although the predecessor statute criminalized extortion activity, the Supreme Court's ruling in *Local 807* permitted labor unions using coercive extortion to escape liability under the statute if the conduct involved wages paid to a bona fide employee. To correct this deficiency, Congress enacted the Hobbs Act, a new statute that specifically contained a "definition of the term 'extortion' and for the first time proscribed 'extortion' in specific language." *U.S. v. Mazzei*, 521 F.2d 639 (3d Cir.1975).

The elements of the present day offense are (1) interference with commerce and (2) robbery or extortion. Extortion is defined within the statute as "the obtaining of property from another, with his consent, induced by wrongful use of actual or threatened force, violence, or fear, or under color of official right." Despite the predecessor statute's emphasis on racketeering activities, 18 U.S.C. § 1951 has no requirement that the government prove racketeering as an element of the offense. *U.S. v. Culbert*, 435 U.S. 371 (1978). The statute permits prosecutions for actual acts of robbery or extortion as well as attempts and conspiracies to rob or extort.

Section 1951 carries a maximum term of imprisonment of not more than twenty years and a fine. The significant prison term afforded by this statute makes its use highly desirable to the government.

§ 7.08   HOBBS ACT—
INTERSTATE COMMERCE

It is rare that a court rejects a section 1951 prosecution as not meeting the jurisdictional requirement of interstate commerce. The statute merely requires a showing that one "in any way obstructs, delays, or affects commerce or the movement of any article or commodity in commerce." Interstate commerce has been found where there is criminal activity "affecting commerce" even when the effect is "de minimus." In *U.S. v. Rabbitt*, 583 F.2d 1014 (8th Cir.1978), the Eighth Circuit stated that, "[i]f the resources of a business which affects interstate commerce are depleted and diminished as a result of extortion, then interstate commerce is affected." An actual or prospective depletion of assets has been found sufficient.

In *U.S. v. Pascucci*, 943 F.2d 1032 (9th Cir.1991), Defendant Pascucci was convicted after a jury trial of two offenses, one of which was the Hobbs Act. In support of the charge of attempted extortion, the government presented evidence at trial that included the defendant's threat to deliver an audio tape of the victim's marital infidelity to the victim's employer.

The majority opinion, by the Ninth Circuit, in *Pascucci,* noted the necessity of having a threat transmitted in interstate commerce in order to have a Hobbs Act violation. The court found that "[b]y showing that the defendant made a credible threat to deliver embarrassing materials *directly* to the victim's employer, who was then engaged in interstate commerce, the Government demonstrated that [defendant] introduced a potential impact on interstate commerce." The fact that the defendant's scheme was unsuccessful because he was caught did not dissolve the criminal liability. In addition to the fact that Pascucci was charged with the crime of attempted extortion, it is sufficient if "the scheme, if successful, would have affected commerce."

Circuit Judge Ferguson, dissenting in *Pascucci*, found the nexus with interstate commerce insufficient in this case. The dissent rejected the argument that because the defendant's "victim was employed by a firm engaged in interstate commerce, the jurisdictional nexus is established." Judge Ferguson stated that the "[i]nterstate commerce must be affected by extortion, not by a result of extortion."

U.S. v. Elders, 569 F.2d 120 (7th Cir.1978) is an example of the rare instance when the interstate commerce element was not met by the government. The case involved alleged kickbacks to a local public official for contracts on tree removal work. Following a jury conviction, the defendant argued on appeal that his tree removal company (IST) was not involved in interstate commerce. The government, arguing a de minimus effect on commerce, claimed "(1) that the use of equipment purchased or manufactured out-of-state was sufficient to establish jurisdiction; (2) that IST engaged in out-of-state work during the period in question; and (3) that either the extortionate payments depleted the assets of IST and/or the inflated prices paid by Maywood depleted its treasury, thereby impairing the ability of either or both to do business interstate."

Despite the *Elders* court's recognition that the nexus with interstate commerce may be de minimus, the court did require that it exist and that "the connection with/or effect on interstate commerce must have been at least a 'realistic probability' at the time of the extortionate act." In *Elders*, the Seventh Circuit rejected all of the governments' arguments noting first that the out-of-state purchases of equipment were well in advance of the alleged extortions and there was no showing by the government of a "realistic probability" of additional equipment being purchased. The court also rejected the government's claim of IST doing out of state work as a basis for interstate commerce in that the few out of state jobs presented as evidence by the government had no connection with the alleged extortions. Finally, the court rejected the depletion of assets argument noting that not only was this issue not presented at trial but "the affect still must be more than a speculative attenuated 'one step removed' kind of effect."

Some courts require that if the government is proceeding on a depletion of assets theory premised upon the victim's purchase of interstate goods, it is necessary for the purchasing to be continuing in nature. "Where the victim of an extortion scheme *customarily* obtains supplies through interstate commerce, the diminution of the victim's resources impairs his purchasing power and may therefore be found to affect interstate commerce for the purpose of the Hobbs Act." *U.S. v. Merolla*, 523 F.2d 51 (2d Cir.1975).

A depletion of assets premised merely upon the receipt of government (FBI) funds as an extortion payment does not establish an actual effect on interstate commerce. This, however, does not mean that the government would be precluded from proceeding on a charge of attempt under the Hobbs Act. *U.S. v. DiCarlantonio*, 870 F.2d 1058 (6th Cir.1989).

Although a jury decides if the facts presented by the government occurred, the trial judge can determine if the conduct affected commerce. In *U.S. v. Kuta*, 518 F.2d 947 (7th Cir.1975), the Seventh Circuit rejected the argument that an instruction given in a trial that charged the defendant with a violation of the Hobbs Act was erroneous because it did not include a definition of commerce. The court stated that "a definition was not necessary, . . . because what constitutes interstate commerce and whether it was affected were matters of law that the trial court resolved."

Challenges premised on insufficient evidence of "interstate commerce" were asserted by defendants after the Supreme Court decisions in *U.S. v. Lopez* (see § 1.02) and *U.S. v. Morrison*, 529 U.S. 598 (2000), cases that enforce a requirement of a substantial effect on interstate commerce. The lower courts have distinguished the statutes from these two Supreme Court cases when applied to an alleged Hobbs Act violation, finding that a de minimis nexus on interstate commerce is sufficient for maintaining a Hobbs Act prosecution. *U.S. v. Clausen*, 328 F.3d 708 (3rd Cir.2003).

§ 7.09   HOBBS ACT—
ROBBERY OR EXTORTION

Section 1951 requires a showing of either robbery or extortion. Robbery is defined by the statute as "the unlawful taking or obtaining of personal property from the person or in the presence of another, against his will, by means of actual or threatened force, or violence, or fear of injury, immediate or future, to his person or property, or property in his custody or possession, or the person or property of a relative or member of his family or of anyone in his company at the time of the taking or obtaining." Despite the specificity of this statute, in the case of *U.S. v. Nedley*, 255 F.2d 350 (3d Cir.1958), the Third Circuit applied the common law definition of the term "robbery." Where a defendant argued on appeal that the common law definition of robbery should have been given as a jury instruction, the appellate court found that use of "the Hobbs Act definition of robbery was not plain error." *U.S. v. Thomas*, 8 F.3d 1552 (11th Cir.1993).

More commonly, the statute is used with acts of extortion. Prior to the 1970s, Hobbs Act extortion prosecutions were premised upon conduct by force, violence, or fear. In recent years there has been a growth and acceptance of prosecutions where the extortion is "under color of official right."

Property extorted from another by "wrongful use of actual or threatened force, violence or fear" is the first of two clauses that a prosecutor can use in alleging extortion. In making a determination as to whether fear exists, one looks at whether "fear was created in the victim's mind, if such fear was a reasonable one, and if the defendants by making use of that fear extorted money or property." *Callanan v. U.S.*, 223 F.2d 171 (8th Cir.1955). "Fear" can be met by a showing of the victim being placed in fear of economic loss.

In *U.S. v. Capo*, 817 F.2d 947 (2d Cir.1987) the government charged the defendant under the Hobbs Act for conduct involving payments made to the defendant as part of a job selling scheme. The victims were alleged to have paid defendants sums of money for contacting the personnel officer at Eastman Kodak Company for favorable treatment on their job applications. On appeal of the Hobbs Act convictions, the government contended that the charge was premised upon fear of economic loss.

In rejecting the economic fear argument as presented by the government, the Second Circuit in

Capo stated that "[t]he absence or presence of fear of economic loss must be considered from the perspective of the victim, not the extortionist; the proof need establish that the victim reasonably believed: first, that the defendant had the power to harm the victim, and second, that the defendant would exploit that power to the victim's detriment." Since the evidence in the *Capo* case failed to show any negative influencing on jobs on the part of defendants and failed to show that any victims feared a detriment to them by defendants actions, the requirement of "preclusion or diminished opportunity" had not been satisfied.

The court in *Capo* stressed the necessity of keeping state offenses away from federal prosecutors. The court stated that "[b]ecause these 'victims' faced no increased risk if they did not pay, but rather, stood only to improve their lots by paying defendants, this case is a classic example of bribery."

§ 7.10   HOBBS ACT—"UNDER COLOR OF OFFICIAL RIGHT"

Extortion "under color of official right" is an alternative basis upon which a prosecutor can claim extortion. It "includes the misuse of one's office to induce payments not due the person or his office. The official need not control the function in question if the extorted party possesses a reasonable belief in the official's powers." *U.S. v. Rabbitt*, 583 F.2d 1014 (8th Cir.1978). As noted in *Evans v. U.S.*, 504 U.S. 255 (1992), there is no need for an affirmative act of inducement. Merely accepting a bribe to misuse one's office is sufficient. The element "under color of official right" has been the subject of two recent Supreme Court cases that involved extortion as related to public officials' campaign contributions.

In *McCormick v. U.S.*, 500 U.S. 257 (1991), petitioner McCormick was a member of the West Virginia House of Delegates who sponsored and spoke on behalf of legislation that would exempt foreign medical school graduates with significant work experience from having to take the state licensing examination. McCormick allegedly received cash payments from the doctors both before and after the passage of this legislation. Evidence presented at trial was that he failed to list the funds received as campaign contributions and likewise failed to report it on his income tax return.

Petitioner McCormick was charged with five counts of violating the Hobbs Act and one count of filing a false income tax return. The Supreme Court reversed petitioner's conviction, finding that a quid pro quo is necessary for a conviction that is predicated upon receiving a campaign contribution. The Court stated that "to hold that legislators commit the federal crime of extortion when they act for the benefit of constituents or support legislation furthering the interests of some of their constituents, shortly before or after campaign contributions are solicited and received from those beneficiaries, is an unrealistic assessment of what Congress could have meant by making it a crime to obtain property from another, with his consent, 'under color of official right.' "

The Supreme Court in *McCormick* was clear to note that not all campaign contributions would be outside the scope of the Hobbs Act. "Political contributions are of course vulnerable if induced by the use of force, violence, or fear. The receipt of such contributions is also vulnerable under the Act as having been taken under color of official right, but only if the payments are made in return for an explicit promise or undertaking by the official to perform or not to perform an official act."

This latter form of extortion was the conduct displayed in the case of *Evans v. U.S.*, 504 U.S. 255 (1992). Petitioner Evans was a member of the Board of Commissioners of DeKalb County, Georgia. Petitioner was approached by an undercover FBI agent who sought petitioner's assistance on a rezoning. The agent paid petitioner eight thousand dollars, of which petitioner reported a one thousand dollar check as a campaign contribution but failed to include the cash payment in the sum of seven thousand dollars on his state campaign financing disclosure form or his federal income tax return. Evans was charged with a Hobbs Act violation and a tax violation of failure to report income.

The Supreme Court in *Evans* accepted the majority view as expressed by eight circuits that an "affirmative act of inducement by a public official, such as a demand," is not required for extortion "under color of official right." The Court stated, "[w]e hold today that the Government need only show that a public official has obtained a payment to which he was not entitled, knowing that the payment was made in return for official acts." Thus passive acceptance of a benefit by a public official can meet the extortion element of the Hobbs Act when "the official knows that he is being offered the payment in exchange for a specific requested exercise of his official power."

The Supreme Court in this six to three decision also reaffirmed its prior ruling in *McCormick*, finding the instruction given in the *Evans* case sufficient to meet the quid pro quo requirement. The Court stated that "because the offense is completed at the time when the public official receives a payment in return for his agreement to perform specific official acts; fulfillment of the *quid pro quo* is not an element of the offense."

Lower courts have also considered the applicability of *McCormick*'s requirement for a *quid pro quo* outside the context of campaign contributions and found that it applies in all Hobbs Act cases. *U.S. v. Collins*, 78 F.3d 1021 (6th Cir.1996). The level of proof, however, required for finding the *quid pro quo* can vary. WCH § 7.4(b)(3). In the context of the gratuities statute, the Supreme Court held that "in order to establish a violation of 18 U.S.C. § 201(c)(1)(A), the Government must prove a link between a thing of value conferred upon a public official and a specific 'official act' for or because of which it was given." *U.S. v. Sun-Diamond Growers of California*, 526 U.S. 398 (1999).

§ 7.11   TRAVEL ACT

The Travel Act, passed in 1961, was aimed at "organized crime." Then Attorney General Robert Kennedy stated that federal legislation "was needed to aid state and local governments which were no longer able to cope with the increasingly complex and interstate nature of large-scale, multiparty crime." *Perrin v. U.S.*, 444 U.S. 37 (1979). The statute used the Commerce Clause of the United States Constitution to reach state and local criminality that had an interstate nexus.

The Travel Act can be seen as a precursor to crimes such as the Racketeer Influenced and Corrupt Organization Act in its use of the commerce power to criminalize what are essentially state offenses. Initially the statute concentrated on unlawful activity in the form of business activities involving gambling, liquor, narcotics, and extortion and bribery that violated state law. The statute was later expanded to include conduct related to controlled substances and arson that violated state law. In 1986 the scope of this offense was again enlarged to encompass the Bank Secrecy Act and the money laundering offenses of sections 1956 and 1957.

18 U.S.C. § 1952, the Travel Act, requires proof of three elements: (1) interstate or foreign travel, or using the mail or any facility in interstate or foreign commerce, (2) intent to promote, direct, or manage illegal business, and (3) an overt act in furtherance of the unlawful activity. Courts have permitted prosecutions charging both the Travel Act and

Hobbs Act for the same conduct, finding no double jeopardy violation. *U.S. v. Bencivengo*, 749 F.3d 205 (3d Cir.2014).

Interstate travel, the jurisdictional element of this offense, mandates that the activity involve at least two states. A state is defined to include "a State of the United States, the District of Columbia, and any commonwealth, territory, or possession of the United States." The required nexus between interstate activity and the criminality is less clear.

In *Rewis v. U.S.*, 401 U.S. 808 (1971) the Supreme Court reversed a section 1952 conviction involving a gambling operation that was frequented by out-of-state bettors. The Court, in examining the legislative history of the statute, found that it strongly suggested "that Congress did not intend that the Travel Act should apply to criminal activity solely because that activity is at times patronized by persons from another State."

Eight years later the Supreme Court chose to take a less restrictive approach to the Travel Act when deciding the case of *Perrin v. U.S.*, 444 U.S. 37 (1979). Petitioner and co-defendants were charged with a violation of section 1952 for their involvement in a scheme to exploit geological data stolen from a company. The unlawful activity alleged in the indictment was the use of interstate commerce for the purpose of promoting a commercial bribery scheme in violation of state law.

The Supreme Court in *Perrin* rejected petitioner's argument that bribery should be limited to bribery of a public official. The statute, the Court held, would include "bribery of individuals acting in a private capacity." The Court distinguished *Perrin* from *Rewis* finding the interstate nexus that was lacking in *Rewis* sufficient in this case. The Court stated, " . . . so long as the requisite interstate nexus is present, the statute reflects a clear and deliberate intent on the part of Congress to alter the federal-state balance in order to reinforce state law enforcement."

Cases have held that requisite to meeting the "business enterprise" element of this offense is a showing of continuity of the activity. Thus, a single action involving the transportation of drugs would not sustain a conviction. *U.S. v. Bates*, 840 F.2d 858 (11th Cir.1988). Where there was a showing of three drug deliveries and a drug distribution enterprise, the Fifth Circuit found sufficient continuity to meet the "business enterprise" element. *U.S. v. Carrion*, 809 F.2d 1120 (5th Cir.1987).

The Travel Act requires that the accused "thereafter performs or attempts to perform" an act as specified in the statute. Although an overt act is required by the statute, the Second Circuit stated in *U.S. v. Jenkins*, 943 F.2d 167 (2d Cir.1991) that the government does not have to show that the accused took a substantial step in furtherance of the intended unlawful activity. "Rather, . . . to establish a Travel Act violation the government must prove that the defendant used a facility of interstate or foreign commerce to 'make easier or facilitate' the intended unlawful activity, and thereafter did one additional act in furtherance of the unlawful activity."

CHAPTER 8

RACKETEER INFLUENCED AND CORRUPT ORGANIZATIONS (RICO)

§ 8.01 INTRODUCTION

The Racketeer Influenced and Corrupt Organizations Act (RICO) is Title IX of the Organized Crime Control Act of 1970. It was enacted by Congress as a tool to combat organized crime. In the initial years after passage, RICO was seldom used by prosecutors. Today, however, it is common for federal prosecutors to bring RICO charges. The addition of RICO as a criminal charge provides the government with federal criminal enforcement in areas that were previously within the state police powers. Its penalty and forfeiture provisions offer the government a strong incentive for using this statute (see § 8.07).

Although some believe that Congress intended RICO to serve as a weapon against organized crime, courts have not required proof to support a RICO charge, of the defendant being a member of organized crime. RICO is "dependent upon behavior and not status." *U.S. v. Mandel*, 415 F.Supp. 997 (D.Md.1976).

The RICO statutes are found in 18 U.S.C. § 1961 through § 1968. Section 1961 of Title 18 serves as a definitions statute for the terms used in the remaining RICO statutes. In defining these terms, it lists nine state and over thirty federal offenses that can serve as predicate acts for a RICO charge.

Although it offers basic definitions for most of the elements of the offense, court interpretations have provided language to further assist in this regard.

Section 1962, subsections (a), (b), (c), and (d), provides four separate and distinct types of prohibited conduct. These are: (a) using income from a pattern of racketeering activity to acquire an interest in an enterprise engaged in, or the activities of which affect interstate or foreign commerce; (b) acquiring or maintaining through a pattern of racketeering activity an interest in an enterprise engaged in, or the activities of which affect interstate or foreign commerce; (c) conducting or participating in the conduct, through a pattern of racketeering activity, of such affairs of an enterprise affect interstate or foreign commerce; and (d) conspiring to further any of the activities listed in (a), (b), or (c). Although it is only necessary for there to be one of these four prohibited activities for a RICO offense, some prosecutions use more than one type of prohibited activity in the charging document.

Although most RICO prosecutions involve racketeering activity, this statute can also be used by the government when the criminal activity involves the collection of an unlawful debt. Section 1961 defines the term "unlawful debt" to mean debts relating to either gambling or usurious loans that are incurred in connection with an illegal gambling business or in connection with a business of lending money where the usurious rate is at least twice the enforceable rate.

The essence of a RICO charge is in proving that the defendant, (1) invested the proceeds of a pattern of racketeering in, or acquired or maintained an interest in through a pattern of racketeering, or participated in through a pattern of racketeering, (2) an enterprise, (3) engaged in, or the activities of which affect, commerce. The intricacies of this statute appear, when each of these elements are dissected relative to the four different types of prohibited conduct. One finds that not only do jurisdictions approach these elements differently, but that courts will vary within the same jurisdiction dependent upon the prohibited conduct that has been charged.

Section 1963 provides the penalties available in a RICO prosecution. A maximum term of imprisonment of up to twenty years is provided for by this statute. This term may be increased to life where the violation is based upon racketeering activity that has a maximum penalty of life imprisonment. In addition to imprisonment and fines, RICO also provides for asset forfeiture. RICO not only serves as a criminal statute, but also provides private parties and the government with a civil cause of action. (18 U.S.C. § 1964).

§ 8.02   ENTERPRISE

RICO requires that the defendant have invested in, maintained an interest in, or participated in the affairs of an enterprise. The term "enterprise" is defined in section 1961(4) as including "any individual, partnership, corporation, association, or other legal entity, and any union or group of individuals associated in fact although not a legal entity." The expansiveness of this definition is seen upon examining cases.

In *U.S. v. Turkette*, 452 U.S. 576 (1981), the accused successfully argued in the appellate court that RICO was solely intended to protect legitimate businesses and thus criminal participation in an association that performed only illegal acts, and had not infiltrated or attempted to infiltrate a legitimate enterprise, could not form the basis for a RICO charge. The Supreme Court, in reversing the appellate court, conceded that the congressional purpose of RICO was to combat organized crime that infiltrated legitimate businesses. The Court noted, however, that this did not preclude RICO charges where the enterprise was illegal. Since neither the language of the statute nor the structure of RICO limited its application to legitimate enterprises the Court found it proper to follow Congress' intent for RICO to have a broad reading. To hold otherwise, the Court noted, would omit whole areas of organized criminal activity from the reach of the statute. RICO does not, however, require that the enterprise or predicate acts have an economic motive. *National Organization for Women, Inc. v. Scheidler*, 510 U.S. 249 (1994).

In addition to allowing both legitimate and illegitimate enterprises, courts have permitted the enterprise to be a governmental body. For example, in *U.S. v. Thompson*, 685 F.2d 993 (6th Cir.1982), defendants entered conditional guilty pleas arguing that it was improper to use the "The Office of Governor" of the State of Tennessee as the enterprise for RICO. The Sixth Circuit in an en banc ruling found that the language and plain meaning of the statute did not exclude governmental offices as RICO enterprises.

Although the court in *Thompson* permitted the use of governmental bodies as RICO enterprises, it noted in dicta its dislike of this practice. The court reflected upon the disruption of comity in federal-state relations and the needless unfair reflection on innocent individuals. The court offered as a better course that prosecutors treat the group of defendants as a group of individuals associated in fact although not a legal entity. Despite this advice, prosecutors have continued to charge RICO with a government entity as the enterprise, and courts have continued to uphold the use of governmental bodies as RICO enterprises. Prosecutions using a State, such as Illinois, as a legal entity have been permitted. *U.S. v. Warner*, 498 F.3d 666 (7th Cir.2007).

RICO has been held not to apply extraterritorially in light of *Morrison v. National Australia Bank Ltd*, 529 U.S. 598 (2010), which examined extraterritoriality in the context of 10(b) of the Securities Exchange Act and found that unless a contrary intent appears the statute is "meant to apply only within the territorial jurisdiction of the United States." § 1.04; WCH § 8.2(A)(2). In *Cedeno v. Intech Group, Inc.*, 733 F.Supp.2d 471 (S.D.N.Y. 2010), a Southern District of New York court held that RICO did not apply extraterritorially as "nowhere does the statute evidence any concern with foreign enterprises, let alone a concern sufficiently clear to overcome the presumption against extraterritoriality." Courts have not resolved how to assess an extraterritorial claim and whether one should look at the enterprise or pattern of racketeering. *Hourani v. Mirtchev*, 943 F.Supp.2d 159 (D.C.2013).

In addition to presenting the entity as a legal entity, prosecutors can also charge it as a "group of individuals associated-in-fact although not a legal entity." (§ 1961(4)). Most courts agreed that to be an "association-in-fact" required a common purpose and functioning as a continuing unit. WCH § 8.2(A)(3). The disagreement arose in whether it had to be an ascertainable structure and the essence of that structure. In *Boyle v. U.S.*, 129 S.Ct. 2237 (2009) the Court resolved this issue holding "that an association-in-fact enterprise must have at least three structural features: a purpose, relationships among those associated with the enterprise, and longevity sufficient to permit these associates to pursue the enterprise's purpose." That said, the Court held that a jury instruction did not have to include this precise language.

Actions brought pursuant to 1962(c) require that the enterprise must be separate and distinct from the person-defendant. RICO separateness can be shown when the defendant is a president and sole shareholder of a closely held corporation. In *Cedric Kushner Promotions, LTD v. King*, 533 U.S. 158

(2001), the Court, in a civil RICO case, found that "separateness" is met for purposes of RICO when there is an individual and a corporation, even if the corporation has only one shareholder and is a closely held corporation as the "corporate owner/employee, a natural person, is distinct from the corporation itself, a legally different entity with differing rights and responsibilities due to its different legal status."

§ 8.03   INTERSTATE COMMERCE

The jurisdiction for the RICO statute is found in its requirement of interstate commerce. In *U.S. v. Robertson*, 514 U.S. 669 (1995), the Supreme Court held that the enterprise's activities could either be "engaged in" or "substantially affect" interstate commerce. The Court found that Robertson had purchased supplies and equipment from out of state, had workers brought in from out of state, and took some of the gold mine's output out of state. The Court found that the activities of the enterprise were engaged in interstate or foreign commerce.

§ 8.04   PATTERN OF RACKETEERING ACTIVITY

The definitions section of RICO defines a "pattern of racketeering activity" as requiring "at least two acts of racketeering activity, one of which occurred after the effective date of this chapter and the last of which occurred within ten years (excluding any period of imprisonment) after the commission of a prior act of racketeering activity." Courts and the legislature have provided guidance as to what constitutes a pattern and what acts are permissible as racketeering activity.

There are nine state and over thirty federal offenses specifically listed in section 1961 as racketeering activity. The nine state offenses are murder, kidnapping, gambling, arson, robbery, bribery, extortion, dealing in obscene matter, or dealing in narcotics or other dangerous drugs. The statute requires that the state offense be chargeable under state law and punishable by imprisonment for more than one year.

Although it is necessary that the state offense be chargeable under state law, it is unimportant what label is placed on the state statute. In defining the nine state offenses, the legislature intended that a generic definition be used. Thus, violations of the Illinois official misconduct statute can fit a general definition of bribery, and thus form a RICO predicate. *U.S. v. Garner*, 837 F.2d 1404 (7th Cir.1987).

It is not necessary that the accused actually be charged with the state offense. Further, procedural problems that might preclude the filing of a state charge do not serve as an impediment to the filing of a RICO charge. Courts have held that it is only necessary to show that the offense can be chargeable under state law.

Where the defendant has been charged with the state predicate in state court, the federal courts have still permitted RICO charges to be brought in federal court using the same state act as a RICO predicate offense. This has been allowed even in some instances where the state trial resulted in an acquittal of the state offense. The dual sovereignty rule provides concurrent jurisdiction to both the state and federal governments so collateral estoppel does not apply. The double jeopardy clause also has not barred a subsequent RICO prosecution based upon a federal predicate offense previously used to prosecute the defendant. Since RICO requires proof of a pattern of racketeering, courts have found that it is not the same offense as the predicate act. *U.S. v. Pungitore*, 910 F.2d 1084 (3d Cir.1990).

Over thirty federal offenses are listed as possible predicate acts for a RICO charge. These offenses are listed in the definitions provision of RICO (18 U.S.C. § 1961), using both the statutory numbers of the offense and descriptions of the conduct. For example, section 201 contains the parenthetical "relating to bribery." Courts have interpreted this language to be merely a description of the statute and not to serve as a limit to the actual statutory provision. Thus, section 201's bribery and gratuities offenses are both included as possible predicate acts.

The expansiveness of RICO is demonstrated by noting the federal offenses included as possible predicate acts. For example, mail fraud, wire fraud, and obstruction of justice are among the list of offenses. Certain drug offenses and currency reporting crimes can also serve as predicate acts of a RICO charge. Federal RICO predicates have been added since the passage of the initial legislation.

For example, in the "Uniting and Strengthening America by Providing Appropriate Tools Required to Intercept and Obstruct Terrorism Act of 2001" (Patriot Act) Congress included acts of terrorism as a RICO predicate.

Although RICO requires at least two predicate acts within the applicable time period, having merely two acts does not make RICO automatically available. Further, the existence of numerous predicate acts does not conclusively imply satisfaction of the pattern of racketeering element of RICO. The statute requires both the requisite number of acts and a pattern. Courts have provided guidance in defining the term "pattern."

The Supreme Court in the case of *H.J. Inc. v. Northwestern Bell Telephone Co.*, 492 U.S. 229 (1989), defined "pattern of racketeering" as requiring "continuity plus relationship." The Court stated that " 'continuity' is both a closed- and open-ended concept." Continuity is achieved by proving related acts extending over a substantial period of time or by acts that demonstrate a threat of continued racketeering activity. Predicate acts over a few weeks or months that do not entail a threat of future criminal conduct do not meet the continuity requirement. Where the acts are over a short period of time, but demonstrate a "specific threat of repetition extending indefinitely into the future" or are part of an "ongoing entity's regular way of doing business," they can satisfy continuity.

The Court in *H.J. Inc.* defined the "relationship" requirement by referring to another provision of the

Organized Crime Control Act of 1970. (18 U.S.C. § 3575(e)). "[C]riminal conduct forms a pattern if it embraces criminal acts that have the same or similar purposes, results, participants, victims, or methods of commission, or otherwise are interrelated by distinguishing characteristics and are not isolated events."

Although the Court in *H.J. Inc.* provided a standard for reviewing cases to determine the existence of a pattern of racketeering, it admitted that a precise method of determination could not be fixed in advance. Four justices concurring in this opinion, criticized the "continuity plus relationship" test finding it as helpful to the conduct of affairs as saying "life is a fountain."

§ 8.05   NEXUS BETWEEN PATTERN OF RACKETEERING AND ENTERPRISE

In the case of 1962(a) and 1962(b) there is no need to reflect upon the nexus requirement in that the statute specifically incorporates the nexus between the racketeering and the enterprise. In 1962(a) a person is using income from a pattern of racketeering activity to acquire an interest in an enterprise and in 1962(b) the accused is acquiring or maintaining through a pattern of racketeering an interest in an enterprise. Thus, in these two provisions the relationship between the racketeering and enterprise is apparent.

Although prosecutions under section 1962(c) also require a nexus between the enterprise and the racketeering activity, the basis of that nexus is less obvious. Section 1962(c) prohibits conducting or participating in conducting, through a pattern of racketeering activity, the affairs of an enterprise affecting interstate commerce. Prior to 1993, a jurisdictional dichotomy existed as to what relationship was required between the enterprise and the racketeering activity or person engaged in the racketeering activity.

In 1993, in the case of *Reves v. Ernst & Young*, 507 U.S. 170 (1993), the Supreme Court resolved the jurisdictional dichotomy. The Court held that 1962(c) required that one participate in the operation or management of the enterprise. The Court noted, however, that the "operation or management" test would not be limited to upper management. "An enterprise is 'operated' not just by upper management but also by lower-rung participants in the enterprise who are under the direction of upper management. An enterprise also might be 'operated' or 'managed' by others 'associated with' the enterprise who exert control over it as, for example, by bribery." The Court did not resolve "how far § 1962(c) extends down the ladder of operation." Lower courts have differed on whether company employees should be considered part of the "operation or management." WCH § 8.5.

§ 8.06   RICO CONSPIRACY

Section 1962(d) prohibits a conspiracy to commit the conduct stated in sections (a), (b), or (c). Unlike the general conspiracy statute (18 U.S.C. § 371), a RICO conspiracy is not focused upon the agreement to commit a specific offense or defraud the government. Rather, the object of a RICO conspiracy is on the conspiracy to violate a substantive RICO provision. For example, a conspiracy to violate section 1962(c) would have as the object of the offense an agreement to conduct or participate in the affairs of an enterprise through a pattern of racketeering. It would not have as the object of the offense, an agreement to commit the individual predicate acts required for a pattern of racketeering. *U.S. v. Elliott*, 571 F.2d 880 (5th Cir.1978). In *Salinas v. U.S.*, 522 U.S. 52 (1997) the Supreme Court held that a RICO "conspiracy may exist even if a conspirator does not agree to commit or facilitate each and every part of the substantive offense." An overt act is not necessary for a RICO conspiracy.

§ 8.07   FORFEITURE

In addition to fines and imprisonment, the RICO statute provides for forfeiture of property. Section 1963(a)(1) provides for forfeiture of "any interest the person has acquired or maintained in violation of section 1962." Additionally, any interest in an enterprise in which the person participated in, that violated section 1962, is subject to forfeiture under § 1963(a)(2). Finally, property from the proceeds of racketeering activity or the unlawful collection of a debt in violation of 1962, is subject to forfeiture under § 1963(a)(3). Property forfeitable under RICO relates back to property owned at the time of the commission of the section 1962 violations. (18 U.S.C. § 1963(c)).

Both tangible and intangible property can be forfeited. Real property, as well as things affixed to it, are subject to forfeiture under § 1963(a)(1). In *Russello v. U.S.*, 464 U.S. 16 (1983) the Supreme Court held that profits and income were an "interest" and therefore subject to forfeiture. The Court noted that although the statute did not specifically define the term "interest," the ordinary meaning of the word encompassed profits or proceeds. The *Russello* Court found that Congress, wanted "to remove the profit from organized crime by separating the racketeer from . . . dishonest gains." Thus, reading the statute as applying only to interests in an enterprise, would limit its effectiveness and place whole areas of organized criminal activity beyond the reach of the statute. Section 1963(a)(3) codified *Russello* in providing for the forfeiture of the "proceeds" of racketeering activity.

In *U.S. v. Caporale*, 806 F.2d 1487 (11th Cir.1986), the Eleventh Circuit found it permissible under the forfeiture provisions of the statute to impose joint and several liability. The government, the court noted, is not required to trace racketeering proceeds to specific assets. All that is necessary is for the government to show the "amount of the proceeds and identify a finite group of people receiving the proceeds."

In personam forfeitures are, however, subject to Eighth Amendment challenges under the Excessive Fines Clause. In *Alexander v. U.S.*, 509 U.S. 544 (1993), the Supreme Court remanded a forfeiture order for the lower court to consider whether the penalty was excessive.

§ 8.08 CIVIL RICO

In addition to criminal RICO actions, the RICO Act provides a statutory basis for both the government and civil litigants proceeding with a civil cause of action. (18 U.S.C. § 1964). Unlike criminal RICO actions that provide penalties including imprisonment, those premised upon section 1964, the civil RICO statute, have remedies of damages. The government, in pursuing civil RICO actions, can also request equitable relief. The statute does provide that "[a]ny person injured in his business or property by reason of a violation of section 1962 . . . may sue . . . and shall recover threefold the damages he sustains and the cost of the suit, including a reasonable attorney's fee."

Most civil RICO actions do not require that the defendants be convicted of the predicate acts used to form the basis of the pattern of racketeering. *Sedima, S.P.R.L. v. Imrex Co., Inc.*, 473 U.S. 479 (1985). The right to sue for treble damages under RICO, however, does require a showing of injury to the plaintiff, and that the defendant's actions in violation of the statute were the proximate cause of that injury. Therefore, the plaintiff must show a direct relationship between the conduct alleged and the injury asserted in the complaint. *Holmes v. Securities Investor Protection Corp.*, 503 U.S. 258 (1992). "A RICO plaintiff cannot circumvent the proximate-cause requirement simply by claiming that the defendant's aim was to increase market share at a competitor's expense." *Anza v. Ideal Steel Supply Co.*, 547 U.S. 451 (2006).

Congress amended § 1964(c) so that a civil RICO action could not be premised upon "conduct that would have been actionable as fraud in the purchase or sale of securities" unless the individual was criminally convicted in connection with the fraud. But a plaintiff in a civil RICO case predicated on mail fraud does not have to "plead and prove" that he or she "relied on the defendant's alleged misrepresentations." *Bridge v. Phoenix Bond & Indem. Co.*, 553 U.S. 639 (2008).

CHAPTER 9

FALSE STATEMENTS

§ 9.01   INTRODUCTION

A myriad of statutes exist today that prohibit the making of false statements. Most of these offenses are specifically tailored to meet explicit prohibited conduct. For example, false statement offenses exist with regard to making false statements under the Federal Trade Commission Act (15 U.S.C. § 50), presenting a false deed, power of attorney or other contract writing that defrauds the United States (18 U.S.C. § 495), presenting a false invoice with the intent to smuggle (18 U.S.C. § 545), making a false statement to obtain a federally backed loan (18 U.S.C. § 1014) and making a false statement with respect to work performed on a highway project (18 U.S.C. § 1020).

Despite the volume of tailored legislation, the most pervasively used provision is the generic false statement statute located in section 1001 of Title 18. Section 1001 has been effectively employed to combat public corruption. The simplicity of proof necessary to obtain a conviction, as well as the substantial penalty provided, has made it a beneficial charge for the government's use.

18 U.S.C. § 1001 emanates from an 1863 Act that made it a criminal offense for a person in the United States armed forces to make a fraudulent claim against the government. In subsequent years the statute was expanded to encompass "every person"

and not just those in the military. A 1934 revision modified the language to include fraudulent claims "in any matter within the jurisdiction of any department or agency of the United States." In 1948 the legislature divided the statute designating 18 U.S.C. § 287 as the false claims statute (see § 9.07) and 18 U.S.C. § 1001 as the prohibition against the making of false statements. As part of the False Statements Accountability Act of 1996, the statute was amended to include "any matter within the jurisdiction of the executive, legislative, or judicial branch" of the United States government.

Section 1001 is divisible into three types of conduct. It can apply to one who "[1] falsifies, conceals or covers up by any trick, scheme or device a material fact, [2] makes any materially false, fictitious, or fraudulent statement or representation, or [3] makes or uses any false writing or document knowing the same to contain any materially false, fictitious, or fraudulent statement or entry."

False statements require proof of the following elements: (1) a statement, (2) falsity, (3) materiality, (4) made knowingly and willfully, (5) within the executive, legislative, or judicial branch of the United States government. Commission of an act prohibited by section 1001 carries a penalty of not more than five years imprisonment and a fine, although matters related to terrorism or failing to register as a sex offender can increase the penalty to eight years.

§ 9.02　STATEMENTS

Section 1001 statements can take a variety of forms. They can be written or oral, sworn or unsworn. False statements that relate to past, present or future activity are covered by the statute. The statement also may be either voluntary or made pursuant to a requirement of law.

In *Brogan v. U.S.*, 522 U.S. 398 (1998) the Supreme Court held that the "the plain language of § 1001 admits of no exception for an 'exculpatory no.'" Prior to this decision, lower courts had accepted in varying degrees an exception to the false statement element of the statute, when the accused replied with a "mere negative response[ ] to questions propounded to him by an investigating agent during a question and answer conference," that was not initiated by the accused. In *Brogan,* the Court rejected the self-incrimination claim finding that there is no Fifth Amendment "privilege to lie."

The statute, under § 1001(b) "does not apply to a party to a judicial proceeding, or that party's counsel, for statements" to a judge or magistrate in the proceeding. Thus a courtroom plea of "not guilty," by an individual who was clearly guilty of the crime, would not be subject to prosecution for making a false statement. Courts, however, do not always agree on whether false statements made to probation officers should be exempt from prosecution pursuant to this section of the statute. *U.S. v. Manning*, 526 F.3d 611 (10th Cir.2008).

§ 9.03   FALSITY

Falsity can be achieved through either the making of a false statement or by the concealment of a material fact. Where the alleged conduct is premised upon the making of a false statement, it is incumbent upon the government to prove actual falsity. *U.S. v. Hixon*, 987 F.2d 1261 (6th Cir.1993). Literally true statements, as well as statements that are merely misleading, have been found insufficient. Although the issue of falsity is a question of fact for a jury to decide, a statement that is subject to more than one interpretation places a burden on the government to refute the meaning attributed by the defendant.

Concealment of a material fact can provide a basis for the crime of false statements, but there has to be a legal duty to disclose the information. In *U.S. v. Safavian*, 528 F.3d 957 (D.C. 2008), the defendant's conviction was reversed with the court holding that government officials who sought advice from a voluntary ethics system could not be prosecuted under the concealment provisions of § 1001 for omitting information when seeking the advice of the ethics committee. A voluntary system, even when "replicated throughout the government," did not create a legal duty to disclose information, and without the legal duty to disclose there was no basis for a concealment offense under § 1001(a)(1).

§ 9.04   KNOWLEDGE AND INTENT

Section 1001 requires that the government prove the defendant's knowledge of the falsity of the statement, or that the defendant's action was taken for the purpose of concealing or covering up a material fact. Additionally, proof of willfulness is required.

The level of knowledge required of the defendant can be met by evidence of a reckless disregard of the truth or by a conscious avoidance in learning the truth. Actual knowledge of the statement's falsity is not required. In meeting the knowledge requirement, the government may employ circumstantial evidence. In *Global-Tech Appliances, Inc. v. S.E.B. S.A.*, 131 S.Ct. 2060 (2011), the Supreme Court in a patent infringement case held that mere recklessness or negligence would not suffice for willful blindness. WCH § 9.4(B).

Willfulness does not mandate proof of an intent to defraud. The false statement statute contains language in the disjunctive: "false, fictitious **or** fraudulent." Thus, willfulness is met with proof that a defendant intended to deceive. Where the government's indictment specifically characterizes the defendant's conduct as fraudulent, as opposed to being false or fictitious, then courts have required that the government prove the allegation.

When proceeding under the concealment provision of the false statement statute, it is also necessary for the government to present sufficient proof of intent to deceive. Additionally, when the indictment is premised upon concealment, it is necessary for the government to substantiate that the defendant knew of the duty to disclose and intentionally failed to comply with that duty.

Although knowledge and willfulness are required for a violation of section 1001, there is no necessity to show that the defendant had actual knowledge of federal agency jurisdiction. In *U.S. v. Yermian*, 468 U.S. 63 (1984), the Supreme Court resolved a then existing jurisdictional dichotomy on whether it was necessary for the government to prove that the defendant actually knew that the matter was before a government agency.

Defendant Yermian was convicted of three counts of making false statements based upon false information supplied to his employer in connection with a Department of Defense security questionnaire. Defendant failed to disclose his mail fraud conviction on the submitted form and additionally listed employment with two companies that had never employed him. The defendant "signed a certification stating that his answers were 'true, complete and correct to the best of [his] knowledge' and that he understood' that any misrepresentation or false statement ... may subject [him] to prosecution under section 1001 of the United States Criminal Code.'" At trial, defendant admitted to the falsity of the statements, but contended that he did not have actual knowledge that the statements would be given to a federal agency.

The Supreme Court, in a 5–4 decision, found no basis for requiring proof of actual knowledge of federal agency jurisdiction. The Court held that the term "knowingly" following the phrase "in any matter within the jurisdiction of any department or agency of the United States," is merely a jurisdictional requirement. The Court found that "[a]ny natural reading of § 1001, therefore, establishes that the terms 'knowingly and willfully' modify only the making of false, 'fictitious or fraudulent statements,' and not the predicate circumstance that the statements be made in a matter within the jurisdiction of a federal agency."

Unresolved by *Yermian* was whether a lesser degree of mens rea would be required with respect to the element of federal agency jurisdiction. In a footnote in the *Yermian* decision, the Supreme Court remarked that the jury had been instructed, without objection from the government, that proof was required that defendant "knew or should have known" that statements were made within the jurisdiction of a federal agency. In this footnote, the Court specifically remarked on the narrowness of the issue being decided. Since the only question before the Court in *Yermian* was whether proof of *actual* knowledge of federal agency jurisdiction was mandated, resolution of the level, if any, of culpable mental state of federal agency jurisdiction remains for future determination. Also left for future interpretation is whether specific inclusion of "executive, legislative, or judicial branch" in the statute alters the required level of knowledge.

In *U.S. v. Green*, 745 F.2d 1205 (9th Cir.1984), the Ninth Circuit found no abuse of discretion in a trial court's failure to give an instruction on jurisdictional knowledge. The appellate court held that "[n]o culpable mental state must be proved

with respect to federal agency jurisdiction in order
to establish a violation of section 1001." Other
jurisdictions have ruled in accord with this Ninth
Circuit decision.

§ 9.05   MATERIALITY

Originally materiality was only listed in the
concealment clause of section 1001. ("Falsifies,
conceals or covers up by a trick, scheme or device a
material fact"). The remaining two
misrepresentation clauses of the statute omitted the
term. ("[2] makes any false, fictitious or fraudulent
statements or representations, or [3] makes or uses
any false writing or document knowing the same to
contain any false, fictitious or fraudulent statement
or entry.") Despite the failure to explicitly require
materiality in the second and third clauses of the
statute, most courts required proof of materiality to
sustain a false statement conviction. Materiality
was added to sections 2 and 3 of the statute as part
of the False Statements Accountability Act of 1996.

In determining whether a false statement or
concealment is material, courts examine whether
the statement has "a natural tendency to influence,
or [be] capable of influencing, the decision of the
decisionmaking body to which it is addressed."
Kungys v. U.S., 485 U.S. 759 (1988). It is not
necessary to prove that the government agency was
actually influenced or that the statement was relied
upon by the government. There is also no
requirement that the statement be made directly to
a federal official.

In *U.S. v. Gaudin*, 515 U.S. 506 (1995), the Supreme Court found that the issue of materiality is a mixed question of law and fact that should properly be submitted to the jury. The defendant in *Gaudin* was accused of making false statements on federal loan documents. The district court ruled as a matter of law that the statements were material. The Ninth Circuit, en banc, reversed finding that the issue of materiality should have been submitted to the jury. In affirming the Ninth Circuit, Justice Scalia wrote that "[t]he Constitution gives a criminal defendant the right to have a jury determine, beyond a reasonable doubt, his guilt or every element of the crime with which he is charged."

In *Gaudin*, the parties had "agreed that materiality was an element of 18 U.S.C. § 1001, but disputed whether materiality was a question for the judge or jury." In *U.S. v. Wells*, 519 U.S. 482 (1997), the Supreme Court found that 18 U.S.C. § 1014, a statute pertaining to false statements to a federally insured financial institution, did not require the government to prove materiality.

§ 9.06   MATTERS WITHIN THE JURISDICTION OF THE EXECUTIVE, LEGISLATIVE, OR JUDICIAL BRANCH

It is first necessary to consider the scope of the term "jurisdiction." In *U.S. v. Rodgers*, 466 U.S. 475 (1984), the United States Supreme Court held that "jurisdiction," although undefined in the statute, does not suggest support for a narrow construction.

Section 1001 "expressly embraces false statements made 'in *any* matter within the jurisdiction of *any* department or agency of the United States.' " Thus, a man who lied to the F.B.I. by telling them his wife had been kidnapped and lied to the Secret Service in telling them his wife was involved in a plot to kill the President, was not entitled to a dismissal of a false statement charge as not within the bounds of the term, "jurisdiction," as used in section 1001. Since the F.B.I. is authorized to investigate crimes, including kidnapping, and the Secret Service is charged with protecting the President, statements to these agencies were within their statutory bases. The Court noted that reading section 1001 broadly furthered the "valid legislative interest in protecting the integrity of [such] official inquiries."

For many years courts struggled with the limits of the term "department or agency." In *U.S. v. Bramblett*, 348 U.S. 503 (1955), the Supreme Court found that the Disbursement Office of the House of Representatives was, in fact, a "department or agency of the United States." Defendant Bramblett, a former member of Congress, was charged with falsely representing to the Disbursement Office that an individual was entitled to compensation for being his official clerk. The Court, providing guidance on how to interpret the term "department," stated that "as used in this context, [it] was meant to describe the executive, legislative and judicial branches of the government." *Bramblett* permitted the term "department" to include numerous government agencies, sub-agencies, and boards. In *Hubbard v. U.S.*, 514 U.S. 695 (1995), however, the Supreme

Court overruled *Bramblett* finding that a court was not an agency or department for purposes of § 1001.

Congress reacted to the *Hubbard* decision by passing the False Statements Accountability Act of 1996, which modifies the statute to explicitly provide "the jurisdiction of the executive, legislative, or judicial branch" of the United States government. The section, however, specifically excludes "statements, representations, writings or documents submitted by" a party or counsel in a judicial proceeding. The new provision also limits the scope of matters of the legislative branch by stating that it applies only to administrative matters or certain Congressional investigations or reviews. Lower courts have looked at questions of statements made to agencies such as the FBI, IRS, and SEC, and also statements made to state officers and those that are not made directly to a federal agency. WCH § 9.6.

§ 9.07   FALSE CLAIMS

False statements pursuant to section 1001 has traditionally been a major offense used in government procurement fraud cases. In 1988 Congress passed the Major Fraud Act (18 U.S.C. § 1031) that created the specific offense of procurement fraud for government contract fraud involving one million dollars or more.

Also used when proceeding against procurement fraud is the false claims statute located in 18 U.S.C. § 287. This offense, originally combined with the false statements statute, was separated by Congress in 1948. The false claims statute is more restrictive in its application than section 1001 in that it applies only to false claims to the government.

The statute requires the government to prove "(1) that the defendant knowingly made and presented to a department or agency of the United States a false, fraudulent or fictitious claim against the United States, and (2) that the defendant acted with knowledge that the claim was false, fraudulent, or fictitious." *U.S. v. Kline*, 922 F.2d 610 (10th Cir.1990). The statute carries a fine and term of imprisonment not to exceed five years. WCH § 9.8.

False claims actions can be presented by private individuals acting on behalf of the United States. Section 3730 of Title 31 permits qui tam plaintiffs the right to bring civil actions on behalf of themselves and the government for violations of the False Claims Act.

§ 9.08 OTHER CRIMES

When false statements under section 1001 are charged in conjunction with another criminal offense, courts are left to decide the propriety of the prosecutor's selection of multiple charges. In *U.S. v. Woodward*, 469 U.S. 105 (1985), the Supreme Court considered the acceptability of indictments under 18 U.S.C. § 1001 and 31 U.S.C. § 1058, 1011 for willfully failing to report the carrying of cash in excess of five thousand dollars. The charges arose from the defendant's response of "no" on a customs form followed by a search and finding of monies in excess of five thousand dollars on the defendant and his wife. The Supreme Court found substantiation of

Congress' intent to punish under both 18 U.S.C. § 1001 and 31 U.S.C. §§ 1058, 1101 "by the fact that the statute's 'are directed to separate evils.' "

Other courts, however, have dismissed counts or refused to permit a conviction and sentence to stand when the same conduct was being punished under two different false statement statutes or a false statement statute and a perjury statute. WCH § 9.7. For example, in *U.S. v. Avelino*, 967 F.2d 815 (2d Cir.1992), the Second Circuit held that it was a violation of the double jeopardy clause to convict and sentence a defendant for both false statements pursuant to section 1001 and making false statements to Customs officials pursuant to 18 U.S.C. § 542. The court noted that "every element needed to prove a crime under Section 1001 is an element of a Section 542 offense and that there is no clear indication of a congressional intent to provide for cumulative punishments for Sections 1001 and 542."

CHAPTER 10

PERJURY AND FALSE DECLARATIONS

§ 10.01   INTRODUCTION

Perjury statutes exist throughout the United States Code. They are evident in Title 18, as well as in sections of the Code that are not focused predominantly upon crimes. For example, in Title 26 one observes a tax offense that is predicated upon the filing of a perjurious tax return (26 U.S.C. § 7206). In some instances the statute will authorize an individual to give an oath and refer violations of the oath to the perjury provisions found in Title 18. For example, Title 8 contains a statute pertaining to false evidence or swearing before the Immigration and Naturalization Service (8 U.S.C. § 1357) and authorizes prosecution pursuant to the criminal perjury statute. (18 U.S.C. § 1621).

Key statutes related to false and perjurious testimony are located at 18 U.S.C. § 1621 (perjury) and 18 U.S.C. § 1623 (false declarations). Today's perjury statute (§ 1621) dates back to statutes enacted by Congress for the purpose of criminalizing all false swearing. *U.S. v. Smull*, 236 U.S. 405 (1915). The false declarations statute (§ 1623) was added by Congress in 1970 as part of the Organized Crime Control Act of 1970 to "facilitate perjury prosecutions and thereby enhance reliability of testimony before federal courts and grand juries." *Dunn v. U.S.*, 442 U.S. 100 (1979). Although this new statute eased the evidentiary requirements in prosecuting perjury, its scope was limited to proceedings before or ancillary to federal courts or grand juries.

Perjury (18 U.S.C. § 1621) requires the government prove that the defendant: (1) under oath, by one authorized to administer the oath; (2) before a competent tribunal, officer, or person; (3) made a false; (4) material statement; (5) willfully and with knowledge of its falsity. Perjury carries a penalty of not more than five years imprisonment and a fine.

False declarations (18 U.S.C. § 1623) requires the government prove that the defendant: (1) under oath; (2) before or ancillary to any court or grand jury of the United States; (3) made a false; (4) material statement; (5) with knowledge of its falsity. False declarations carries a penalty of not more than five years imprisonment and a fine.

Perjury and false declarations permit prosecutions of statements that are made both inside or outside the United States. Further, these statutes incorporate 28 U.S.C. § 1746, thereby permitting certain unsworn statements to be subject to prosecution.

The key distinctions between these two offenses are noted in examining the scope, defenses, and evidentiary rules surrounding the two statutes. Where perjury applies to false statements before any "competent tribunal, officer, or person," false declarations is limited to statements "before or ancillary to any court or grand jury of the United States."

An additional distinction between these two statutes is noted in the fact that unlike the perjury statute, the false declarations statute does not require two witnesses. Also, the false declarations statute permits the use of inconsistent statements to prove falsity, without specification as to which statement is false. Finally, the false declarations statute provides for a recantation defense in certain circumstances.

When sections 1621 and 1623 both apply to the applicable criminal conduct, prosecutors have discretion to choose under which offense to proceed. Defense attorneys have unsuccessfully contested the use of the perjury statute when the statement was before a court or grand jury, and therefore subject to a false declarations charge. Arguments that the government has deprived the defendant of the recantation defense, by proceeding with a perjury charge, have failed to merit reversals. In one case, however, the Ninth Circuit treated a charge pursuant to section 1621 as if it had been filed under section 1623. *U.S. v. Clizer*, 464 F.2d 121 (9th Cir.1972).

Immunization of a witness does not preclude a perjury or false declarations charge against that witness. The federal immunity statute, 18 U.S.C. § 6002, specifically excepts "a prosecution for perjury, giving a false statement, or otherwise failing to comply with the order." Both the truthful and untruthful immunized testimony may be used in a subsequent false swearing prosecution for making false statements in the immunized testimony. *U.S. v. Apfelbaum*, 445 U.S. 115 (1980) (see § 19.12).

Section 1622 prohibits subornation of perjury. This allows for the prosecution of someone who assists another in committing a perjury offense. Typically, however, the individual would be charged with an obstruction of justice. See chap. 6.

§ 10.02 OATH

Both perjury (18 U.S.C. § 1621) and false declarations (18 U.S.C. § 1623) require proof that the defendant's statement was under oath. In most circumstances this oath will be a sworn declaration. It is possible, however, to prosecute for perjury or false declarations, absent an oath, when the criteria encompassed in 28 U.S.C. § 1746 have been met.

Congress passed section 1746 of Title 28 in 1976. That same year the legislature amended sections 1621 and 1623 to incorporate this alternative to the sworn oath requirements of the perjury and false declarations statute. Section 1746 provides that where a law, "rule, regulation, order, or requirement made pursuant to law" permits or requires an oath, then an unsworn declaration can suffice. The unsworn declaration must, however, be in substantially the same form as specifically set forth in the text of section 1746. The form provided includes a declaration, under penalties of perjury, that the statement is true and correct. The statute offers alternative forms for the unsworn declaration dependent on whether it is executed inside or outside the United States.

Although sections 1621 and 1623 of Title 18 require an oath, there is no necessity that the indictment allege the name of the person administering the oath. In *U.S. v. Debrow*, 346 U.S. 374 (1953), the Supreme Court reversed a district court's dismissal of a perjury indictment that failed to state the name and authority of the individual administering the oath. The Court found that the oath requirement could be met by the indictment's allegations "that the defendant had 'duly taken an oath.'" The term "duly taken" was interpreted by the Court to mean "an oath taken according to a law which authorizes such oath."

Although the indictment does not have to name the person who administered the oath, a court has required that it be proven in a section 1621 prosecution. In *Smith v. U.S.*, 363 F.2d 143 (5th Cir.1966), the Fifth Circuit found insufficient evidence of the oath requirement where the government's case consisted of a court clerk identifying a certified copy of the transcript containing the alleged perjury. The clerk in *Smith* failed to state that he was present at the hearing or that he observed the administration of an oath to the defendant. The court found that "the bare statement in the transcript, unsupported by testimony, that the defendant had been duly sworn was insufficient evidence to support a conviction of perjury."

In contrast, one court held that the false declarations statute (18 U.S.C. § 1623) does not make the identity of the one who administered the oath an essential element of the offense. In *U.S. v. Molinares*, 700 F.2d 647 (11th Cir.1983), the Eleventh Circuit discussed the distinction in proof required for 1621 and 1623. The court found that section 1621 required greater proof of the oath in that the statute used the language "taken an oath before a competent tribunal, officer, or person. . . ." In contrast, section 1623, the false declarations statute, merely required "the government prove that the maker of a knowingly false declaration before a court be under oath at the time of the statement." The court in *Molinares* found direct evidence by two witnesses of the administration of the oath, coupled with a transcript of the proceedings indicating the defendant being duly sworn prior to testifying, sufficient evidence for sustaining a prosecution pursuant to section 1623.

Although courts require that the oath be taken before an individual authorized to administer the oath, the person may be a de facto officer. A prosecution involving a violation of 18 U.S.C. § 1623 was predicated upon false testimony given under an oath administered by an "assistant" deputy foreperson of a grand jury. The court had designated an assistant deputy foreperson due to the absence of the foreperson. In response to the defendant's challenge of this oath, the Eastern District of Virginia found the use of the word "assistant" to be mere surplusage. The court stated that "generally it is considered immaterial whether the person administering the oath is an officer de jure or de facto, if his act takes place in the presence of the Court or one authorized to administer the oath, and with its apparent sanction." *U.S. v. Allen*, 409 F.Supp. 562 (E.D.Va.1975).

§ 10.03   WITHIN TRIBUNALS AND PROCEEDINGS

Section 1621 requires that the statement be made before "a competent tribunal, officer, or person, in any case in which a law of the United States authorizes an oath to be administered." In contrast, section 1623 requires that the statement has to be "in any proceeding before or ancillary to any court or grand jury of the United States."

The competency of the person administering the oath has been challenged in several section 1621 cases. Courts have found district court judges, deputy clerks, Senate subcommittees, an internal revenue agent, and public notaries as competent tribunals, officers, or persons authorized to administer an oath.

Even a court proceeding that is later found to be premised upon a defective indictment can serve as a competent tribunal for purposes of section 1621. All that is required is court power to proceed to a determination on the merits. Thus, a later showing of a statute being unconstitutional or a holding of insufficient evidence to prove the crime will not bar a prosecution of false testimony presented at the trial. *U.S. v. Williams*, 341 U.S. 58 (1951). A false declaration indictment, however, was found to be improper when based upon a declaration made two days after the grand jury term had expired. *U.S. v. Fein*, 504 F.2d 1170 (2d Cir.1974). Courts have also examined whether congressional rules have been met for purposes of a section 1621 case. WCH § 10.3.

In *Dunn v. U.S.*, 442 U.S. 100 (1979), the Supreme Court considered the scope of section 1623 and found that a sworn statement taken at an interview in a private attorney's office did not constitute a proceeding ancillary to a court or grand jury. The Court in *Dunn* examined the legislative history surrounding section 1623 and also noted a comment of the Department of Justice on the proposed legislation "that the scope of the inconsistent declarations provision was 'not as inclusive' as the perjury statute." Despite this comment, the government argued that since pre-trial depositions were covered in a letter sent by Senator McClellan to the Assistant Attorney General, it could also be interpreted that affidavits and certificates were meant to be included. The Court in *Dunn* agreed with the Court of Appeal's conclusion that the interview in this case "lacked the degree of formality required by § 1623." Implied throughout this decision, however, is that depositions, taken pursuant to Rule 15 of the Federal Rules of Criminal Procedure and 18 U.S.C. § 3503 can be ancillary proceedings for the purposes of a section 1623 prosecution.

§ 10.04   FALSITY

Prosecutions of both perjury and false declarations require a false statement. Actual falsity has been demanded by the courts. Thus, literally true but misleading statements will not constitute falsity. Likewise, ambiguous questions that call for varying interpretations cannot be used as the basis for obtaining a perjury or false declarations conviction.

Bronston v. U.S., 409 U.S. 352 (1973), is the Supreme Court's seminal decision holding that literally true statements cannot be the basis of a perjury conviction. In *Bronston*, the defendant was being questioned in a bankruptcy hearing by a lawyer representing a creditor. The questions sought to elicit whether the defendant, sole owner of Bronston Productions, had any Swiss bank accounts. The attorney first asked defendant if he had any Swiss bank accounts. To this question the defendant answered "no." The attorney for the creditor then asked defendant Bronston, "[h]ave you ever?" The defendant responded that "[t]he company had an account there for about six months, in Zurich." The defendant failed, however, to mention that although he presently had no bank accounts in Switzerland, he had held such an account for the past five years. Thus, although defendant's answers were literally true, in that he did not presently have an account and the company did at one point have one, he had failed to respond specifically to whether he had a Swiss bank account in the past.

In rejecting the government's use of this second question as the basis for a perjury conviction, the Court stated that it is the responsibility of the "questioner to pin the witness down to the specific object of the questioner's inquiry." Even though the witness may be deliberately avoiding the question, "it is the lawyer's responsibility to recognize the evasion and to bring the witness back to the mark, to flush out the whole truth with the tools of adversary examination." Literally true, but unresponsive answers should not be the subject of a federal perjury prosecution.

Falsity is a question to be determined by the jury. In making this determination, the jury should examine the answer to the question objectively. "The jury should determine whether the question—as the declarant must have understood it, giving it a reasonable reading—was falsely answered." *U.S. v. Lighte*, 782 F.2d 367 (2d Cir.1986).

Courts vary on the extent that answers should be examined in the context in which they are set, as opposed to being viewed in a vacuum. In *U.S. v. Shotts*, 145 F.3d 1289 (11th Cir.1998) the Eleventh Circuit stated that "[a] perjury conviction must rest on the utterance by the accused of a false statement; it may not stand on a particular interpretation that the questioner places upon the answer." In *U.S. v. DeZarn*, 157 F.3d 1042 (6th Cir.1998), however, the Sixth Circuit held that a perjury inquiry requires examination of the contextual setting. The court stated, "[a] perjury inquiry which focuses only upon the precision of the question and ignores what the

Defendant knew about the subject matter of the question at the time it was asked, misses the very point of perjury: that is, the Defendant's intent to testify falsely and, thereby, mislead his interrogators."

Falsity cannot exist when the question itself is "fundamentally ambiguous." A test for determining if a question is "fundamentally ambiguous" is set forth in the case of *U.S. v. Lattimore*, 127 F.Supp. 405 (D.D.C.1955), where the District Court for the District of Columbia found vagueness in a phrase that "is not a phrase with a meaning about which ordinary men of ordinary intelligence could agree, nor one which could be used with mutual understanding by a questioner and answerer unless it were defined at the time it were sought and offered as testimony."

To determine if a statement is "fundamentally ambiguous" it is necessary to examine the statement in its context. The asking of some ambiguous questions does not preclude a perjury conviction. *U.S. v. Lighte*, 782 F.2d 367 (2d Cir.1986). Further, a question in not "fundamentally ambiguous" just because some of the words used in the question may have different meanings.

The false declarations statute (18 U.S.C. § 1623) specifically provides that in certain circumstances a defendant who knowingly makes "two or more declarations, which are inconsistent to the degree that one of them is necessarily false, [the indictment] need not specify which declaration is false. . . ." The statute specifies that each declaration must be material to the point in question, and the declarations must be made within the applicable statute of limitations for the offense being charged. It is a defense if the accused believed the declaration to be true at the time it was made.

§ 10.05 MATERIALITY

Materiality is an element of both perjury and false declarations. Although required, the element is met with minimal evidence. "The test of materiality is whether the false testimony was capable of influencing the tribunal on the issue, or whether the false testimony would have the natural effect or tendency to influence, impede, or dissuade the Grand Jury from pursuing its investigation." *U.S. v. Gremillion*, 464 F.2d 901 (5th Cir.1972). The statement does not have to actually influence the tribunal or impede the investigation. It suffices when it is capable of this result.

The government bears the burden of proving materiality. *U.S. v. Bednar*, 728 F.2d 1043 (8th Cir.1984). It need only be proven as of the time the statements were given. Materiality does not require that the statement relate to a main issue in the case. Statements relating to subsidiary matters have been found to be material.

Some prosecutions have been based upon a "perjury trap," "when the government calls a witness before the grand jury for the primary purpose of obtaining testimony" from the witness in order to prosecute this individual later for perjury. *U.S. v. Chen*, 933 F.2d 793 (9th Cir.1991). But not all courts have embraced that doctrine. *U.S. v. Burke*, 425 F.3d 400 (7th Cir.2005).

§ 10.06   KNOWLEDGE AND WILLFULNESS

It is incumbent in a perjury or false declarations prosecution that the defendant have acted with knowledge of the statement's falsity. Although the statutes differ in this mens rea terminology (perjury uses "not believe to be true," false declarations uses "knowingly"), courts have been consistent in finding that both provisions require that the defendant must have believed when delivering the testimony that it was untrue. *U.S. v. Reveron Martinez*, 836 F.2d 684 (1st Cir.1988).

Whether the accused acted with knowledge of the statement's falsity is a question for the jury to resolve. Oftentimes circumstantial evidence is presented to satisfy the knowledge requirement. "The trier of fact may infer this element of knowledge from the surrounding circumstances." *U.S. v. Larranaga*, 787 F.2d 489 (10th Cir.1986).

Willfulness is an element of a section 1621 offense. It is not, however, used in the statutory language found in section 1623. Refusal of a defendant's willfulness instruction in a section 1623 prosecution has been upheld by an appellate court, since willfulness is not an element of a section 1623 offense. *U.S. v. Fornaro*, 894 F.2d 508 (2d Cir.1990).

§ 10.07 TWO WITNESS RULE

Perjury prosecutions are subject to a two-witness rule. *Hammer v. U.S.*, 271 U.S. 620 (1926). This evidentiary rule bars a conviction for perjury that is based solely upon one witness. *Weiler v. U.S.*, 323 U.S. 606 (1945). The rule requires "that the falsity of the defendant's statements must be proved by the testimony of two witnesses or the testimony of one witness, plus corroborating evidence." *U.S. v. Davis*, 548 F.2d 840 (9th Cir.1977).

The two-witness rule is not applicable to charges brought pursuant to section 1623, the false declarations statute. Congress specifically stated in the false declarations statute that although proof beyond a reasonable doubt would be sufficient for a conviction, it would not be necessary that such proof include a particular number of witnesses or evidence.

The policy rationale offered for adoption of a two-witness rule in perjury prosecutions is that it prevents a perjury conviction resting solely on one person's oath against another. Further, the rule encourages witnesses to come forward in that it prevents witnesses from being harassed or subjecting themselves to a possible false perjury prosecution.

Although called the two-witness rule, in actuality it does not require two separate witnesses. The rule can be satisfied either with two witnesses, or alternatively, one witness and sufficient corroborative evidence. Jurisdictions have differed over the precise level of sufficiency required for corroboration.

Generally, the corroborating evidence does not have to be sufficient for a conviction. It cannot, however, consist of merely peripheral testimony not tending to show the falsity of the accused's statements while under oath. *U.S. v. Diggs*, 560 F.2d 266 (7th Cir.1977). Most courts require that the corroborative evidence "be inconsistent with the innocence of the accused and must tend to show the perjury independently of the testimony which it is intended to corroborate." *U.S. v. Forrest*, 639 F.2d 1224 (5th Cir.1981). Independent evidence has been defined as "evidence coming from a source other than that of the direct testimony." *U.S. v. Diggs*, 560 F.2d 266 (7th Cir.1977).

Courts have accepted circumstantial evidence as corroboration. The evidence must, however, be trustworthy. Some jurisdictions have permitted the defendant's own statements and conduct to serve as the corroboration. The jury decides the weight to be accorded to the corroborative evidence.

§ 10.08   RECANTATION

The false declarations statute, section 1623, permits a limited defense of recantation. The statute provides one with the opportunity to admit false testimony and avoid a false declarations prosecution. The statute requires that the admission be made in the same continuous court or grand jury proceeding of the original declaration. The statute, however, is only applicable in certain circumstances.

Congress offered this recantation defense in an effort to "encourage truthful testimony by witnesses appearing before courts and grand juries." *U.S. v. Moore*, 613 F.2d 1029 (D.C.Cir.1979). The House Committee on the Judiciary reported that recantation "serves as an inducement to the witness to give truthful testimony by permitting him voluntarily to correct a false statement without incurring the risk [of] prosecution by doing so."

Recantation does not apply to perjury prosecutions under section 1621. Defendants have unsuccessfully raised the issue that the government has deprived them of their right of recantation by charging perjury when the conduct could have been charged pursuant to the false declarations statute. In *U.S. v. Kahn*, 472 F.2d 272 (2d Cir.1973), the Second Circuit expressed concern with the prospect of prosecutors using section 1621 when a recantation existed and section 1623 when it did not. In *Kahn* the court found it unnecessary to reach the merits of this argument in that even if the defendant had been charged pursuant to the false declarations statute, he would not have been entitled to a recantation defense.

Eligibility for a recantation defense is statutorily limited in that "at the time the admission is made, the declaration has not substantially affected the proceeding, or it has not become manifest that such falsity has been or will be exposed." Despite the disjunctive wording of this provision, most courts hold that "and" should be substituted for the "or" in section 1623(d). Thus, a defendant desiring a recantation defense must avail themselves of the opportunity before it substantially affects the proceeding and prior to it being exposed. The Eighth Circuit, however, found that "or" should be given "its ordinary meaning, reading the statute as setting forth two alternative conditions, satisfaction of either of which will allow a declarant to employ the recantation defense to bar prosecution for perjury." *U.S. v. Smith*, 35 F.3d 344 (8th Cir.1994).

The rationale as to why most courts require both conditions for a recantation defense is seen in examining the statute's aim of truthtelling in judicial proceedings. To permit a defendant the right to recant upon realization of a possible prosecution, would encourage a witness to initially lie. Only when threatened with exposure or prosecution would the witness come forward to recant. *U.S. v. Fornaro*, 894 F.2d 508 (2d Cir.1990).

In *U.S. v. Moore*, 613 F.2d 1029 (D.C.Cir.1979), the defendant initially testified before a grand jury investigating police corruption. Learning of a tape recording that contradicted his testimony, he attempted to recant his prior grand jury statements. The government, however, stopped a rehearsal of this recantation claiming his new version to be lacking credibility. The district court dismissed defendant's indictment when the government refused to permit defendant Moore the opportunity to reappear before the grand jury to recant his prior statements.

On appeal, the District of Columbia Circuit Court reversed and remanded, finding that the defendant was not entitled to a recantation defense when the government was already aware that Moore had lied to the grand jury. The court recognized that the recantation defense was premised upon a New York statute that used a conjunctive interpretation. It permitted a recantation defense only when the falsity had not substantially affected the proceeding and when it had not become manifest that such falsity had been or would be exposed.

In addition to these two conditions, courts have precluded a recantation defense when a defendant is using this avenue to attempt to explain prior inconsistent testimony. Outright retraction and repudiation of the prior statement has been required. *U.S. v. Tobias*, 863 F.2d 685 (9th Cir.1988). Implicit recantation, such as claiming memory loss, has been held not to suffice.

A recantation defense must be raised by the defendant prior to trial. Courts differ, however, on which party bears the burden of proving recantation. Some find that once the defendant raises the issue, then the prosecution has the burden of proving the inapplicability of the recantation defense beyond a reasonable doubt. Other courts place the burden on the defendant to prove proper recantation pursuant to section 1623(d). It is, however, clear that recantation is a question of law for the court.

CHAPTER 11

TAX CRIMES

§ 11.01 INTRODUCTION

White collar crime prosecutions commonly include tax charges. Title 26 of the United States Code provides an array of available offenses. Additionally, tax offenses can sometimes be prosecuted through general criminal statutes found in Title 18.

Charges are often premised on attempts to evade or defeat tax. (26 U.S.C. § 7201). Also noteworthy to criminal tax prosecutions are charges of failure to file a return or pay a tax (26 U.S.C. § 7203), and the filing or aiding and assisting in the filing of a false tax return. (26 U.S.C. § 7206). On occasion the prosecution also will include a charge of delivering a fraudulent return. (26 U.S.C. § 7207).

Fewer prosecutions have been premised on other tax offenses, such as a willful failure to collect or truthfully account for and pay over any tax (26 U.S.C. § 7202), a willful furnishing of a fraudulent statement or failing to furnish a statement to employees as required by section 6051 of the Internal Revenue Code (26 U.S.C. § 7204), and a willful failure to supply withholding information or the supplying of false withholding information to an employer (26 U.S.C. § 7205).

Section 7212 criminalizes two types of behavior. Under section 7212(a) one who corruptly or by force or threats of force endeavors to interfere with the administration of the internal revenue laws is subject to prosecution. Section 7212(b) criminalizes forcible rescue of property seized under the Internal Revenue Code. A tax offense also exists specifically to combat offenses such as extortion and obstruction by officers and employees "of the United States acting in connection with any revenue law of the United States." (26 U.S.C. § 7214).

There are also statutes for specific criminal conduct that arises in the context of tax issues. For example, false statements to purchasers or lessees relating to tax (26 U.S.C. § 7211), failure to obey a summons pursuant to certain sections of the Internal Revenue Code (26 U.S.C. § 7210), and disclosure or use of information by preparers of returns can in certain circumstances result in misdemeanor penalties (26 U.S.C. § 7216). It is also a crime for a trade or business to structure a transaction to evade reporting requirements. (26 U.S.C. § 6050I) (see §12.06).

Criminal statutes located in the crimes section of the United States Code also provide a basis for the prosecution of tax charges. For example, a conspiracy (18 U.S.C. § 371) charge can be used where the accused conspires with another to commit an offense defined in other federal statutes or conspires to defraud the United States. *U.S. v. Helmsley*, 941 F.2d 71 (2d Cir.1991). As previously noted, conspiracy under this general conspiracy statute requires an overt act in furtherance of the conspiracy. (see chap. 3).

False statements (18 U.S.C. § 1001), false claims (18 U.S.C. § 287), perjury (18 U.S.C. § 1621), and mail fraud (18 U.S.C. § 1341) have also been used when the conduct involves tax violations. The Department of Justice, however, restrains prosecutorial discretion by internally limiting the application of mail fraud charges to tax offenses. Authorization is required to prosecute tax violations as mail fraud. Further, the Department of Justice Guideline states that this authorization will only be given in "exceptional circumstance[s]" when the case involves "one person's tax liability or when all submissions to the IRS were truth." This restriction not only serves to limit the prosecution of tax violations through mail fraud charges, but also limits tax violations that might be prosecuted under the Racketeer Influenced and Corrupt Organization Act (RICO). Because mail fraud serves as one of the possible predicate acts for a RICO offense, but tax violations do not, the restriction has the effect of precluding some tax violations from being used in RICO prosecutions. This guideline, however, is not enforceable as a matter of law in that it is merely an internal guideline of the Department of Justice.

§ 11.02 WILLFULNESS

An element common to the tax fraud offenses (§§ 7201–7207) is the mens rea element of willfulness. Although willfulness is not defined in these sections, the Supreme Court has ruled that it has the same meaning in each section. Thus, irrespective of whether the offense is a misdemeanor or a felony, the level of willfulness required remains the same. *U.S. v. Bishop*, 412 U.S. 346 (1973). Although the willfulness element remains consistent in all tax fraud prosecutions, it "is a word of many meanings, its construction often being influenced by its context." *Spies v. U.S.*, 317 U.S. 492 (1943).

Historically courts interpreted willfulness to mean acts done with "bad purpose or evil intent," *U.S. v. Murdock*, 290 U.S. 389 (1933), "evil motive and want of justification in view of all the financial circumstances of the taxpayer," *Spies v. U.S.*, 317 U.S. 492 (1943), or "willful in the sense that he knew that he should have reported more income than he did." *Sansone v. U.S.*, 380 U.S. 343 (1965). This historical view is outlined in the Supreme Court's decision in *U.S. v. Bishop*, 412 U.S. 346 (1973).

Bishop, a lawyer convicted of three counts of the felony of filing a false return (26 U.S.C. § 7206(1)), contested the failure of the trial court to give his requested instruction on the misdemeanor offense of delivering a fraudulent return (26 U.S.C. § 7207). He argued that section 7207 was a lesser included offense of the felony and that "willfully" as found in the misdemeanor statute should be construed to require less scienter than the term would require in the felony offense.

In rejecting defendant's argument, the Supreme Court in *Bishop* stated that " 'willfully' has the same meaning in § 7207 that it has in § 7206(1)." While adhering to the historical standard of willfulness, the Supreme Court in *Bishop* also stated that willfully "connotes a voluntary, intentional violation of a known legal duty."

In *U.S. v. Pomponio*, 429 U.S. 10 (1976), the Supreme Court elucidated upon its holding in *Bishop*. Petitioners in *Pomponio* were convicted of willfully filing false income tax returns (26 U.S.C. § 7206(1)). The Supreme Court reversed the appellate court's ruling that the jury had been improperly instructed concerning willfulness. The instruction given by the trial court had not required a finding of bad purpose or evil motive. The Court in *Pomponio* stated that *Bishop* did not require "proof of any motive other than an intentional violation of a known legal duty." Thus, the trial court did not err in failing to instruct the jury on bad purpose or evil motive.

Although courts continue to refer to bad purpose and evil motive, it is clear that the government is not required to present such proof in establishing the element of willfulness. It is, however, incumbent upon the government to prove beyond a reasonable doubt that the accused intentionally and voluntarily violated a known legal duty.

Whether the accused acted with the requisite intent is a question of fact subject to jury determination. Often the prosecution offers circumstantial evidence as proof of this mens rea. A jury may infer willfulness from the facts presented. In practice, juries are often provided with evidence of the accused engaging in fraudulent type conduct ("badges of fraud").

Negating the element of willfulness can be a crucial aspect of the defense. In the landmark case of *Cheek v. U.S.*, 498 U.S. 192 (1991), the Supreme Court resolved the standard to be used by a jury in deciding whether a defendant had a good faith misunderstanding of the law that negated willfulness.

Petitioner Cheek, a commercial airline pilot, was convicted by a jury of six charges of failing to file federal income tax returns (26 U.S.C. § 7203) and for alleged tax evasions (26 U.S.C. § 7201). Petitioner, acting pro se at trial, argued that he acted without willfulness in that he believed his actions were lawful and further that he believed that the tax laws were being unconstitutionally enforced.

The district court instructed the jury on three occasions regarding aspects of willfulness. The latter two occasions were as a result of questions submitted to the court by the jury. On appeal Cheek argued that the trial court erred in instructing the jury "that only an objectively reasonable misunderstanding of the law negates the statutory willfulness requirement." The Seventh Circuit rejected Cheek's argument and affirmed his convictions.

The Supreme Court granted certiorari and thereafter vacated the judgment of the Court of Appeals and remanded the case for further proceedings consistent with its opinion. Justice White, writing the majority opinion, commenced by noting that the term "willfully" as used in federal criminal tax offenses served to "carv[e] out an exception to the traditional rule" that ignorance of the law or mistake of law is no defense to criminal prosecution. The Court further reaffirmed that the standard for willfulness is the "voluntary, intentional violation of a known legal duty."

In resolving the issues presented in this case, the Court concentrated on the "knowledge" requirement of willfulness. The government must prove that the defendant is "aware of the duty at issue, which cannot be true if the jury credits a good-faith misunderstanding and belief submission, whether or not the claimed belief or misunderstanding is objectively reasonable." To characterize a belief as not objectively reasonable transforms the question to a legal issue and precludes the jury from properly resolving this factual question. It was, therefore, improper for the trial court to instruct the jury in such a way that they were precluded from considering petitioner's asserted beliefs that wages were not income and that he was not a taxpayer within the meaning of the Internal Revenue Code. The Court determined that these are rightfully issues to be decided by a jury in considering whether Cheek had acted willfully.

The Court in *Cheek*, however, rejected the defendant's claim that he had a good-faith belief that the income tax laws were unconstitutional as applied to him. Claims of unconstitutionality reveal that the accused's conduct is not arising from innocent mistakes. Rather, it provides a showing of full knowledge of the law. A defendant's view of the law is irrelevant to the issue of willfulness. It was, therefore, not error in this case for the trial court to instruct the jury to disregard defendant's claims that the tax laws were unconstitutional.

In his concurring opinion, Justice Scalia voiced his dissatisfaction with the Court's test for willfulness. He argued that willfulness should not be interpreted so "that belief in the nonexistence of a textual prohibition excuses liability, but belief in the invalidity (*i.e.*, the legal nonexistence) of a textual prohibition does not."

A dissent authored by Justice Blackmun, and joined by Justice Marshall, criticized the Court for exceeding the limits of common sense. The dissent expressed the view that a person of defendant's intelligence should not be permitted to assert, as a defense to willfulness, that the wages he receives for labor is not income.

On retrial, defendant Cheek argued a good faith belief premised upon his reliance on the advice of counsel. The trial court, however, refused defendant's request for an instruction on advice of counsel. The Seventh Circuit affirmed, finding insufficient evidence to warrant the giving of the instruction. *U.S. v. Cheek*, 3 F.3d 1057 (7th Cir.1993).

Willfulness also can be negated when there is uncertainty in the tax law. *James v. U.S.*, 366 U.S. 213 (1961). In *U.S. v. Garber*, 607 F.2d 92 (5th Cir.1979), the Fifth Circuit in an en banc rehearing examined the defendant's conviction for tax fraud that stemmed from her alleged failure to report income from the sale of her blood. The court reversed and remanded this section 7201 conviction finding that the district court had acted improperly in failing to permit experts from testifying on the question of whether the income was taxable. The court also found it improper for the trial court to have refused to instruct the jury that a reasonable misconception of tax law would negate defendant's intent. Because of the novel and unsettled nature of the law, the defendant should have been afforded the opportunity to present this position.

Some jurisdictions adhere to the position taken in *Garber*, finding uncertainty in the law as a proper defense to a tax charge. Subsequent Fifth Circuit cases, however, have limited *Garber*. *U.S. v. Burton*, 737 F.2d 439 (5th Cir.1984). Additionally, not all jurisdictions accept the position expressed in *Garber*. For example, in *U.S. v. Curtis*, 782 F.2d 593 (6th Cir.1986), the Sixth Circuit rejected this view in part because it placed in the hands of the jury a legal question that should be resolved by the court. In *Curtis* the court expressed the view that a jury should not be asked "to read and interpret statutes to determine whether or not the governing law is uncertain or debatable."

§ 11.03 TAX EVASION

Tax evasion is considered the "capstone" of the tax offenses. Its purpose is to "induce prompt and forthright fulfillment of every duty under the income tax law and to provide a penalty suitable to every degree of delinquency." *Spies v. U.S.*, 317 U.S. 492 (1943). The elements of a charge pursuant to 26 U.S.C. § 7201 are: (1) the existence of a tax deficiency, (2) an affirmative act of evasion or attempted evasion of tax, and (3) willfulness. The felony of tax evasion carries a penalty of not more than five years imprisonment and a fine, although pending legislation seeks to increase the sentence for this offense. When the evasion is by a corporation, the fine can be higher than that for an individual.

The government is required to prove beyond a reasonable doubt the existence of a tax deficiency. Courts often require that the deficiency be "substantial." In *U.S. v. Marashi*, 913 F.2d 724 (9th Cir.1990), however, the Ninth Circuit rejected defendant's *de minimis* argument. The court stated that "[t]he language of section 7201 does not contain a substantiality requirement. It simply states that willful attempts to evade 'any tax' under the Tax Code is a felony." In reality, the Justice Department seldom prosecutes a tax evasion case absent a showing of a sufficient level of tax due and owing.

A mere tax deficiency, however, will not suffice to sustain an evasion conviction. It is also essential that the government show an affirmative act of evasion and willfulness. The evidence supporting these latter two elements often coalesces.

In *Spies v. U.S.*, 317 U.S. 492 (1943), the Supreme Court examined the predecessor evasion statute as it relates to the misdemeanor of willful failure to pay a tax. According to the Court, the factor that distinguishes these two offenses is the "affirmative action implied from the term 'attempt,' as used in the felony subsection." While the misdemeanor can be a willful omission, the felony of evasion requires a positive attempt to evade tax.

The willful attempt to defeat or evade tax can be accomplished "in any manner." In *Spies* the Court offered illustrations of conduct (so-called "badges of fraud") from which a willful attempt could be inferred. The examples provided were "keeping a double set of books, making false entries or alterations, or false invoices or documents, destruction of books or records, concealment of assets or covering up sources of income, handling of one's affairs to avoid making the records usual in transactions of the kind, and any conduct, the likely effect of which would be to mislead or conceal." The filing of a false tax return has been found to be a sufficient affirmative commission to satisfy this element. *Sansone v. U.S.*, 380 U.S. 343 (1965).

§ 11.04 METHODS OF PROOF

It is necessary for the government to prove a tax deficiency for a prosecution under section 7201. One way this can be accomplished is through the direct or specific item method. Alternatively, the government can use indirect methods of proof. The indirect methods include the net worth method, the expenditures method, and bank deposit method.

The direct or specific item method is considered the simplest method of proving a tax deficiency. It employs specific items to prove the underpayment.

For example, a defendant's records could be used to prove that a specific deduction listed on the return was improper.

Indirect methods of proving a tax deficiency use circumstantial evidence to establish this element. One such method is the net worth method that examines the defendant's net worth at the beginning of a year in contrast to the net worth at the end of the year.

In *Holland v. U.S.*, 348 U.S. 121 (1954), the Supreme Court examined the use of the net worth method. The Court noted the flaws inherent in this method, but upheld its legality cautioning that it be subject to the "exercise of great care and restraint." It is essential that the government establish the net worth at the beginning of the year with "reasonable certainty." Because the net worth method rests solely on circumstantial evidence, courts require the government to investigate all reasonable explanations offered by the defendant that are inconsistent with guilt. "A number of courts have held that a substantiality instruction is necessary" when the "net worth" method is used and the amount of the tax owed is contested by the defense. WCH § 11.3.

Using the cash expenditures method, a variant of the net worth method, the government shows that the defendant's expenditures exceeded the reported income. Presumably the source of funds for these expenditures must be taxable income.

Finally, the government can use the bank deposit method for proving the tax deficiency. The government examines the bank deposits of the defendant, excluding deposits that are not taxable income. These deposits are then compared to the reported income of the accused. The excess in the amount deposited over the reported income represents the unreported income.

The government also may use a combination of methods. In *U.S. v. Scott*, 660 F.2d 1145 (7th Cir.1981), the defendant William J. Scott, former Attorney General for the State of Illinois, was convicted of one count of violating section 7206(1). The government used the net worth, cash expenditures, and specific items methods to prove that Scott had falsely reported his adjusted gross income for 1972.

§ 11.05   FAILURE TO FILE A RETURN OR PAY A TAX

Section 7203 criminalizes the willful failure to pay any tax, make any return, keep any records, or supply any information as required by law or regulations. The government must prove beyond a reasonable doubt that the accused, (1) willfully, (2) failed to make a return, to pay a tax, to keep records or supply information, (3) having a legal duty to do so, (4) at the time required by law. This misdemeanor offense carries a penalty of up to one year imprisonment and a fine, although this may be increased if pending legislation passes. In the case of a corporation, this fine can be higher. If, however, the failure to pay involves an estimated tax, the section is inapplicable if there is no addition to tax under section 6654 or 6655. The statute becomes a felony offense where the willful violation involves section 6050I of the Code. (see § 12.06). In this circumstance the offense carries a penalty of up to five years imprisonment.

This section is commonly employed to prosecute tax protesters who fail to file a return or who file incomplete returns. It is rare that the government proceeds with a section 7203 case absent a certain threshold of unpaid tax. Failure to file can be proven by testimony of an individual from the Internal Revenue Service stating that a search was made of the government's records and no return was found. As with other tax offenses, the government is required to prove that the accused acted willfully.

§ 11.06 FALSE RETURNS

Section 7206 is divided into two separate offenses. Subsection one is a perjury tax offense in that it prohibits one from willfully making and subscribing a return, statement, or other document under penalties of perjury which the person did not believe to be true and correct as to every material matter. Subsection two criminalizes the conduct of one who aids or assists in the preparation of a false return.

In order to sustain a conviction under section 7206(1), the government must prove that the accused: (1) willfully, (2) signed a return, statement, or other document, (3) under penalties of perjury, (4) that the return, statement, or document was materially false, and (5) that the accused did not believe it to be true and correct. Section 7206(2) requires the government to prove that the accused: (1) willfully, (2) aided or assisted in, or procured, counseled or advised the preparation or presentation of any document in connection with any matter arising under the internal revenue laws, (3) which document is materially false.

Both subsections to this statute are felony offenses. They carry penalties of up to three years imprisonment and a fine, although pending legislation aims to increase the penalty. In the case of a corporation, the fine can be higher.

Unlike the tax evasion statute, there is no requirement for the government to prove a tax deficiency. It is only necessary to show that the return is materially false.

In *U.S. v. DiVarco*, 484 F.2d 670 (7th Cir.1973), defendants' convictions included violations of section 7206(1). Defendants argued on appeal that the government's failure to show that they understated their income precluded the use of this statutory provision. The Seventh Circuit noted that although most cases involving misstatement of source of income also involve an understatement of taxable income, "the purpose behind the statute is to prosecute those who intentionally falsify their tax returns regardless of the precise ultimate effect that falsification may have." In *DiVarco*, the court found that misstatement of the source of one's income could be a material matter.

In *U.S. v. Greenberg*, 735 F.2d 29 (2d Cir.1984), the Second Circuit rejected defendant's argument that the misstatements were not material in that "they resulted in, at most, minimal underpayments of taxes." The court found that materiality referred to the impact the statement may have on the ability of the agency to perform its assigned functions. "The question is not what effect the statement actually had, . . . rather whether the statement had the potential for an obstructive or inhibitive effect." The court in *Greenberg* found the false statements of income material, even though they resulted in the minimal underpayment of taxes.

In *U.S. v. Gaudin* (see § 9.05), the Supreme Court held that issues of materiality of alleged false statements were questions for the jury to decide. In *Neder v. U.S.*, 527 U.S. 1 (1999), the Supreme Court reaffirmed its holding in *Gaudin* that materiality is a jury question, and also stated that "[i]n a prosecution under § 7206(1), several courts have determined that 'any failure to report income is material.'"

A tax preparer can be charged under either subsection of this statute. In *U.S. v. Shortt Accountancy Corp.*, 785 F.2d 1448 (9th Cir.1986), the defendant corporation was convicted of seven counts of violating section 7206(1). The corporation, through its chief operating officer, improperly structured certain investments to appear as if they occurred before a change in law. This permitted clients to receive an undeserved tax benefit.

The corporation argued on appeal that a tax preparer could not be charged under subsection one of this statute, but rather 7206(2) was the applicable offense. The accounting corporation also maintained that the actual subscriber of the return was unaware of the fraud involved and therefore did not have the requisite intent of willfully making and subscribing a false return.

The Ninth Circuit, in *Shortt*, rejected defendant's arguments, finding that section 7206(1) was not limited to taxpayers. Being a perjury statute, the court found that anyone who makes a false return could be prosecuted pursuant to this provision. The court also held that the corporation could be convicted of section 7206(1) even though the particular employee subscribing the return had no knowledge of the fraudulent scheme. To hold otherwise would permit a tax preparer to escape liability "by arranging for an innocent employee to complete the proscribed act of subscribing a false return."

CHAPTER 12

CURRENCY REPORTING CRIMES AND MONEY LAUNDERING

§ 12.01 INTRODUCTION

Currency reporting crimes emanate from statutes that are of recent vintage. In an effort to monitor financial transactions, Congress enacted legislation concentrating on reporting and recordkeeping by banks. This initial act, commonly referred to as the Bank Secrecy Act, includes a requirement that financial institutions report to the government certain cash transactions.

A second major effort to use currency transaction reporting as a method to combat criminality is seen in 26 U.S.C. § 6050I. Unlike the Bank Secrecy Act, which is limited to financial institutions, section 6050I requires the reporting of certain monetary transactions by those engaged in a "trade or business." The Bank Secrecy Act and section 6050I both, however, require that parties who meet the defined class, as specified in each of these statutes, report the transaction irrespective of any criminal conduct being involved.

The Bank Secrecy Act and section 6050I include provisions prohibiting the structuring of a transaction to evade the reporting requirements. Additionally, Congress enacted sections 1956 and 1957 of Title 18 to combat money laundering. (see § 12.07) These latter two provisions fill a gap that became apparent in initial prosecutions under the

Bank Secrecy Act. Congress extended the reach of the Bank Secrecy Act and money laundering statutes in Title III of the Patriot Act, The International Money Laundering Abatement and Anti-Terrorist Financing Act of 2001.

§ 12.02   BANK SECRECY ACT

Congress passed the Bank Secrecy Act in 1970. The Act was "designed to obtain financial information having 'a high degree of usefulness in criminal, tax, or regulatory investigations or proceedings.'" *California Bankers Association v. Shultz*, 416 U.S. 21 (1974). The Patriot Act added an additional mission of requiring reports "in the conduct of intelligence or counterintelligence activities, including analysis to protect against international terrorism." (31 U.S.C. § 5311).

Title I of the Act, presently codified in Title 12 of the United States Code, pertains to the requirements of financial institutions to keep records, including the maintaining of records of customer identity and the microfilming of checks. Title II of the Bank Secrecy Act, presently codified in Title 31 of the United States Code, requires the reporting to the federal government of certain foreign and domestic transactions. The Act authorizes the Secretary of the Treasury to prescribe via regulation the specified bank recordkeeping and reporting requirements.

Pursuant to 31 U.S.C. § 5313 and its accompanying regulations, it is incumbent that financial institutions file reports on certain domestic transactions. Statutes also exist regarding the recordkeeping and reporting on foreign financial agency transactions (31 U.S.C. § 5314), reports on foreign currency transactions (31 U.S.C. § 5315), and reports on exporting and importing monetary instruments (31 U.S.C. § 5316). Some of the statutes allow for exemptions. 31 U.S.C. § 5318.

One who causes or attempts to cause a financial institution to fail to file a report required by section 5313(a), or causes or attempts to cause a financial institution to file a report that contains a material omission or misstatement of fact, can find themselves subject to the penalties imposed under this Act. The Bank Secrecy Act also prohibits the structuring of a transaction to evade the currency reporting requirements of section 5313(a). (31 U.S.C. § 5324).

Approximately two years after the passage of the Bank Secrecy Act, an action was brought in the District Court for the Northern District of California contesting the constitutionality of the Act. Although this action's principle focus was a claimed violation of the Fourth Amendment's guarantee against unreasonable searches and seizures, plaintiffs also claimed a violation of the First, Fifth, Ninth, Tenth and Fourteenth Amendments of the Constitution. The Supreme Court, in its eventual ruling in *California Bankers Association v. Shultz*, 416 U.S. 21 (1974), found that the recordkeeping requirements imposed by the regulations of the Secretary of the Treasury did not deprive the plaintiff bank of due process of law and did not invade the Fourth Amendment's guarantee against unreasonable searches and seizures.

In rejecting this constitutional challenge to the Act, the Court in *California Bankers Association* noted that the recordkeeping requirements, as imposed by the Secretary of the Treasury, did not place an unreasonable burden on banks. The Supreme Court further found that a requirement of maintenance of records did not constitute a seizure. The Court found the application of the reporting requirements to both foreign and domestic transactions to be reasonable and that the bank depositors lacked standing to challenge the Act under the Fourth and Fifth Amendment.

In the later case of *U.S. v. Miller*, 425 U.S. 435 (1976), the Supreme Court held that a bank depositor had no interest protected by the Fourth Amendment in records maintained by a bank pursuant to the Bank Secrecy Act, despite the allegation that these records were obtained by the government through defective subpoenas. The Court found that defendants had no legitimate expectation of privacy in business records of the bank. The Court stated that "[t]he depositor takes the risk, in revealing his affairs to another, that the information will be conveyed by that person to the Government."

In its initial years, the Bank Secrecy Act was seldom employed by the government as a prosecutorial tool. In recent years, however, the Act has significantly influenced the banking industry and has served as a source for the prosecution of financial institutions.

The Bank Secrecy Act and its accompanying regulations impose civil and criminal penalties for noncompliance with many of the reporting requirements. Willful violations of most of the provisions found in Title 31 carry criminal penalties of up to five years imprisonment and a fine. This penalty can be enhanced up to ten years with a fine when there is a willful violation that occurs while violating another law of the United States or engaging in conduct that is part of a pattern of illegal activity involving transactions exceeding $100,000 in a twelve month period. (31 U.S.C. § 5322). The penalty for structuring transactions to evade reporting requirements also carries imprisonment of up to five years, with an additional five years possible in certain aggravated cases. (31 U.S.C. § 5324).

Willful violations of a regulation under the recordkeeping statutes found in Title 12 can result in imprisonment of up to one year and a fine. (12 U.S.C. § 1956). This can be increased up to five years imprisonment with a fine where the violation is committed in furtherance of the commission of any violation of federal law punishable by imprisonment for more than one year. (12 U.S.C. § 1957).

§ 12.03 DOMESTIC FINANCIAL INSTITUTIONS

Section 5313 concerns reports required to be filed by domestic financial institutions. A financial institution is defined in 31 U.S.C. § 5312 and in the regulations of the Secretary of the Treasury. The breadth of this term is apparent in the inclusion of businesses well beyond the typical banking association. For example, financial institutions include "a dealer in precious metals, stones, or jewels," "a pawnbroker," "a travel agency," "a telegraph company," "a business engaged in vehicle sales, including automobile, airplane, and boat sales," and "persons involved in real estate closings and settlements."

In *U.S. v. Gollott*, 939 F.2d 255 (5th Cir.1991), defendants challenged their status as a financial institution. In upholding defendants' convictions, the Fifth Circuit examined the definition of financial institution as stated in the amended regulations. The court stated that, "[t]his language is broader than and perhaps counterintuitive to everyday understanding of what a financial institution is, but it is not vague as applied to appellants' dealings." The court decided that the jury had rationally found defendants to be a financial institution as defined by applicable regulations.

In *U.S. v. Bucey*, 876 F.2d 1297 (7th Cir.1989), the Seventh Circuit reversed a defendant's convictions premised on 31 U.S.C. §§ 5313 and 5322(b). The court found defendant Bucey, acting in his individual capacity, not to be a financial institution, where the definition of the term included the language "agency, branch, or office." The court in *Bucey* did, however, note that the term financial institution was amended in 1987 after the time of defendant's alleged violations. The amended regulation added the word "agent" prior to "agency, branch, or office."

Most circuits find that an individual may be a financial institution. *U.S. v. Tennenbaum*, 934 F.2d 8 (2d Cir.1991). A financial institution has been defined to encompass a bank, including each of its branches. Thus, if there are multiple cash transactions at different branches of the same financial institution that meet the reporting requirements, then the bank must file a currency transaction report. *U.S. v. Giancola*, 783 F.2d 1549 (11th Cir.1986).

The terms "domestic financial agency" and "domestic financial institution" are defined in section 5312 as to "apply to an action in the United States of a financial agency or institution." An "unlicensed money-transmitting business" has been found to meet this definition. *U.S. v. Mazza-Alaluf*, 621 F.3d 205 (2d Cir.2010).

§ 12.04   RECORDKEEPING AND REPORTING REQUIREMENTS

The Bank Secrecy Act and its accompanying regulations specify both recordkeeping and reporting requirements. Certain records by financial institutions involving extensions of credit, transfers of currency or monetary instruments, or intents to transfer currency or monetary instruments, are subject to be retained in original, microfilm, or other form of reproduction. In many instances, regulations found in the Code of Federal Regulations provide details of the reporting rules. The reports filed are called Currency Transaction Reports (CTR) with different forms used for the different reporting requirements.

For example, reports on exporting and importing monetary instruments are the subject of 31 U.S.C. § 5316. Certain monetary instruments transported from the United States to a place outside this country or from outside the United States to within this country are subject to the reporting requirements. Additionally, monetary instruments received from outside the United States may be subject to these reporting requirements.

The regulations provided by the Secretary of the Treasury pursuant to this statutory provision on reports of transportation of currency or monetary instruments contain an array of exemptions from this filing requirement. (31 C.F.R. § 103.23). For example, a federal reserve bank is not subject to this reporting requirement. Regulations also provide the procedure, including time limitations for the filing of reports. (31 C.F.R. § 103.27).

Financial institutions are required to have an anti-money laundering program that includes "the development of internal policies, procedures, and controls; the designation of a compliance officer; an ongoing employee training program; and an independent audit function to test programs." (31 U.S.C. § 5318(h)). There is also the requirement of "due diligence for United States private banking and correspondent bank accounts involving foreign persons." This requires that "[e]ach financial institution that establishes, maintains, administers, or manages a private banking account or a correspondent account in the United States for a non-United States person, including a foreign individual visiting the United States, or a representative of a non-United States person shall establish appropriate, specific, and, where necessary, enhanced, due diligence policies, procedures, and controls that are reasonably designed to detect and report instances of money laundering through those accounts." (31 U.S.C. § 5318(I)).

Other statutes also contain reporting requirements, as for example customs forms. The Supreme Court, in *U.S. v. Bajakajian*, 524 U.S. 321 (1998), held that failure to report funds on a customs currency reporting form would not subject the individual to forfeiture "of the entire $357,144 that respondent failed to declare" when the forfeiture was disproportionate to the gravity of the offense. The Court found the forfeiture to be punitive and a violation of the Excessive Fines Clause. Congress, however, in the Patriot Act, created a new bulk cash smuggling offense that criminalizes the undeclared movement of more than ten thousand dollars across U.S. borders and makes the property subject to forfeiture. (31 U.S.C. § 5332).

§ 12.05 KNOWLEDGE AND WILLFULNESS

Criminal prosecutions under the Bank Secrecy Act often require willfulness. Recent legislation removed the willfulness requirement when a structuring offense is involved.

In *Ratzlaf v. U.S.*, 510 U.S. 135 (1994), the Supreme Court examined willfulness in the context of an alleged structuring offense under 31 U.S.C. § 5324. In reversing defendant's conviction, the Court held that to willfully violate "the antistructuring law, the Government must prove that the defendant acted with knowledge that his conduct was unlawful." The Court in *Ratzlaf* stated that they were "unpersuaded . . . that structuring is 'so obviously "evil" or inherently "bad" that the "willfulness" requirement is satisfied irrespective of the defendant's knowledge of the illegality of structuring.' "

In response to the *Ratzlaf* decision, Congress modified § 5324 as part of the Riegle Community Development and Regulatory Improvement Act of 1994. The modified statute omits the term willfully. By placing penalty provisions directly in § 5324, the mens rea for the structuring statute is now met when the government shows that the defendant intended to evade the reporting requirement.

In *U.S. v. Bank of New England, N.A.*, 821 F.2d 844 (1st Cir.1987), the First Circuit found that a trial court's collective knowledge instruction was proper where a bank had a structure similar to that of a large corporation. The court stated that "[c]orporations compartmentalize knowledge, subdividing the elements of specific duties and operations into smaller components. The aggregate of those components constitutes the corporation's knowledge of a potential operation." (see § 2.03).

§ 12.06   SECTION 6050I

Section 6050I of the Internal Revenue Code (Title 26) was modeled after the Bank Secrecy Act. A shortcoming of the Bank Secrecy Act, as being limited to financial institutions, was met by the adoption of a statute that extended currency transaction reporting to individuals engaged in a trade or business. Section 6050I, as passed in 1984, was intended to encourage the reporting of cash income in order to reduce the deficit. In reality, this section has become a tool for monitoring criminal activity.

26 U.S.C. § 6050I is applicable to trades or businesses that receive in excess of ten thousand dollars in cash. It requires the reporting of these transactions to the Internal Revenue Service. The section excludes certain transactions, such as those that would be reported pursuant to the Bank Secrecy Act. WCH § 12.3(B). A provision of section 6050I prohibits the evading or assisting in the structuring of a transaction to avoid the reporting requirement. The Internal Revenue Service's form for complying with section 6050I is found in Form 8300.

Section 6050I and Form 8300 have proved controversial in the legal community. Because the statute applies to all trades or businesses, the question has arisen as to the section's applicability to payments received by attorneys.

In *U.S. v. Goldberger & Dubin, P.C.*, 935 F.2d 501 (2d Cir.1991), the Second Circuit found that section

6050I did not conflict with the United States Constitution. Analogizing to cases reported under the Bank Secrecy Act, the court found no Fourth or Fifth Amendment violation. The court noted that the reporting requirements targeted transactions without regard to the underlying purpose and irrespective of any criminality involved in the transaction.

The *Goldberger* court also dismissed defense arguments that section 6050I was a deprivation of the right to counsel under the Sixth Amendment. The court found the section less intrusive than the recent Supreme Court decisions that permitted forfeiture of attorney fees. The Second Circuit stated that section 6050I did not preclude clients from their choice of counsel, "they need only pay counsel in some other manner than with cash."

Equally unpersuasive to the *Goldberger* court was appellant's contention that section 6050I conflicted with the attorney-client privilege. "Absent special circumstances," the court found that client identity and fee information were not privileged matters. (see § 22.01). Since the practice of law is considered a "trade or business" for purposes of the income tax laws and the Sherman Act, *Goldberger* found that absent a specific congressional intent to exclude attorneys, section 6050I applied to lawyers.

In *U.S. v. Sindel*, 53 F.3d 874 (8th Cir.1995), the Eighth Circuit examined when the attorney-client privilege would protect client identity and fee information. "Special circumstances" exceptions were found to include "the legal advice exception," "the last link exception," and the "confidential communications exception." "After examining Sindel's *in camera* testimony about client's special circumstances," the court found the release of information with respect to one client, could not be accomplished without revealing "confidential communication." According to the court, "special circumstances," however, did not exist with respect to a second client.

It is necessary for the government to use the procedural process correctly when seeking to obtain information from an attorney about their client. In *U.S. v. Gertner*, 65 F.3d 963 (1st Cir.1995), the First Circuit did not address the applicability of § 6050I to attorneys, finding that summons enforcement should be denied in that the government failed to adhere to the proper procedure for the service of John Doe summonses (see § 17.04).

§ 12.07 MONEY LAUNDERING

Sections 1956 and 1957 of title 18, the money laundering statutes, emanate from the Anti-Drug Abuse Act of 1986. Specifically 18 U.S.C. § 1956 concentrates on financial transactions involving proceeds of unlawful activity. It does, however, criminalize transactions involving proceeds of unlawful activity "knowing that the transaction is designed in whole or in part ... to avoid a transaction reporting requirement under State or Federal Law ... " Section 1957 pertains to those who knowingly engage or attempt to engage in monetary transactions involving "criminally derived property that is of a value greater than ten thousand dollars and is derived from specified unlawful activity." WCH § 12.4(C). Section 1957 "does not include any transaction necessary to preserve a person's right to representation as guaranteed by the Sixth Amendment to the Constitution."

Both sections 1956 and 1957 focus on transactions involving tainted funds. Often drug related activity is prosecuted through the use of these money laundering offenses. In recent years, white collar criminality has also produced charges under sections 1956 and 1957. This is perhaps in part a result of the simplicity in proving a section 1956 and 1957 offense and the severe penalty accompanying these charges. A case that may have been limited to fraud charges may now find money laundering charges added to the indictment. *U.S. v. Powers*, 168 F.3d 741 (5th Cir.1999).

It is necessary, however, that "money laundering must be a crime distinct from the crime by which the money is obtained. The money laundering statute is not simply the addition of a further penalty to a criminal deed; it is a prohibition of processing the fruits of a crime or of a completed phase of an ongoing offense." *U.S. v. Abuhouran*, 162 F.3d 230 (1998).

Section 1956(a)(1) pertains to domestic money laundering. In contrast, section 1956(a)(2) involves international money laundering. The third form of money laundering, found in 1956(a)(3) "is designed for government sting operations using money 'represented to be' the proceeds of unlawful activity, but which is, in fact, government property." *U.S. v. Manarite*, 44 F.3d 1407 (9th Cir.1995).

The basic elements of an offense under 1956(a)(1) are that "(1) the defendant took part in a financial transaction; (2) the defendant knew that the property involved in the transaction involved the proceeds of illegal activity; (3) that the property involved was in fact the proceeds of that illegal activity; and (4) the defendant knew that the transaction was designed in whole or in part to conceal or disguise the nature, source, location, ownership, or control of the illegal proceeds." *U.S. v. Ruiz-Castro*, 92 F.3d 1519 (10th Cir.1996). Not every form of conduct constitutes concealment for purposes of § 1956(a). *U.S. v. Naranjo*, 634 F.3d 1198 (11th Cir.2011).

Property being the proceeds of illegal activity is met by being a "specified unlawful activity," a term that is a component of all subsections of this offense. The array of conduct included in the definition of "specified unlawful activity" allows the statute to have enormous breadth. Many statutes serve as predicate offenses for the money laundering statute. For example, "specified unlawful activity" includes an offense under 18 U.S.C. § 1030, the computer fraud statute. (see § 15.02).

Two Supreme Court decisions, issued on the same day, narrow the scope of the money laundering statute. In *U.S. v. Santos*, 553 U.S. 507 (2008), the Court in a plurality opinion held that the term "proceeds" in § 1956(a)(1) means " 'profits,' as opposed to 'receipts.'" The charges stemmed from payments to "lottery operators" and employees receipt of payments in an alleged gambling operation. Because the federal statute failed to define the term "proceeds," the Court used the rule of lenity in deciding favorable to the defendants that "proceeds" would be interpreted to mean "profits."

Also narrowing the money laundering statute was the Court's decision in *Cuellar v. U.S*, 553 U.S. 550 (2008), a case interpreting section 1956(a)(2), the transportation provision of the money laundering statute. The Court held that merely hiding money in international travel would not rise to the level of being international transportation of the proceeds of unlawful activity.

CHAPTER 13
BANKRUPTCY CRIMES

§ 13.01 INTRODUCTION

Statutes pertaining to bankruptcy crimes are, for the most part, found in sections 151 through 157 of Title 18. General criminal statutes also have been employed in the prosecution of criminal conduct related to bankruptcies.

Historically 18 U.S.C. § 152 served as the key bankruptcy crime statute for the prosecution of bankruptcy fraud. This statute concentrates on the concealment of assets, false oaths, and bribery and extortion conduct occurring in connection with a bankruptcy.

Section 153 pertains to embezzlement by a trustee, officer, or their agent. A penalty of up to five years imprisonment and fine can be imposed against a trustee, custodian, marshal, or other officer who "knowingly and fraudulently appropriates" to their "own use, embezzles, spends, or transfers any property or secrets or destroys a document" in their charge that is from the debtor's estate.

A custodian, trustee, marshal, or other officer of the court, who "knowingly purchases, directly or indirectly, any property of the estate of which he is such an officer in a case under Title 11" is subject to a fine and a forfeiture of the office held by the individual. Section 154 not only contains this adverse interest statute, but also imposes the same penalty when an officer refuses a court direction permitting parties in interest a reasonable opportunity to inspect documents or refuses a United States Trustee a reasonable opportunity to inspect documents.

Section 155 prohibits a party in interest from knowingly and fraudulently agreeing with another party in interest to the fixing of a fee or other compensation from the assets of the estate. A violation of this latter provision can result in imprisonment of up to one year and a fine.

Section 156 penalizes a bankruptcy petition preparer "if a bankruptcy case or related proceeding is dismissed because of a knowing attempt" by the preparer to disregard the bankruptcy statutes and rules. The bankruptcy petition preparer, defined as "a person, other than the debtor's attorney or an employee of such attorney, who prepares for compensation a document for filing" faces up to one year imprisonment and a fine for the knowing disregard of a bankruptcy law or rule.

Section 157 is modeled after the mail fraud statute. Like mail fraud, it authorizes a penalty of up to five years imprisonment and a fine against individuals who devise or intend to devise a scheme or artifice to defraud. The execution of the scheme can be through filing a bankruptcy petition, bankruptcy document, or the making of a "false or fraudulent representation, claim, or promise concerning or in relation" to a bankruptcy proceeding. As a result of an amendment to the statute, it now includes a "fraudulent involuntary bankruptcy petition." In *U.S. v. Lee*, 82 F.Supp. 389 (E.D. Pa. 2000), a district court ruled that this statute should not be given the breadth that has been afforded to other fraud statutes, such as the mail and securities fraud statutes.

Despite the existence of specific bankruptcy crime statutes, prosecutors have on occasion bypassed these statutes and proceeded with actions under general criminal statutes. Most often, bankruptcy crimes are charged in conjunction with charges using general criminal offenses found in Title 18. For example, agreements by two or more individuals to commit a bankruptcy offense have been prosecuted under both section 152 and the general conspiracy statute. (18 U.S.C. § 371). When there is a scheme to defraud coupled with a mailing in furtherance of the scheme, mail fraud has been included by prosecutors. (18 U.S.C. § 1341). Prosecutors have also included charges of wire fraud, tax evasion, and perjury in bankruptcy fraud cases.

In addition to these general criminal provisions, when there is a pattern of racketeering involving fraud connected with a case under Title 11, the offense may be the subject of a RICO prosecution. To proceed with a RICO charge it is, of course, necessary for the government to prove all the elements of this offense (see chap. 8). As a predicate act of RICO, bankruptcy fraud can be pursued in both criminal and civil RICO actions.

§ 13.02   BANKRUPTCY FRAUD

Historically prosecutors used section 152 of Title 18 to prosecute bankruptcy fraud. The essence of this statute is to provide criminality when the debtor or others associated with the bankruptcy attempt to avoid the required distribution of non-exempt assets to creditors as provided for by the Bankruptcy Code.

The statute contains a variety of fraudulent acts upon which a criminal prosecution can be premised. Most notable among the listing is the general concealment provision. Under this aspect of the statute, criminality is imposed when one "knowingly and fraudulently conceals from the custodian, trustee, marshal, or other officer of the court charged with the control or custody of property, or from creditors in any case under Title 11, any property belonging to the estate of a debtor."

In addition to this general prohibition against concealment, section 152 specifically prohibits the knowing and fraudulent (2) making of a false oath or account, (3) making of a false declaration, (4) presenting of a false proof of claim, (5) receiving any material amount of property from a debtor, after the filing of a case under Title 11, (6) giving, offering, receiving, or attempts to obtain any money, property, or advantage for acting or forbearing to act in a bankruptcy case, (7) transferring or concealing of property in contemplation of a Title 11 case, (8) concealing, destroying, or falsifying documents relating to property or financial affairs of a debtor after or in contemplation of the filing of a

Title 11 case, and (9) withholding recorded information relating to the property or financial affairs of the debtor, from an officer, after the filing of a Title 11 case. Thus, this act provides criminality to acts of concealment, false oaths, and bribery that occur in relation to a bankruptcy.

To sustain a conviction under the general concealment clause of section 152, the government must prove beyond a reasonable doubt that the accused (1) knowingly and fraudulently, (2) concealed from an officer or the creditors, (3) in a Title 11 case, (4) property belonging to the estate of the debtor. To sustain a conviction under the false oath clause of section 152, the government must prove beyond a reasonable doubt that the accused (1) knowingly and fraudulently, (2) made a false oath or account, (3) that was material, (4) in relation to a Title 11 case. A violation of section 152 is a felony and can result in a penalty of up to five years imprisonment and a fine.

§ 13.03   CONCEALMENT AND FALSE OATH

Concealment, in a variety of ways, can form the basis of a prosecution under section 152. Secreting, falsifying, and mutilating of property or information have been found to be evidence of concealment. Mere omission of an asset on a bankruptcy schedule does not, however, indicate conclusively the existence of concealment.

In *Coghlan v. U.S.*, 147 F.2d 233 (8th Cir.1945), the Eighth Circuit discussed the circumstances of when a failure to schedule property would constitute a concealment. The court noted that although omission of assets from a schedule indicates concealment, taken alone this is inconclusive. "The conduct of the bankrupt, the relative extent of the omission, the character of the asset itself, and the reasons given for the difference between financial statements of the business and the bankruptcy schedules are the other circumstances in every case." When these circumstances explain the omission, the element of concealment is lacking. The court in *Coghlan* noted, however, that facts supporting a continued concealment consummate the offense.

The knowing and fraudulent filing of a false account or schedule of assets under oath, also can form the basis of a prosecution under the false oath provision of section 152. *Goetz v. U.S.*, 59 F.2d 511 (7th Cir.1932). Actions premised upon the false oath provision of section 152 have been held as not requiring all of the elements of a perjury charge. *U.S. v. Lynch*, 180 F.2d 696 (7th Cir.1950).

Some courts, however, examine the false oath in the context of perjury law. Thus, literally true, but unresponsive answers to questions cannot form a perjury charge when the examiner is put on notice to ask additional questions to clarify the answers provided. *Bronston v. U.S.*, 409 U.S. 352 (1973) (see § 10.04). Perjury, however, is established if in the context in which the statement is made, it is materially untrue. Thus, a false oath prosecution can be upheld despite the existence of statements that are literally true in isolation. *U.S. v. Schafrick*, 871 F.2d 300 (2d Cir.1989).

Actions involving false oaths and accounts require the government to prove materiality. Materiality has been defined as referring "not only to the main fact which is the subject of inquiry, but also to any fact or circumstance which tends to corroborate or strengthen the proof adduced to establish the main fact." *Metheany v. U.S.*, 365 F.2d 90 (9th Cir.1966). Materiality does not require the government to prove that creditors were harmed by the false statement.

Matters "pertinent to the extent and nature of [a] bankrupt's assets, including the history of a bankrupt's financial transactions," have been found material. Statements designed to secure adjudication by a particular bankruptcy court have been found to be material. *U.S. v. O'Donnell*, 539 F.2d 1233 (9th Cir.1976). Failing to disclose prior bankruptcies has been found to be material in that this information can "impede an investigation into a debtor's financial affairs." *U.S. v. Lindholm*, 24 F.3d 1078 (9th Cir.1994). Additionally, statements aimed at obtaining a particular status before a court, such as *in forma pauperis*, have been held to be material. *U.S. v. Yagow*, 953 F.2d 427 (8th Cir.1992).

In *U.S. v. Phillips*, 606 F.2d 884 (9th Cir.1979), the Ninth Circuit found misstatements in a bankruptcy petition material, and as included in the indictment, these false statements were properly read to the jury. The statements were a false social security number, false prior addresses, and failure to give past names by which the accused had been known. The court stated that the false social security number and fabrication of prior addresses may have misled creditors as to the petitioner's identity and financial background. The failure to provide prior names can obstruct attempts to acquire a full credit history and hinder the determination of assessing one's eligibility for bankruptcy.

Crucial to a bankruptcy fraud prosecution is a bankruptcy proceeding. Provisions within section 152 permit prosecutions to be premised upon concealment in contemplation of a bankruptcy case. A defendant's belief in the invalidity of a bankruptcy proceeding does not negate the bankruptcy fraud. *U.S. v. Beery*, 678 F.2d 856 (10th Cir.1982).

It is necessary that the actions of concealment or false oath relate to the bankruptcy. In an action premised upon the false statement provision within section 152, the Eighth Circuit held that the "in relation to" requirement should be interpreted broadly. The court found that statements made in cases arising from a central bankruptcy proceeding would be "in or in relation to any case under Title 11." *U.S. v. Yagow*, 953 F.2d 427 (8th Cir.1992).

§ 13.04   KNOWINGLY AND FRAUDULENTLY

Section 152 requires that the defendant act knowingly and fraudulently. This intent requirement mandates proof by the government that the accused acted willfully as opposed to through mistake, excusable neglect, or inadvertence. A defendant who acts with willful blindness can be found to have acted knowingly and fraudulently. Most often this element is proved through circumstantial evidence. A jury may infer intent from the evidence presented. In *U.S. v. Gellene*, 182 F.2d 578 (7th Cir.1999), the Seventh Circuit permitted an "intent to deceive" to suffice in meeting the "fraudulent" element of the statute.

In *U.S. v. Goodstein*, 883 F.2d 1362 (7th Cir.1989), the Seventh Circuit upheld convictions, including a violation of section 152, against an attorney with experience in bankruptcy matters who practiced for over forty years. The court found that the jury could have concluded that the defendant fraudulently intended to evade the requirements of the bankruptcy laws. In assessing this jury determination, the appellate tribunal noted that the defendant was a "knowledgeable businessman and lawyer." The court found that this "extensive legal background and integral role in" these bankruptcy affairs indicated that a failure to notify the bankruptcy court and creditors of a transfer was not something done inadvertently.

Where the accused, in a bankruptcy fraud action alleging concealment, lacked knowledge of the bankruptcy order for relief or the appointment of a receiver, a court reversed the defendant's convictions. The defendant in *U.S. v. Guiliano*, 644 F.2d 85 (2d Cir.1981), was neither the owner or an officer of the debtor. As a salesperson, the court found that he was not required to be familiar with the financial condition of the company. Although it was possible to speculate that when the business closed the accused should have realized that a bankruptcy would follow, mere conjecture was insufficient to meet the knowledge requirement.

With respect to one count, the Second Circuit in *Guiliano* was satisfied that there was evidence to support a jury inference of the defendant's knowledge of the bankruptcy order for relief or the appointment of a trustee. This count accused the defendant of fraudulently concealing certain equipment from the bankruptcy trustee. According to the court, there was evidence that the defendant had been requested to remove this equipment and sell it for as much cash as possible. Upon removal of these items, the defendant knew of the company's financial crisis. The court noted that the defendant also worked closely with another individual after the bankruptcy order for relief and appointment of a trustee. Although the *Guiliano* court found evidence inferring knowledge, this count was reversed and remanded for a retrial in that there was a risk that the jury was influenced in its disposition of this count by improper evidence and by allegations of a reversed RICO count.

§ 13.05 PONZI SCHEMES AND CLAWBACKS

The term Ponzi scheme originates from a 1920 scheme of Charles Ponzi. The SEC defines a Ponzi scheme as "an investment fraud that involves the payment of purported returns to existing investors from funds contributed by new investors." WCH

§ 13.4. Ponzi received a five year sentence for this scheme. More recently Bernard Madoff received a prison sentence of 150 years for a Ponzi scheme.

When a Ponzi scheme results in a bankruptcy, clawback actions may occur to recover funds from fraudulent transfers. The aim is to obtain funds that were improperly transferred in order to diminish the harm resulting to innocent investors.

CHAPTER 14
ENVIRONMENTAL CRIMES

§ 14.01 INTRODUCTION

Like so many of the white collar crime areas, the environmental sector also demonstrates an overlap between civil and criminal law. A person violating a federal environmental statute is often subject to civil proceedings, criminal prosecution, or dual civil and criminal actions (see chap. 18). There may also be violations of state environmental statutes. There can also be prosecutions for conduct occurring extraterritorially, such as those being prosecuted under the Lacey Act for violations that involve a violation of foreign law.

There exists a wealth of environmental statutes throughout the United States Code. Many of the environmental related Acts contain provisions that criminalize conduct for noncompliance. There is, however, no single comprehensive set of environmental crimes found within the United States Code.

In recent years there has been an increasing number of federal prosecutions for environmental offenses. In 1982, the Department of Justice established a separate environmental crimes unit for the prosecution of these offenses. In 1987 the Environmental Crimes Section (ECS) "became a fully independent Section within the Environmental and Natural Resources Division" (ENRD).

The prosecution of environmental crimes is not limited to the indictment of individuals for alleged violations. A significant number of prosecutions have concentrated on the corporate entity. Principles of corporate criminal liability, as well as personal criminal liability in the corporate setting, play a factor in the environmental arena. Prosecutions under the Occupational Health and Safety Act (OSHA) and the Federal Food, Drug, and Cosmetic Act (FDA) have examined principles of corporate criminal liability (see § 2.07).

Water, air, and energy are among the array of environmental areas that have incorporated criminal provisions for enforcement of specific Acts. With respect to water, one observes criminal penalties for noncompliance in Acts such as the Rivers and Harbors Appropriations Act (33 U.S.C. § 401 et seq.), Safe Drinking Water Act (42 U.S.C. § 300f et seq.), and the Water Pollution Control Act (Clean Water Act) (33 U.S.C. § 1251 et seq.). Criminal penalties are provided for in the Clean Air Act (42 U.S.C. § 7401 et seq.), the Resource Conservation and Recovery Act of 1976 (Solid Waste Disposal Act) (RCRA) (42 U.S.C. § 6901 et seq.), the Toxic Substances Control Act (TSCA) (15 U.S.C. § 2601 et seq.), the Federal Insecticide, Fungicide, and Rodenticide Act (FIFRA) (7 U.S.C. § 136 et seq.), the Atomic Energy Act (42 U.S.C. § 2011 et seq.), and the Comprehensive Environmental Response, Compensation, and Liability Act of 1980 (CERCLA) (42 U.S.C. § 9601 et seq.). These are, however, by no means an exhaustive list of the federal environmental Acts that contain criminal enforcement provisions. Scattered throughout federal law are environmental statutes that use criminal sanctions for the purposes of enforcement. Many states have also incorporated environmental crimes statutes as part of their laws.

Federal prosecutions related to environmental crimes have not always been limited to the specific provisions found within an environmental Act. On occasion the government will prosecute under general criminal provisions or add general criminal provisions as additional counts against a defendant. For example, prosecutors have included conspiracy charges, pursuant to 18 U.S.C. § 371, when there are two or more offenders who agree to commit a specific offense and an overt act is performed in furtherance of the conspiracy. (see chap. 3). A false reporting of a material fact to a government agency can result in a prosecution under the false statements statute. (18 U.S.C. § 1001). (see chap. 9). Environmental crime prosecutions have also added charges of mail fraud when there is a scheme to defraud and a mailing in furtherance of that scheme. (18 U.S.C. § 1341) (see chap. 4).

§ 14.02   MENS REA

Most environmental offenses emanate from a violation of regulatory statutes. It is common for defendants to concentrate their defense on arguing the level of intent necessary for proving a violation of the applicable statute.

Courts have not always ruled consistently when examining the issue of intent as it pertains to an environmental statute. For example, the Sixth Circuit in *U.S. v. Wulff*, 758 F.2d 1121 (6th Cir.1985), found that a felony provision of the Migratory Bird Treaty Act (MBTA), that did not require proof of scienter, violated due process. The court found that because the felony was a "crime unknown to the common law" which carried a substantial penalty, the government was required to prove that the defendant acted with some degree of scienter. In contrast, the Third Circuit in *U.S. v. Engler*, 806 F.2d 425 (3d Cir.1986), found that the absence of a scienter requirement, in the strict liability provisions of a felony under the MBTA, did "not offend the requirements of due process." Congress clarified the mens rea required for the MBTA, making it a strict liability offense in 16 U.S.C. § 707(a), a misdemeanor, and requiring a mens rea of knowingly in 16 U.S.C. § 707(b), a felony provision.

Most environmental crimes require proof of the defendant acting knowingly. Courts usually permit knowledge to be inferred from the surrounding circumstances. In *U.S. v. International Minerals & Chemical Corp.*, 402 U.S. 558 (1971), the Supreme Court held that "where . . . dangerous or deleterious devices or products or obnoxious waste materials are involved, the probability of regulation is so great that anyone who is aware that he is in possession of them or dealing with them must be presumed to be aware of the regulation."

Knowledge also can be found when there is a deliberate avoidance to learn all the facts. In these circumstances, courts may give a willful blindness instruction. (see § 1.05; WCH § 14.2).

Most courts interpreting the term knowledge in the context of environmental statutes have held that there is no requirement that a defendant know the specific law being violated. For example, in examining knowledge in the context of the Comprehensive Environmental Response, Compensation, and Liability Act (CERCLA), a Sixth Circuit Court held that " . . . knowledge as used in such regulatory statutes means knowledge that one is doing the statutorily prescribed acts, not knowledge that the statutes or potential health hazards exist." *U.S. v. Buckley*, 934 F.2d 84 (6th Cir.1991).

§ 14.03   REFUSE ACT

The Rivers and Harbors Appropriations Act of 1899, (33 U.S.C. § 401 et seq.), has been one source of prosecution of environmental crimes. The Act, a codification of prior statutes, includes section 13 which forbids "the deposit" of all kinds of "refuse matter" into navigable rivers "other than that flowing from streets and sewers and passing therefrom in a liquid state." (33 U.S.C. § 407).

This Refuse Act provides criminal penalties for the improper discharge into navigable or tributary waters of the United States. The government can charge each separate act of discharging or depositing refuse as a separate count. The number of acts chargeable "cannot be deduced from the mere size or length of time of a discharge without more, unless discontinuity of the flow or change in composition or other evidence indicates that certain action necessarily were taken to further the discharging or depositing of refuse." *U.S. v. Allied Chemical Corp.*, 420 F.Supp.122 (E.D.Va.1976).

Refuse has been defined as "all foreign substances and pollutants apart from those 'flowing from streets and sewers and passing therefrom in a liquid state' into the watercourse." *U.S. v. Standard Oil Co.*, 384 U.S. 224 (1966). In *U.S. v. Standard Oil Co.,* the Supreme Court held that commercially valuable gasoline discharged into a navigable river could come within the definition of "refuse" under the Rivers and Harbors Act.

Most courts find this Act to be a strict liability statute. *U.S. v. White Fuel Corp.*, 498 F.2d 619 (1st Cir.1974). One court noted that depositing refuse in navigable waters is malum prohibitum, within the category of public welfare offenses, and therefore a statute of strict liability. "The public is injured just as much by unintentional pollution as it is by deliberate pollution, and it would have been entirely reasonable for Congress to attack both." *U.S. v. U.S. Steel Corp.*, 328 F.Supp. 354 (N.D.Ind.1970). The Supreme Court reserved for future determination, the question of what scienter requirement is imposed by this Act. *U.S. v. Standard Oil Co.*, 384 U.S. 224 (1966).

§ 14.04   WATER POLLUTION CONTROL ACT

The Federal Water Pollution Control Act, commonly referred to as the Clean Water Act

(CWA), (33 U.S.C. § 1251 et seq.), objective "is to restore and maintain the chemical, physical, and biological integrity of the Nation's waters." The Act prohibits the discharge of pollutants into navigable waters unless authorized. The CWA requires one to have a permit for the discharge of pollutants from a "point source" into "navigable waters." The CWA provides that both the EPA Administrator and the Secretary of the Army have the administrative responsibility for establishing guidelines for permits. WCH § 14.4

The terms "point source" (33 U.S.C. § 1362(14)) and "pollutant" (33 U.S.C. § 1362(6)) are defined by statute. In *U.S. v. Plaza Health Laboratories*, 3 F.3d 643 (2d Cir.1993), the Second Circuit held that a person is not a "point source."

Navigable waters is defined in the statute as meaning "the waters of the United States, including the territorial seas." It has been held to include tributaries. *U.S. v. Phillips*, 367 F.3d 846 (9th Cir.2004). In *Rapanos v. U.S.*, 547 U.S. 715 (2006), a plurality opinion held that "navigable waters" did "not include channels through which water flows intermittently or ephemerally, or channels that periodically provide drainage for rainfall." But because of a four-person dissent Justice Kennedy's concurring opinion becomes important as he expressed a view for a case-by-case review when the Army Corps of Engineers sought "to regulate wetlands based on adjacency to nonnavigable tributaries."

Criminal penalties exist for negligent violations of the discharge limits, with increased penalties provided for knowing violations. Repeat offenses also carry increased penalties. When the actions place another individual in "imminent danger of death or serious bodily injury" there is a possible penalty of imprisonment of up to fifteen years and fine. The fine may be increased when the knowing endangerment is by a corporation. (33 U.S.C. § 1319(c)). In *U.S. v. Borowski*, 977 F.2d 27 (1st Cir.1992), the First Circuit held that a knowingly endangerment prosecution could not "be premised upon danger that occurs before the pollutant reaches a publicly-owned sewer or treatment works."

In *U.S. v. Hanousek*, 176 F.3d 1116 (9th Cir.1999), the defendant was charged with negligently "discharging a harmful quantity of oil into a navigable water of the United States." The Ninth Circuit rejected defendant's arguments that "gross negligence" should be required to meet this particular Clean Water Act statute. The court stated that 33 U.S.C. § 1319(c)(1)(A) can be met with a showing of ordinary negligence.

Responsible corporate officers are statutorily included as "persons" that are subject to criminal penalties under this Act. (33 U.S.C. § 1319(c)(6)). In interpreting the responsible corporate officer provisions in the Clean Water Act, the court in *U.S. v. Iverson*, 162 F.3d 1015 (9th Cir.1998) stated that "a person is a 'responsible corporate officer' if the person has authority to exercise control over the corporation's activity that is causing the discharges." The Ninth Circuit noted that "[t]here is no requirement that the officer in fact exercise such authority or that the corporation expressly vest a duty in the officer to oversee the activity." The inclusion of a provision regarding a responsible corporate officer does not serve to limit the prosecution of individuals who violate the act. *U.S. v. Brittain*, 931 F.2d 1413 (10th Cir.1991). WCH § 14.4(D).

Applicable discharges must be reported by "any person in charge." Corporations are included as a "person" under the Act. 33 U.S.C. § 1321(a)(7). "Further, the knowledge of the employees is the knowledge of the corporation." *Apex Oil Co. v. U.S.*, 530 F.2d 1291 (8th Cir.1976).

§ 14.05 RESOURCE CONSERVATION AND RECOVERY ACT (RCRA)

Congress enacted the Resource Conservation and Recovery Act (RCRA) to provide a national system for the safe management of hazardous waste and to promote a system that conserved valuable material and energy resources. This statute authorizes the EPA, through its adoption of regulations, to place controls on solid and hazardous wastes. The Act is divisible into two sections, one pertaining to non-hazardous solid waste management, and another regarding hazardous waste management. *U.S. v. White*, 766 F.Supp. 873 (E.D.Wash.1991).

The RCRA enacted in 1976 has been termed a "'cradle-to-grave' regulatory scheme for toxic materials, providing 'nationwide protection against the dangers of improper hazardous waste disposal.'" *U.S. v. Johnson & Towers, Inc.*, 741 F.2d 662 (3d Cir.1984). Although originally the statute authorized misdemeanor penalties for the disposal of waste without a permit, later amendments increased the penalties for noncompliance to felonies. The amendments also expanded coverage to include not only the disposal of waste, but also the improper treatment and storage of waste.

The Act's criminal provisions have been found applicable to "any person" that stores, treats, or disposes of hazardous wastes. "Any person" is defined in 42 U.S.C. § 6903(15) as meaning "an individual, trust, firm, joint stock company, corporation (including a government corporation), partnership, association, State, municipality, commission, political subdivision of a State, or an interstate body and shall include each department, agency, and instrumentality of the United States." Courts have not limited the provisions of the RCRA only to those who are owners or operators of facilities. *U.S. v. Johnson & Towers, Inc.*, 741 F.2d 662 (3d Cir.1984). Further, federal employees working at a federal facility have not been precluded from prosecution under this statute. In *U.S. v. Dee*, 912 F.2d 741 (4th Cir.1990), the Fourth Circuit found that sovereign immunity did not immunize federal employees from prosecution for criminal acts that violated the RCRA.

Criminality under the RCRA is found in section 6928(d) and (e) of Title 42. Where subsection (d) provides for penalties when one "knowingly," commits certain acts specified by the statute, subsection (e) increases the penalty for a knowing endangerment in committing a violation. The terms "knowing" and "knowingly," as used throughout this statute, have been the focal point of many appellate decisions. The penalty can be increased when it involves a "knowing endangerment." The Tenth Circuit found the "serious bodily injury" provision of this statute not to be unconstitutionally vague when it was applied to a corporate defendant whose employees were alleged to have suffered "psychoorganic syndrome," which may cause impairment to mental facilities. *U.S. v. Protex Industries, Inc.*, 874 F.2d 740 (10th Cir.1989).

Despite the requirement for a "knowing" violation, courts do not require that the government prove that a defendant had knowledge of the specific provisions of RCRA. The government does need to prove the defendant knew the general hazardous character of the waste material being handled. *U.S. v. Dee*, 912 F.2d 741 (4th Cir.1990). Being a public welfare offense, "it is completely fair and reasonable to charge those who choose to operate in such areas with knowledge of the regulatory provisions." *U.S. v. Hayes International Corp.*, 786 F.2d 1499 (11th Cir.1986).

Courts have not ruled consistently on whether knowledge of a permit is required. One court found that although the term "knowingly" is omitted in subsection (2)(A) of the statute, its inclusion in subsection (2)(B) implies that there must be knowledge of the requirement of a permit. In *U.S. v. Johnson & Towers*, 741 F.2d 662 (3d Cir.1984), the Third Circuit held that, "[i]t is unlikely that Congress could have intended to subject to criminal prosecution those persons who acted when no permit had been obtained irrespective of their knowledge (under subsection (A)), but not those persons who acted in violation of the terms of a permit unless that action was knowing (subsection (B))." The court in *Johnson & Towers, Inc.* concluded that either the word "knowingly" was inadvertently omitted from subsection (A), or that "knowingly" as introducing subsection (2) applies to (B).

Other courts, however, have rejected the view taken in *U.S. v. Johnson & Towers*, 741 F.2d 662 (3d Cir.1984), finding that there is no requirement of knowledge of a lack of a permit for conviction under subsection (A) of this statute. As noted by the Ninth Circuit, "[t]he statute makes a clear distinction between non-permit holders and permit holders, requiring in subsection (B) that the latter knowingly violate a material condition or requirement of the permit. To read the word 'knowingly' at the beginning of section (2) into subsection (A) would be to eviscerate this distinction." *U.S. v. Hoflin*, 880 F.2d 1033 (9th Cir.1989). In rejecting the view taken by the court in *Johnson & Towers, Inc.*, the Sixth Circuit noted that "[t]he 'knowingly' which begins section 6928(d)(2) cannot be read as extending to the subsections without rendering nugatory the word 'knowing' contained in subsections 6928(d)(2)(B) and (C)." *U.S. v. Dean*, 969 F.2d 187 (6th Cir.1992).

One appellate court has specifically refused to apply a responsible corporate officer doctrine to establish knowledge. In *U.S. v. MacDonald & Watson Waste Oil Company*, 933 F.2d 35 (1st Cir.1991), the First Circuit held that proof of a defendant being a responsible corporate officer would be insufficient to show the required knowledge for conviction under the RCRA. The court stated that "[s]imply because a responsible corporate officer believed that on a prior occasion illegal transportation occurred, he did not necessarily possess knowledge of the violation charged. In a crime having knowledge as an express element, a mere showing of official responsibility under *Dotterweich* and *Park* is not an adequate substitute for direct or circumstantial proof of knowledge." See § 2.08.

CHAPTER 15

COMPUTER CRIMES

§ 15.01 OVERVIEW

The Department of Justice's (DOJ) Computer Crime and Intellectual Property Section (CCIPS), "is responsible for implementing the Department's national strategies in combating computer and intellectual property crimes worldwide." Prior to 1984, computer criminal offenses were subject to prosecution under existing statutes that had no computer emphasis. For example, computer improprieties were on occasion prosecuted pursuant to the federal wire fraud statute. (18 U.S.C. § 1343) (see § 4.08). Today there exists specific legislation to criminalize illegal computer activities.

In 1984, Congress enacted a criminal statute (the Counterfeit Access Device and Computer Fraud and Abuse Act of 1984) that exclusively focused on computer offenses. This statute, 18 U.S.C. § 1030, concentrated on improper computer access as opposed to other improprieties, such as, computer use. This statute was amended in 1986 (the Computer Fraud and Abuse Act of 1986) to cure some of the deficiencies evident in the initial legislation. More recent amendments also modify the language of the statute. The statute is no longer restricted to crimes related to computer access.

In the "Uniting and Strengthening America by providing Appropriate Tools Required to Intercept and Obstruct Terrorism Act of 2001 (USA PATRIOT

ACT)," Congress made additional changes to the computer fraud act. For example, computer fraud is now listed a specified unlawful activity of money laundering and the statute now has extraterritorial application.

Despite the existence of section 1030 in the federal criminal code, computer crimes are still facing prosecution under other statutory offenses. For example, prosecutions may be predicated upon charges of copyright infringement (17 U.S.C. § 506), conspiracy (18 U.S.C. § 371), wire fraud (18 U.S.C. § 1343), illegal interception devices and equipment (18 U.S.C. § 2512), and unlawful access to stored communications (18 U.S.C. § 2701). Two key statutes recently used in computer prosecutions come from the National Stolen Property Act (18 U.S.C. § 2314) and the Economic Espionage Act (18 U.S.C. § 1832). Criminal activity can also come from improper procedural conduct during a criminal investigation. WCH § 15.1(C).

The U.S. has been at the forefront internationally in fighting computer crimes, and it participated in the drafting of the Council of Europe's Convention on Cybercrime. The U.S. later ratified the Convention with several reservations. The main objective of the Convention "is to pursue a common criminal policy aimed at the protection of society against cybercrime, especially by adopting appropriate legislation and fostering internal co-operation."

§ 15.02   SECTION 1030

Section 1030 contains seven variants of conduct that are subject to prosecution. As opposed to a consistent mens rea and jurisdictional predicate, each of the seven subsections specifies its own requisite jurisdiction and mens rea. Likewise, the penalties for some of these varying forms of improper computer conduct differ. In addition to imprisonment, the statute also provides for imposition of a fine.

Subsection (a)(1) basically criminalizes the conduct of one who "having knowingly accessed a computer without authorization or exceeding authorized access," thereby obtained confidential national security information "with reason to believe that such information so obtained could be used to the injury of the United States, or to the advantage of any foreign nation willfully" attempts to or communicates it to someone "not entitled to receive it, or willfully" "fails to deliver it to the officer or employee of the United States entitled to receive it." This electronic espionage provision permits imprisonment of up to ten years. Additionally, a repeat offender is subjected to imprisonment of up to twenty years.

Subsection (a)(2) pertains to one who "intentionally accesses a computer, without authorization or exceeds authorized access, and thereby obtains" financial information of a financial institution or a card issuer, "information from a department or agency of the United States," or "information from a protected computer." This conduct is punishable by imprisonment of up to one year. The statute provides for an increase to five years if the offense is committed for private or commercial gain, "in furtherance of a criminal or tortious act in violation of the Constitution" or federal or state laws, or "the value of the information exceeds five thousand dollars." The statute also provides for an increase to ten years for the repeat offender. A conviction under this subsection cannot be premised exclusively on a defendant's failure to abide by a website's terms of service. *U.S. v. Drew*, 259 F.R.D. 449 (C.D. Cal.2009). See WCH § 15.2(C).

Subsection (a)(3) of this statute pertains to browsing in a government computer. It applies to those who access "intentionally, without authorization to access a nonpublic computer" of a federal department or agency, said computer being exclusively for government use or the conduct "affects" the government's use of the computer. The penalty for commission of this offense is one year, but may be increased to ten years for the repeat offender.

Subsection (a)(4) concentrates on theft from protected computers. It applies to one who "knowingly and with intent to defraud, accesses a protected computer without authorization or exceeds authorized access," furthering the fraud and obtaining anything of value. An exception is provided when the object of the fraud is the computer and the value of such use does not exceed five thousand dollars in any one year period. The statute, in subsection (e), explicitly defines a "protected computer." In addition to computers used by the government and financial institutions, the term "protected computer" also includes computers "used in interstate or foreign commerce or communication." This offense is punishable with up to five years of imprisonment, with an additional five years possible for the repeat offender.

Subsection (a)(5) is divided into three parts. Subsection (a)(5)(A) pertains to one who "knowingly causes a transmission of a program, information, code or command, and as a result of such conduct intentionally causes damage without authorization to a protected computer." Subsection (a)(5)(B) criminalizes the intentional access of "a protected computer without authorization, and as a result of such conduct recklessly causes damage." Finally, Subsection (a)(5)(C) criminalizes conduct of those who "intentionally" access a "protected computer without authorization, and as a result of such conduct, causes damage and loss."

Subsection (a)(5)(A) carries a penalty of up to ten years imprisonment in certain specified circumstances with an additional ten years possible for the repeat offender. It can also be increased to a twenty year sentence when the "offender knowingly and recklessly causes serious bodily injury" resulting from the conduct in (a)(5)(A), and may be increased to a life sentence "if the offender knowingly and recklessly causes or attempts to cause death from conduct in violation of (a)(5)(A)." Subsection (a)(5)(B) carries a penalty of up to five years imprisonment under certain specified circumstances with an additional ten years possible for the repeat offender. Finally (a)(5)(C) provides for an increase to ten years in the case of a repeat offender. All other offenses not explicitly provided for in other provisions under (a)(5) are subject to imprisonment of not more than one year and a fine.

Subsection (a)(6) of this statute criminalizes interstate trafficking of passwords. The government must show that the defendant "knowingly and with intent to defraud traffics" "in any password or similar information." The trafficking must affect "interstate commerce or foreign commerce," or the computer must be used by or for the federal government. This provision carries imprisonment of not more than one year with the possibility of ten years imposed for the repeat offender.

The final subsection (a)(7), originally added as part of the National Information Infrastructure Protection Act of 1996 (Economic Espionage Act of 1996, Title II), criminalizes the conduct of one who "with intent to extort from any person any money or other thing of value, transmits in interstate or foreign commerce any communication containing any threat to cause damage to a protected computer; threat to obtain information from a protected computer with authorization or in excess of authorization or to impair the confidentiality of information obtained from a protected computer without authorization or by exceeding authorized access; or demand or request for money or other thing of value in relation to damage to a protected computer, where such damage was caused to facilitate the extortion." This provision carries imprisonment of up to five years, with repeat offenders facing the possibility of ten years.

Often conduct relating to accessing a computer may qualify under more than one provision of the statute. Additionally, section 1030(b) permits criminal culpability for conspiracies and attempts for the conduct provided for in part (a) of the statute. The punishment for these inchoate crimes can vary, although typically it mirrors the punishment specified for a completed crime of the same type.

The statute also provides for civil actions by those who are damaged as a result of a violation of the statute.

§ 15.03   PROSECUTING COMPUTER CRIMES

"Accessing without authorization" and "exceeding authorized access" are two areas of section 1030 that have proved controversial. Typically outsiders engage in unlawful access and insiders are individuals who exceed their access. WCH § 15.3(A)(1).

Courts have differed as to whether violations of "corporate computer use restrictions or violations of a duty of loyalty" meet the definition of "exceeds authorized access" under section 1030(e)(6). For example, in *U.S. v. Nosal*, 676 F.3d 854 (9th Cir.2012), the Ninth Circuit en banc rejected the government's position finding that "[b]asing criminal liability on violations of private computer use policies can transform whole categories of otherwise innocuous behavior into federal crimes simply because a computer is involved." In contrast, in *U.S. v. Rodriguez*, 628 F.3d 1258 (11th Cir.2010), the Eleventh Circuit held that an employee who improperly accesses a database in violation of a company policy limiting the employee's computer access can be found to have exceeded their authorized access.

Courts have also examined the mens rea required for a prosecution under section 1030. In *U.S. v. Morris*, 928 F.2d 504 (2d Cir.1991), the Second Circuit examined whether the intent requirement in then subsection (a)(5) applied only to accessing information or also to preventing the authorized use of the computer's information and thereby causing loss. Defendant Robert Morris, a graduate student at Cornell University had transmitted a "worm into INTERNET, which is a group of national networks that connect university, governmental, and military computers around the country." In transmitting this worm, Morris had underestimated the damaging effect.

The court in *Morris* found that "[d]espite some isolated language in the legislative history that arguably suggests a scienter component for the 'damages' phrase of section 1030(a)(5)(A), the wording, structure, and purpose of the subsection, examined in comparison with its predecessor provision persuade us that the 'intentionally' standard applies only to the 'accesses' phrase of section 1030(a)(5)(A), and not to its 'damages' phrase."

In interpreting § 1030(a)(2)(C), the Tenth Circuit chose not to mirror the mens rea that was used in § 1030(a)(4). Unlike § 1030(a)(4), which requires an intent to defraud, under § 1030(a)(2) the government does not need to prove "that the defendant had the intent to defraud in obtaining the information, or that the information was used to any particular ends." *U.S. v. Willis*, 476 F.3d 1121 (10th Cir.2007).

In *U.S. v. Sablan*, 92 F.3d 865 (9th Cir.1996), the Ninth Circuit found that it was constitutional to omit a mens rea for the damages element of the offense in that the defendant "must have had a wrongful intent in accessing the computer in order to be convicted under the statute." Later amendments to the statute provide a mens rea for the damages clause in the amended (a)(5)(A)(i) and (ii). There is no mens rea, however, for the damages clause in (a)(5)(A)(iii).

Merely browsing is a government computer is not sufficient for a charge under section 1030(a)(4). In *U.S. v. Czubinski*, 106 F.3d 1069 (1st Cir.1997), the First Circuit reversed convictions for wire fraud and computer fraud that were premised upon the defendant's alleged browsing in an Internal Revenue Computer. The court found that the government failed to show that the defendant had received "anything of value." The First Circuit court held that viewing information "about friends, acquaintances, and political rivals" in an IRS computer does not merit a computer fraud conviction where there is no evidence showing "that he printed out, recorded, or used the information he browsed."

§ 15.04 ECONOMIC ESPIONAGE ACT

The Economic Espionage Act (EEA) of 1996 criminalizes economic espionage (18 U.S.C. § 1831) and theft of trade secrets (18 U.S.C. § 1832). It "became law in October 1996 against a backdrop of increasing threats to corporate security and a rising tide of international and domestic economic espionage." *U.S. v. Hsu*, 155 F.3d 189 (3d Cir.1998). Prosecutions under § 1832 can be problematic as the government tries to maintain the confidentiality of the trade secret while prosecuting the criminal conduct.

Computer crimes that include charges under this statute, sometimes also charge the National Stolen Property Act (NSPA) 18 U.S.C. § 2314. For example, in *U.S. v. Aleynikov*, 676 F.3d 71 (2d Cir.2012), the Second Circuit reversed convictions as the defendant's alleged uploading of source code from his former employer was "purely intangible property" and not "goods," "wares" or "merchandise" for the purposes of the NSPA. The court also rejected the use of the EEA as the high frequency trading system was not "produced for" nor "placed in" interstate or foreign commerce. WCH § 15.4(B). But in *U.S. v. Agrawal*, 726 F.3d 235 (2d Cir.2013), the Second Circuit affirmed convictions under these same two statutes finding a violation of the NSPA because unlike *Aleynikov* the stolen code was not in intangible form as the defendant produced paper copies of the code. The *Agrawal* court also found that publicly traded securities met the "product and nexus requirements" of the EEA.

PART 3

PROCEDURAL AND
EVIDENTIARY ISSUES

CHAPTER 16

GRAND JURY INVESTIGATIONS

§ 16.01 INVESTIGATIVE ADVANTAGES

Federal investigations of white collar crime commonly involve use of the powers of the grand jury in addition to (or often, in lieu of) traditional police investigative authority. The grand jury offers various advantages over police investigations as a result of seven structural features of the grand jury process: (1) the availability of the *subpoena duces tecum* (a court order requiring the production of documents or other tangible matter before the grand jury); (2) the availability of the *subpoena ad testificandum* (a court order requiring the recipient to appear before the grand jury and give testimony); (3) closed proceedings; (4) immunity grants; (5) grand jury secrecy; (6) lay participation; and (7) the role of the prosecutor in leading the investigation. The seventh feature—the role of the prosecutor—is the prerequisite that leads the government to take advantage of the others. The prosecutor is not only the legal advisor to the grand jury, but also the leader of its investigation. Indeed, the prosecutor so dominates the investigation that some courts have characterized the grand jury as being "for all practical purposes" no more than an "investigative arm" of the prosecutor.

The prosecutor, at least initially, determines which documents and which witnesses to subpoena. Although the subpoenas are court orders, with persons refusing to comply subject to contempt sanctions, it is the prosecutor who sends out the subpoena without the prior authorization of the court. See § 16.02. The grand jury may direct the prosecutor to subpoena additional witnesses or additional documents, but that authority is rarely used where the prosecutor is opposed. The prosecutor also determines what information actually will be put before the grand jury through the subpoenaed sources. The prosecutor may decide not to present particular subpoenaed documents or to present only summaries of the documents, and the prosecutor also decides what questions will be asked of testifying witnesses (although the grand jurors may ask to see the original documents or seek to have further questions put to the witness). Where a witness refuses to answer by exercising the self-incrimination privilege, the prosecutor determines whether to grant immunity and thereby preclude reliance on the privilege. The prosecutor's authority over all of the above decision, as well as others of less significance, firmly puts the prosecutor in control of the initiation, direction, and content of the grand jury investigation. That control, aside from the procedural advantages discussed below, can be a factor that leads the federal prosecutor, in some settings, to prefer a grand jury investigation over an investigation requiring primary reliance upon a federal police agency or federal administrative agency.

Subpoena duces tecum. The various federal police agencies (e.g., F.B.I., or Secret Service) can obtain documents through a search, but that requires a showing of probable cause that a crime has been committed and that evidence of the crime will be found in the place searched. See § 21.03. The subpoena duces tecum does not require even a lesser showing of probability, such as "reasonable suspicion." It allows for what constitutes, in effect, a "fishing expedition" for documents that will hopefully explain whether particular transactions did or did not involve criminal activity. Moreover, as discussed in § 21.01, even where probable cause exists and a search warrant could be obtained, the subpoena duces tecum often offers various advantages, both as to administrative efficiency and effectiveness in securing all relevant documents, in the typical white collar setting.

Subpoena ad testificandum. Police investigators lack the authority to compel persons to answer their questions. Indeed, apart from the arrestee, who can be subjected to custodial interrogation, police investigators lack the authority to even compel a person to listen to their questions. The subpoena duces tecum compels both attendance before the grand jury and responding to questions put there. It therefore is especially useful in obtaining statements from persons who will not voluntarily furnish information to federal investigators. Faced with the threat of contempt, a recalcitrant witness often will have a change of heart and will respond to questions that would not be answered if asked by an investigator. Of course, the recalcitrant grand jury witness may rely on the privilege against self-incrimination to refuse to answer. However, many persons who would refuse to provide information to investigators are driven by concerns other than possible self-incrimination, and are willing to provide that information when under a judicial order to do so. That is often the case, for example, where employees are asked to provide information that might incriminate their employer or service-providers are asked to provide information about their customers.

Where potential witnesses are willing to be interviewed by investigators, they commonly will not be required to testify because the content of that statement can be conveyed to the grand jury through the investigator (hearsay evidence being acceptable) and the prosecutor would prefer not to create another recorded statement of the witness (which could be used at trial to impeach the witness). However, as to certain cooperative witnesses, the grand jury setting provides distinct investigative advantages. Although giving false information to federal investigators is a crime (see Ch. 9), testifying under oath, after being warned of the consequences of perjury, may better serve to ensure that the witness provides full disclosure. Also, once a person has testified under oath, he is likely to think twice about changing that testimony at trial, and risking a prosecution based on inconsistent sworn statements. (see § 10.04).

Closed proceedings. The federal grand jury proceeding is a closed proceeding, in which the witness must attend without being accompanied by counsel, family, or friends (in contrast to the voluntary interview with investigators, where the witness can insist upon the presence of others). While witnesses ordinarily will be given permission to briefly leave the grand jury room in order to consult with a retained counsel (who may be located in the anteroom or contacted by phone) (see § 16.12), not all witnesses have retained counsel and many of those who do will not seek frequent consultations for fear that the consultations will create the appearance that their testimony is "scripted" and not fully credible. The overall setting, it is argued, creates a psychological pressure that produces more complete and less ambiguous answers than voluntary interviews, especially as to persons reluctant to cooperate with the investigators.

Immunity grants. As discussed in § 19.10, the immunity grant replaces the privilege against self-incrimination, placing the witness who previously claimed the privilege in a position where he now must testify or be held in contempt. Since the grant is conditioned on a sworn witness initially refusing to testify, it is available through grand jury investigations, but not police investigations. Federal investigators, working with the prosecutor, may offer a promise not to prosecute in return for an individual's willingness to provide information, but the witness who refuses to cooperate can be forced to testify only through the immunity grant (assuming the witness at that point chooses testifying over incarceration).

Secrecy. Grand jury secrecy requirement are discussed in § 16.09. Courts have cited three potential investigative advantages stemming from those requirements: (1) keeping the target of the grand jury "in the dark" as to the existence of the investigation (or at least as to the precise scope of the investigation) until an indictment is issued (or at least until the investigation reaches the point at which evidence must be sought directly from the target); (2) avoiding public disclosure of investigations that do not result in indictments and thereby "protecting the innocent accused who is exonerated from disclosure of the fact that he has been under investigation" (a factor that arguably will lead prosecutors to be less hesitant to utilize the grand jury's authority to investigate mere suspicions, based on "tips and rumors," see §16.05, particularly as to "public figures"); and (3) encouraging "free and untrammeled disclosures" by potential witnesses who fear retaliation by the target or others. See WCH § 16.9(A).

A critical barrier to achieving the first two advantages is a major exception to grand jury secrecy obligations; unlike grand jurors, grand jury personnel, and government personnel, a grand jury witness is not subject to those obligations. A person subpoenaed to testify is free to inform any person (i.e., not just his lawyer) that he has been called to testify, and is free afterwards to reveal to any person both the substance of his testimony and what was revealed about the investigation by the questions posed by the prosecutor. Where witnesses have a business relationship with the target (e.g., as employees, customers, or suppliers), they often are inclined to keep the target informed (particularly, as to employees, where the target-employer will provide free legal assistance). Witnesses are less likely to feel obligated to inform the public (through the media), but such disclosures do occur (particularly where a complainant/witness is not satisfied with the prosecutor's pursuit of the investigation). So too, occasional witnesses, disregarding prosecutor requests for utmost confidentially, discuss their testimony with friends and acquaintances, a practice that can readily lead to media acquisition of that information.

The third investigative advantage concerns witnesses who definitely do not want to disclose to others their witness-status or the content of their testimony, and who need assurance that others (in particular, the target) will not gain that information. A key factor in providing that assurance is the limited disclosure required under Federal Rule 16 (governing pretrial-discovery) and the Jencks Act (governing required disclosure at trial). Rule 16, in contrast to some state pretrial-discovery provisions, does not make available to the defendant the grand jury transcript, the list of grand jury witnesses, or even the list of potential trial witnesses. The Jencks Act does require that, when a witness testifies at trial, the witness' prior recorded statements (including grand jury testimony) be made available to the defense. Thus, unless the prosecutor promises the prospective grand jury witness that he will not be called at trial, the witness must anticipate the possibility that his assistance in the prosecution will eventually be revealed. Of course, even if the prosecutor cannot make that promise, testifying at trial is not inevitable, as the target may never be indicted or the indicted target may plead guilty. On the other hand, even if the grand jury witness will not be called to testify at trial, there remains the possibility that the target will identify the individual as a possible cooperating witness through other sources (e.g., the nature of the material subpoenaed directly from the target, information shared with the target by other witnesses, and even information shared by the prosecutor in the course of convincing the target to plead guilty). However, if the witness in such a situation should find it necessary to acknowledge to the target that he testified, grand jury secrecy and Rule 16 gives the witness the opportunity to describe his testimony as he pleases, recognizing that the target will never have access to a transcript of that testimony. Indeed, this aspect of secrecy has been touted as facilitating untrammeled disclosures even by employee-witnesses who are regularly "debriefed" after testifying by their employers. See WCH §16.8(F).

Lay participation. When the subject of the investigation is likely to become known to the public (typically, where the grand jury investigates a matter that has previously attracted considerable media attention), the prosecutor may view the participation of the grand jury, a body of lay persons, as helpful in maintaining community confidence in the integrity of the investigatory process. That participation may be thought to be helpful, in particular, where targets are likely to claim that they are being harassed or the public may view the investigation as potentially "white-washing" misconduct by officials seen as having close ties to the U.S. Attorney or the Department of Justice.

§ 16.02   RULE 17 SUBPOENAS

Federal grand jury subpoenas are issued pursuant to Fed.R.Crim.P. 17, which governs both subpoenas ad testificandum and subpoenas duces tecum issued in connection with any type of proceeding governed by the Federal Rules of Criminal Procedure. Rule 17 provides that the clerk "must issue a blank subpoena * * * to the party requesting it." In the grand jury setting, that "party" is the grand jury itself, but the issuance of the subpoena is controlled by the prosecutor (the grand jury's "legal advisor"), although some federal districts require that the grand jury foreperson endorse the subpoena before it is served. The prosecutor will fill in the blanks as to name of the person subpoenaed and the designated time and place for that person's appearance before the grand jury. Pursuant to USAM § 9–11.150 (discussed in § 19.05), an "Advice of Rights Form" is attached to the subpoena. It includes a brief, very general description of the subject matter of the grand jury's investigation, usually by reference either to the generic character of the offenses under investigation (e.g., "tax offenses") or the general character of the transactions under investigation (e.g., "zoning in Baltimore County").

Where the prosecutor also seeks documents from the witness, the subpoena, as provided in Rule 17(c), will "order the witness to produce any books, papers, documents, or other objects [as] the subpoena designates." Ordinarily, the documents demanded will be described in an attachment to the subpoena. Documents may be described by type (e.g., all "invoices"), by general subject matter (e.g., all "records of purchases"), or by relationship to a specific activity (e.g., all documents that "relate to the setting of prices" for a particular item). The description usually will refer to a specific time period (e.g., "invoices for 1996–97"), unless the characterization is by reference to an event that implicitly limits the time frame. The subpoena will direct that the documents be produced before the grand jury, but prosecutors often give the party the option of simply delivering the documents to the prosecutor. This tends to be more convenient as the documents will be screened initially by the prosecutor's staff, and often only a summary will be presented to the grand jury.

Challenges to subpoenas typically are presented through a motion to quash filed by the subpoenaed party in the federal district court. Where a subpoenaed witness appears before the grand jury, but then refuses to answer particular questions on grounds that are challenged by the prosecutor, the prosecutor files an enforcement motion in district court, asking that the witness be ordered to respond and held in contempt if he fails to obey the order. Where the presentations relating to the particular motion are likely to reveal matter occurring before the grand jury, the hearing will be closed, so as to preserve grand jury secrecy.

A district court ruling rejecting the subpoenaed party's objection ordinarily is not itself an appealable order. The traditional rule is that an appeal is allowed only from an order holding the subpoenaed party in contempt. However, a subpoenaed party who pursues the contempt route to an appeal may have to bear significant costs. An individual held in contempt may be immediately incarcerated pending disposition of the appeal (which disposition will then occur within 30 days). An entity held in contempt often will be required to pay significant daily fines, with no reimbursement if the appeal should fail. Thus, in deciding whether to appeal, the subpoenaed party must weight not only the likelihood of success, but also significant burdens that go beyond the ordinary expenses involved in any appeal.

A limited exception to the contempt prerequisite is known as the *Perlman* exception, based on *Perlman v. U.S.*, 247 U.S. 7 (1918). The Court there allowed the owner of documents to intervene and pursue an appeal from enforcement of a subpoena directed to a disinterested third-party (a court clerk) who had possession of the documents. An exception was created because the third-party did not share the owner's interest in challenging the order and could not be expected to stand in contempt. Lower courts have divided as to whether the *Perlman* exception applies to a subpoena directing an attorney to produce documents belonging to a client, disagreeing as to whether the attorney-client relationship creates a sufficient similarity of interest to require that an appeal be conditioned on the lawyer standing in contempt. See WCH § 16.5(D).

§ 16.03   THE FOURTH AMENDMENT'S OVERBREADTH PROHIBITION

In *Boyd v. U.S.*, 116 U.S. 616 (1886), the Supreme Court concluded that a court order to produce a document constituted a search under the Fourth Amendment. The order in question directed an importer to either produce the invoice for an item that the government alleged to have been illegally imported, or be bound by the government's allegation of what would be shown by the invoice. While the order was not a subpoena duces tecum, as the subpoenaed party was not subject to contempt for failure to produce the document, the consequences of failing to produce were severe and the Supreme Court treated the order as the equivalent of a subpoena duces tecum. The Court acknowledged that a court order directing the recipient to produce a document "lacked certain aggravating incidents of actual search and seizure, such as forcible entry into a man's house and searching among his papers," but stressed that it nonetheless "accomplish[ed] the substantial object of those acts in forcing from a party evidence against himself." Accordingly, a "compulsory production of a man's private papers" would be treated as "within the scope of the Fourth Amendment to the constitution, in all cases in which a search and seizure would be." Moreover, this particular "search and seizure, or what is equivalent thereto," was unreasonable within the meaning of that Amendment because the court order was seeking to compel the defendants to give what was, in effect, self-incriminatory testimony (see § 20.01).

Only twenty years after *Boyd* was decided, in *Hale v. Henkel*, 201 U.S. 43 (1906), the Supreme Court dramatically modified *Boyd*'s Fourth Amendment analysis. *Hale* basically rejected *Boyd*'s interpretation of that Amendment's reasonableness requirement, although it reaffirmed the applicability of the Fourth Amendment to a "compulsory production of a man's private papers." The *Hale* majority initially held that *Boyd* had erred in reading together the Fourth and Fifth Amendment protections. The Fifth Amendment provided a completely separate source of protection against compelled production of documents (see § 20.01), which did not apply in *Hale* since the challenged grand jury subpoena was directed to corporate documents and corporations do not have the benefit of the self-incrimination privilege (see § 20.09). However, the Court continued, the corporation was entitled to the protection of the Fourth Amendment, and "an order for the production of books and papers" could still constitute "an unreasonable search and seizure."

In defining what constitutes unreasonableness in this context, *Hale* utilized a standard that would have sustained the *Boyd* order for a single, obviously relevant document as a "reasonable search." The key issue, the Court noted, was whether the subpoena duces tecum was "far too sweeping in its terms to be regarded as reasonable." The subpoena in *Hale* failed in this regard as it required production of virtually "all the books, papers, and documents found in the offices" of the subpoenaed corporation. Such a broad request, the Court noted, was capable of preventing the corporation from carrying on its business. While the government might have need for many of these documents, it would have to make some showing of that need before it could "justify an order for the production of such a mass of papers."

In the area of police searches, the Fourth Amendment generally requires that the search be based on probable cause. *Hale* imposed no such requirement, insisting only that the search not be overbroad. The Supreme Court did not explain in *Hale* why overbreadth is the only concern of Fourth Amendment reasonableness in the context of a subpoena duces tecum. One possibility is that the subpoena does not require a probability showing because it is a less invasive form of "search." The *Hale* Court acknowledged that the execution of a subpoena did not present the usual physical attributes of the search. The service of the subpoena involved "no element of trespass or force," nor was it "secret and intrusive." The subpoena could not be "finally enforced except after challenge, and a judgment of the court upon the challenge." Indeed, these qualities led dissenting Justice McKenna to conclude that the Fourth Amendment simply was not implicated.

Another consideration that arguably influenced the Court was the context in which the subpoena was issued. The *Hale* Court also rejected a contention that the grand jury could not pursue an investigation unless a specific charge was pending before it. The Court emphasized the broad inquisitorial powers of the grand jury, rejecting state cases that restricted grand jury investigations to instances in which the grand jury had "reason to believe that a crime has been committed." As it later noted, the task of the grand jury was to determine whether that "reason to believe" existed. If probable cause was not needed to institute an investigation, then neither could it be imposed to restrict the grand jury's authority to obtain a particular type of evidence. See also § 16.05. Under this rationale, the less invasive character of the subpoena, combined with the special role of the grand jury, produces a Fourth Amendment requirement of reasonableness that does not have to meet the requirements commonly associated with the Fourth Amendment's warrant clause (which include probable cause).

§ 16.04 APPLYING THE OVERBREADTH PROHIBITION

Post-*Hale* cases applying the constitutional prohibition against overly broad subpoenas duces tecum frequently start out by noting that the stated standard proscribing breadth "far too sweeping * * * to be regarded as reasonable" necessarily requires a fact-specific judgment, with each ruling tied to the circumstances of the individual case. At the same time, federal lower courts have sought, with limited success, to develop some general criteria to guide that judgment. Initially, the subpoena poses difficulties only if it has sufficient breadth to suggest either that compliance will be burdensome or that the subpoena's scope may not have been shaped to the purposes of the inquiry. If it has that potential, the court then will turn to the three "components" of reasonableness developed by the lower federal courts: "(1) the subpoena may command only the production of things relevant to the investigation being pursued; (2) specification of things to be produced must be made with reasonable particularity; and (3) production of records covering only a reasonable period of time may be required." The second component in the above formulation is commonly described as having "two prongs": first, "particularity of description" so that the subpoenaed party "know[s] what he is being asked to produce" and second, "particularity of breadth" so that the subpoenaed party "is not harassed or oppressed to the point that he experiences an unreasonable business detriment." See WCH § 16.1(B)

While many courts have treated the elements of relevancy, particularity of description, particularity as to breadth, and limited time period as separate requirements of reasonableness, with a deficiency as to any one invalidating the subpoena, it is clear that these elements are interrelated. Greater particularity as to breadth, by narrowing the range of documents to be produced, will extend the time period into which the subpoena may reach. On the other hand, as a subpoena reaches farther into the past, a court is more likely to require a stronger showing of relevancy. So too, the significance of the burden of production will be weighed against the strength of the showing as to relevancy and the reasonableness of the time period.

While the subpoenaed party bears the ultimate burden of establishing that a challenged subpoena is unreasonable, many courts insist that the government make an initial showing of relevancy since it alone knows the precise nature of the grand jury inquiry. Ordinarily, this showing requires no more than a general description of the relationship of the material sought to the subject matter of the investigation. Moreover, the government generally is thought to be entitled to considerable leeway on the issue of relevancy. Courts recognize that "some exploration or fishing necessarily is inherent" since the grand jury will not ordinarily have a "catalog of what books and papers exist" nor "any basis for knowing what their character or contents immediately are." Nonetheless, subpoenas are likely to fail where they make no effort to differentiate among documents by reference to a document's function or its general subject matter, but simply seek a mixed group of documents identified by location in a particular place. In this respect, the overbreadth analysis under the Fourth Amendment largely duplicates the Rule 17(c) standard of "reasonableness", discussed in § 16.06. Indeed, following the *R. Enterprises* ruling, which defined the Rule 17(c) standard (see § 16.6), rulings rejecting subpoenas on overbreadth grounds have tended to rely on that standard rather than the

Fourth Amendment. See e.g., *In re Grand Jury Subpoena Duces Tecum Dated Nov. 15, 1993*, 846 F.Supp. 11 (S.D.N.Y. 1994) (relying on overbreadth rulings in rejecting, under Rule 17(c), a subpoena which demanded all computer hard drives, ignoring possible use of a key word search to identify particular categories of documents that might be relevant).

§ 16.05   OTHER FOURTH AMENDMENT OBJECTIONS

Where a subpoena is not "too sweeping," are there other Fourth Amendment grounds for challenging the subpoena? In the companion cases of *U.S. v. Dionisio*, 410 U.S. 1 (1973), and *U.S. v. Mara*, 410 U.S. 19 (1973), the Supreme Court rejected one such possibility, which rested on treating the subpoena directing a person to appear before the grand jury as the equivalent of a "seizure" of the person. Both cases involved grand jury subpoenas directing witnesses to produce identification evidence (voice and handwriting exemplars). The lower court, looking to the analogy of a court order allowing police to take persons into custody to obtain such exemplars, concluded that the Fourth Amendment required the government to show (1) some reasonable suspicion justifying the selection of these persons to provide the exemplars, and (2) that the request for the exemplars was relevant to the subject of the grand jury's inquiry and was not excessive in light of that inquiry. The Supreme Court held that the Fourth Amendment did not apply and neither showing should be required.

The *Dionisio* majority concluded that the lower court's analogy to police-detention cases was flawed because "a subpoena to appear before a grand jury is not a 'seizure' in the Fourth Amendment sense." There was a dramatic difference between the "compulsion exerted" by a subpoena and an "arrest or even an investigative stop." The "latter is abrupt, is effected with force of the threat of it and often in demeaning circumstances, * * * [while the] subpoena is served in the same manner as other legal process; it involves no stigma whatever * * * and it remains at all times under the control and supervision of a court." Admittedly, appearing before a grand jury could be both "inconvenient" and "burdensome," but these were simply "personal sacrifices" inherent in the "historically grounded obligation of every person to appear and give evidence before the grand jury." The subpoena's directive to give identification evidence did not alter the nature of that burden because the taking of voice or handwriting exemplars did not in itself involve a search; both procedures related only to physical characteristics "constantly exposed to the public" and thus were to be distinguished, for example, from the taking of a blood sample.

Having found that the Fourth Amendment had no application to either the summons to appear or the directive to provide identification exemplars, the *Dionisio* Court concluded that there was "no justification for requiring the grand jury to satisfy even the minimal requirement of 'reasonableness' imposed by the [lower court]." The grand jury "could exercise its 'broad investigative powers' on the basis of 'tips, rumors, evidence offered by the prosecutor, or [the jurors'] own personal knowledge,'" and it should not be required to explain the basis for each of its subpoenas. To "saddle a grand jury with minitrials and preliminary showings would assuredly impede its investigation and frustrate the public's interest in the fair and expeditious administration of the criminal laws."

One of the features that *Dionisio* cited in distinguishing subpoenas from arrests was the opportunity to challenge the subpoena before complying. In the federal system, prosecutors use "forthwith subpoenas", directing immediate production of the subpoenaed item, where there is concern that documents might otherwise be destroyed or there is an immediate need for the information contained in the documents. Federal courts have rejected the contention that such subpoenas are comparable to Fourth Amendment arrests, noting that those subpoenas do not preclude taking the subpoenaed material to court and challenging the subpoena (rather than simply delivering it to the prosecutor for grand jury use). They have warned however, against investigative agent aggressiveness in seeking compliance with the subpoena, which could result in an immediate delivery that was coerced rather than voluntary.

The broad language in *Dionisio* made clear that there is no Fourth Amendment grounding for challenging the scope of the questions put to a witness testifying before the grand jury. The appearance before the grand jury is not an arrest and mandated testimony is not a search; there is no limitation as to questioning similar to the *Hale* standard applied to the subpoena of documents. In *U.S. v. Calandra*, 414 U.S. 338 (1974), the Court rejected an attempt to carve out a narrow exception to the absence of a Fourth Amendment restriction on the scope of the demanded testimony.

The defendant in *Calandra* argued that the Fourth Amendment should prohibit questioning that was the fruit of illegal search; the defendant should be allowed to refuse to testify where the illegal search led to his identity and should be allowed to refuse to answer questions that were based upon information provided by such a search. Rejecting that contention, the Court reasoned that sufficient deterrence of unconstitutional searches is provided by the prohibition against the use of the fruits of such a search at trial. There was no need to extend the exclusionary rule to grand jury proceedings, undercutting the grand jury's investigative authority and leading to the type of preliminary challenges warned against in *Dionisio*. Due to a special provision in Title III of the Omnibus Crime Control and Safe Streets Act of 1968, 18 U.S.C. § 2515, the fruits of illegal electronic surveillance are treated differently. That Act prohibits the government from using conversations intercepted by illegal electronic surveillance, or information derived from those conversations, in a grand jury proceeding. Accordingly, a grand jury witness can object to government questioning based upon information obtained from an illegal wiretap. *Gelbard v. U.S.*, 408 U.S. 41 (1972).

§ 16.06   RULE 17(c) OBJECTIONS

Rule 17(c), governing the subpoena duces tecum, provides that the court "may quash or modify the subpoena if compliance would be unreasonable or oppressive." *U.S. v. R. Enterprises*, 498 U.S. 292 (1991), provides the leading interpretation of that provision as applied to a grand jury subpoena. The Supreme Court there rejected the contention that a grand jury subpoena was not "reasonable" under 17(c) unless it met the same standards applied to a subpoena duces tecum directing production of documents for use at trial. In the trial context, the moving party must show that the document subpoenaed is relevant, admissible, and adequately specified, and the subpoenaed party argued that the government here had failed to make the first two showings and could not do so. The government responded, and the Court agreed, that there was no need for a government showing as to relevancy and admissibility. The requirement of evidentiary admissibility made no sense as to the grand jury, as it had long been held that the grand jury's "operation generally is unrestrained by the technical procedural and evidentiary rules governing the conduct of criminal trials." Requiring a preliminary showing as to relevancy "would invite procedural delays and detours while courts evaluate the relevancy * * * of [the] documents sought," exactly the kind of disruptive "minitrial" warned against in *Dionisio* (see § 16.05). So too, a mandated preliminary showing, by requiring the government to "explain in too much detail the particular reasons underlying a subpoena," could very well "compromise 'the indispensable secrecy of grand jury proceedings'" and "afford the targets of the investigation far more information about the grand jury's internal workings * * * than the Federal Rules of Criminal Procedure appear to contemplate."

Turning to the fashioning of an appropriate Rule 17(c) standard for the unique setting of the grand jury, the Court noted that several considerations had to be balanced. Initially, it had to be recognized that "the investigatory powers of the grand jury are * * * not unlimited," that the grand jury cannot, for example, "engage in arbitrary fishing expeditions" or "select targets of investigation out of malice or an intent to harass." Fashioning a procedure to enforce such limits, however, required consideration of conflicting elements in the grand jury process. On the one hand, the decision as to the appropriate charge "is routinely not made until after the grand jury has concluded its investigation," and "one simply cannot know in advance whether information sought during the investigation will be relevant and admissible in the prosecution for a particular offense." On the other hand, the party to whom the subpoena is directed "faces a difficult situation" in challenging the improper use of a subpoena. Grand juries ordinarily "do not announce publicly the subjects of their investigations," and the subpoenaed party therefore "may have no conception of the Government's purpose in seeking production of the requested information." Thus, what was needed was a Rule 17(c) standard of reasonableness that "gives due weight to the difficult position of subpoena recipients but does not impair the strong governmental interests in affording grand juries wide latitude, avoiding minitrials on peripheral matters, and preserving a necessary level of secrecy."

Several general guidelines, the Court noted, gave substance to such a standard. Initially "the law presumes, absent a strong showing to the contrary, that a grand jury acts within the legitimate scope of its authority." Consequently, "a grand jury subpoena issued through normal channels is presumed to be reasonable, and the burden of showing unreasonableness must be on the recipient who seeks to avoid compliance." In this case, that party "did not challenge the subpoena as being too indefinite, nor did [it] claim that compliance would be overly burdensome." The challenge was strictly on relevancy grounds and for such a challenge, the presumption of regularity produced the following standard: "[T]he motion to quash must be denied unless the district court determines that there is no reasonable possibility that the category of materials the Government seeks will produce information relevant to the general subject of the grand jury's investigation."

Recognizing that the above standard imposed an "unenviable task" upon the party raising a relevancy objection, the Court noted that the district court had authority to ease that task through appropriate procedures. Because a subpoenaed party who does not even know the general subject matter of the grand jury's investigation is "unlikely" to make the necessary showing "no matter how valid that party's claim," a district court "may be justified in a case where unreasonableness is alleged in requiring the Government to reveal the general subject of the grand jury's investigation before requiring the challenging party to carry its burden of persuasion." The district court, however, in fashioning appropriate procedures for this purpose would also have to take account of "the strong governmental interests in maintaining secrecy, preserving investigatory flexibility, and avoiding procedural delays." One possibility, the Court noted, was to require the government simply to "reveal the subject of the investigation to the trial court *in camera*, so the court may determine whether the motion to quash has a reasonable prospect for success before it discloses the subject matter to the challenging party." This case did not present that concern, however, as there was "no doubt that the respondents knew the subject of the grand jury's investigation." The Court described that subject as the "transportation of obscene materials," a description typical of those provided in the Advice of Rights attachment to a subpoena. See § 16.02.

In the leading lower court discussion of the *R. Enterprises* standard, *In re Grand Jury Proceedings*, 616 F.3d 1186 (10th Cir.2010) set forth three restrictions on relevancy review: (1) relevancy must be assessed by reference to the category of documents as described in the subpoena; the trial may not impose its own more narrowly tailor subcategories identifying groupings less likely to be over-inclusive when the subpoena's general subject matter grouping meets *R. Enterprises'* "reasonable possibility" standard; (2) once that standard is met as to the general category, the grand jury is entitled to everything within the category; the district court may not engage in a document-by-document, line-by-line exclusion or redaction, even where the objective is to exclude supposedly irrelevant "family information" contained in "otherwise relevant producible documents"; and (3) in camera review of documents will rarely if ever be justified for the purpose of assessing relevancy. While *R. Enterprises* prohibited an *"arbitrary* fishing expedition," it recognized that the grand jury process "necessarily involves a fishing expedition" with supoenas duces tecum "often drawn broadly."

A three-justice concurrence in *R. Enterprises* maintained that the subpoenaed party might succeed on a showing less demanding than the Court's "no-reasonable-possibility" standard where that party also could show that either (1) responding to the subpoena would be particularly burdensome due to the volume and location of the subpoenaed documents, (2) the "subpoena would intrude significantly on * * * privacy interests or call for the disclosure of trade secrets or other confidential matter," or (3) that "compliance would have First Amendment implications." Lower courts have occasionally quashed subpoenas seeking obviously relevant information in light of the first or second of the above factors. See e.g., *In re Grand Jury, John Doe No. G.J.2005–2,* 478 F.3d 581 (4th Cir.2007) (quashing subpoena requiring local police department to produce records of an internal investigation, in light of the adverse impact disclosure might have on willingness of police officers to cooperate in such investigations, where they had been promised confidentiality, and the weakness of the government's investigative need). When subpoenas have had "First Amendment implications", the lower courts commonly have rested their rulings on the bearing of the First Amendment on grand jury investigations, rather than Rule 17(c) analysis, as discussed below (see § 16.07).

§ 16.07   "CHILLING EFFECT" OBJECTIONS

Grand jury witnesses have argued in various contexts that even though the testimony or documents demanded of them clearly would be relevant, the grand jury should be required to show a compelling need for that information where the impact of its inquiry is to chill the exercise of a constitutionality protected right. Federal caselaw responding to such allegations largely have involved two settings; (1) challenges to requiring disclosures that bear upon the exercise of First Amendment rights; and (2) challenges to requiring attorneys to disclose information relating to their past or current clients that is not protected by the attorney-client privilege (e.g., client identity and fee information).

First Amendment Challenges. First Amendment challenges have been raised by a variety of grand jury witnesses in opposing the compelled disclosure of various types of information, including reporters refusing to disclose their sources, distributors of publications refusing to identify their customers, and organizations engaged in advocacy or religious activity refusing to reveal financial information and membership lists. The sole Supreme Court ruling addressing such a claim, *Branzburg v. Hayes*, 408 U.S. 665 (1972), rejected the contention that newspaper reporters could not be compelled to identify their confidential sources unless the prosecution first established a compelling need for obtaining that information. The Court majority both questioned the potential adverse impact of such a disclosure upon newsgathering, and concluded that any such adverse impact was more than offset by the interest of the public in criminal investigation, as reflected in the traditional investigative authority of the grand jury. Because the Court questioned the chilling impact of the confidential-source disclosure, and one of the five justices joining the majority opinion arguably suggested a narrower rationale in a concurring opinion, lower courts have varied in their reading of *Branzburg* (and their approach to First Amendment claims). See WCH § 16.12(E).

Several federal lower courts have concluded that *Branzburg* does not preclude requiring a special justification for a grand jury subpoena where disclosure of the information sought clearly would have a chilling impact on the exercise of a basic First Amendment right. These courts typically speak of requiring the government to show that the information sought by the subpoena is "substantially related" to a "compelling government interest." *Branzburg*, however, is viewed as having established that the government interest in investigating crime is per se a "compelling interest," so that standard is automatically met by a government showing of a substantial relationship to a grand jury's investigation, absent factors strongly suggesting that the grand jury investigation was initiated in bad faith.

Other courts have rejected entirely the contention that the government must ordinarily make a special showing to sustain a subpoena that has the potential for chilling the exercise of First Amendment rights. The Fourth Circuit adopted that position upon remand in the *R. Enterprises* case, considering there a First Amendment claim (not presented to the Supreme Court) that compliance with the challenged subpoena would chill the petitioner's continued operations in the distribution of sexually explicit magazines. *In re Grand Jury 87–3 Subpoena Duces Tecum*, 955 F.2d 229 (4th Cir.1992). It reasoned that *Branzburg,* in recognizing the sufficiency of the district court's capacity to respond to a "bad faith exercise of grand jury powers," rejected the need to impose any special burden on the government. Consistent with this reading of *Branzburg*, First Amendment interests are adequately protected by the district court applying, "with special sensitivity where values of expression are potentially implicated," the standards of *R. Enterprises*, keeping in mind the "traditional rule," as set forth in *R. Enterprises*, that "grand juries are not licensed to engage in arbitrary fishing expeditions, nor may they select targets out of malice or an intent to harass."

Counsel disclosures. A "chilling effect" argument also has been raised where the grand jury requires the testimony of an attorney, seeking information regarding past or current clients that is not within the attorney-client privilege. Finding that the attorney-client privilege provides adequate protection of the lawyer-client relationship, the lower courts generally have refused to require a special governmental showing of need to compel the attorney to testify as to matters not within the privilege. They note that the subpoenaed attorney often is not currently representing the target, and even where that is the case, the target is not yet an accused and therefore has no Sixth Amendment right to representation (see § 16.13). Also, requiring counsel's testimony is not likely to interfere with the target's future Sixth Amendment right to counsel of choice (assuming eventual indictment), as counsel's testimony may very well not create an unwaivable conflict of interest. Here again, requiring a special showing of need would be contrary to the warning in *Dionisio* and *Branzburg* against imposing procedures that impede and delay grand jury investigations.

Although rejecting a required showing of need, several circuits have noted that the district court's supervisory authority under Rule 17(c) allows it to quash or delay enforcement of a subpoena where requiring the attorney's immediate appearance could interfere with that attorney's current representation of the target who also is a defendant in a pending trial. See *In re Grand Jury Subpoena for Attorney Representing Criminal Defendant (Reyes-Requena)*, 913 F.2d 1118 (5th Cir.1990) (district court had discretion to quash as oppressive subpoena requiring attorney to appear and testify as to fee payment where appearance was demanded on same day as defendant's scheduled bail hearing and government offered no justification for the timing). But note *Impounded*, 241 F.3d 308 (3d Cir.2001) (district court abused its discretion when it quashed a grand jury subpoena on a determination that it would be "fundamentally unfair" to seek counsel's testimony regarding a client's possible destruction of subpoenaed records; district court erred in failing to look to the standards of Rule 17(c) and to consider whether the government's submission established the applicability of the crime-fraud exception to the attorney-client privilege).

Various states have adopted versions of Rule 3.8 of the Model Rules of Professional Conduct, which holds that prosecutors who seek to subpoena lawyers for the purpose of obtaining client information engage in unprofessional conduct unless certain prerequisites are met. Under the federal Citizen's Protection Act (the "McDade Act"), federal prosecutors are subject to the attorney regulation standards of the state in which they are located. However, *Stern v. U.S.*, 214 F.3d 4 (1st Cir.2000), held that a state version of Rule 3.8 which required prosecutors to gain judicial approval prior to issuance of a grand jury subpoena to a lawyer was not made applicable to federal prosecutors under the Citizen's Protection Act. Such a state rule was "more than an ethical standard", as it prescribed a novel rule of procedure (conflicting with Rule 17), and the Citizen's Protection Act applies only to ethical standards. A similar position has been advanced as to the Rule 3.8 requirements that the prosecutor conclude (1) that there is no feasible alternative to obtaining the information sought from the attorney and (2) that the information is "essential" to the "successful completion" of the investigation. Rule 6, it is noted, places no such limitations on the grand jury's authority to call for evidence.

In dealing with state ethical standards that clearly are incorporated under the Citizen's Protection Act, federal lower courts have held that the CPA does not provide a grounding for remedies within the criminal justice process (e.g., the exclusion of evidence). Rather, the CPA simply provides a grounding for subjecting a violating federal prosecutor to discipline by the state bar. Under this view, even if portions of Rule 3.8 are viewed as incorporated state ethical standards under the CPA, the subpoena could not be quashed notwithstanding that the prosecutor could not reasonably assert that the subpoena met those Rule 3.8 standards.

§ 16.08   SUBPOENA MISUSE OBJECTIONS

Blair v. U.S., 250 U.S. 273 (1919), generally is viewed as barring a subpoenaed party from

challenging the authority of the grand jury to indict
for (and therefore investigate) the activities that are
the subject of its inquiry. In *Blair*, the witness
claimed that the transaction under investigation
was beyond the grand jury's investigative authority
because the applicable federal criminal statute was
unconstitutional. The Supreme Court initially noted
that consideration of the constitutionality of the
statute at this point, prior to any indictment, would
be contrary to the long-established practice of
"refrain[ing] from passing upon the constitutionality
of an act of Congress unless obliged to do so." It then
proceeded, however, to speak in quite general terms
of a witness' lack of capacity to challenge the
"authority * * * of the grand jury," provided the jury
had "de facto existence and organization." The Court
treated the position of the grand jury witness as
analogous to that of the trial witness. Neither could
raise objections of incompetency or irrelevancy, for
those matters were of "no concern" to a witness, as
opposed to a party. For the same reasons, witnesses
also should not be allowed "to take exception to the
jurisdiction of the grand jury or the court over the
particular   subject   matter   that   is   under
investigation." The grand jury operates as a "grand
inquest," which requires broad investigative powers.
It must have authority, in particular, "to investigate
the facts in order to determine the question of
whether the facts show a case within [its]
jurisdiction." The witness could not be allowed "to
set limits to the investigation that the grand jury
may conduct."

A long line of cases, in contrast to *Blair*, recognize the right of the subpoenaed party to challenge a subpoena on the ground that it is being used for a purpose inconsistent with the grant of subpoena authority to a grand jury. Since such a "misuse" of the subpoena is deemed contrary to Rule 17, and since the relief sought is quashing the subpoena (rather than dismissing the indictment), these rulings, which largely predate *U.S. v. Williams* (see § 16.10), are deemed consistent with the limitations *Williams* placed on the exercise of federal court supervisory authority with respect to grand juries. Recognized instances of subpoena misuse include: (1) employment of the grand jury subpoena primarily to elicit evidence for use in a pending or future civil action; (2) employment of the grand jury subpoena "for the sole or dominating purpose of preparing an already pending indictment for trial"; (3) employment of the grand jury process to further independent investigations by police or prosecutor rather than to produce evidence for grand jury use; and (4) calling a witness for the purpose of "harassment," with "harassment" described as encompassing various objectives other than producing relevant evidence, such as burdening the witness with repeated appearances or seeking to punish the witness by forcing the witness into a situation where she will refuse to answer (or lie) and be held for contempt (or perjury).

A common thread running through the judicial treatment of misuse objections is that "a presumption of regularity" attaches to the grand jury proceeding and the objecting party bears a substantial burden in seeking to overcome that presumption. It clearly is not sufficient simply to show that the use of the grand jury process has (or will) benefit the government with respect to civil discovery, criminal discovery on a pending indictment, or some other alleged improper purpose. Courts have stressed that misuse exists only if the "primary" prosecutorial purpose in the use of the subpoena is improper; the prosecutor will not be enjoined from carrying forward a legitimate grand jury investigation simply because one byproduct may be the production of evidence useful in other proceedings in which the government has some interest. To gain an evidentiary hearing on a claim of alleged misuse, the objecting party ordinarily must at least point to surrounding circumstances "highly suggestive" of improper purpose.

Even where the surrounding circumstances strongly suggest improper use to obtain civil discovery or discovery on a pending criminal indictment, courts have expressed a reluctance to judge the dominant purpose of the investigation while it is still ongoing. The objecting party, it is noted, should not be allowed to "break up the play before it was started and then claim the government was offsides." *U.S. v. Doe (Ellsberg)*, 455 F.2d 1270 (1st Cir.1972). A preferable remedy, they note, is to allow the investigation to continue to its completion and then judge its purpose if the government should attempt to utilize the fruits of its alleged misuse in another proceeding. Where the alleged improper purpose is the development of evidence for a civil proceeding, the Rule 6(e) motion needed to disclose the grand jury material to civil attorneys ordinarily will provide the objecting party with an opportunity to challenge the purpose of the investigation after it has been completed (see § 18.06). Where the alleged improper purpose is gaining additional information for use in a trial on a pending indictment, the judge presiding at that trial can determine whether to require an inquiry into the dominant purpose of the post-indictment grand jury investigation when (and if) the government makes use in its prosecution of the fruits of that allegedly tainted investigation.

§ 16.09 CHALLENGING SECRECY VIOLATIONS

Rule 6(e)(2) of the Federal Rules of Criminal Procedure sets forth the general secrecy requirements of federal grand jury proceedings. It provides that the grand jurors, grand jury personnel, government attorneys, and personnel assisting government attorneys may not disclose "a matter occurring before the grand jury." Rule 6(e)(2) further provides that no obligation of secrecy may be imposed on any person "except in accordance with this Rule." Rule 6(e)(3) recognizes several "exceptions" to the general rule of secrecy imposed by Rule 6(e)(2)(see § 18.06).

Individuals or entities who have furnished information to the grand jury, or whose activities are the subject of the grand jury investigation, often seek to challenge a disclosure of grand jury matter by government personnel where the government acknowledges the disclosure but justifies it as consistent with Rules 6(e)(2) and 6(e)(3). As discussed in § 18.06, such persons may challenge proposed court orders that would authorize disclosure of grand jury testimony to third persons or other governmental units under Rule 6(e)(3)(E)(i) (disclosure "preliminary to or in connection with a judicial proceeding"). So too, as noted in § 18.05, targets of an investigation may seek relief with respect to disclosures that government personnel have made without a court order—i.e., where the government claims that the disclosures either were not subject to Rule 6(e)(2) because they did not include "matter occurring before the grand jury," or fit within the Rule 6(e)(3) exceptions that authorize limited disclosures without a court order. In both of the above situations, no question exists as to who disclosed (or intends to disclose) what information to whom, and the primary issue is whether the disclosure meets the standards of Rule 6(e)(3) or is outside the coverage of Rule 6(e)(2). If the disclosure is contrary to Rule 6, a prospective disclosure will be prohibited and a past disclosure will be remedied (in some instances, by prohibiting a recipient's further use of the information).

A quite different type of challenge is presented where the individual or entity claims that there have been "leaks" of grand jury matter to the media. Here, the issue ordinarily is not whether the alleged disclosures to the media by persons clearly subject to the Rule 6(e)(2) secrecy requirements (in particular, government attorneys and assisting personnel) would fall within the exceptions recognized in Rule 6(e)(3), or otherwise would be justified under Rule 6(e)(2) (they clearly would not), but whether those persons actually did leak grand jury matter, and, if so, what is an appropriate remedy. See WCH § 16.9(J).

Rule 6(e)(7) provides that "a knowing violation of Rule 6 may be punished as a contempt of court." A few lower court opinions suggest that this provision refers only to criminal (and not civil) contempt, and, of course, whether criminal contempt sanctions should be pursued lies in the discretion of the supervisory court, which is responsible for enforcing Rule 6's secrecy provisions. The Fourth Circuit has held that the Rule 6(e)(7) provision refers as well to civil contempt, but that it does not create a private cause of action seeking a civil contempt sanction. *Finn v. Schiller*, 72 F.3d 1182 (4th Cir.1996). Under either of these readings of Rule 6(e)(7), neither the witness whose testimony is leaked, nor the person who is the subject of the information leaked, has a cause of action for which relief can be demanded. Such individuals or entities may notify the court of the alleged violation and urge it to hold an evidentiary hearing for the purpose of determining whether imposition of criminal contempt (or civil contempt) is appropriate, but the court has discretion to pursue the alternative route of referring the matter to the Department of Justice's Office of Professional Responsibility for internal investigation and the possible imposition of internal sanctions.

Other courts have concluded that Rule 6(e)(7) authorizes a civil contempt remedy, and that enables the victim of the alleged secrecy violation to pursue a civil action for relief, to obtain an evidentiary hearing upon establishing a prima facie case, and to gain a civil contempt order if a knowing violation is established. *Barry v. U.S.*, 865 F.2d 1317 (D.C.Cir.1989). A few courts also have suggested that the contempt sanction specified in Rule 6(e)(7) might not be the exclusive remedy. Thus, if leaks persist and their source cannot be identified, a court could quash a subpoena on behalf of a witness who would suffer prejudice if her testimony were leaked. Since courts have agreed that whatever relief is available should not "unnecessarily interfere with the grand jury process," such relief would be rare, and arguably a court should never be compelled to go so far as to dismiss the grand jury and terminate the investigation because of continued leaks.

These courts rarely have had to rule definitively on the appropriate remedy because of the complainant's almost insurmountable hurdle of establishing that there was a leak. Initially, to establish the grounding even for an evidentiary hearing, some courts insist upon a prima facie showing that there has been an unauthorized disclosure. This requires showing both that the information disclosed probably was within the protection of grand jury secrecy (i.e., was "grand jury matter," see § 18.05, rather than, for example, information acquired by government agents through their own investigative efforts) and that the disclosure was likely to have come from government personnel, the grand jurors, or grand jury personnel, rather than from a person not sworn to secrecy under Rule 6(e)(2) (in particular, a witness). Thus, newspaper articles that refer only to the general character of the investigation (rather than grand jury testimony or grand jury actions) ordinarily will be insufficient, and even articles that refer specifically to grand jury matter (e.g., a witness having refused to testify on self-incrimination grounds) may be insufficient because it may reflect speculation by the journalist or information furnished by the witness or someone with whom the witness shared that information.

Other courts have concluded that, "depending on context, mere suspicion may be enough "to justify an inquiry," *In re U.S.*, 441 F.3d 44 (1st Cir.2006), and here, the target is more likely to obtain an evidentiary hearing. The leading appellate opinions, however, provide little guidance as to the scope of that hearing. Typically, the government will seek to rely on affidavits stating that all relevant government personnel deny any disclosure on their part. Courts may be wary of requiring the government even to disclose on the record the names of all such personnel on the ground that it would provide the subject of the investigation with discovery of internal grand jury operations. Although journalists can be called as witnesses and questioned as to their confidential source, they are most unlikely to respond even though that information will not be privileged under federal law. *U.S. v. Sterling*, 724 F.3d 482 (4th Cir.2013) (denying claim based on *Branzburg* (§ 16.07), but acknowledging a minority position that federal common law can create a reporter's privilege.)

§ 16.10 STATUTORILY PROTECTED THIRD-PARTY RECORDS

A common feature of grand jury investigations of white collar crime is obtaining from third parties records that provide information on the activities of the target. Those third-parties typically are commercial entities that provide services to the target (e.g., financial institutions and internet service providers) and government agencies that receive information from the target in the course of enforcing regulations, imposing taxes, or distributing benefits. In some instances, the records were created by the third-party entity based on information provided by the target and others (sometimes unknowingly provided, as in the case of historic cell-phone location data). Here, the records often provide information that could not readily be obtained from any other single source.

Third-party records are also commonly sought even when the record consists of documents (hard copy or electronic) created and submitted by the target, with the target likely to have retained a copy (e.g., a government form, a bank deposit, or an electronic communication). The government investigators, for various reasons, will prefer to obtain the document from the third-party rather than from the target. In some instances, as discussed below, the document can be obtained from the third-party without the target being informed of the disclosure, and that may have advantages in "keeping the target in the dark" as to either the existence or scope of the investigation. A third-party will promptly and fully comply with a subpoena duces tecum, while particular targets might seek to evade or delay production (including delaying by contesting an obviously valid subpoena). As discussed in Ch. 20, a non-entity target may raise a self-incrimination objection to a subpoena duces tecum and while that objection is likely to prevail only as to a limited class of documents, the third-party cannot even put forth that objection as there is no personal incrimination. See § 20.07.

More than two-dozen federal "privacy statutes" address the disclosure to federal enforcement agencies of particular types of third-party records. The most significant, in the field of white collar investigations, are: (1) the Right to Financial Privacy Act (RFPA) (governing disclosure of the records of individuals and small partnerships by a variety of financial institutions, including banks and credit card companies); (2) the Stored Communications Act (SCA) (governing disclosures of information by providers of electronic communication services and public providers of remote computing services, which covers most internet service providers and "cloud computing" providers); and (3) the "confidentiality" provisions of the Internal Revenue Code (governing disclosure of "tax returns" and "tax return information," which goes beyond information furnished by the taxpayer). Several other privacy statutes address the disclosure of records that may become relevant in investigating a limited range of white collar offenses (e.g., educational records). See WCH § 16.10(d).

Where a privacy statute has no provision applicable to a grand jury subpoena duces tecum seeking third-party records, the primary issue unique to that setting is the target-standing issue discussed in § 16.11. Where a statute does apply, it may address some key administrative matters (e.g., imposing special requirements as to the storage and return of the records), but the two critical questions posed by the statute's application are: (1) does the statute impose restrictions that preclude use of the grand jury subpoena, and (2) does the statute impose special requirements as to notification of the target.

Several of the federal privacy statutes impose prerequisites for disclosure that are not met by a grand jury subpoena. The SCA, for example, includes a requirement of a search warrant to obtain the content of an electronic communication (e.g., e-mails and text messages) that are retained in electronic storage for less than 180 days by a provider of electronic communication services. Other statutes, including the IRS provision, require a court order based on a special showing to obtain a certain type of record. On the other hand, the RFPA explicitly recognizes that the records subject to its provisions may be obtained by a grand jury subpoena.

In the absence of a statutory provision to the contrary, a third-party subpoenaed to produce its records is free to either notify or not notify the individual or entity that is the subject of those records. Since Rule 6(e) prohibits imposing a secrecy obligation except in accord with that provision (which does not include witnesses among the persons so obligated, see § 16.09), federal courts have held that the prosecution acts improperly if it informs subpoenaed third-parties that they are prohibited from informing the target of the subpoena (although it can request confidentiality). A few courts, however, have suggested that they have an inherent power to impose a gag upon a sufficient showing of the government that target awareness will result in actions undermining the investigation. See WCH § 16.9(D)(2).

Many privacy statutes address the notification issue and impose an obligation upon the third-party to notify the subject of the record before complying with a subpoena, court order, or warrant. However, both the RFPA and the SCA also provide a 90-day-court-ordered delay in notification (with extensions possible). Issuance of the order requires a finding of reason to believe that notification will result in specified harms (e.g., destruction or tampering with potential evidence) or "otherwise seriously jeopardizing" the investigation. Where the grand jury investigation is directed at crimes committed against a financial institution, the RFPA automatically prohibits the institution's notification of persons identified in the subpoena. Privacy statutes governing disclosures by government agencies sometimes do not include either notification or gag order provisions; the agency is free to notify, but the assumption is that the government agency will be inclined to adhere to a prosecution request for confidentiality (in contrast to private services providers, likely to view failing to notify as bad for business).

§ 16.11 TARGET STANDING

The issue of target-standing arises with respect to both subpoenas duces tecum and subpoenas ad testificandum. Where the target is aware that a third party has been subpoenaed to produce documents that relate to the target's activities or to give testimony concerning those activities, the target may seek to quash the subpoena. However, the target may not have standing to raise all of the issues previously discussed. Being the target of the inquiry does not, in itself, allow you to stand in the shoes of the subpoenaed party.

Initially *U.S. v. Miller*, 425 U.S. 435 (1976), held that a customer lacks standing to challenge on Fourth Amendment grounds a subpoena directing a third party service provider (there, a bank) to disclose its records of the customer's transactions. Although some of the records were originally created by the customer, in giving control over the records to the service provider, the customer assumed the risk of disclosure by the provider. A few lower courts have concluded that *Miller* does not extend to target created documents that were submitted to the third party not for its own use, but simply to act as "intermediary" in distributing the document. See *U.S. v. Warshak*, 631 F.3d 266 (6th Cir.2010) (subpoena to internet service provider to produce customer's e-mails; also holding that a search warrant is required).

In general, as in *Miller*, the target of the grand jury investigation has no standing to object to directing a third party to produce information relating to the target, as the target has no protected interest in that information. Certain misuses of grand jury authority, however, will directly impact the rights of the target, and here the target may challenge the third-party. Thus, a target may challenge a grand jury's misuse of the subpoena to enhance the prosecutor's criminal discovery on an indictment pending against the target, or to gain discovery for a civil action to be brought against the target. So too, an employer/target was held to have standing to object to subpoenas issued to its employees where it alleged that the government's design was to harass the employer by repeatedly calling its employees to testify. Where statutes establish special prerequisites for issuance of subpoenas to third-party record holders (see § 16.10), those statutes commonly establish target/customer standing to insist upon compliance with those prerequisites.

§ 16.12 CHALLENGES ALLEGING PROSECUTORIAL MISCONDUCT

Prosecutorial misconduct in presenting a case to the grand jury typically is discovered after the target is indicted, so this challenge is presented by the "defendant," rather than the "target," with the defendant arguing that the misconduct requires dismissal of the indictment.

At one point, federal lower courts had characterized as impermissible "misconduct" a broad range of prosecutorial actions and inactions in presenting its case. Misconduct included: various actions or inactions that led to the misleading presentation of evidence (e.g., failing to correct testimony that the prosecutor should have known to be false); giving incorrect legal advice; testifying as a witness; making inflammatory statements; expressing a personal opinion as to guilt; allowing unauthorized persons to be present; and presenting before the grand jury the target's immunized testimony from another proceeding. *U.S. v. Williams*, 504 U.S. 36 (1992), however, produced a sea change in the authority of federal courts to characterize prosecutorial actions or inactions as misconduct.

In *Williams*, the Supreme Court concluded that "as a general matter at least," federal courts lack the authority to independently prescribe standards of appropriate prosecutorial conduct before the grand jury and to then dismiss indictments because of the prosecutor's failure to abide by those standards. Stressing the grand jury's "functional independence from the judicial branch," *the Williams* Court concluded that federal courts generally lack authority to utilize their supervisory power to dismiss indictments unless they do so "as a means of enforcing or vindicating legally compelled standards of prosecutorial conduct before the grand jury," as established in statutes, the Federal Rules of Criminal Procedure, or constitutional prohibitions. Accordingly, *Williams* held, a federal court could not dismiss an indictment because the prosecutor failed to present before the grand jury known exculpatory evidence, as there was no statute, court rule, or constitutional provision that required the prosecutor to present such evidence to the grand jury.

The *Williams* Court cited examples of "those few, clear rules which were carefully drafted and approved by the Court and Congress to ensure the integrity of the grand jury" and therefore could be enforced by a dismissal of an indictment. They consisted largely of the provisions of Rule 6 and a series of limited statutory prohibitions (such as the prohibition against presenting unlawful wiretap evidence before the grand jury and the prohibition against subornation of perjury). Those provisions do not encompass much of what had been viewed as prosecutorial misconduct in earlier lower court opinions (e.g. inflammatory remarks about the witness or target, expressions of personal opinion as to the target's guilt, and misstatements of the law).

Williams had no need to explore the question of what type of action by the prosecutor would produce a "constitutional violation" (referring presumably to a violation of the Fifth Amendment right to indictment by a grand jury, but possibly also encompassing due process violations). Lower courts addressing that issue are divided. Some suggest that actions which completely mislead the grand jury, such as the knowing introduction of perjured testimony, will produce a constitutional violation (distinguishing *Williams* as a case of simply presenting one side of the evidence, consistent with the ex parte structure of the grand jury). Others suggest that a constitutional violation requires action that undermines the "structural independence" of the grand jury. Thus, in *U.S. v. Navarro-Vargas*, 408 F.3d 1184 (9th Cir.2005) (en banc), four dissenting judges concluded that the grand jury had a recognized right of nullification and a jury instruction indicating that it lacked such a right produced a constitutional violation.

Procedural setting. Except for the most unusual case, prosecutor misconduct in presenting a case to the grand jury will not occur in the presence of the target or a witness who is friendly to the target. Thus, where such action is uncovered, it usually is after the target has been indicted, in the course of pretrial discovery or in the review of the grand jury testimony of trial witnesses. If those sources strongly suggest some impropriety, they can be used as the basis of a motion under Federal Rule 6(e)(3)(E), providing for disclosure of part or all of the grand jury transcript on a showing that "a ground may exist to dismiss the indictment because of a matter that occurred before the grand jury". Moreover, even though the defense fails to make the needed preliminary showing, which is fairly rigorous, the district court has the discretion to itself review the grand jury transcript to determine whether it reveals possible misconduct.

Dismissal of an indictment. To dismiss an indictment, the district court must find more than prosecutorial action or inaction constituting misconduct under the standard of *Williams*. It also must conclude that the prosecutor's violation of Rule 6, a federal statute, or the federal constitution was not a "harmless error." In *Bank of Nova Scotia v. U.S.*, 487 U.S. 250 (1988), the Supreme Court held that "dismissal of the indictment is appropriate only if it established that the violation substantially influenced the grand jury's decision to indict or if there is 'grave doubt' that the decision to indict was free from the substantial influence of such violations." Since the *Bank of Nova Scotia* Court noted that that case did not present any constitutional error on the part of the prosecutor, arguably the more rigorous harmless error standard applicable to prosecutorial constitutional error at trial would apply where prosecutorial misconduct constituted constitutional error in the grand jury setting. Under that standard, dismissal would be required unless the court is convinced "beyond a reasonable doubt" that the constitutional error "did not contribute" to the grand jury's decision to indict. *Chapman v. California*, 386 U.S. 18 (1967).

Of course, as *Bank of Nova Scotia* noted, prosecutorial misconduct that does not relate to the presentation of the prosecution's case before the grand jury almost always constitutes harmless error under either standard, because only in the most unusual circumstances will it have contributed to the grand jury's decision to indict. Thus, the Court noted that the Rule 6(e) secrecy violations raised there (disclosing grand jury matter to third parties and imposing secrecy obligations upon witnesses), clearly constituted harmless error because they simply "could not have affected the charging decision."

Conviction reversal. Where the application of harmless error doctrine is considered after the defendant is convicted, that may present an insurmountable barrier for the defense. *U.S. v. Mechanik*, 475 U.S. 66 (1986), is the leading ruling on harmless error in that situation. In *Mechanik*, the defense learned of a Rule 6(d) violation (the presence of unauthorized persons—here multiple witness—before the grand jury) during the middle of the trial, and the trial court postponed consideration of defense's subsequent challenge to the indictment until the trial ended. The Supreme Court in *Mechanik* held that at that point, with the defendant already convicted, the misconduct before the grand jury had become a moot issue. Even if the Rule 6(d) violation might have influenced the grand jury on its finding of the probable cause needed to indict, the "petit jury's subsequent guilty verdict" rendered that irrelevant because that verdict "not only means that there was probable cause to believe that the defendants were guilty as charged, but that they are in fact guilty as charged beyond a reasonable doubt." Thus, the "petit jury's verdict rendered harmless any conceivable error in the charging decision that might have flowed from the [Rule 6(d)] violation."

Federal lower courts have disagreed as to how broadly *Mechanik* should be read. Reasoning that *Mechanik* was "carefully crafted along very narrow lines" and involved misconduct that "at worst, was

[a] technical [violation]," the Tenth Circuit holds postconviction review available for allegations of misconduct suggesting the prosecutor "attempted to unfairly sway the grand jury or to otherwise affect the accusatory process" and misconduct that "transgressed the defendant's right to fundamental fairness." *U.S. v. Taylor*, 798 F.2d 1337 (10th Cir.1986). Other circuits have rejected such a narrow reading. They acknowledge that *Mechanik* does not extend to misconduct which denies fundamental fairness and thereby presents a constitutional claim, but see it as extending to the full range of nonconstitutional improprieties that might justify dismissal if considered prior to conviction.

§ 16.13   ASSISTANCE OF COUNSEL

The Supreme Court has twice indicated that a grand jury witness does not have a constitutional right to the assistance of counsel while testifying before a grand jury. In *In re Groban*, 352 U.S. 330 (1957), a case holding that a witness in a fire marshall's investigative proceeding did not have a constitutional right to the assistance of counsel, the Court drew an analogy to grand jury proceedings and stated: "A witness before a grand jury cannot insist, as a matter of constitutional right, in being represented by counsel." In *U.S. v. Mandujano*, discussed in § 19.06, the plurality opinion rejected the defendant's contention that, as a putative defendant called before the grand jury, he should have been told not simply that "he could have a lawyer outside the room with whom he could consult", but that counsel would be appointed to assist him if he was indigent. The plurality reasoned that, since "no criminal proceedings had been instituted," the "Sixth Amendment right to counsel had not come into play." That Amendment, which provides the usual constitutional grounding for requiring appointed counsel for the indigent, describes that right as one of the "accused", and the Court had previously held that a person does not become an "accused" until subjected to "adversary judicial proceedings", which does not include grand jury proceedings. *Miranda v. Arizona* recognized a Fifth Amendment right of the indigent arrestee (also not an "accused") to insist upon receiving the advice of an appointed counsel when subjected to custodial interrogation, but the *Mandujano* plurality, for reasons set forth in § 19.06, concluded that *Miranda* did not extend to the grand jury setting.

Though the government has no constitutional obligation to provide counsel for persons subpoenaed to appear before the grand jury, due process might well be violated should it bar subpoenaed persons from consulting with retained counsel prior to complying with the subpoena. That issue is unlikely to arise, however, as the longstanding federal practice is to facilitate consultation even at the point where the witness appears before the grand jury. Federal Rule 6(d) operates to preclude counsel's presence within the grand jury room as it allows for the presence only of the witness, the jurors, the prosecutor, and needed grand jury personnel. However, the federal practice, is to allow the witness to interrupt her testimony and consult with retained counsel located in the anteroom. Indeed, the notification of rights attached to the subpoena (see § 19.06) states: "If you have retained counsel, the grand jury will permit you a reasonable opportunity to step outside the grand jury to consult with counsel if you desire."

When counsel represents more than one witness in a grand jury proceeding, more than one target or subject of the investigation, or a combination of witnesses and non-witness targets or subjects, the government may move to bar such representation as presenting an actual or potential conflict of interest. The Supreme Court has recognized the authority of a trial court to preclude joint representation of criminal defendants, in the interest of both protecting the defendant's right to effective assistance of counsel and preserving the "appearance of fairness" in legal proceedings, even where the defendants are willing to "waive" their right to conflict-free counsel. *Wheat v. U.S.*, 486 U.S. 153 (1988). Lower courts have assumed that the same authority exists with respect to the grand jury setting—especially since the participants here cannot rely on any Sixth Amendment right to counsel of choice, but must rely, at best, on a due process right not to have the government arbitrarily interfere in the participant's efforts to obtain legal advice.

Wheat recognized the right of the trial judge to preclude multiple representation not only where an actual conflict existed (i.e. where the clients' current positions make action favoring one harmful to the other), but also where there exists a "serious potential for conflict." The latter situation encompasses many of the settings in which the government has challenged multiple representation, such as the representation of a target and witnesses who might testify against the target, the representation of targets who had different levels of culpability in the activities under investigation, and the representation of the corporate employer and the employee whose actions can give rise to the corporation's liability. The government has also challenged multiple representation of same-level targets or subjects who adopt a "united front" position of all refusing to testify on self-incrimination grounds. It occasionally has been argued that disqualification should be ordered in such cases because the united front threatens the effectiveness of the grand jury's investigation. The few federal courts considering such an argument have found this contention unpersuasive, but disqualification in such cases commonly can be reached under the *Wheat* standard (particularly where the government might well grant concessions to one person willing to testify against the others, and the joint representation thereby keeps each client from obtaining conflict-free advice as to whether she should be that person).

To avoid conflict challenges, employers commonly provide separate counsel for employees called to testify before the grand jury. Indeed, indemnification provisions in executive employment contracts or charter or by-law provisions may require an employer to pay attorneys' fees for such employees. Very often the employee will limit the employee's choice of counsel, but to avoid counsel's possible disqualification, the employer will retain the chosen counsel under an agreement stating that counsel's "sole obligation" is to the employee. Of course, that provision does not preclude counsel from determining that it is in the best interest of the client to share information with the employer's counsel, or possibly enter into a joint-defense agreement (§ 22.12).

CHAPTER 17

ADMINISTRATIVE AGENCY INVESTIGATIONS

§ 17.01 ADMINISTRATIVE SUBPOENAS

Most federal administrative agencies have been authorized by Congress to issue administrative subpoenas (also called "summonses") to compel testimony and the production of documents. While that authority has been given to the agencies only to facilitate their investigation of activities that may violate the various regulatory statutes that are within their enforcement domain, its use for that purpose can readily have a direct bearing on criminal prosecutions, particularly as to white collar crime. Violations of those regulatory statutes may constitute crimes as well as civil wrongs, and even when that is not the case, the circumstances surrounding a violation may suggest that a non-regulatory crime has been committed. Of course, the agency may not itself initiate criminal enforcement, but it may deliver the evidence it has collected to the appropriate prosecuting official, along with the agency recommendation for prosecution (see § 18.02). Should further investigation be desired, the prosecutor may utilize the expertise of the agency investigators already familiar with the case in the grand jury's subsequent investigation (see § 18.06). Should a prosecution eventually be brought, the evidence collected by the agency may be used in the criminal trial.

Unlike grand jury subpoenas, an administrative subpoena is not process of the district court. To enforce it, the agency must bring an independent civil action as authorized in the statute granting it subpoena authority. One consequence of this distinction is that a court order enforcing the subpoena is a final judgment and may be appealed in the same manner as a civil judgment (in contrast to the enforcement of the grand jury subpoena, where the party directed to comply ordinarily can gain review only by being held in contempt and then appealing that order).

The administrative subpoena, like the grand jury subpoena, is subject to the subpoenaed party's testimonial privileges. The individual may rely on the self-incrimination privilege, the lawyer-client privilege, and other privileges recognized in federal courts to refuse to provide particular documents or to answer specific questions put to the witness while testifying before an agency examiner. The subpoenaed party also may raise in the enforcement proceeding several other challenges, the most significant of which are discussed below.

In several areas of federal regulation, Congress has granted to the Department of Justice subpoena authority similar to that granted to administrative agencies. These subpoenas are commonly described as "administrative subpoenas", and they are subject to roughly the same challenges as the subpoenas issued by administrative agencies.

§ 17.02 FOURTH AMENDMENT OVERBREADTH

In its initial response to broad administrative subpoenas duces tecum, the Supreme Court warned against administrative "fishing expeditions" and suggested that Fourth Amendment principles limited the agency to compelling production only where it had "some ground * * * for supposing" the documents subpoenaed contained information relevant to a violation of the statute the agency was charged with enforcing. *FTC v. American Tobacco Co.*, 264 U.S. 298 (1924). That view was flatly rejected, however, in *Oklahoma Press Publishing Co., v. Walling*, 327 U.S. 186 (1946), and *U.S. v. Morton Salt Co.*, 338 U.S. 632 (1950).

Oklahoma Press distinguished subpoenas duces tecum from traditional searches, as *Hale* had done in the context of the grand jury subpoena (§16.03). Indeed, it described the Fourth Amendment as applying to the subpoena only in an "analogical sense," and referred at one point to the Fourth Amendment "if applicable," leading to a lower court suggestion that constitutional standard announced in *Oklahoma Press* might be grounded in due process rather than the reasonableness clause of the Fourth Amendment. That standard, however, was described as imposing the "gist" of the Fourth Amendment's "reasonableness requirement," and later Supreme Court rulings have continued to refer to the Fourth Amendment.

The *Oklahoma Press* standard did not encompass probable cause or any other degree of probability as to a possible violation within the agency's administrative authority. The constitutional restriction of reasonableness in this context, it noted, "at the most guards against abuse only by way of too much indefiniteness or breadth in the things required to be 'particularly described,' if also the inquiry is one the demanding agency is authorized by law to make and the materials specified are relevant." In *Morton Salt*, the Court specifically acknowledged that the *Oklahoma Press* standard allowed for some "fishing expeditions." The administrative agency, the Court noted, had been given by Congress "the power of inquisition". This was a power "more analogous to the grand jury" than to that of a court which issues a subpoena in a specific "case or controversy", and it therefore allowed the agency to "investigate merely on suspicion that the law is being violated, or even just because it wants assurance that it is not."

The standard set forth in *Oklahoma Press*, as explained in *Morton Salt*, is very much like the overbreadth doctrine applied to grand jury subpoenas duces tecum (see § 16.03). *Oklahoma Press* did cite as separate elements the requirements that the investigation be within the scope of the agency authority as granted by Congress and that the documents requested be "relevant" to the investigation. The former requirement basically insists that the subject matter be within the agency's jurisdiction. Its practical significance is limited by the well-established standard of review that gives to the agency the opportunity to explore the potential coverage of its mandate, and therefore allows it to investigate for the very purpose of deciding whether or not the particular activity falls within its bailiwick. *Endicott Johnson Corp. v. Perkins*, 317 U.S. 501 (1943). As for relevancy, that is a factor also considered in applying the overbreadth standard (see § 16.04).

§ 17.03   THE *POWELL* PREREQUISITES

In *U.S. v. Powell*, 379 U.S. 48 (1964), the Supreme Court set forth four prerequisites for district court enforcement of an Internal Revenue Service summons. The statutory provision on enforcement noted simply that the district court was given "jurisdiction by appropriate process" to enforce the summons, but the Court found guidance as to what must be shown to merit enforcement in the statutory provisions governing IRS investigations and the IRS summons. "Reading the statutes as we do," the Court noted, "the Commissioner * * * must show that the investigation will be conducted pursuant to a legitimate purpose, that the inquiry may be relevant to the purpose, that the information sought is not already within the commissioner's possession, and that the administrative steps required by the Code have been followed—in particular, that the 'Secretary or his delegate,' after investigation, has determined the further examination to be necessary and has notified the taxpayer in writing to that effect."

Although *Powell* was speaking only of the IRS summons, the four prerequisites announced there—legitimate purpose, relevancy, lack of current possession, and adherence to agency procedures for issuance—have been applied by lower courts to administrative subpoenas generally. Lower court opinions interpreting the four *Powell* prerequisites have focused primarily on challenges to the government's allegation of a legitimate purpose (see § 17.04), but they have also lent additional content to the other prerequisites.

In seeking enforcement of a subpoena, the agency will present a statement as to the purpose of the investigation. That statement typically refers to the investigation of possible violations of designated statutory provisions (or the agency rules and regulations adopted thereunder) by specified individuals or entities in the course of activities that may be described in a fairly general fashion. Relevancy is then determined by assessing the possible relationship of the documents requested to this subject of investigation. The relevancy requirement is met, according to a frequently quoted standard, if the subpoenaed documents "might throw light" upon the subject of the investigation. *Foster v. U.S.*, 265 F.2d 183 (2d Cir.1959).

Even under this standard, a subpoena may be rejected where its breadth indicates that no effort was made to categorize the requested documents by reference to what might be relevant (ignoring obvious distinctions based on time-frame, document-function, or general subject matter). The presence of a privacy concern, as where the subpoena seeks personal information relating to activities of an individual, also leads to "heightened scrutiny" in analyzing relevancy. WCH § 17.4(D). But note *In re Administrative Subpoena John Doe, D.P.M.*, 253 F.3d 256 (2001) (while a stronger showing ordinarily is required for personal financial data, that showing was not needed where the individuals could readily transfer assets from the business account to their personal accounts).

The third *Powell* prerequisite, that the information sought must not already be within the possession of the government, has been considered primarily in the context of an IRS summons calling for the production of records previously examined by IRS agents. Courts have held that the prerequisite of "possession" means actual physical possession, and is not satisfied by previous knowledge of the contents. So too, where the bulk of the documents subpoenaed clearly are not in the government's possession, and the "marginal burden of supplying information which might already be in the [government's] possession is small," the court may grant enforcement of the subpoena "in its entirety," rather than seek to determine the status of individual documents. WCH § 17.5(E).

The content of the fourth prerequisite, compliance with administrative procedures for issuance of the subpoena, varies with the statute applicable to the particular agency and the rules adopted thereunder. One common requirement is that the administrative subpoena be issued with the approval of a person in a specified position within the agency—the requirement to which the *Powell* Court referred. In the case of subpoenas issued to third-party recordkeepers, there sometimes will be a requirement of notification to the target who is the subject of the subpoenaed records. See § 17.05. While adherence to that requirement also falls within *Powell's* fourth prerequisite, one court has suggested that it should not bar enforcement where the target has received notification through other sources. See *U.S. v. Texas Heart Institute*, 755 F.2d 469 (5th Cir 1985).

§ 17.04 LEGITIMATE PURPOSE CHALLENGES

In discussing the prerequisites for enforcement, the *Powell* Court noted that a "court may not permit its process to be abused" and that "such an abuse would take place if the summons had been issued for an improper purpose, such as to harass the taxpayer or to put pressure on him to settle a collateral dispute, or for any other purpose reflecting on the good faith of the particular investigation." This language is sometimes described as permitting a "bad faith" challenge to the subpoena that stands apart from the *Powell* prerequisites, but it actually does no more than recognize one possible ground for challenging the agency's allegation of legitimate purpose.

Challenges to purpose typically allege improper motivation and typically are grounded on one of the two bad-faith illustrations offered in *Powell*. A purpose of harassment is often tied to a claim that the investigation is vindictive, i.e. the investigation was designed to punish a person who exercised his rights. While vindictiveness clearly is improper, that does not mean that an agency cannot shift to a more adversary stance in response to the exercise of a right. *U.S. v. Texas Heart Institute*, 755 F.2d 469 (5th Cir.1985) (where statute of limitations for civil actions is about to run and taxpayer will not voluntarily extend it, bad faith is not shown by informing taxpayer that case will be transferred to the Criminal Investigation Division, not subject to the same statute of limitations). In *SEC v. Wheeling-Pittsburgh Steel Corp.*, 648 F.2d 118 (3d Cir.1981), the Third Circuit recognized that improper motivation need not spring from the agency, but could also be the product of third party influence, there the alleged political coercion imposed by a competitor and a legislator.

The *Powell* Court noted that "the burden of showing an abuse of the court's process is on the taxpayer." Most lower courts have held that the government bears the initial burden of demonstrating a lawful purpose by submission of the agency's formal order of investigation (where used), or the affidavit of the responsible agency official, setting forth a purpose that is within the agency's statutory domain. The subpoenaed party then has the burden of asserting and proving that the subpoena is actually motivated by an improper purpose. In *U.S. v. Gertner*, 65 F.3d 963 (1st Cir.1995), the First Circuit suggested that perhaps the burden on a subpoenaed party should be only to "create a substantial question in the court's mind regarding the validity of the government's purpose," and then the ultimate burden of proof should shift back to the government as the plaintiff in the enforcement action. Under either view, the subpoenaed party faces a significant burden, as it does not have an automatic right to discovery, enforcement proceedings being summary in nature. Federal Rules of Civil Procedure, Rule 81.

In *U.S. v. Clarke*, 134 S.Ct. 2361 (2014), the Court resolved a split in the circuits as to when the subpoenaed party is entitled to examine the IRS agent in charge of the investigation for the purpose of establishing improper motivation. The Court noted that: (1) "the taxpayer * * * [must] point to specific facts or circumstances plausibly raising an inference of bad faith"; (2) while a "bare assertion or conjecture is not enough, neither is a fleshed out case demanded"; and (3) the required showing must be based on "credible evidence," but "circumstantial evidence can suffice," since "direct evidence * * * at this threshold stage will rarely, if ever, be available". *Clarke* did not address the ultimate standard for establishing bad faith. It did, however, note that: "[A]bsent contrary evidence, the IRS can satisfy the [good faith] standard by submitting a simple affidavit from the investigating agent."

§ 17.05 THIRD-PARTY SUBPOENAS

As in the case of grand jury subpoenas (see § 16.10), administrative subpoenas are often directed to service providers for records relating to the use of their services by customers. Of course, there will be no opportunity for the customer to challenge the subpoena if the customer is not made aware of the subpoena. As discussed in § 16.10, Congress has adopted customer-notification requirements for third-party subpoenas in various situations. In addition, administrative regulations or statutes governing particular agencies may require target notification, as in the case of the third-party summons of the IRS. As noted in § 16.10, a few of the "privacy" statutes also authorize court-ordered "gag" directives prohibiting notification by the third-party for 90 days (with a possible renewal). Similarly, the IRS third-party provision establishes a "John Doe Summons" in which the taxpayer/target need not be identified (and not given notice), but that requires a judicial finding that (1) there is "a reasonable basis for believing" that the John Doe (or John Does) "may fail or may have failed to comply with* * * [the] internal revenue law" and (2) the "information sought is not readily available from other sources."

Absent the command of a statute or administrative regulation, the agency issuing the third-party subpoena has no obligation to give notice to the customer. *SEC v. Jerry T. O'Brien, Inc.*, 467 U.S. 735 (1984). The *O'Brien* Court noted that agencies, such as the SEC, commonly undertake investigations into "suspicious activities" involving a high number of parties ("often without any knowledge of which parties involved may have violated the law"), and notifying all of those parties would be "virtually impossible". Also, notice "would substantially increase the ability of persons who have something to hide to impede the investigation". Of course, in the absence of special provisions that authorize court orders directing the third party not to inform its customers of the subpoena, the agency will lack authority to keep the third-party provider from notifying if it chooses to do so.

A customer made aware of the subpoena prior to compliance may seek to quash the subpoena in a judicial proceeding, but its challenge must satisfy the standing requirements for the particular objection. Thus, *U.S. v. Miller*, 425 U.S. 435 (1976), held that a customer could not raise a Fourth Amendment challenge to a subpoena requiring disclosure of bank records as those records were not the customer's property. Statutory provisions requiring customer notification typically establish standing by providing for a timely customer challenge. The challenges they authorize, however, are largely limited to relevancy and legitimacy grounds, thus providing a parallel to the key prongs of the *Powell* objection. In *Jerry T. O'Brien*, supra, the Court assumed *arguendo* that a target could intervene and challenge an administrative subpoena under the *Powell* standards. Where third-party disclosure allegedly would result in a violation of a testimonial privilege of the customer, intervention also is allowed.

§ 17.06   CRIMINAL REFERRALS AND CONTINUING INVESTIGATIONS

Most administrative agencies may conduct investigations that look to the possibility of both civil and criminal enforcement. Moreover, they may continue that investigation after a U.S. Attorney has initiated a grand jury inquiry (typically on the recommendation of the administrative agency), thereby creating one of the common types of parallel proceedings discussed in Ch. 18. The most prominent exception is the IRS. Because of the special character of IRS investigations, including the breadth of the group subject to such investigations (all taxpayers), and the character of the information that may be sought (personal financial information), IRS investigations are subject to limitations that distinguish investigations aimed at possible criminal prosecutions and shut down all investigative activity following a referral to the U.S. Attorney. See WCH § 17.6(B)

Initially, IRS regulations provide that, where an agent conducting a standard IRS audit, aimed at determining civil liability, finds "a firm indication of fraud", the audit must be suspended and a referral made to the Criminal Investigation Division ("CID"). If the CID pursues the matter through its agents (known as "special agents"), those agents, in soliciting further information from the taxpayer, must provide a warning that identifies the character of the investigation. Once the CID concludes that a criminal prosecution is appropriate and refers the case to the U.S. Attorney's office for possible prosecution, a further restriction applies. Under IRS Code § 7602, "no [IRS] summons may be issued * * * with respect to any person if a Justice Department referral is in effect with respect to such person". This provision shutting down the IRS investigation following a referral codified a portion of the ruling in *U.S. v. LaSalle National Bank*, 437 U.S. 298 (1978). The Court there concluded that a ban against post-referral use of the IRS summons followed logically from elements of the IRS investigative structure. It noted, in particular, that the IRS lost its authority to settle a civil action against the taxpayer once a referral was made, and allowing the IRS to use its summons authority to develop further evidence for the criminal case would improperly "broaden the Justice Department's right of criminal litigation discovery" and "infringe on the role of the grand jury as a principle tool of criminal investigation".

Lower courts have refused to extend the rationale of *LaSalle National Bank* to preclude post-referral issuance of administrative subpoenas by administrative agencies other than the IRS. In some instances, the agency statute specifically gives it the authority to investigate both criminal and civil violations, and in others, important enforcement responsibilities require that the agency be allowed to continue its civil investigation and bring it to a prompt close even while the DOJ is acting on the agency's referral and pursuing a criminal investigation. *SEC v. Dresser Industries*, 628 F.2d 1368 (D.C.Cir.1980) (noting that "unlike the IRS, which can postpone collection of taxes for the duration of parallel criminal proceedings without seriously impairing the public, the *SEC* must often act quickly, lest the false or incomplete statements of corporations mislead investors and infect the markets"). Also, because an agency's subpoena authority will be no broader than that of a grand jury, the courts see no potential for broadening the prosecution's "discovery rights" so long as the criminal investigation is still before the federal grand jury (i.e., the referral has not yet resulted in an indictment), as the grand jury could give the prosecution access to the same material. So too, while agency investigations may not be subject to secrecy provisions of the type imposed in the grand jury investigations, the courts do not see that as undercutting the independence or effectiveness of the grand jury investigation. Indeed, where the agency has the authority to investigate both civil and criminal violations, courts have even upheld a "joint investigation" strategy that selects the post-referral agency summons over the grand jury subpoena to obtain evidence both agency and grand jury desire, with the agency then sharing its evidence with the grand jury. WCH § 17.7.

§ 17.07 STAFF MISCONDUCT

While the administrative investigation may proceed alongside the criminal investigation, lower courts, looking to language in *U.S. v. Kordel* (see § 18.03), have concluded that certain actions taken to further the criminal investigation may violate due process and therefore preclude the use of the fruits of the administrative investigation in a subsequent prosecution. Initially the agency may not engage in an enforcement "solely to obtain evidence for the criminal investigation." See *U.S. v. Stringer*, 535 F.3d 929 (9th Cir.2008). However, where the agency investigation is aimed at enforcement of its regulatory responsibilities, that does not preclude shaping the investigation to develop evidence that would be particularly helpful in a subsequent criminal prosecution. *Stringer*.

Though an investigation may be valid in its objective, due process will also restrict the means used to achieve that objective. Under a principle drawn from IRS investigations, affirmative misrepresentations regarding the potential criminal component of the investigation can reach the level of a due process violation WCH §§ 17.6(B), 17.7. *Stringer* found no due process violation where the SEC relied on a printed form advising prospective witnesses that "the commission often makes its files available to * * * United States Attorneys", while informing a witness' counsel that its policy was not to respond to the question of whether it was working with the U.S. Attorney in this specific case (directing counsel to address any such inquiry to the U.S. Attorney's office), and structuring its investigation so as not to reveal the U.S. Attorney's ongoing criminal investigation and the SEC's cooperation with that investigation.

Typically, alleged staff misconduct, through actions like affirmative misrepresentations of possible criminal ramifications or failure to abide by internal regulatory restrictions (as in the IRS' "firm indication of fraud" provision, see § 17.06), is raised via a motion to suppress evidence obtained as a result of that misconduct. Suppression depends upon a finding of a due process violation, likely to require a strong showing of both bad faith and prejudice. *Powell* (§ 17.04), however, establishes the grounding for exploring misconduct in another procedural setting—the enforcement of a subpoena—which arguably does not require a misconduct showing reaching the level of a due process violation.

In *Powell*, the Supreme Court noted: "[I]t is the court's process which is invoked to enforce the administrative summons and a court may not permit its process to be abused." While the *Powell* Court made that statement in the course of discussing the district court's authority to refuse to enforce a subpoena issued for an improper purpose, several lower courts have held that it also supports refusing to enforce a subpoena that is the product of flagrant staff misconduct. Illustrative is *SEC v. ESM Government Securities, Inc.*, 645 F.2d 310 (5th Cir.1981), where ESM alleged that an SEC investigator deceived ESM in gaining access to its records (the investigator pretended to be interested only in gaining a basic education on the government securities market, while ESM was actually his investigative target), and that the information he obtained through that deception led to the issuance of the challenged subpoena. The Fifth Circuit concluded that if ESM's allegations were true—that the "SEC intentionally or knowingly mislead ESM about the purposes of its review of ESM's files", that "ESM [was] in fact mislead," and that the subpoena as to the particular documents requested was "a result of the SEC's allegedly improper access"—then enforcement of the subpoena as to those documents would be denied "as an abuse of process." The Fifth Circuit reasoned that "fraud, deceit, or trickery" by government agents could constitute "grounds for refusing enforcement," as the district court's obligation in "determining whether to enforce * * * [is to] evaluate the seriousness of the violation [by the staff] under all the circumstances, including the government's good faith and the degree of harm imposed by the unlawful conduct."

§ 17.08   THE ROLE OF COUNSEL

Unlike the grand jury witness, the witness subpoenaed to testify in an agency proceeding may be accompanied by counsel. Indeed, that right is recognized in the Administrative Procedures Act [APA § 6(a), 5 U.S.C. § 555(b)] as well as many agency regulations dealing specifically with investigations. Very often those agency regulations also will define the role of counsel. Thus, Rule 203.7 of the SEC's Rules Relating to Investigation states that the witness' right to counsel is a right to have the attorney "(1) advise such person before, during and after the conclusion of such examination, (2) question such person briefly at the conclusion of the examination to clarify any of the answers such person has given, and (3) make summary notes during such examination solely for the use of such person." 17 C.F.R. 203.7(c). The objective of such provisions is to preclude counsel from converting the agency's taking of testimony into a trial, with counsel offering objections and arguments, and requiring the staff examiner to explain the basis and relevance of each and every question.

In some instances, agency regulations seek to deter multiple representation by the same counsel. Thus, SEC Rule 203.7(c) allows counsel to make summary notes solely for the use of the witness counsel is then representing. Also, SEC Rule 203.7(b) provides that "all witnesses shall be sequestered, and unless permitted in the discretion of the officer conducting the investigation, no witness or the counsel accompanying any such witness shall be permitted to be present during the examination of any other witness called in such proceeding." 17 C.F.R § 203.7(b). While such provisions do not absolutely prohibit multiple representation, they can take away from a witness whose counsel has appeared with a previous witness the assistance of that counsel of choice during the witness' appearance before an examiner. However, that potential has been narrowed substantially by the D.C. Circuit's ruling that use of a sequestration provision to exclude the witness' counsel of choice contravenes the Administrative Procedure Act's guarantee of counsel unless the exclusion is based on "concrete evidence" that the agency investigation will be "obstructed or impeded" by the same counsel appearing with more than one witness. *Professional Reactor Operator Society v. U.S. Nuclear Regulatory Commission*, 939 F.2d 1047 (D.C.Cir.1991).

CHAPTER 18
PARALLEL PROCEEDINGS

§ 18.01 INTRODUCTION

With violations of regulatory statutes and administrative rules so often also creating criminal liability, administrative agency proceedings (both investigations and enforcement actions) may readily overlap in subject matter with criminal proceedings (both investigations and prosecutions). So too, with white collar offenses frequently also constituting common law torts and violations of statutes creating private causes of action (e.g. civil RICO), civil actions may readily overlap in subject matter with criminal proceedings. Where the civil or administrative proceedings and the criminal proceedings appear likely to produce such an overlap, they are commonly described as "parallel proceedings." Whether brought simultaneously or seriatim, parallel criminal and civil/administrative proceedings require the participants in those proceedings to give consideration to the bearing of one proceeding upon the other. That is especially true for the "dual target"—i.e., the person who is or anticipates being a defendant in a criminal prosecution (or at least the target of a criminal investigation) and who is or anticipates being a defendant in a civil or administrative proceeding (or at least the target of an administrative agency investigation).

Where the dual target must respond first in a civil suit or an administrative proceeding, the dual target must consider whether that response will be available to the prosecutor in the parallel criminal proceeding (see § 18.02), and if so, what benefits might that give to the prosecutor. Depending upon the nature of the dual target's response, a prosecutor could gain from that response: (1) incriminating evidence or leads to incriminating evidence; (2) recorded statements that can be used to impeach the target and the target's witnesses should they vary from those statements in their testimony in the criminal case, and that can provide, in any event, a useful springboard at an early date for preparing cross-examination; and (3) notice of the target's likely defense well in advance and in far greater depth than the notice that could be obtained through criminal discovery. Should these benefits for the prosecutor be likely, the dual target may seek to delay being required to respond until after the criminal proceeding reaches a conclusion (see § 18.03). If that should fail, the dual target may consider exercising the privilege against self-incrimination to limit the content of the response (see § 18.04).

Where the dual target must respond first in a criminal investigation, a major potential peril of cross-proceeding discovery is that opponents in a subsequent civil action or administrative proceeding will be able to obtain the product of the government's criminal investigation. Of special significance here is the reach of grand jury secrecy (see § 18.05) and the conditions under which materials covered by grand jury secrecy can be transferred to potential opponents in parallel civil and administrative actions (see §§ 18.06, 18.07). When required to respond initially to a criminal prosecution, the dual target must consider not only the cross-proceeding discovery that will be given to opponents in any subsequent parallel civil or agency actions by going to trial, but also the possibility that the prosecution could end in a guilty verdict that will bar the target from contesting critical issues in those other proceedings (see § 18.08).

§ 18.02   PROSECUTION DISCOVERY FROM PARALLEL PROCEEDINGS

What is disclosed at trial in a civil proceeding is open to the public, including, of course, the prosecutor. As for the documents recording disclosures made in civil discovery (e.g., deposition transcripts, interrogatories), those too ordinarily are public documents, freely open to inspection after being filed with the clerk. And even where local rule allows the documents of discovery not to be filed, an opposing party would be free to deliver that material to the prosecutor, and if the opposing party resisted a prosecutorial request, the grand jury could subpoena that material.

Under Rule 26(c) of the Federal Rules of Civil Procedure, a district court may issue a protective order that places discovery depositions under seal and forbids the disclosure of discovery beyond the litigants. Federal courts are divided as whether such an order precludes obtaining the sealed material in a grand jury investigation. WCH § 18.2(c). The Second Circuit has held that where such a protective order was issued because critical witnesses otherwise would have relied on their self-incrimination privilege to refuse to provide deposition testimony, the order prevailed over a grand jury subpoena for the record of their deposition testimony. Three other circuits take the opposite position, concluding that the grand jury subpoena always "trumps a district court's protective order." They reason, inter alia, that: (1) the grand jury has need for such deposition testimony even if it can gain the witness' testimony by granting immunity because it must determine whether the immunized testimony is truthful, and (2) allowing the protective order to prevail over the subpoena constitutes, in effect, a judicial grant of immunity as to that deposition testimony, which is contrary to executive branch authority to control immunity grants (see § 19.12). Two other circuits have taken what has been described as a "middle position": a grand jury subpoena will not invariably trump a protective order, but there is a strong (albeit rebuttable) presumption that the grand jury subpoena will prevail. Under this position, to preclude disclosure, the subpoenaed party must "sho[w] the existence of exceptional circumstances that clearly favor enforcing the protective order against the grand jury subpoena."

Statutes governing agency investigations commonly treat information acquired through agency investigative subpoenas as "confidential," rather than as matter of public record. However, they also allow for disclosures in the public interest, which clearly encompasses disclosure to a prosecuting authority. Indeed, agency regulations often encourage staff to inform the Department of Justice or U.S. Attorney's office of agency investigations with criminal implications long before a formal referral is made. A notable exception is § 6103 of Internal Revenue Code, which restricts IRS disclosure of information collected in tax administration and enforcement, giving the greatest protection to "taxpayer return information" (tax returns and other information furnished by the taxpayer). Where taxpayer return information appears to relate to criminal activity, it may be disclosed to federal prosecutors, but that requires an "ex parte order [issued] by a Federal district court judge or magistrate" upon a finding that: "(i) there is reasonable cause to believe, based upon information believed to be reliable, that a specific criminal act has been committed, (ii) there is reasonable cause to believe that the return or the return information is or may be relevant to a matter relating to the commission of such act, and (iii) the return or return information is sought exclusively for use in a Federal criminal investigation or proceeding concerning such act, and the information sought to be disclosed cannot reasonably be obtained, under the circumstances, from another source." See WCH § 16.10(D)(2).

§ 18.03 DELAYING THE PARALLEL CIVIL OR ADMINISTRATIVE PROCEEDING

In *U.S. v. Kordel*, 397 U.S. 1 (1970), the Supreme Court rejected the defendants' contention that they had been denied due process by a sequence of events that included the government's initial filing of an in rem action against two food products produced by the corporation of which they were officers, notification shortly thereafter that the FDA was recommending their criminal prosecution, denial of their request to stay the civil action or extend their time for answering interrogatories until after the disposition of the anticipated criminal proceedings, and the subsequent use in the criminal prosecution of their answers to those interrogatories. Though recognizing that individuals who are the targets of parallel civil and criminal proceedings face certain perils when required to respond to the civil action in advance of the criminal proceeding (although compulsory incrimination was not one of these perils, since they could exercise the privilege against self-incrimination in the civil action), the Court concluded that there was no constitutional mandate that dual targets be relieved of those perils by the issuance of a stay of the discovery in the civil proceeding. To mandate an automatic stay of the civil proceedings "would stultify enforcement of Federal law" by requiring government agencies "invariably to choose either to forego recommendation of criminal prosecution once it seeks civil relief or to defer civil proceedings pending ultimate outcome of a criminal trial."

The *Kordel* Court held open, however, the possibility that certain circumstances might produce a due process violation either in denying a stay or in allowing the government to use in a criminal case the fruits of its civil discovery. It noted: "We do not deal here with a case where the Government has brought a civil action solely to obtain evidence for its criminal prosecution or has failed to advise the defendant in its civil proceeding that it contemplates his criminal prosecution; nor with a case where the defendant is without counsel or reasonably fears prejudice from adverse pretrial publicity or other unfair injury; nor with any other special circumstances that might suggest the unconstitutionality or even the impropriety of this criminal prosecution."

Although a stay may not be constitutionally mandated, the federal district court, under Fed.R.Civ.P. 26(c), has discretion to grant a stay, as does an administrative agency. In determining whether to grant a stay requested by a dual target, courts and agencies tend to apply a balancing test, weighing (1) the harm that will be suffered by the moving party from the failure to grant the stay, (2) the interest of the opposing party in proceeding expeditiously (including any prejudice it might suffer through the delay), (3) the concerns of interested persons who are not a party to the litigation (including, in particular, the "public interest"), and (4) the interests of the court in maximizing judicial efficiency.

Courts have noted that the "strongest case" for deferring civil proceedings comes when the parallel criminal proceeding has reached the indictment stage. At that point, the likely period of deferment is more predictable and ordinarily shorter than the deferment granted during an ongoing criminal investigation. Because the prosecutor cannot use the grand jury to gather further evidence once the indictment is issued (see § 16.08), there is greater concern that the prosecutor will use the civil proceeding (at least where the government is a party) to gain discovery not available through the Rules of Criminal Procedure. Also, with the government having made a firm commitment to prosecute, the defendant is under greater pressure to accept the adverse consequences (even a default) that may accompany reliance on the self-incrimination privilege (see § 18.04), rather than risk giving the prosecution valuable discovery through her presentation in the civil case. Even with these considerations working in favor of a post-indictment deferment, however, the stay will not be granted if the alleged civil violations are ongoing and threaten continued injury to the public.

The defense may prefer to go forward with the civil action, rather than seek a stay, when the government is the opposing party and the defense concludes that the civil discovery process will produce more benefit than harm as a result of what it will learn about the case the government is likely to present in the criminal prosecution. Here, it is the government who often will be seeking to stay the civil case. Courts have tended to grant such requests on the ground that administrative policy gives priority to the public interest in law enforcement. Where the criminal defendant brought the civil action against the government, there often is concern that the action was brought simply to obtain such discovery.

Weighing the government's interest becomes more complex when the dual target is proceeded against in an administrative enforcement action, the U.S. Attorney intervenes to request a stay to preclude the target's efforts to obtain discovery as to evidence likely to be used in any criminal proceeding, but the administrative agency prefers to press forward with the enforcement action. The issue becomes easier, however, if the target's discovery efforts are resisted in a way that restricts the target in preparing a defense in the enforcement action (e.g. witnesses who are sources for both the criminal investigation and the enforcement action cannot be deposed effectively because of their exercise of the privilege against self-incrimination), as the stay is then supported by the interests of both the U.S. Attorney and the target. Where the administrative enforcement action is brought against both the target and other defendants who are not targets, the U.S. Attorney, to gain a stay that will extend to those other defendants, will have to show that they too are seeking discovery that relates to the criminal prosecution (possibly as a "stalking horse" for the target). See WCH § 18.5(C).

§ 18.04   ASSERTING THE SELF-INCRIMINATION PRIVILEGE

A person may claim the privilege against self-incrimination in a civil case or administrative proceeding if the person's testimony realistically could provide the government with a link in the chain of evidence needed to prosecute for a crime (see § 19.02). In the civil case, the privilege may be claimed not only as to questions posed at trial or in depositions, but also as to interrogatories, requests for admissions, and subpoenas to produce documents (see § 20.02). The privilege is not available to entities (see § 20.07), so the entity that is the defendant or plaintiff in a civil action cannot rely on the privilege to refuse to answer interrogatories. Should the officer of the entity designated to answer them refuse on the ground that the answers would tend to incriminate the officer personally, the burden lies on the entity to find some other agent who can provide the answers. Where the exercise of the privilege by all knowledgeable witnesses places the entity in a position where it cannot establish its claim (as a plaintiff) or present a defense (as a defendant), it may seek a stay (or a protective order that convinces the witnesses to testify), but if such relief is unavailable, it simply must bear the consequences. See *Afro-Lecon, Inc. v. U.S.*, 820 F.2d 1198 (1987) (stay should not have been denied simply because the entity was a plaintiff, and its inability to produce the accounting needed to sustain its claim stemmed from the exercise of the privilege by key witnesses who had connections to the entity).

The exercise of the privilege by a civil plaintiff or defendant is not without costs. If the party claiming the privilege thereby finds herself unable to present evidence supporting her side of the case, the consequence is likely to be a summary judgment. Moreover, courts may take remedial action because the party claiming the privilege has disadvantaged the opposing party by depriving that party of a useful source of evidence. Since an individual has a right to claim the privilege and since litigants do not have a right to discovery of privileged materials, courts have emphasized that any such remedy should be aimed at repairing the disadvantage rather than punishing the exercise of the privilege. *SEC v. Graystone Nash Inc.*, 25 F.3d 187 (3d Cir.1994). Ordinarily, the entry of a dismissal or a default judgment would be viewed as punishment, but it may be justified in extreme cases, as where the exercise of the privilege results in a wholesale denial of discovery. Older cases suggest that a dismissal is always appropriate where the plaintiff exercises the privilege to restrict discovery as the plaintiff should be viewed as "automatically waiving" the privilege in seeking judicial relief. The prevailing view, however, is to tailor the remedy to the impact of the exercise of the privilege.

One common response to the exercise of the privilege, in both civil and administrative actions, is to bar the admission of particular evidence where the party's exercise of the privilege kept from the opposing party the means of challenging that evidence. *Gutierrez-Rodriguez v. Cartagena*, 882 F.2d 553 (1st Cir.1989). Another common response is to allow the finder of fact to draw an adverse inference as to the information not received (see § 19.09). Thus, where a defendant in a civil case exercises the privilege in responding to interrogatories, the plaintiff can ask the jury to assume that the answer not given would have been that most unfavorable to the defendant. So too, where a party relies on the privilege and refuses to respond to the evidentiary supported material facts set forth in a motion for summary judgment, the court may view that refusal as an admission of those facts. See *LaSalle Bank Lake View v. Seguban*, 54 F.3d 387 (7th Cir.1995) (also noting, however, that the assertion of the privilege cannot be treated as an admission of liability, producing an automatic summary judgment.)

As noted in § 19.09, a government licensee or employee cannot automatically lose the license or employment because that person exercises the privilege in an administrative investigation or enforcement proceeding. But here too the power to draw an adverse inference may lead to the same loss (particularly in enforcement proceedings, as the government there will have additional evidence that led to the institution of the proceeding). Should the government erroneously threaten to go beyond drawing an adverse inference, and the individual respond by testifying in light of that "compulsion," the subsequent use of that testimony (and fruits derived therefrom) will be prohibited. See § 19.12; WCH § 18.4.

Ordinarily, when a non-party witness invokes the privilege, no adverse inference may be drawn. However, where the witness is so closely connected to the party as to be "within its control" (e.g., officers of an entity) and has particular knowledge of its activities, an adverse inference may be drawn against that party.

§ 18.05   GRAND JURY MATTER

Insofar as information obtained by the prosecution during a criminal investigation is governed by the Rule 6(e)(2) provision on grand jury secrecy (see § 16.09), the prosecution can only share that information with potential litigants in parallel proceedings where the conditions prescribed in Rule 6(e)(3) are met (see §§ 18.06, 18.07). When the information is not governed by Rule 6(e)(2), the prosecution ordinarily is free to share the information if it deems sharing to be in the public interest (which will almost invariably be the case where the criminal process has reached its end and the information would be useful to other government offices in bringing a parallel civil or administrative action).

Rule 6(e)(2) applies to a "matter occurring before the grand jury." That phrase is a term of art, not to be construed literally as encompassing only events that have taken place before the grand jury. *In re: Sealed Case No. 99–3091*, 192 F.3d 995 (D.C. Cir.1999) ("matter before the grand jury" extends to "anticipated testimony" and "strategy and direction" of grand jury presentations, though not the "internal deliberations of prosecutors"). Thus, "grand jury matter" will include an office interview given by a subpoenaed witness in lieu of a grand jury appearance, a prosecution memorandum describing documents or testimony that was presented to the grand jury, and an expert's report to the prosecutor that served as the basis for the experts' final conclusion, which alone was given to the grand jury.

On the other hand Rule 6(e)(2) does not apply to material generated independently of the grand jury even though similar material was later presented to the grand jury. Thus, where FBI agents independently obtain through interviews with possible witnesses information that is relevant both to an ongoing grand jury investigation and an administrative investigation, they may disclose that information to the administrative agency even though the persons interviewed subsequently testified before the grand jury (and presumably conveyed the same information in that testimony). *In re Grand Jury Subpoena (U.S. v. Under Seal)*, 920 F.2d 235 (4th Cir.1990). So too, where the prosecutor learns of the existence of a document through sources independent of the grand jury, and desires to acquire that document in a fashion that will permit sharing it with an administrative agency without having to meet the requirements of Rule 6(e)(3), the prosecutor may achieve that end by obtaining the document through process other than a grand jury subpoena (e.g., by use of a search warrant or by requesting that the agency utilize its own subpoena power to obtain the document). *U.S.*

v. Educational Development Network, discussed in § 17.06.

Even where documents were obtained by grand jury subpoena and were presented to the grand jury, they may not be treated as grand jury matter in all possible disclosure situations. Consider, for example, the situation in which the document in question was preexisting (i.e., it was not prepared for the purpose of complying with the subpoena), the prosecutor did not return the document to the subpoenaed party after presenting it to the grand jury, a civil litigant or government agency was aware of the document and sought to obtain it from the subpoenaed party, that party then responded that the document had been subpoenaed by the grand jury and was currently in the possession of the prosecutor, and the civil litigant or government agency then sought to obtain the document from the prosecutor. Although a few earlier decisions viewed such disclosure as per se subject to Rule 6(e)(2), later decisions, while varying in the standards applied, hold that disclosure does not fall within Rule 6(e)(2) (and therefore does not require a Rule 6(e)(3) court order) in at least some circumstances. Indeed, most circuits have adopted standards that ordinarily make Rule 6(e)(2) inapplicable (e.g. that the Rule applies only where the document is sought to "learn what occurred before the grand jury" or only when disclosure of the document would "reveal the inner workings of the grand jury"). See WCH § 18.3(B).

§ 18.06 THE "PRELIMINARY TO" REQUIREMENT

Rule 6(e)(3) sets forth several exceptions to the basic secrecy requirement of Rule 6(e)(2) (see § 16.09). Each exception authorizes disclosure of grand jury matter to persons who were not present during the grand jury proceeding. Most of these exceptions relate to disclosure to implement criminal law enforcement, as in (1) disclosure to U.S. Attorneys and other DOJ attorneys for use in enforcing federal criminal law; (2) disclosure to assisting personnel, including agency personnel designated by the prosecutor as needed to assist in the grand jury's criminal investigation (with such personnel specifically prohibited from "utilizing that grand jury material for any purpose other than assisting the attorney for the government in the performance of such attorney's duty to enforce federal criminal law"); (3) disclosure to another grand jury; and (4) disclosure to a state prosecuting official for the purpose of enforcing state criminal law. The only Rule 6(e)(3) exception possibly authorizing disclosure to a prospective litigant in a parallel civil or administrative action is found in subdivision 6(e)(3)(E)(i)—providing for court-ordered disclosure "preliminary to or in connection with a judicial proceeding."

Where the parallel proceeding is a civil action, and is already underway, it will meet the "in connection with" portion of the Rule 6(e)(3)(E)(i) standard. Where the civil action has not yet been filed, but is readily anticipated, that is sufficient to meet the "preliminary to" standard. The major hurdle arises where the proceeding first anticipated is an administrative proceeding, for Rule 6(e)(3)(E)(i) refers only to a "judicial" proceeding. As the Supreme Court noted in *U.S. v. Baggot*, 463 U.S. 476 (1983), this limitation "reflects a judgment that not every beneficial purpose, or even every valid government purpose, is an appropriate reason for breaching grand jury secrecy." Rather, only "uses related fairly directly to some identifiable litigation" in a court were thought to merit such a breach.

Baggot held that disclosure to the IRS for use in an IRS audit of civil tax liability did not fall within the "preliminary to" requirement since the IRS's calculation and collection of any amount determined by it to be due did not require judicial intervention. The mere possibility that the taxpayer might challenge the agency's non-judicial means of enforcing its determination would not make the agency proceeding "preliminary to a judicial proceeding." On the other side, where an administrative proceeding requires a judicial determination for enforcement (as in attorney disbarment), disclosure to assist the agency in its proceeding generally is treated as within the "preliminary to" requirement. Indeed, courts here have held that the same is true where judicial review is not mandatory, but still plays "a significant role" in the "operation of the regulatory/statutory scheme." See WCH § 18.3(C). Of course, as to any administrative proceeding, the agency investigation may be at such a preliminary stage, far removed from a substantial likelihood of a finding that would require judicial enforcement, that disclosure could not yet be viewed as preliminary to a judicial proceeding. *Baggot* specifically left open what was needed in this regard, although noting that the possibility the individual might consent to the agency's proposed sanction should not be sufficient to negate the anticipated judicial proceeding.

§ 18.07   PARTICULARIZED NEED

Disclosure under Rule 6(e)(3)(E)(i) also requires that the party seeking disclosure establish a "particularized need"—i.e., establish that "the need for disclosure is greater than the need for continued secrecy, and that th[e] request is structured to cover only material so needed." *Douglas Oil Co. of California v. Petrol Stops Northwest*, 441 U.S. 211 (1979). The Supreme Court and the circuit courts have pointed to a variety of factors that should be weighed by a district court in the balancing required by the particularized need standard. See WCH § 18.3(E).

Initially, the court should look to the status of the investigation that produced the requested grand jury material. The need for secrecy clearly is greatest while the grand jury is still gathering evidence and considering whether to indict. Once the grand jury is finished with the matter, the need for secrecy declines and the movant's burden in establishing a particularized need declines. As the Supreme Court noted in *Douglas Oil*, however, the value of grand jury secrecy is only "reduced," not "eliminated," by the termination of the investigation, for consideration must be given to the long term impact of disclosure, extending beyond the particular case. Frequent authorization of disclosure will undercut the effectiveness of the promise of secrecy in gaining the cooperation of grand jury witnesses.

Another factor weighed is whether the third party seeks disclosure that might subject grand jury witnesses to "retribution or social stigma." One of the considerations that the Supreme Court found to weigh against disclosure to a participant in a civil antitrust suit was that witnesses in an antitrust investigation often are employees of the target companies, or their customers, competitors or suppliers, and might face discharge or other forms of retaliation if their testimony were disclosed to their employers. *U.S. v. Procter & Gamble*, 356 U.S. 677 (1958). On the other hand, if there already has been substantial disclosure of the grand jury materials to the investigated companies (as where the companies were indicted and gained the witness's statements in the course of criminal discovery), disclosure to the other parties in the parallel civil suit is less likely to cause concern.

Another important consideration is the narrowness of the disclosure requested. Under a standard of "particularized" need, a request for broad disclosure will almost certainly work against the petitioner, as it did in *Procter & Gamble,* where the Court characterized the rejected request as seeking "wholesale discovery." As the Supreme

Court has noted, the "typical showing of particularized need arises when a civil litigant seeks to use the grand jury transcript at the trial to impeach a witness, to refresh his recollection, to test his credibility and the like." The disclosure there "can be limited to those portions of a particular witness' testimony that bear upon his * * * direct testimony at trial." *Douglas Oil.* In addition, such requests are less likely to be based on a speculative judgment as to need, while the use involved serves the important interest of ensuring that the factfinder is not misled. In assessing need even as to fairly limited disclosure, however, the court also must take into consideration the availability of alternative means (such as civil discovery) that might produce the same information. The fact that disclosure will avoid the significant expense and delay of the alternative means is not in itself sufficient to establish the requisite need.

Where the request for disclosure comes from a governmental agency pursuing an administrative or civil claim, many courts have required a somewhat lesser showing of particularized need. The Supreme Court has rejected the contention that a government agency can justify disclosure simply by showing the relevancy of the requested material, but it has also said that the balancing process may be somewhat different for disclosure to government bodies as opposed to private parties. The Court has noted in particular that "the district court may weigh the public interest, if any, served by disclosure to a government body—along with the requisite particularized need—in determining whether the need for disclosure is greater than the need for continued secrecy." *Illinois v. Abbot & Associates*, 460 U.S. 557 (1983). Thus, where the contemplated disclosure was to civil attorneys within the government for the purpose of deciding whether to file a civil action, the district court could properly take into account the likelihood that the disclosure would "sav[e] the Government, the potential defendants, and witnesses, the pains of costly and time consuming depositions and interrogatories which might later have turned out to be wasted if the Government decided not to file a civil action after all." *U.S. v. John Doe, Inc. I*, 481 U.S. 102 (1987). Accordingly too, while the governmental agency's capacity to obtain the same information through its own investigative authority is a consideration weighing against the need for disclosure, that factor cannot be treated as a per se bar against authorizing disclosure. Indeed, that authority may strengthen the case for disclosure as it responds to another concern noted by the Court— that the use of grand jury materials by other government agencies not "threaten to subvert the limitations applied outside the grand jury context on the Government's powers of discovery and investigation." *John Doe, Inc. I.*

§ 18.08   COLLATERAL ESTOPPEL

A defendant who goes to trial in a criminal case must consider the dual perils of disclosure and collateral estoppel as they relate to subsequent parallel civil and administrative actions. The trial puts on the public record the prosecution's case and the defendant's defense, making them available to prospective opponents in the parallel proceedings. Information that was protected by grand jury secrecy becomes available to all when the prosecution presents that information through its witnesses and documents at trial.

Of course, the prosecution's evidence may fail to convince the criminal jury, but that does not necessarily mean that it will fail to convince the finder of fact when duplicated (or improved upon) in the parallel proceeding, where there is a lower standard of proof. Even if the parallel civil proceeding involves precisely the same issue and is brought by the government, that lower proof standard means the acquitted defendant cannot use the doctrine of collateral estoppel. *U.S. v. One Assortment of 89 Firearms*, 465 U.S. 354 (1984). On the other hand, should the defendant be convicted, by trial or by guilty plea, in the subsequent civil or administrative action, collateral estoppel will treat that conviction as conclusive as to any issue determined by the criminal case. In some instances, this will mean that the only issue left to be resolved in the civil action is that of damages.

A criminal conviction based on a plea of *nolo contendere*, however, is treated differently. Although a plea of *nolo contendere* supports a conviction, it technically is not an admission of guilt (defendant saying, in effect, "I do not contest"). Accordingly, a defendant who has pleaded *nolo contendere* is not estopped from denying in a subsequent civil proceeding the facts on which the criminal charge was based, and the conviction based on a *nolo* plea is not evidence that the defendant committed the crime. *Hudson v. U.S.*, 272 U.S. 451 (1926).

For a criminal defendant more concerned about the consequences of anticipated parallel proceedings than the consequences of a conviction (often the case for an entity), the preferred strategy may be to enter a plea of *nolo contendere* rather than provide discovery and risk both a conviction and collateral estoppel by contesting guilt at trial. The *nolo contendere* plea, however, can be entered only with the approval of the district court. Moreover, Rule 11(b) of the Federal Rules of Criminal Procedure directs the court to accept such a plea only after giving due consideration to "the parties' views and the public interest in the effective administration of justice." The plea is more likely to be accepted where the government does not object, but that lack of objection may require negotiated concessions by the defendant relating to restitution and other remedial orders.

CHAPTER 19

THE SELF-INCRIMINATION PRIVILEGE: TESTIMONY

§ 19.01 APPLICABILITY OF THE PRIVILEGE

The Fifth Amendment's self-incrimination clause provides that "no person * * * shall be compelled in any criminal case to be a witness against himself." It was not until more than a century after the Amendment's adoption that the Supreme Court, in *Counselman v. Hitchcock*, 142 U.S. 547 (1892), put to rest the possibility that this Fifth Amendment privilege was available only to a defendant refusing to be compelled to testify in the defendant's own criminal case. *Counselman* presented the exercise of the privilege by a grand jury witness and the Court concluded that a grand jury proceeding was part of the criminal case (a broader term than the Sixth Amendment's "criminal prosecution"). The Court went on to note that, in any event, the Fifth Amendment "criminal case" requirement referred only to the eventual use of the compelled testimony, not to the nature of the proceeding in which the testimony was compelled. Accordingly, the privilege was available to an individual "in any proceeding" who is being compelled by subpoena to give testimony that might be used against him in a subsequent criminal case. A realistic potential for such use sufficed and that potential depended on the nature of the witness' answer to the question asked, not the nature of the proceeding in which the question was asked.

Counselman's analysis led to a long line of cases holding the self-incrimination privilege available to witnesses in various noncriminal proceedings, including civil cases and administrative hearings. These rulings traditionally were understood as resting on the premise that the Fifth Amendment violation occurred with the prohibited compulsion, as suggested in *Counselman*, but that premise was rejected by a majority in *Chavez v. Martinez*, 538 U.S. 760 (2003). In *Chavez*, four justices described the rulings making the privilege available in noncriminal proceedings as establishing a "prophylactic rule", and two others described those rulings as establishing "complementary protection" that went beyond the Fifth Amendment's "core guarantee". These descriptions followed from the view that the compulsion alone did not violate the self-incrimination privilege; the violation also required the government's use of the compelled testimony against the individual in a criminal case, as only that made the individual "a witness against himself". Allowing the witness in a noncriminal proceeding to rely on the privilege at the point of testifying was necessary, however, to protect against the possible subsequent violation of the privilege through the admission of compelled testimony in a subsequent criminal case. If the witness in a noncriminal proceeding could not raise the privilege at that point, but instead was told to testify and raise his self-incrimination challenge when (and if) that testimony was later used against him in a criminal case, the court there would have to decide whether the testimony had truly been a product of the compulsion of the subpoena or was made voluntarily notwithstanding the subpoena (see § 19.05). The end result might be inadequate protection of the privilege due to erroneous factfinding error on that issue. The *Counselman* analysis, under this view, requires assertion of the privilege at the point of testifying in the noncriminal proceedings in order to "memorialize the fact that [any] testimony [that followed] had indeed been compelled", not because the self-incrimination clause would be violated in the compulsion alone. This analysis had no bearing on the availability of the privilege to witnesses in noncriminal proceedings, but did relate to the issue posed in *Chavez* (whether a damage remedy would be available for compulsion alone on the theory that the compulsion itself violated the Fifth Amendment privilege).

§ 19.02   POTENTIAL FOR INCRIMINATION

The Fifth Amendment privilege is available, of course, only if the compelled testimony carries the potential of later being used against the witness as a defendant in a criminal case. This requires a content that potentially would be harmful to a criminal defendant. Although that covers a great deal, it is not without limits. Thus, the Supreme Court has noted that content is incriminating only as it relates to criminal liability, *Ullman v. U.S.*, 350 U.S. 422 (1956) (civil disabilities and social stigma, no matter how severe, are not sufficient), and that the potential incriminating character must relate to the witness' own criminal liability, not the

criminal liability of others, *Rogers v. U.S.*, 340 U.S.
367 (1951). Moreover, the potential for criminal
incrimination must be "real and appreciable," not
"imaginary and unsubstantial." *Brown v. Walker*,
161 U.S. 591 (1896).

A witness' assertion of the privilege does not, in
itself, establish that the witness' testimony would
have this potentially incriminating quality. As
Hoffman v. U.S., 341 U.S. 479 (1951), stressed, "it is
for the court to say whether [the witness'] silence is
justified, and to require him to answer 'if it clearly
appears to the court that he is mistaken.' " *Hoffman*
also indicated, however, that courts are to give the
witness every benefit of the doubt in reviewing an
assertion of the privilege. "The privilege," the Court
noted, applies "not only to answers that would in
themselves support a conviction but likewise * * *
those which would furnish a link in the chain of
evidence needed to prosecute the claimant." The
witness must have "reasonable cause" to believe
that his testimony would have this potential, but he
cannot be expected to "prove * * * [that] hazard in
the sense in which a claim is usually required to be
established in court," as that would "compel * * *
[the witness] to surrender the very protection which
the privilege is designed to guarantee." Accordingly,
to sustain the witness' claim, "it need only be
evident from the implications of the question, in the
setting in which it is asked, that a responsive
answer to the question or an explanation of why it
cannot be answered might be dangerous because
injurious disclosure could result."

The *Hoffman* case also provides a fine illustration of the need for the court to look to all surrounding circumstances and to imagine the worst in the witness' possible responses in determining whether there is a "real and appreciable" possibility that the witness' testimony will furnish that "link in the chain of evidence" sufficient to make it incriminating. The Supreme Court there ruled that the district court had erred in holding the privilege inapplicable to questions concerning the witness' current occupation and his contacts with a person who was a fugitive witness. Since the lower court was aware that the grand jury was investigating racketeering, it should have recognized that questions concerning Hoffman's current occupation might require answers relating to violations of various gambling laws. It also should have recognized that the answers to questions concerning Hoffman's contacts with the fugitive witness could have referred to efforts to hide that witness, which would be criminal.

Although *Hoffman* suggests that witness claims of the privilege will usually be sustained without requiring any specific explanation of the possibilities for incrimination, special settings may impose that burden upon the witness. One such setting is the questioning of the witness regarding criminal acts for which the witness already has been convicted (assuming that the conviction is "final", so the double jeopardy will bar any reprosecution for that offense). Here, the usual assumption is that the individual "no longer has the privilege against self-incrimination as he can no longer be incriminated by his testimony about the crime." *Reina v. U.S.*, 364 U.S. 507 (1960). However, as illustrated by *Malloy v. Hogan*, 378 U.S. 1 (1964), the privilege may be available even as to such questioning under some circumstances. *Malloy* found error in a lower court's rejection of a self-incrimination claim by a witness who previously pled guilty to a gambling charge and was now being asked about the circumstances surrounding his arrest and plea. The Court noted that the questions were obviously designed to determine the identity of the witness' employer, and "if this person were still engaged in unlawful activity, disclosure of his identity might furnish a link in a chain of evidence sufficient to connect the [witness] with a more recent crime for which he still might be prosecuted."

In re Morganroth, 718 F.2d 161 (6th Cir.1983), presented another setting in which a court may assume that the self-incrimination claim is not based on a realistic threat. The witness there had previously testified in separate proceedings about the same transactions that were the subject of the current questions. The district court held that the privilege did not apply to questions identical to those asked earlier, and the Sixth Circuit affirmed, concluding that the witness had failed to furnish sufficient information to establish a reasonably grounded risk of incrimination. Both the questions propounded and the witness' answers to these questions in the earlier proceedings had an entirely "innocent" content, and the Sixth Circuit rejected the witness' claim that the risk of incrimination per se existed because answers truthful in light of his current memory of events could be inconsistent with his earlier testimony, and thus lead to a perjury prosecution. To require no more to sustain an assertion of the privilege, the court reasoned, would give every witness who had happened to testify previously on an overlapping subject matter the capacity, no matter how innocuous the questions asked, to become, in effect, the "final arbiter" of the validity of his self-incrimination claim.

§ 19.03 INCRIMINATION UNDER THE LAWS OF ANOTHER SOVEREIGN

For many years, American courts took the position that the self-incrimination privilege protected only against incrimination under the laws of the sovereign which was compelling the witness' testimony. Thus, if a witness in a federal proceeding was granted immunity against federal prosecution, he could not refuse to testify on the ground that his answers might be incriminating under the laws of a state or a foreign nation. In *Murphy v. Waterfront Commission*, 378 U.S. 52 (1964), the Supreme Court rejected this "separate sovereign" doctrine as applied to state and federal incrimination. Noting that the doctrine would allow a witness to be "whipsawed into incriminating himself under both state and federal law," the Court concluded that the "policies and purposes" of the Fifth Amendment require that the privilege protect "a state witness against incrimination under federal as well as state law and a federal witness against incrimination under state as well as federal law."

As *Murphy* noted, where a witness in a federal proceeding claims potential state incrimination, the federal government has the authority to grant the witness immunity that extends to state proceedings, and that immunity permits it to compel the witness' testimony. As for the states, *Murphy* held that where a state granted immunity to a witness, the federal government would be prohibited (under the Court's supervisory power) from making any use of the testimony given under that immunity, so that the state immunity, like the federal, would operate upon both sovereigns (see § 19.11). In contrast, neither the federal government nor the states have the authority to grant immunity against foreign prosecution. Elimination of the dual sovereignty doctrine as applied to foreign prosecutions would place the state and federal systems in a position where they could not supplant the privilege and compel the testimony with a grant of immunity. This consideration was noted in *U.S. v. Balysys*, 524 U.S. 666 (1998), where the Court held that incrimination under the laws of a foreign country was beyond the protection of the self-incrimination clause. The reference to "any criminal case" in the Fifth Amendment, the Court reasoned, extended only to prosecutions in jurisdictions subject to that Amendment (the federal government and the states, via the Fourteenth Amendment), and not to foreign nations.

§ 19.04   COMPELLING THE GRAND JURY TARGET TO APPEAR

The self-incrimination privilege has long been held to prohibit the prosecution from forcing a defendant to take the stand as a witness at his own trial and to then invoke the privilege as to specific questions; the defendant's privilege protects him from even being called to testify. Should the prosecutor similarly be prohibited from forcing the "target" of an investigation to appear before the grand jury, or is the Fifth Amendment satisfied by simply allowing the target-witness, like any other witness, to refuse to respond to individual questions where his answer might be incriminating? Federal courts have concluded that the target should be treated no differently than any other witness. "The obligation to appear," the Supreme Court has noted, "is no different for a person who may himself be the subject of the grand jury inquiry." *U.S. v. Dionisio*, 410 U.S. 1 (1973). The defendant's right of silence grew out of the early common law rule on the incompetency of parties to testify, which had bearing only on the trial.

Internal Justice Department guidelines provide a series of standards relating to subpoenaing targets. See WCH § 19.3. A target is defined as "a person as to whom the prosecutor or grand jury has substantial evidence linking him or her to the commission of a crime, and who, in the judgment of the prosecutor, is a putative defendant." A target who refuses to appear voluntarily may be subpoenaed, but only with the approval of both the grand jury and the federal prosecutor. In deciding whether to subpoena the target, consideration is to be given both to the importance of the target's anticipated testimony and the availability of alternative sources of information. If the target is subpoenaed, but then gives advance notice of an intention to claim the privilege, the target "ordinarily should be excused from testifying." The grand jury and prosecutor can jointly insist upon appearance, however, where justified by consideration of the importance of the testimony and the possible inapplicability of the privilege. Also, while not constitutionally compelled to do so (see § 19.06), federal prosecutors are directed to advise witnesses who are known targets of their target status.

§ 19.05 INVOCATION OF THE PRIVILEGE

A witness in any type of proceeding ordinarily must invoke the privilege on a question by question basis. A blanket objection is not satisfactory, although a court may terminate all further questioning along a certain line when the witness indicates that he intends to assert the privilege as to all questions relating to that particular topic. Above all, the witness must refuse to testify and note that his refusal is based on the privilege. The witness bears the responsibility for recognizing that the privilege would apply to his testimony and invoking it by refusing to give that testimony.

Should the witness simply testify, the privilege is lost as to that testimony (and often more, see

§ 19.08), even though his failure to assert the privilege may have been the product of ignorance or confusion regarding the existence and application of the privilege. This consequence occasionally has been described as a product of "waiver," but the Supreme Court has recognized that it is not sustained by the traditional standard for waiver of constitutional rights (requiring a "knowing and intelligent" relinquishment of the right). *Garner v. U.S.*, 424 U.S. 648 (1976). Rather, the invoke-or-forfeit standard rests on an analysis of the element of compulsion that was summarized by Justice Frankfurter in an oft-quoted passage from his dissent in *U.S. v. Monia*, 317 U.S. 424 (1943): "The Amendment speaks of compulsion. It does not preclude a witness from testifying voluntarily in matters which may incriminate him. If, therefore, he desires the protection of the privilege, he must claim it or, he will not be considered to have been 'compelled' within the meaning of the Amendment."

The Supreme Court has established three exceptions to what it has described as the "general rule" that the privilege is not "self-executing" (and therefore requires an affirmative assertion at the point of compulsion). These exceptions are: (1) "confessions obtained from suspects in police custody"; (2) situations in which the government threatens to impose a penalty if the individual asserts the privilege and thereby "forecloses a free-choice to remain silent"; and (3) instances in which "the assertion of privilege itself would lend to incriminate." See WCH § 19.2(H). The second and third exceptions often arise in the context of white collar investigations. The second exception involves penalties of the type discussed in § 19.09—the automatic imposition of regulatory sanctions or the automatic denial of a government benefit if the individual asserts the privilege. In the cases discussed in § 19.09, the individual responded to the threat by challenging the imposition of the penalty. But *Garrity v. N.J.* (see § 19.13) held that the individual did not need to pursue such a challenge. The individual there responded to the threat by providing incriminating testimony (as his government employer demanded) and the Court held that pressure had produced coerced testimony in violation of the Fifth Amendment. The failure to assert the privilege was excused as that failure was not voluntary, but the product of the pressure of the penalty which made "exercise of the privilege so costly that it could not be affirmatively asserted." The end result, as discussed in § 19.13, was to bar the government's use in a criminal case of the compelled testimony (and the fruits of that testimony).

The third exception has been held to apply where the government requires from the individual a regulatory report acknowledging participation in activity (e.g., gambling) that inherently indicates likely criminality. Here the individual may simply not file the report (rather than object to filing by asserting the privilege) and rely on the privilege as a defense if subsequently charged for the failure to file. This exception applies only where the filing requirement is limited to persons "inherently suspect of criminal activities." Thus, a person who would be incriminated by revealing the source of income on an income tax return must assert the privilege rather than simply ignore the directive to report all income. WCH § 19.1(H).

§ 19.06   ADVICE AS TO RIGHT

In *Miranda v. Arizona*, 384 U.S. 436 (1966), the Supreme Court held that the Fifth Amendment bars admission of a statement obtained by police through custodial interrogation of a suspect where the police have failed to advise the suspect of various rights relating to the self-incrimination privilege. The *Miranda* mandated advice, which has come to be known as the "*Miranda* warnings," includes informing the suspect of the right to "remain silent." In contrast, witnesses in judicial and administrative proceedings need not be advised of their right to exercise the privilege. As noted in *Monia* (see § 19.05), it is the witness' responsibility to assert the privilege under an invoke-or-forfeit standard. A presiding judicial officer has discretion to warn the witness when the question appears to call for an incriminating answer, but the failure to warn the witness does not excuse the witness' failure to invoke the privilege.

In *U.S. v. Mandujano*, 425 U.S. 564 (1976), the defendant argued that the rationale of *Miranda*, rather than that of *Monia*, should govern the testimony of a grand jury witness who was a "putative defendant," in that the witness was being questioned about an event for which the government already had probable cause to charge him. In the absence of appropriate warnings, Mandujano argued, his failure to invoke the privilege was irrelevant, and his grand jury testimony should be viewed as compelled (as in *Miranda*) rather than as voluntary (as in *Monia*). Because Mandujano had committed perjury in his grand jury testimony (which would not be excused even if his testimony had been compelled), the Supreme Court was able to affirm his perjury conviction without ruling on whether a "putative defendant" called before a grand jury has to be advised of his right to assert the privilege. However, six justices did speak to the need for self-incrimination warnings.

Chief Justice Burger's plurality opinion, speaking for four members of the Court, flatly rejected extension of *Miranda* to the grand jury setting. *Miranda*, he noted, applied only to the special setting of custodial interrogation. The position of a subpoenaed grand jury witness could hardly be compared to that of the arrestee subjected to police questioning in the "hostile" and "isolated" setting of the police station. See also *Minnesota v. Murphy*, 465 U.S. 420 (1984) (Court majority notes: "We have never held that [*Miranda* warnings] must be given to a grand jury witness").

Chief Justice Burger added that since Mandujano had been advised of his right to exercise the privilege against self-incrimination, there was no need to decide whether even that limited advice—less complete than the full set of *Miranda* warnings—was constitutionally required. However, the Chief Justice also stated that a grand jury witness' exercise of the privilege, whether or not a prospective defendant, should be governed by the compulsion analysis of *Monia*, and that analysis does not *require* that any warning be given. In a concurring opinion, Justice Brennan, joined by Justice Marshall, viewed the Chief Justice's reliance upon *Monia* as indicating no warning would be needed and expressed disagreement with that position.

Justice Brennan's opinion in *Mandujano* did not stop with requiring warnings as to the privilege alone. In his view, the Fifth Amendment also required the prosecution to inform a witness who was a putative defendant that "he was currently subject to possible criminal prosecution for the commission of a stated crime." In *U.S. v. Washington*, 431 U.S. 181 (1977), the Court rejected (over Justice Brennan's dissent) the contention that the Fifth Amendment requires some form of notification of "target" status. The witness there had been given full *Miranda*-type warnings, but had not been told that he was a primary suspect in the theft of a motorcycle as a result of his possession of the stolen motorcycle. The Court reasoned that a failure to give a potential defendant a target warning simply did not put the witness at a "constitutional disadvantage." His status as a target "neither enlarge[d] nor diminish[ed]" the scope of his constitutional protection. He "knew better than anyone else" whether his answers would be incriminating, and he also knew that anything he did say, after failing to exercise the privilege, could be used against him. The "constitutional guarantee," the Court noted, ensures "only that the witness be not *compelled* to give self-incriminating testimony."

Although the Supreme Court in *Washington* again found it unnecessary to decide whether a target witness has to be informed of the right to refuse to answer incriminating questions, that issue has largely been mooted by the Department of Justice guidelines on the questioning of grand jury witnesses. See WCH § 16.5(C). Under those guidelines, all witnesses who are either a "target" or a "subject" of the grand jury investigation are informed of several rights by a form attached to the grand jury subpoena. That form advises the witness of; (1) the general subject of investigation (e.g., "illegal gambling"); (2) the right "to refuse to answer any question if a truthful answer to the question would incriminate you"; (3) that any testimony given could be used against the witness by the grand jury or in a "subsequent legal proceeding"; and (4) that the witness will be given a reasonable opportunity to consult with retained counsel (see § 16.12). Since a "subject" is defined in the guidelines as "a person whose conduct is within the scope of the grand jury's investigation", the requirement that the advice be furnished to subjects as well as targets ensures coverage of virtually all persons in a position where possible incrimination reasonably could be anticipated. As noted in § 19.04, the Department of Justice guidelines also call for target warnings, although *Washington* made clear that such warnings are not constitutionally mandated.

§ 19.07 SEPARATE PROCEEDINGS

When a witness testifies as to particular activities in one proceeding, that does not prohibit the witness from claiming the privilege and refusing to testify as to the same activities in another proceeding (assuming the witness' testimony would be incriminating). The privilege is "proceeding specific," so that testifying in one proceeding does not relinquish the privilege as to the same information in a second proceeding. On occasion, however, there may be a question as whether separate hearings are necessarily separate proceedings. With a lone exception, federal circuits take the position that a grand jury inquiry and a subsequent trial are separate proceedings.

§ 19.08 SCOPE OF THE
TESTIMONIAL FORFEITURE

When a witness subject to the general rule (see § 19.05) fails to invoke the privilege and testifies, that witness relinquishes the privilege for that proceeding not only as to his testimony, but often also as to further information on the subject of his testimony. *Rogers v. U.S.*, 340 U.S. 367 (1951), is the leading case on the scope of such testimonial "forfeiture" or "waiver." The witness there testified before a grand jury that, as treasurer of the Communist Party of Denver, she had been in possession of party records, but had subsequently delivered those records to another person. She refused, however, to identify the recipient of the records, asserting that would be incriminating. A divided Supreme Court affirmed her contempt conviction, holding the privilege inapplicable. The Court noted that Rogers had already incriminated herself by admitting her party membership and past possession of the records; disclosure of her "acquaintanceship with her successor present[ed] no more than a 'mere imaginary possibility' of increasing the danger of prosecution." A witness would not be allowed to disclose a basic incriminating fact and then claim the privilege as to "details." To uphold such use of the privilege would "open the way to distortion of facts by permitting a witness to select any stopping point in her testimony."

Although *Rogers* often is described as posing great danger for the witness who answers even seemingly "innocuous questions," the decision actually is fairly limited. Lower courts have held, for example, that where a witness' initial admission related to only one element of an offense, that did not constitute a waiver as to questions that might require him to admit other elements of the offense. The fact that the second question asks for further detail as to the same event does not in itself establish that the privilege is not available. Indeed, most of the reported cases finding a forfeiture as to further information have involved, as did *Rogers*, a witness' refusal to name others in a setting suggesting that the witness actually was concerned about incriminating those persons rather than himself. See WCH § 19.4(B).

§ 19.09 PENALTIES AND BURDENS

The Fifth Amendment, the Supreme Court has noted, guarantees to the witness both the "right * * * to remain silent until he chooses to speak in the unfettered exercise of his own will, and to suffer no penalty * * * for such silence." *Malloy v. Hogan*, 378 U.S. 1 (1964). *Griffin v. California*, 380 U.S. 609 (1965) presents the classic illustration of the prohibition against governmental action that penalizes the exercise of the privilege. At issue there was the constitutionality of the prosecutor's adverse comment on the defendant's failure to take the stand and give testimony, thereby offering no explanation of incriminating circumstances peculiarly within his knowledge. In an earlier ruling, *Grunewald v. U.S.*, 353 U.S. 391 (1957), the Court had held that a defendant who testified at trial could not be impeached by reference to the fact that he had exercised his privilege against self-incrimination when questioned about some of the same circumstances before the grand jury. But that ruling was not constitutionally based, as it rested largely on the lack of inconsistency between exercising the privilege in the earlier proceeding (thereby asserting that his answers were potentially incriminatory) and providing testimony at trial that denied guilt and offered innocent explanations for the circumstances in question. In *Griffin*, the prosecution argued that drawing an adverse inference from defendant's failure to come forward and testify on critical facts "peculiarly within the accused's knowledge" was entirely logical and something the jury would do even if the prosecution did not ask it to do so. The Court responded, however, that the critical factor was the prosecution's attempt, with the trial court's acquiescence, to use the defendant's exercise of the privilege as evidence of his guilt. That was a characteristic "of the inquisitorial system of criminal justice, which the Fifth amendment outlaws." Adverse comment on the defendant's exercise of the privilege constituted "a penalty imposed by courts for exercising a constitutional privilege," which "cuts down on the privilege by making its assertion costly," and therefore violates the self-incrimination clause itself.

Spevack v. Klein, 385 U.S. 511 (1967), and its progeny provide a line of "penalty" cases of special relevance to the field of white collar crime. *Spevack* held that the state could not utilize the exercise of the privilege as the basis for disbarring a lawyer who had refused on self-incrimination grounds to produce documents subpoenaed in a state bar disciplinary proceeding. Disbarment here was being used as a penalty and therefore violated the Fifth Amendment. The Court reasoned that "in this context, 'penalty' is not restricted to fine or imprisonment," but extends to "the imposition of any sanction which makes assertion of the Fifth Amendment 'costly'", and therefore certainly includes "the threat of disbarment," which entails "the loss of professional standing, professional reputation, and of livelihood." Relying on *Spevack*'s analysis of prohibited penalties, the Supreme Court subsequently held invalid: state statutes that required the dismissal of police officers and other government employees who refused to waive their privilege against self-incrimination in an official inquiry relating to their employment, *Gardner v. Broderick*, 392 U.S. 273 (1968), and *Uniformed Sanitation Men Association v. Commissioner of Sanitation of New York*, 392 U.S. 280 (1968); a state statute that required disqualification of a contractor from doing business with the state for five years should the contractor refuse to waive the privilege before a grand jury investigating transactions with the state, *Lefkowitz v. Turley*, 414 U.S. 70 (1973); and a state statute that imposed a five year bar on holding office in a political party should an officeholder refuse to waive the privilege before a grand jury investigating possible misuse of his office, *Lefkowitz v. Cunningham*, 431 U.S. 801 (1977).

As illustrated by *Baxter v. Palmigiano*, 425 U.S. 308 (1976), not all burdens resulting from the exercise of the privilege are deemed penalties and therefore prohibited by the Fifth Amendment. In *Baxter*, a prison inmate summoned before a disciplinary board on a charge of causing a disturbance was told that the charge against him involved a potential criminal violation, and that he therefore had a right to remain silent, but that the board would be entitled to draw an adverse inference from that silence in resolving the disciplinary charge. The Supreme Court held that drawing an adverse inference in this setting did not penalize the exercise of the self-incrimination privilege. Unlike *Griffin*, the inference here was not being drawn in a criminal case. Unlike, the *Spevack* line of cases, the state here did not automatically impose a sanction upon the person who exercised the privilege. A prison inmate who remained silent was not automatically found guilty of a disciplinary infraction. The disciplinary board simply was allowed to give his silence whatever "evidentiary value was * * * warranted by the facts surrounding the case." Lower courts have followed *Palmigiano* in a variety of administrative inquiries, including proceedings of the type involved in *Sepvack* and *Gardner*, supra.

The *Palmigiano* Court noted that its ruling was "consistent with the prevailing rule that the Fifth Amendment does not forbid adverse inferences against parties to civil actions when they refuse to testify in response to probative evidence offered against them." *Palmigiano* has been viewed by the lower courts as also lending support for the imposition of various other adverse consequences within a civil suit that may attach to a party's invocation of the privilege (see § 18.04).

§ 19.10   IMMUNITY: CONSTITUTIONAL GROUNDING

In *Brown v. Walker*, 161 U.S. 591 (1896), a sharply divided Court concluded that precluding reliance on the privilege by granting a witness immunity from criminal prosecution was entirely consistent with the purposes of the Fifth Amendment privilege, as illustrated by historical practice. That practice, the majority noted, established that the Fifth Amendment could not be "construed literally as authorizing the witness to refuse to disclose any fact which might tend to incriminate, disgrace, or expose him to unfavorable comments." The history of the Amendment made clear that the privilege's objective was only to "secure the witness against criminal prosecution." Thus, the English adopted an immunity procedure, known as providing "indemnity" against criminal prosecution, soon after the privilege against compulsory self-incrimination became firmly established, and a similar practice was followed in the colonies. So too, the self-incrimination privilege had been held inapplicable where the witness' compelled testimony would relate only to an offense as to which he had been pardoned or as to which the statute of limitations had run. Such rulings implicitly sustained the constitutionality of the immunity procedure. Since the immunity grant removed the only danger against which the privilege protected the witness, the witness could no longer claim that he was being compelled to be "a witness against himself" in a "criminal case."

§ 19.11 THE CONSTITUTIONALLY REQUIRED SCOPE OF THE IMMUNITY

In *Counselman v. Hitchcock*, 142 U.S. 547 (1892), the Court struck down a federal immunity statute that granted protection only against the prosecution introducing the witness' immunized testimony into evidence in a subsequent prosecution of the witness. The Court stressed that the statute failed to afford protection against derivative use of the witness' testimony. Thus, the statute "could not, and would not, prevent the use of his testimony to search out other testimony to be used in evidence against him." At the conclusion of its opinion, however, the Court spoke in terms of even broader protection than prohibiting derivative use. "To be valid," it noted, an immunity grant "must afford absolute immunity against future prosecution for the offense to which the question relates." This statement was taken as indicating that a valid immunity grant must absolutely bar prosecution for any transaction noted in the witness' testimony. Accordingly, Congress adopted a new immunity statute providing for such "transactional immunity." This provision was upheld in *Brown v. Walker*, and for many years it was assumed that immunity had to be transactional. Even so, it was recognized that transactional immunity was subject to two major limitations, inherent in any type of immunity grant. First, the witness may still be prosecuted for perjury committed in the immunized testimony. Second, the immunity does not extend to an answer totally unresponsive to the question asked. Thus, the witness could not gain immunity from prosecution for all previous criminal acts by simply including a reference to these transactions in her testimony even though they had nothing to do with the subject about which she was questioned.

In *Murphy v. Waterfront Commission*, 378 U.S. 52 (1964), discussed in § 19.03, the Court clearly indicated that immunity need not be as broad in scope as traditional transactional immunity. Following *Murphy*, Congress adopted a new immunity provision for federal witnesses, replacing transactional immunity with a prohibition against use and derivative use as to both federal and state prosecutions. The statute provided that "no testimony or other information compelled under the [immunity] order (or any information directly or indirectly derived from such testimony or other information) may be used against the witness in any criminal case, except a prosecution for perjury, giving a false statement, or otherwise failing to comply with the order." In *Kastigar v. U.S.*, 406 U.S. 441 (1972), a divided Court upheld the new federal provision. The "broad language in *Counselman*," which suggested the need for transactional immunity, was discounted as inconsistent with the "conceptual basis" of the *Counselman* ruling. The crucial question, as *Counselman* noted, was whether the immunity granted was "coextensive with the scope of the privilege against self-incrimination." The traditional Fifth Amendment remedy of simply excluding from evidence the compelled statement and its evidentiary fruits (as exemplified by coerced confession cases) indicated that the privilege did not require an absolute bar against prosecution. A prohibition against use and derivative use satisfied the privilege by placing the witness "in substantially the same position as if * * * [the witness] had claimed his privilege."

The *Kastigar* majority rejected the argument, relied upon by the dissenters, that the bar against derivative use could not be enforced so effectively as to ensure that the witness really was placed in the same position as if he had not testified. The statute's "total prohibition on use," it noted, "provides a comprehensive safeguard, barring the use of compelled testimony as an 'investigatory lead,' and also barring the use of any evidence obtained by focusing investigation on a witness as a result of his compelled disclosures." Appropriate procedures for "taint hearings" would ensure that this prohibition was made effective. Once a defendant demonstrates that he previously testified under a grant of immunity, the prosecution must carry "the burden of showing that [its] evidence is not tainted by establishing that [it] had an independent, legitimate source for the disputed evidence." This requirement, the Court noted, would provide the immunized witness with "protection commensurate with that resulting from invoking the privilege itself."

§ 19.12   THE FEDERAL IMMUNITY PROVISIONS: 18 U.S.C. §§ 6000–6005

Chapter 601 of the Federal Criminal Code (18 U.S.C. §§ 6000–6005) sets forth the immunity provisions commonly relied upon in federal white collar cases. Section 6002 defines the scope of the immunity. The immunity is restricted to a witness who refuses, "on the basis of his privilege against self-incrimination, to testify or provide other information in a proceeding before or ancillary to" (1) a federal court, (2) a federal grand jury, (3) an "agency of the United States", (which covers a series of agencies, e.g., the S.E.C., specified in the definitions section, § 6001), and (4) Congressional Committees. Once immunity is granted pursuant to court order, the witness is compelled to testify and "no testimony or other information compelled under the order (or an information directly or indirectly derived from such testimony or other information) may be used against the witness in any criminal case, except in a prosecution for perjury, giving a false statement, or otherwise failing to comply with the order."

The immunity order for a witness in a grand jury or agency proceeding is issued by the district court, but that court does not assess the justification for granting immunity. Its sole function is to assure that the procedural prerequisites of § 6003 and § 6004 are met. The executive branch has the sole responsibility for determining whether or not immunity should be granted to a particular witness who otherwise would exercise the self-incrimination privilege. The basic procedural prerequisites of § 6003 (governing grand jury witnesses) are: (1) the prosecution's request for the issuance of an immunity order must have been approved by one of several high-level Justice Department officials specified in the statute; and (2) the prosecutor must state in the request that, "in his judgment," (i) the "testimony or other information * * * [sought from the witness] may be necessary to the public interest," and (ii) the witness "has refused or is likely to refuse to testify or provide other information on the basis of his privilege against self-incrimination." In the case of a witness called before an administrative agency, the agency must be one of those listed in § 6001, the agency must gain approval of the Attorney General, and it must have "in its judgment" reached the same conclusions as to the public interest and the witness' reliance on the privilege as are required for the prosecutor who seeks a § 6003 immunity order.

The DOJ has internal guidelines that identify the factors to be considered in deciding whether an immunity order is in the public interest. Subject to various exceptions, those guidelines advise against compelling testimony from a "close family relative" of the target. Where a prospective witness is likely to be subject to economic repercussions or other forms of retaliation if his identify becomes known, an important consideration is the effectiveness of grand jury secrecy (see § 16.01) in protecting the witness' identity. See WCH § 19.3 (D).

Once granted immunity, the witness can be ordered to respond to all questions within the scope of the immunity order. A witness refusing to respond faces contempt sanctions, absent some legal justification for refusing to respond (e.g., the attorney-client privilege). Self-incrimination is no longer a valid justification for refusing to respond, as the immunity grant supplants the privilege as to both state and federal prosecution. Witnesses sometimes claim that they fear physical retaliation by associates, but the lower courts have invariably found that a true case of duress is not presented, as the threat must be of a "palpable, imminent danger." *In re Grand Jury Proceedings of December 1989 (Freligh)*, 903 F.2d 1167 (7th Cir.1990).

The immunity order under § 6002 is proceeding specific. Thus, *Pillsbury v. Conboy*, 459 U.S. 248 (1983), held that where a witness had given immunized testimony in a grand jury proceeding, and later was called to testify in a civil case and asked there whether he had testified previously as to the content of his immunized testimony, he could assert the privilege against self-incrimination. The Supreme Court majority reasoned that it need not decide whether an affirmative answer would itself be excludable in a subsequent criminal prosecution as the fruit of immunized grand jury testimony. The witness could not be compelled to testify by virtue of the earlier grant of immunity, as it did not extend to the civil proceeding. The § 6002 immunity order was not intended to serve as the basis for compelling testimony except where it makes a "duly authorized assurance of immunity at the time" (i.e., in the proceeding in which the order is obtained).

§ 19.13 GARRITY IMMUNITY

As noted in § 19.05, *Garrity v. N.J.*, 385 U.S. 493 (1967), held that a statement made in response to a threat of a penalty (there a police officer's sworn testimony in an internal investigation coerced by the threat of automatic discharge) must be viewed as compelled in violation of the Fifth Amendment. As a result, neither the statement nor evidence derived from the statement can be used by the government in a criminal case. Lower courts have held that the scope of *Garrity*'s use/derivative-use prohibition is set by *Kastigar* (see § 19.11). Thus, the governmental agency imposing the penalty is granting what amounts to immunity outside of the requirements of the federal immunity statute. Of course, the individual here does not face incarceration if he refuses to make a statement, but the consequence of that refusal is still severe, the imposition of the threatened administrative sanction or the threatened withdrawal of a governmental benefit. With *Garrity* providing immunity that replaces the privilege, the threatened adverse consequence can now be imposed without penalizing the exercise of the privilege. *Sher v. U.S. Dep't of Veterans Affairs*, 488 F.3d 489 (1st Cir.2007) (noting a division within the circuits as to whether a prerequisite for imposing the automatic sanction is explicitly advising the individual that he will receive *Garrity* immunity).

Since *Garrity* coercion requires "state action," similar threats by private parties (e.g., an employer) do not similarly immunize a statement forced by such a threat. But note *U.S. v. Stein*, 541 F.3d 130 (S.D.N.Y. 2006) (government involvement in forcing employer to threaten employees who failed to cooperate with the government's investigation was so extensive as to render the employer the government's agent, so resulting statements received *Garrity* protection).

§ 19.14 PROSECUTING THE IMMUNIZED WITNESS

Unlike transactional immunity, use/derivative-use immunity does not absolutely preclude later prosecuting an immunized witness for criminal activities touched upon in the immunized testimony. To sustain such a prosecution, however, the government must establish, under a preponderance of evidence standard, that the evidence upon which it relies was not derived from the defendant's immunized testimony, but came instead from a "legitimate source wholly independent of the compelled testimony." *Kastigar v. U.S.* (§ 19.11). The primary hearing on this issue—commonly called a taint hearing—"'may be held' pre-trial, post-trial, [or] mid-trial (as the evidence is offered)," at the discretion of the trial court. Many courts favor a pretrial hearing on the ground that the defendant should not be forced to trial unless the government can show that its evidence is not tainted. One byproduct of such a hearing is to give the defense valuable pretrial discovery that would otherwise not be available, as the government identifies each item of evidence it intends to use and cites its independent source. See WCH § 19.5(B).

Some lower courts have suggested that the government cannot possibly sustain its *Kastigar*-burden if the evidence shows that "but for" the immunized testimony, the government would not have come into possession of its evidence. Others suggest that a causal connection can be so attenuated—particularly where critical steps in uncovering the evidence were taken by non-governmental actors—that the evidence will be considered not to have been derived from the immunized testimony even though that testimony was the catalyst for the initiation of the process that eventually brought the evidence to the government's attention. Courts generally agree that the government is most likely to meet its *Kastigar*-burden when it can show that its evidence was collected before the witness was ever given immunity. Thus, the Department of Justice's guidelines direct prosecutors to follow the practice of preparing a memorandum prior to the grant of immunity listing all evidence against the witness then known to exist and designating its source and date of receipt. Where that evidence consists, however, of witnesses who testified before the grand jury and those witnesses subsequently learn of the defendant's immunized testimony before testifying at trial, their testimony at trial may be tainted by virtue of the immunized testimony having further shaped their memory of events.

Although *Kastigar* spoke primarily of immunity granting protection against the government using the compelled testimony as evidence or as an investigatory lead to other evidence, it also used broader language that several courts have read as establishing a prohibition against the government's "tactical" or "nonevidentiary" use of the compelled testimony. This has led to a division as to whether *Kastigar* immunity is violated where the immunized statement impacts governmental strategy, but not the evidence presented by the government. However, courts suggesting certain tactical uses may be prohibited require a preliminary showing that the immunized testimony was so used, which is difficult to achieve, particularly where (as is typical) the prosecutors assigned to the case did not examine the immunized testimony.

§ 19.15 IMMUNITY AGREEMENTS

Where the witness is willing to testify in exchange for immunity, the prosecutor may prefer to provide immunity through an agreement (whereby the witness agrees to testify in exchange for a promise of non-prosecution) rather than an immunity grant. Use of an immunity agreement, rather than statutory immunity, permits the prosecutor to tailor the scope of the immunity to the needs of the case. Thus, a prosecutor may believe that an informal grant of transactional immunity will be more effective in gaining witness cooperation. In other situations, the immunity provided by statute may be more than the witness requires or the prosecutor is willing to give; an immunity agreement may be limited to barring prosecution only as to certain aspects of the transaction. For the witness, an immunity agreement has an advantage primarily where the agreement grants broader immunity than would be available by statute. Very often, however, the witness will go along with narrower agreement immunity because the prosecution simply will not offer statutory immunity. Federal courts have frequently upheld the use of immunity agreements, viewing them as similar in nature to plea agreements that are conditioned on the defendant providing testimony against others. WCH § 19.5(E). This means that the recalcitrant witness who wants to back away from an agreement cannot be compelled to testify, but once the witness provides the testimony he promised to give, the government will be required to honor its side of the agreement.

Prosecutors often demand, as a prerequisite for considering a grant of immunity, that the possible cooperating witness provide a proffer of his testimony. WCH § 19.5(F). A limited form of immunity is commonly granted as to the proffer itself through a proffer agreement. Federal Rule 11(f), by incorporating Federal Rule of Evidence 410, provides that a statement made in the course of a plea discussion which does not result in a guilty plea may not later be admitted in evidence against the person making the statement. Although discussions of possible immunity are also likely to consider a guilty plea alternative, to ensure protection of the type provided under Rule 11(f), counsel for a potential cooperating witness commonly will insist that the prosecution agree to Rule 11(f) treatment of that person's proffer. However, the prosecutor in turn will insist on an exception allowing impeachment use of the proffer, a practice upheld as to plea discussions in *U.S. v. Mezzanatto*, 513 U.S. 196 (1995). Thus, the agreement will provide that if the potential cooperating witness is not granted immunity, but is instead prosecuted, the prosecution may not use the proffer as evidence against him in its case-in-chief, but may use the proffer to impeach him if he testifies inconsistently with his proffer at trial. Indeed, courts have upheld agreements that permit the prosecution to use the proffer as rebuttal evidence if the defendant simply presents a defense at trial that is "inconsistent" with the proffer. While this type of agreement obviously burdens the defendant's choice of defense, it does not "forfeit his constitutional right to present a defense", and without such a provision to ensure witness candor, the government "might well decline to enter cooperation discussions". *U.S. v. Velez*, 354 F.3d 190 (2d Cir.2004). Where defendant admitted to the crime, the range of defenses not deemed inconsistent may be quite narrow. See *U.S. v. Krilich*, 303 F.3d 784 (7th Cir.1999) (indicating that such a defendant could still challenge the trustworthiness of the government's witnesses, but the claim that he was not present at the crime-scene clearly was inconsistent with his admission as to the crime).

Even if Rule 11(f) protection is tied to the proffer without any impeachment or rebuttal exception, the proffer still poses risks, as Rule 11(f) does not preclude prosecution use of evidence derived from information contained in the proffer. Of course, here again, the scope of the protection is open to negotiation in the proffer agreement. See *U.S. v. Plummer*, 941 F.2d 799 (9th Cir.1991) (since the terms of the agreement were dictated by the government, it was responsible for failing to specifically distinguish derivative use immunity, so an agreement that refers simply to "use immunity" will be read as "presumptively including derivative use immunity").

CHAPTER 20

THE SELF-INCRIMINATION PRIVILEGE: DOCUMENTS

§ 20.01 *BOYD V. UNITED STATES* AND "CONTENT PROTECTION"

Boyd v. U.S., 116 U.S. 616 (1886), was the first Supreme Court case to consider the applicability of the self-incrimination privilege to compelled production of documents, and for close to a century thereafter, *Boyd* dominated Fifth Amendment analysis of the subpoena duces tecum. At issue in *Boyd* was the constitutionality of a court order requiring an importing firm organized as a partnership to produce the invoice it had received for items alleged to have been illegally imported. The Court initially concluded that the court order was the equivalent of a search and therefore was subject to the Fourth Amendment (see § 16.03). It then concluded that the search was unreasonable because it constituted a forcible compulsion that was contrary to the 5th Amendment's self-incrimination clause. Just as the Fifth Amendment prohibited "compulsory discovery by extorting the party's oath," it also prohibited discovery by "compelling the production of his private books and papers." The documentary production order was simply another form of "forcible and compulsory extortion of a man's own testimony."

It is unclear whether *Boyd's* self-incrimination analysis was intended to be limited to the compelled production of documents. As documents contain words, the compelled disclosure of their content can be viewed as more closely analogous to the compelling of testimonial utterances than compelling the disclosure of other forms of property possessed by the subpoenaed party. Also, the Court spoke of "private" papers, which would often have been authored by the owner. However, the document at issue in *Boyd* itself was not authored by the owner and was not a confidential document relating to a personal or private matter, but a business record that had been prepared by the shipper of the items in question. Moreover, the Court spoke generally of the individual's privacy interest in the possession of personal property as to which the public had no entitlement (such entitlement existing, the Court noted, only where a third-party had a superior right, as with stolen property, or the state had a superior interest, as with records required to be kept by law). Thus, the *Boyd* approach to the Fifth Amendment has been characterized by commentators as more property oriented than privacy oriented, and the Supreme Court, later described *Boyd* as having protected the individual "from any disclosure, in the form of oral testimony, documents, or chattels sought by legal process against him as a witness." *U.S. v. White*, 322 U.S. 694 (1944). Consider also *U.S. v. Hubbell*, 530 U.S. 27 (2000) (Justices Thomas and Scalia, in a concurring opinion, urge the Court to consider reviving *Boyd*, a decision they view as supporting the proposition that "the Fifth Amendment privilege protects against the compelled protection not just of incriminating testimony, but of any incriminating evidence").

Starting with *Hale v. Henkel*, 201 U.S. 43 (1906), decided only two decades after *Boyd*, the Supreme Court gradually developed a series of doctrines that chipped away at the broad implications of *Boyd's* property-rights/privacy analysis of Fifth Amendment protection. The Court recognized various "exceptions" to the application of the Fifth Amendment to document production, including those for entity records (see § 20.09), required records (§ 20.08), and third party production (§ 20.07).

More significantly, the Court also adopted limitations that rejected, at least in part, a property rights or privacy analysis of the Fifth Amendment. Building upon the property rights analysis of *Boyd*, the Court initially held that a search was per se unreasonable under the Fourth Amendment if it sought personal property that was not contraband or the fruits or instrumentalities of a crime (i.e., property that was "mere evidence" of a crime). However, it rejected that property rights limitation in the mid-1960s and a decade later upheld a search for documents. *Andressen v. Maryland*, 427 U.S. 463 (1976). So too, in a series of cases culminating in *Schmerber v. California*, 384 U.S. 757 (1966), the Court held that privilege was limited to testimonial compulsion. Thus, *Schmerber* held that the compelled extraction of a blood sample was not subject to the privilege, notwithstanding the privacy and property interests obviously involved. The individual was not making a "communication" in providing blood, but was simply being made "the source of 'real' or 'physical' evidence." Communication was not necessarily limited to statements "compelled from a person's own lips"; it could take other forms as well, but those other forms must also convey "testimony"—i.e., reflect the "contents of the mind." *U.S. v. Doe* (§ 20.04).

In *Fisher v. U.S.*, 425 U.S. 391 (1976), the Court majority concluded that all that remained of *Boyd* was a prohibition against compelling the production of documents, which had "long been a rule searching for a rationale." In light of *Schmerber*, the prohibition could not rest on the incriminating content of the documents, for the court order does not direct the subpoenaed party to author the requested documents, but simply to produce documents that are preexisting. Since the documents were prepared voluntarily, they "cannot be said to contain compelled testimonial evidence." The documents may contain incriminating writing, but whether the writing of the subpoenaed party or another, that writing is not a communication compelled by the subpoena. Its content is no more protected than the content of physical evidence with similar incriminating content (as in *Schmerber*). As explained in § 20.02, the *Fisher* Court did find an element of compelling testimony implicit in the act of producing the preexisting document, and where the communicative aspect of that act of production is potentially incriminating, the privilege remains as a bar to requiring production of the document.

While *Fisher* did not overturn *Boyd*, in offering the act of production as the focal point for the application of the self-incrimination doctrine, *Fisher* certainly appeared to turn away from a rationale that looked to the "private" character of the subpoenaed documents. That led to separate concurring opinions by Justices Brennan and Marshall, who argued that the availability of the self-incrimination privilege depended upon whether the papers were truly "private" or "personal," which could include certain records of a sole proprietor, but not those widely shared with others. Their reading of *Boyd* led, in turn, to the dual grounding of the lower court ruling in *U.S. v. Doe*, 465 U.S. 605 (1984).

Doe involved a subpoena directing a sole proprietor to produce for grand jury use a variety of business records (including some that were strictly business related and others that may have encompassed personal matters, such as telephone records). The lower court held that the privilege applied as to all the documents, relying upon both a privacy analysis that it drew from *Boyd* and the act-of-production analysis of *Fisher*. Affirming solely on the latter ground, the Supreme Court criticized the lower court's alternative analysis, noting that it tied the privilege to the content of the documents and that reasoning was contrary to "the reasoning underlying this Court's holding in *Fisher*." Justice O'Connor wrote separately "to make explicit what is implicit in the analysis of [the Court's] opinion; that the Fifth Amendment provides absolutely no protection for the contents of private papers of any kind. The notion that the Fifth Amendment protects the privacy of papers originated in *Boyd v. U.S.*, but our decision in *Fisher v. U.S.*, sounded the death-knell for *Boyd*." Justice Marshall, joined by Justice Brennan, expressed disagreement, noting that the *Doe* case dealt only with business records "which implicate a lesser degree of concern for privacy interests than, for example, personal diaries."

Subsequent lower court opinions have been divided in their response to contentions that a privacy analysis can still sustain the privilege as to highly personal documents, even when the act of production would not do so. Many have agreed with Justice O'Connor's analysis, concluding that the rationale of *Fisher* and *Doe* precludes self-incrimination protection of the contents of a voluntarily prepared document, no matter how personal the document. These courts have held that the act-of-production doctrine provides the only protection for such personal records as diaries and pocket calendars. Other courts have held open the possibility of a limited privacy analysis, while noting that issue is not before the court on subpoenas seeking such records as cancelled checks or personal tax returns. If the "content of papers are protected at all," they note "it is only in rare situations where compelled disclosure would break the heart of our sense of privacy," and that applies only to the "most intimate papers, such as diaries and drafts of letters or essays." See WCH § 20.1(D).

§ 20.02   THE ACT-OF-PRODUCTION
DOCTRINE

Having concluded that the application of the privilege cannot rest on the declarations contained in a preexisting voluntarily authored writing that the subpoenaed party was now compelled to produce, the *Fisher* Court looked to communicative aspects of the very act of producing the documents and concluded that such a communication could sometimes (but not always) be sufficient to invoke the privilege. The act of producing subpoenaed documents, the Court noted, "has communicative aspects of its own, wholly aside from the contents of the papers produced." Compliance with a subpoena "tacitly concedes the existence of the papers demanded and their possession or control by the [subpoenaed party]." It also would indicate that party's "belief that the papers are those described in the subpoena," and in some instances this could constitute authentication of the papers. These three elements of production—acknowledgment of existence, acknowledgment of possession or control, and potential authentication by identification—were clearly compelled, but whether they also were "testimonial" and "incriminating" would depend upon the "facts and circumstances of particular cases or classes thereof." The resolution of that question, the Court reasoned, should determine whether a particular documentary production is subject to a Fifth Amendment challenge.

The *Fisher* Court was concerned in that case with the testimonial significance of the implicit admissions as to the existence and possession of an accountant's workpapers through their compelled production. Relying upon what came to be known as the "foregone conclusion" standard, the *Fisher* Court concluded:

> It is doubtful that implicitly admitting the existence and possession of the papers rises to the level of testimony within the protection of the Fifth Amendment. The papers belong to the accountant, were prepared by him, and are the kind usually prepared by an accountant working on the tax returns of his client. Surely the Government is in no way relying on the "truthtelling" of the taxpayer to prove the existence of or his access to the documents. The existence and location of the papers are a foregone conclusion and the taxpayer adds little or nothing to the sum total of the Government's information by conceding that he in fact has the papers. Under these circumstances by enforcement of the summons "no constitutional rights are touched. The question is not of testimony but of surrender."

In further explaining this forgone conclusion analysis, the Court cited as analogous its rulings holding the Fifth Amendment inapplicable to a court order requiring an accused to submit a handwriting sample. Incidental to the performance of that act, the Court noted, the accused necessarily "admits his ability to write and impliedly asserts that the exemplar is his writing." But the government obviously is not seeking this information—the "first would be a near truism and the latter self-evident"—, and therefore "nothing he has said or done is deemed to be sufficiently testimonial for purposes of the privilege." Where the existence and possession of the documents to be produced were a "foregone conclusion," the act of production was viewed by the *Fisher* Court as having the same non-testimonial character. The government in such a case obviously was not seeking the assertions of the subpoenaed party as to the facts of existence and possession, and her incidental communication as to those facts, inherent in the physical act that the government had the authority to compel, therefore would not rise to the level of compelled "testimony."

Fisher did not have before it an act of production that had a significant potential for providing authentication evidence, and therefore spoke of the foregone conclusion doctrine only as it related to establishing existence and possession of the documents. However, two later cases, *U.S. v. Doe*, 465 U.S. 605 (1984), and *U.S. v. Hubbell*, 530 U.S. 27 (2000), established that the foregone conclusion analysis applied as well to this potentially testimonial aspect of the act of production.

After *Fisher*, the government had two major avenues for defeating a self-incrimination claim as to the production of preexisting to documents: (1) establishing that the act of production is not testimonial because existence, possession, and authentication (to the extent applicable) are a foregone conclusion; (2) contending that the act of production, even though testimonial, does not present the realistic potential for incrimination required for the privilege to apply. The standards applied to these contentions, as established by the Supreme Court, are discussed below.

§ 20.03 THE FOREGONE CONCLUSION STANDARD

Fisher offered only limited insight as what was needed to meet the foregone conclusion standard. The Court's reference to the accountant's workpapers as a type of document commonly prepared for taxpayers led the government to contend that the existence and location of standard business documents was always a foregone conclusion. *U.S. v. Doe*, 465 U.S. 605 (1984), appeared to reject this contention, as the documents subpoenaed there were standard business documents and the Court sustained the lower court findings that the government had failed to establish "that possession, existence, and authentication were a foregone conclusion." But the Court in *Doe* did not offer an independent analysis of this conclusion. Rather, it emphasized that two lower courts had found that the act-of-production there would present testimonial self-incrimination, that this finding rested basically on "factual issues," and that the Court had "traditionally been reluctant to disturb findings of fact in which two courts below have concurred."

In *U.S. v. Hubbell*, 530 U.S. 27 (2002), however, the Court both confirmed the implicit message of

Doe and offered a reading of *Fisher* consistent with the lower court rulings demanding that the government, to meet the foregone conclusion standard, demonstrate with "reasonable particularly that it knows of the existence and location of subpoenaed documents." The subpoena in *Hubbell* called for 11 categories (almost all broadly described) of largely business documents. The Court reasoned that, "given the breadth of the 11 categories, * * * the collection and production of the materials demanded was tantamount to answering a series of interrogatories asking a witness to disclose the existence and location of particular documents fitting broad descriptions." The government responded that this obviously "communicative aspect of production" was nonetheless not sufficiently testimonial "because the existence and possession of such records by any business is a foregone conclusion." Rejecting this contention, the Court reasoned:

> Whatever the scope of this "foregone conclusion" rationale, the facts of this case plainly fall outside of it. While in *Fisher*, the Government already knew that the documents were in the attorneys' possession and could independently confirm their existence and authenticity through the accountants who created them, here the Government has not shown that it had any prior knowledge of either the existence or the whereabouts of the 13,120 pages of documents ultimately produced by respondent. The Government cannot cure this deficiency through the overboard argument

that a businessman such as respondent will always possess general business and tax records that fall within the broad categories described in this subpoena. The *Doe* subpoenas also sought several broad categories of general business records, yet we upheld the District Court's finding that the act of producing those records would involve testimonial self-incrimination.

Hubbell's description of *Fisher* illustrates one means of meeting the foregone conclusion standard, although its scope is not entirely clear. *Fisher* presented two features that contributed to the foregone conclusion finding there—one fairly common and one unusual. The fairly common factor is the availability of third persons (in *Fisher*, the accountants) who can establish that the documents had been prepared and delivered to the person now being investigated. The unique factor is that the target's lawyers (who had possession of the documents), in order to establish the lawyer-client privilege (through which the self-incrimination issue was raised, see § 22.04), had to acknowledge that their client had possessed the documents and had transferred them to the lawyers in the course of seeking legal advice. In general, lower courts have not demanded such strong evidence of existence and current possession as that acknowledgment. They have relied either on the availability of third persons, as in *Fisher*, or on other extrinsic evidence as to existence and possession, such as a similar document in the government's possession containing references to the subpoenaed documents and indicating that they are in the subpoenaed person's possession. Similarly as to authentication, courts have held that the foregone conclusion standard may be satisfied where the government can identify a third person who can authenticate or where authentication can be achieved by other extrinsic means (e.g., comparison of handwritten documents with the handwriting of the subpoenaed party). See WCH § 20.2(B).

The foregone conclusion showing must be tied to documents identified with "reasonable particularity," but that does not prohibit a grouping of documents. In *Fisher*, as *Hubbell* noted, the government's showing was tied to documents described as "working papers prepared by the taxpayer's accountants that the IRS knew were in possession of the taxpayer's attorneys." It was sufficient to identify the documents by reference to their general function (tax workpapers), timing (identified by tax year), source (the accountants) and current location (held by the attorneys). Greater specificity, such as identifying the particular type of workpaper, or the particular content, was not necessary. Of course, the description that identifies a group of documents, to be acceptable, must be tailored to the showing that establishes a foregone conclusion. The government cannot expand on that showing to include other documents of the same general character. See *In re Grand Jury Subpoena Dated April 18, 2003*, 383 F.3d 905 (9th Cir.2004) (while defendant had acknowledged existence of e-mails and records concerning communications with competitors selling a particular product, that hardly provided foregone-conclusion support for requiring production of any type of document relating to the production and sale of the product).

The foregone conclusion doctrine remains a viable tool for the government even when the documents at issue are encrypted. In such cases, the government typically does not demand the encryption password. The Supreme Court has noted in dicta that compelling an individual to reveal the combination to a wall safe is to compel testimony, as the individual must reveal the "contents of his mind." See WCH § 19.1(E). This analysis would apply equally to revealing the password, but not to compelling the individual to produce an unencrypted version of the files. Here, the act of production doctrine applies. Of course, the act in this instance establishes, in addition to existence, possession and possible authentication, the individual's capacity to decrypt; but that capacity can readily be established as a foregone conclusion as to an individual who regularly uses the encrypted files. Thus, the Eleventh Circuit has noted in such a case that the key is whether the government can meet the foregone conclusion standard as to the files, "showing] with some reasonable particularity that it seeks a certain file and is aware, based on other information, that (1) the file exists in some specified location (e.g., a computer hard drive], (2) the file is possessed by the target * * *, and (3) the file is authentic." *In re Grand Jury Subpoena Duces Tecum Dated March 25, 2011*, 670 F.3d 1335 (11th Cir.2012) (finding that the government could not establish existence because the government relied on a computer code that could as readily reflect a blank as an actual file).

§ 20.04   POTENTIAL INCRIMINATION

The Court in *Fisher* stated that even if the act of production in that case had been testimonial, the privilege still would not apply because there had been no showing that the communicative aspects of production posed a "realistic threat of incrimination to the taxpayer." As to authentication, it noted that production would not provide the government with evidence that could be used to authenticate the subpoenaed workpapers since production by the taxpayer would "express nothing more than the taxpayer's belief that the papers are those described in the subpoena" and the taxpayer could not thereby authenticate as he "did not prepare the papers and could not vouch for their accuracy." As to existence and possession, "surely it was not illegal to seek accounting help in connection with one's tax returns or for the accountant to prepare workpapers and deliver them to the taxpayer." "At this juncture," the Court noted, it was "quite unprepared to hold that either the fact of the existence of the papers or their possession by the taxpayer" posed a sufficient threat to raise a legitimate self-incrimination claim.

In *Doe*, in contrast to *Fisher*, the lower courts had found that the production of the documents had a potential for incrimination. Indeed, the Supreme Court, in a revealing footnote, rejected the government's contention that even if the act of production there were viewed as having sufficient "testimonial aspects," any incrimination would be "so trivial" that the Fifth Amendment would not be implicated. Respondent Doe, the Court noted, had never conceded that the records subpoenaed actually existed or were within his possession. The government could use the act of production against the petitioner, both to establish his possession of the documents produced and to authenticate those documents.

The *Doe* Court, in its brief comment on self-incrimination potential, did not seek to distinguish *Fisher*. Certainly the cases cannot be distinguished by the general character of the records involved: the records subpoenaed in *Doe* were standard business records (e.g., billings and cancelled checks) and the possession of such records was just as innocuous on its face as the possession of an accountant's workpapers. The critical distinction apparently related to the possible content of the records and incriminating potential of possession in light of that content. *Doe*, of course, involved a grand jury investigation and the government obviously was seeking to establish though the documents that the subpoenaed party had a connection to the businesses that had created the records. In *Fisher*, in contrast, the materials were subpoenaed in a standard IRS investigation, and the taxpayer had raised no more than a blanket claim as to potential incrimination. The Court's reference to being unprepared to find a realistic threat of incrimination "at this juncture" arguably was a product of these circumstances, indicating a much more particularized showing would be needed in the context of a setting that did not have obvious criminal overtones. The *Fisher* ruling therefore appears not to undercut the view that, in the typical grand jury investigation, the subpoenaed party should be able to meet the *Hoffman* standard as to likely incrimination (see § 19.02) simply by reference to the subject of the investigation, the relevancy of the documents sought, and the status of the subpoenaed party (as a target or subject of the investigation). In *Hubbell*, such factors so clearly pointed to a realistic threat of incrimination that the issue was not even raised before the Supreme Court (and, of course, the later use of documents, after immunity had been granted, had established their incriminating character).

§ 20.05 ACT OF PRODUCTION IMMUNITY

In *U.S. v. Doe*, 465 U.S. 605 (1984), the government argued that, should the Supreme Court accept the lower court's finding that the privilege applied to the subpoena duces tecum, the Court should nonetheless order the district court to enforce the subpoena on condition that the government agree not to make use or derivative use of the act of production. Rejecting this proposal, the Court noted that the government was, in effect, offering to provide immunity for the act of production and that only could be done in accordance with the immunity statutes (see § 19.12). The Court did note, however, that the government "could have compelled respondent to produce the documents" by utilizing the federal immunity statutes, and that the use/derivative-use immunity granted thereunder could be limited to the act of production. There was no need for the immunity grant to extend to the contents of the documents as such, because the privilege was based solely on the act of production and the "immunity need be only as broad as the privilege."

Concurring in *Fisher*, Justice Marshall noted that immunity tied to the act of production would nonetheless commonly serve to "effectively shield" the contents of the subpoenaed documents, as the contents would be a direct fruit of the "immunized testimony" contained in the act of production. In contrast to Justice Marshall, the Department of Justice took the position that immunity limited to the act of production never extends derivatively to the document itself (including its contents) because *Fisher* held quite clearly that the contents were not compelled and therefore not subject to the Fifth Amendment privilege. All that the immunity required, the D.O.J. argued, was that the documents be treated, in effect, as "manna from heaven"—i.e., no reference be made to their source. If this was done, the documents themselves could be used for any purpose, including their introduction in evidence (if otherwise authenticated).

In *U.S. v. Hubbell*, 530 U.S. 27 (2002), the Supreme Court flatly rejected the D.O.J.'s argument, although it did not necessarily go so far as to accept Justice Marshall's position. The government in *Hubbell* had granted the respondent Hubbell act-of-production immunity for his compliance with a subpoena calling for 11 different categories of documents, but it contended that the immunity did not impact its subsequent prosecution of Hubbell. It was not using the documents produced by respondent, but other evidence discovered through an examination of the contents of the produced documents. The Court held this showing insufficient because the government could not also show that it had not made "derivative use" of the "testimonial aspect[s] of the act-of-production itself." Indeed, the Court concluded, the prosecution in various ways had violated the derivative use prohibition.

Certain aspects of the Court's discussion of the government's derivative use focused on the special character of the subpoena in *Hubbell* and what it had required for compliance. Because of the breadth of the different categories, it was "unquestionably necessary for respondent to make extensive use of the 'contents of his own mind' in identifying the hundreds of documents responsive to the subpoena." He had, through his act of production, provided "the prosecutor with an accurate inventory of the many sources of potentially incriminating evidence sought by the subpoena," and that inventory presented the "first step in the chain of evidence that led to the prosecution." This discussion might suggest that if the testimonial aspects of the act of production do not assist in describing the background of the documents and in categorizing the documents, but simply establish their existence, the government may use the contents of the documents (assuming no reference is made to the defendant's act of production).

The *Hubbell* opinion, however, also used broader language. It noted, for example, that it was only through "respondent's truthful reply to the subpoena that the Government received the incriminating documents", and that the act of production had provided testimony as to "existence" and "whereabouts," which were not part of the government's prior knowledge. Such language suggests that the very availability of the document (allowing the examination of its contents) is a derivative use, and thus the government cannot make use of documents produced under an immunity grant even where the subpoena is narrowly drawn to identify a particular document. See *In re Grand Jury Subpoena Duces Tecum Dated March 25, 2011*, 670 F.3d 1335 (11th Cir.2012) (since government was not aware of the actual existence of encrypted documents, see § 20.03, a grant of immunity for decrypting cannot be limited to use of that act but must extend to "its fruits, the unencrypted content of the hard drives").

§ 20.06 REQUIRING NON-TESTIMONIAL WRITINGS

Building upon the reasoning of *Fisher*, *Doe v. U.S.*, 487 U.S. 201 (1988) recognized that even a compelled writing could be nontestimonial. The Court there held that an individual could not rely on the privilege to refuse to obey a court order directing the individual to sign a form authorizing a foreign bank to release records relating to any account held by the individual. The government's purpose, it noted, was not to have the individual, by signing the form, "relate a factual assertion or disclose information." Indeed, the form was carefully drafted so that the signing party noted that he was acting under court order and did not acknowledge the existence of any account in any particular bank. The form did not constitute evidence that the requested documents existed and offered no assistance to the government in later establishing the authenticity of any records produced by the bank in response to the form. Accordingly, the Court concluded, the signed form constituted a communication, but did not constitute "testimony" for Fifth Amendment purposes. The district court was directing the individual only to perform the act of signing a directive to the bank, not to engage in "truth telling" through the directive.

§ 20.07 THIRD PARTY PRODUCTION

In both *Fisher* and *Couch v. U.S.*, 409 U.S. 322 (1973), the owner of records had transferred the records to an independent professional, and it was that person who was subpoenaed to produce the records. In *Couch*, the taxpayer had delivered various financial records to her accountant for the purpose of preparing her income tax returns, and the IRS subsequently issued a summons directing the accountant to produce the papers. In *Fisher*, the IRS directed a summons to lawyers for production of accountant's workpapers that had been delivered to them by the taxpayer in seeking legal advice. In both instances, the taxpayers sought to challenge the IRS summons as invading the taxpayer's privilege against self-incrimination. They stressed their ownership of the documents and the potential incrimination that would fall upon them though the content of the documents. The Supreme Court responded that the persons compelled to produce the documents were the professionals, not the taxpayers, and the Fifth Amendment protected only those persons who themselves were "compelled" to give testimony or perform a testimonial act. The taxpayers themselves were not required "to do anything." (In *Fisher*, because of the lawyer-client privilege, see § 22.04, the lawyers were able to place before the court the taxpayer's self-incrimination contention, but the taxpayer could not raise that claim directly).

Both *Fisher* and *Couch* acknowledged that "situations might exist where constructive possession is so clear or the relinquishment of possession is so temporary and insignificant as to leave the personal compulsion upon the accused substantially intact." Lower courts have since indicated that constructive possession is a concept largely limited in application to situations in which an employer seeks to raise the privilege in response to a subpoena directed to an employee who maintains the employer's records under the supervision of the employer. Moreover, to take advantage of the concept, the employer must show that he "exercised dominion" over the records and that the employee's control was restricted. WCH § 20.5.

§ 20.08   REQUIRED RECORDS

Where individuals engage in a regulated business, they may be required to keep certain records and to make such records open for inspection by public officials. In *Shapiro v. U.S.*, 335 U.S. 1 (1948), the Supreme Court held that the self-incrimination privilege does not provide protection against the compelled disclosure of such records as the records were created for the public benefit, with the government reserving the right to insist upon their production. The *Shapiro* Court acknowledged that "there are limits which the Government cannot constitutionally exceed in requiring the keeping of records which may be inspected * * * and may be used in prosecuting statutory violations committed by the record-keeper himself," but it had no need to consider those limits in the context of the records before it—records of commodity sales that wholesale fresh produce dealers were required to keep in the implementation of the Wartime Emergency Price Control Act. Subsequently, in *Grosso v. U.S.*, 390 U.S. 62 (1968), the Court characterized three elements as necessary "premises of the [required records] doctrine."

First, "the purposes of the United States' inquiry [requiring that the records be kept] must be essentially regulatory." The government's interest in the records must arise out of a regulatory scheme rather than a criminal law enforcement objective. Thus, the doctrine could not be used to impose a reporting requirement on professional gamblers, a "group inherently suspect of criminal activities."

Most states make gambling a crime, and looking to the "characteristics of the activity" and "the composition of the group to which inquiries are made," the Court could not say that Congress was dealing here with "an essentially non-criminal and regulatory area." *Grosso v. U.S.*

Second, the information that is to be obtained by the government by "requiring the preservation of records" must be "of a kind which the regulated party has customarily kept." This reduces the burden placed upon the record keeper and often supports the regulatory relevance of the record. "[T]hird, the records themselves must have assumed 'public aspects' which render them at least analogous to public documents." This characteristic was said to exist in *Shapiro* because the "transaction which it [the required record] recorded was one in which petitioner could lawfully engage solely by virtue of the license granted to him under the statute."

Lower court rulings sustaining the application of the required records doctrine generally have involved recordkeeping requirements in regulated industries. However, requirements upheld under this doctrine can go beyond a limited regulated class, as in the Bank Secrecy Act requirement that taxpayers keep and share with the IRS various basic account-holder information as to foreign bank accounts (similar to the information U.S. banks provide to the IRS). See WCH § 20.6.

§ 20.09   THE ENTITY EXCEPTION

Hale v. Henkel, 201 U.S. 43 (1906) not only reconstructed *Boyd's* Fourth Amendment analysis (see § 16.03), but also added a major exception to the application of its Fifth Amendment analysis. *Hale* held that the self-incrimination privilege is not available to a corporation and therefore the *Boyd* ruling could not operate to bar a grand jury subpoena duces tecum requiring production of corporate records. The Court's reasoning stressed the different status of the individual and the corporation. The individual, it noted, "owes no duty to the State * * * to divulge his business, or to open his doors to an investigation, so far as it may tend to incriminate him." The corporation, in contrast, "is a creature of the State," and exercises its franchise subject to the "reserved right" of the State to compel its assistance in ensuring that it has not "exceeded its powers."

The Court in *Hale* also took special note of a concern repeatedly cited in subsequent entity cases—the enforcement needs of the government in regulating entities. If the government were precluded by the self-incrimination clause from compelling production of corporate records, "it would result in a failure of a large number of cases where the illegal combination was determinable only upon such papers." Not surprisingly in light of this concern, the Court, in *Wilson v. U.S.*, 221 U.S. 361 (1911), next rejected the claim of a corporate officer possessing subpoenaed corporate records that he could refuse to produce those records because they would personally incriminate him. The State's "reserved power of visitation," the Court noted, "would seriously be embarrassed, if not wholly defeated in its effective exercise, if guilty officers could refuse inspection of the records and papers of the corporation." As the records were those of the corporation, not personal records, and were held "subject to the corporate duty," the official could "assert no personal right * * * against any demand of the government which the corporation was bound to recognize." The subpoena in *Wilson* was directed to the corporation, but *Dreier v. U.S.*, 221 U.S. 394 (1911) held that the result was the same where the subpoena was directed to a specified individual in his capacity as corporate custodian.

In *U.S. v. White*, 322 U.S. 694 (1944), the Court extended the *Hale* exception to entities other than corporations. *White* held that the president of an unincorporated labor union could not invoke his personal privilege against a subpoena demanding union records. The privilege against self-incrimination, the Court noted, was "designed to prevent the use of legal process to force from the lips of the accused the evidence necessary to convict him or force him to produce and authenticate any personal documents that might incriminate him, * * * [to] thereby avoid * * * physical torture and other less violent but equally reprehensible modes of compelling the production of incriminating evidence." These concerns did not apply to entities, as they lacked the qualities of human personality and therefore could not suffer the "immediate and potential evils of compulsory self-disclosure."

The *White* Court characterized the labor union as an organization with "a character so impersonal in scope of its membership and activities that it cannot be said to embody or represent the purely private or personal interests of its constituents, but rather to embody their common or group interests only." In *Bellis v. U.S.*, 417 U.S. 85 (1974), however, the Court concluded that the entity exception remained applicable even where the entity embodied personal as well as group interests. The functional key was that the organization "be recognized as an independent entity apart from its individual members." Thus, a small law firm, organized as a partnership, was an entity for this purpose even though it "embodied[d] little more than the personal legal practice of the individual partners."

Bellis noted that "this might be a different case if it involved a small family partnership, or * * * if there were some other pre-existing relationship of confidentiality among the partners." Lower courts have viewed any such exceptions as quite narrow. Indeed, even where there is no formal partnership agreement, a structured business organization may fall within the entity exception. Thus, the entity exception was held to apply to persons who owned commercial property as tenants in common, had a separate bank account for business activities relating that to that property, and utilized an assumed name in conducting such business. *In re Grand Jury Proceedings (Shiffman)*, 576 F.2d 703 (6th Cir.1978). On the other hand, a husband-wife professional service firm, though organized as a partnership under the Uniform Partnership Act, was held not to constitute an entity where it had no employees and no office outside the couple's home. *In re Grand Jury Subpoena*, 605 F.Supp. 174 (E.D.N.Y.1985).

§ 20.10   THE ENTITY AGENT

Because the entity has no self-incrimination privilege, and the entity agent is responding in a representative capacity in producing the documents of the entity, *U.S. v. Wilson* (see § 20.07) and a series of other early 1900s cases held that the entity agent could not invoke the agent's personal privilege even though the content of the documents were clearly incriminating to the agent. Prior to *Fisher*, the only major open issue as to production by an entity agent was where the agent's responsibility ended. The lower courts had held, with some suggestion of approval by the Supreme Court, that the agent could be required to testify for the purpose of identifying the documents. However, once this was done, the agent could exercise his personal privilege as to further questions relating to the records (e.g., how they were prepared). In an analogous situation, the Supreme Court held that an officer of a local union, having established that he no longer possessed the subpoenaed records, could then assert the privilege as to questions concerning their disposition. *Curcio v. U.S.*, 354 U.S. 118 (1957). But note *U.S. v. Rylander*, 460 U.S. 752 (1983) (custodial agent still carried burden of establishing that he no longer had the records, which could not be met by simply claiming the privilege).

After *Fisher* introduced the act-of-production doctrine (see § 20.01), several lower courts concluded that the entity agent should be allowed to claim the privilege as to the act of production, at least where the subpoena was directed to the agent as an entity official, rather than to the entity itself. In *Braswell v. U.S.*, 487 U.S. 99 (1980), a closely divided Supreme Court rejected that position. The *Braswell* majority concluded that *Fisher*'s adoption of the act-of-production doctrine had not altered the unavailability of the privilege to the entity agent. The Court's pre-*Fisher* rulings on the responsibility of the agent had not ignored the testimonial aspects of the act of production, but had correctly considered any such testimonial elements to be properly attributed to the entity rather to the agent acting on its behalf. Even where the subpoena was directed by name to a particular entity official having control of the records, that official was not performing "a personal act, but rather an act of the [entity]" in complying with the subpoena. The dissent argued that this position was allowing the law "to be captive to its own fictions," but the majority responded that *Fisher* itself had accepted this distinction in the course of analyzing the act-of-production rationale. Thus, the *Braswell* majority noted, "whether one concludes—as did the Court [in *Fisher*]—that a custodian's production of corporate records is deemed not to constitute testimonial self-incrimination or instead that a custodian waives the right to exercise the privilege, the lesson of *Fisher* is clear: A custodian may not resist a subpoena for corporate records on Fifth Amendment grounds." To rule otherwise, as the Court had noted in its earlier rulings, would "largely frustrate legitimate government regulation of such organizations" and have a "detrimental impact," in particular, on "the Government's efforts to prosecute 'white collar crime' * * * as the greater portion of evidence of wrongdoing by an organization or its representatives is usually found in the official records of that organization."

Braswell, however, added an evidentiary limitation not mentioned in the earlier cases rejecting self-incrimination claims by entity agents. Since the agent's act of production is an act of the entity and not the individual, the government "may make no evidentiary use of the 'individual act' against the individual." Illustrating this point, the Court noted that "in a criminal prosecution against the custodian, the Government may not introduce into evidence before the jury the fact that the subpoena was served upon and the corporation's documents were delivered by one particular individual, the custodian." The government would be limited to showing that the entity had produced the document and to using that act of the entity in establishing that the records were authentic entity records that the entity had possessed and had produced.

In its discussion of the limited use the government might make of the act of production in a subsequent prosecution of the custodian, the Court, in a footnote, added what could have been a very important caveat: it was "leav[ing] open the question [of] whether the agency rationale supports compelling a custodian to produce corporate records when the custodian is able to establish, by showing for example that he is the sole employee and officer of the corporation, that the jury would inevitably conclude that he produced the records." Lower courts subsequently held that the *Braswell* footnote did not require a reexamination of the long-standing position that a "one-person corporation" (i.e., one individual is the sole shareholder, director, officer, and employee) falls within the collective-entity doctrine, and that this sole proprietor must comply with the subpoena. Various other measures, they noted, remain available to meet the problem cited in the *Braswell* footnote. One possibility is to preclude the prosecution from making any reference to the corporation's act of production, although that would place on the government the burden of authenticating and establishing corporate possession through other means. Another possibility would be to allow the subpoenaed person to make production through some third-party custodian (e.g., counsel or an unaffiliated agent) who could then testify as to having obtained the documents from the corporate files.

Federal lower courts have divided as to whether *Braswell* extends to former employees who have retained corporate records. See WCH § 20.4(C). One view is that the key to *Braswell* is the production of the documents by the subpoenaed party in a "representative capacity", and since the former employee is no longer an agent of the corporation (and no longer the custodian of the corporate records), he or she may rely on potential act-of-production incrimination even though the documents may belong to the corporation. The contrary position stresses the ownership of the records (including the corporate right to recover them from the former employee) and notes that exempting former employees from the *Braswell* ruling "creates a perverse incentive" for a departing employee to take with him all corporate records that "he knows may contain evidence of wrongdoing" so as to be able to assert a self-incrimination claim that would not be otherwise available.

Of course, *Braswell* only applies to entity documents. An employee subpoenaed to produce what are supposedly entity records can assert the privilege if those records actually are his or her personal documents. Thus, a substantial body of lower court opinions consider the question of whether, under the circumstances of the case, such documents as employee desk and pocket calendars are personal rather than corporate records. A multi-factored analysis is employed, with the court seeking to determine the "essential nature" of the document by looking at such criteria as: "who prepared the document; the nature of its contents; its purpose or use; who possessed it; who had access to it; whether the corporation required its preparation; and whether its existence was necessary to or in furtherance of corporate business." WCH § 20.4(E).

CHAPTER 21

SEARCHES

§ 21.01 SEARCHES VS. SUBPOENAS: ADVANTAGES AND DISADVANTAGES

Very often a search does not present a viable alternative to the subpoena duces tecum in obtaining business records because the constitutional prerequisites for a search are not available. Where these prerequisites arguably can be met, the subpoena duces tecum might still be preferred for several reasons. For one, the administrative costs of a subpoena are far less, as there the subpoenaed party, rather than law enforcement offers, must bear the time consuming task of assembling the documents. Second, the subpoena may be more effective in gaining all relevant documents. Since the subpoenaed party is more familiar with the records and their location, good faith compliance by the subpoenaed party is more likely to include all documents within the specified categories than an investigator's search for the same documents. Also, since the subpoena need not be shaped to fit the probable cause prerequisite, it can be more broadly framed, thereby further insuring that relevant documents are not overlooked.

Third, a grand jury subpoena duces tecum does not open the investigation to the public (assuming the subpoenaed party does not want to make it public) and does not reveal the grounding for the subpoena to the subpoenaed party. The search, however, typically does both. The affidavit presented to obtain the warrant is presumptively a court record open to the public (although the court may place the affidavit under seal on a proper showing of need). Moreover, even if sealing is ordered, the owner of the seized property, on a motion challenging the seizure, will eventually see the affidavit and learn far more about the nature of the investigation than the target of a grand jury investigation who moves to quash.

Fourth, searches causes business disruptions that are deemed unfair and inappropriate where directed at a person who is merely a custodian of records and not a criminal suspect. Indeed, Congress has severely limited the permissible use of searches against third party nonsuspects under the Privacy Protection Act (42 U.S.C. § 2000aa—2000aa–12) and the DOJ guidelines mandated by that Act. Searches directed at a "disinterested third party" require an internal prosecutorial authorization, which is to be granted only if the subpoena alternative would "substantially jeopardize the availability or usefulness of the material sought." Also, further restrictions are placed on searches of the media for journalistic "work product" or searches of disinterested third party physicians, lawyers, or clergymen for records containing confidential information on their patients, clients, or parishioners. On the other side, as discussed in § 16.10, Congress has mandated the use of a search warrant (with its probable cause prerequisite), rather than a subpoena, to obtain certain types of records from third-party service providers. These search warrants seeking electronically stored data are usually executed in much the same fashion as a subpoena in order to avoid the disruptive impact of on-premises enforcement (i.e., the third party submits to the government all account-data that might include the documents sought in the search, and the government then searches that data off-premises, see Fed.R.Crim.P. 41(e)).

Fifth, the remedy for conducting an unconstitutional search can be far more severe than the remedy for issuing an invalid subpoena. The subpoena is challenged prior to compliance, and if it is held invalid, the government can return with a properly framed subpoena. A search is challenged after the fact, and if the search is held to be invalid because of inadequacies of the probable cause affidavit, the warrant, or the execution of the search, the exclusionary rule applies, subject to certain important exceptions (see § 21.04). With exclusion, the evidence that was seized is permanently lost to the government for use in its case-in-chief.

On the other side, assuming a search is legally available, it offers certain advantages over the subpoena duces tecum. First, a search comes without advance notice and therefore does not offer the party in possession of the documents the opportunity to destroy, conceal, or alter the documents. Second, the search gives the government immediate access to the documents. Third, the search places an officer in a position to examine a larger body of documents in seeking to identify those specified in the warrant, and should the officer find in plain view an incriminating document (perhaps as to another crime) that the government never anticipated, he can seize that document (and perhaps use it to obtain a search warrant authorizing a broader search). Fourth, by placing investigators on the premises, the search facilitates possibly "on the spot" questioning of employees.

Fifth, the search has a certain symbolic significance. The disruptive impact of the search can convey a special sense of urgency to those involved. It also conveys to the public the message that prosecutors are adopting an aggressive stance towards white collar crime by subjecting suspects to the same procedures applied to street crimes. In this regard, the absence of the secrecy requirements that attach to a grand jury investigation may be a distinct advantage.

Finally, while an individual (though not an entity) may assert a self-incrimination to a subpoena decum (see § 20.02), that objection is not available to the subject of a search, even a search for documents. As the Supreme Court noted in *Andresen v. Maryland*, 427 U.S. 463 (1976), the "records seized contai[n] statements that the subject voluntarily committed to writing," and the seizure by another does not require the subject to "say or do anything" (i.e., he is not "compelled" to be a "witness").

§ 21.02   FOURTH AMENDMENT REQUIREMENTS

The Fourth Amendment to the United States Constitution provides that, "[t]he right of the people to be secure in their persons, houses, papers, and effects against unreasonable searches and seizures, shall not be violated, and no Warrants shall issue, but upon probable cause, supported by Oath or affirmation, and particularly describing the place to be searched, and the persons or things to be seized." Almost all of the searches involved in white collar cases will require a warrant. The searches here are of business premises or residences, and they are not likely to present any of the narrow exceptions to the warrant requirement that occasionally apply to the search of such buildings. Similarly, computers are treated as closed containers, so even when they are seized without a warrant, a warrant usually will be required to examine the data stored on the computer.

Thus, the searches utilized in white collar investigations typically will be governed by the second clause of the Fourth Amendment (the warrant clause), which states that "no warrant shall issue, but upon probable cause, supported by Oath or affirmation, and particularly describing the place to be searched, and the persons or things to be seized." As applied to searches to obtain documents constituting evidence of a crime (the usual objective of searches in white collar investigations), the primary stumbling blocks under this clause are: (1) establishing probable cause as to the different types of documents that the government hopes to find; and (2) meeting the requirement of "particularly describing * * * [the] things to be seized."

§ 21.03   PROBABLE CAUSE

In *Illinois v. Gates*, 462 U.S. 213 (1983) the Supreme Court noted that "[p]robable cause is a fluid concept—turning on the assessment of probabilities in particular factual contexts—not readily, or often usefully, reduced to a neat set of legal rules." The magistrate issuing the warrant must conclude on the basis of a "practical, common-sense" analysis of the information presented that "there is a fair probability" that evidence of a crime will be found in the place to be searched. A magistrate's finding of probable cause is given deference by a reviewing court, but there are limits. "Sufficient information must be presented to the magistrate to allow that official to determine probable cause; his action cannot be a mere ratification of the bare conclusions of others."

The special difficulty presented in establishing probable cause for a search for documents lies not in establishing probable cause as to the commission of a crime, but in establishing probable cause that particular documents constitute evidence of that crime. Thus, where probable cause was based on reports of a series of fraudulent cash transactions, a court held that those illicit dealings in cash provided an obviously insufficient basis for believing that evidence of the crime was to be found in the company's checking account records. So too, the warrant was faulted because it authorized the seizure of documents that predated by several months the start of the fraudulent transactions and the supporting affidavit failed to allege any grounds for believing that the scheme reached back to that earlier date. *U.S. v. Diaz*, 841 F.2d 1 (1st Cir.1988). In general, a showing of probable cause carries with it a limited time frame and the records must have been created within that time frame, although that time frame need not be limited precisely to the period in which the suspect activities occurred. A preceding period may be relevant, for example, to compare similar records from "innocent transactions" or to access the possibility of advance planning. See WCH § 21.3(B), (C).

Where an organization is "permeated by fraud", that may establish probable cause to seize all of its current records. *In re Grand Jury Investigation Concerning Solid State Devices*, 130 F.3d 853 (9th Cir.1997) (also noting that this analysis did not apply where the business "routinely engaged in fraudulent practices," but also engaged in "some legitimate activity," in contrast to a "boiler shop"). But note *Voss v. Bergsgaard*, 774 F.2d 402 (10th Cir.1985) (arguing that the "pervasively criminal" concept does not authorize the warrant to refer simply to the seizure of "all records", as some cases suggest, but still requires an identification of particular types of records relevant to the particular crime, even where that results in the seizure of all records).

§ 21.04   PARTICULARITY OF DESCRIPTION

Particularity of description initially requires that the documents specified for seizure be limited by the probable cause grounding. But particularly also requires that the officer exercising the search can identify "with reasonable certainty" the items so specified. Document searches pose a special difficulty in this regard because simple descriptions do not sufficiently distinguish one document from another. Courts note that a more particular description is required when other objects of the same general classification are likely to be found at the place to be searched. Moreover, they note that the possibility of a mistaken seizure is of special concern where the "innocent objects" that might mistakenly be seized are documents. Thus, generic descriptions (e.g., "billings") often must be qualified by reference to content or date.

On the other hand, courts do, on occasion, sustain some very open-ended descriptions. *Andresen v. Maryland*, 427 U.S. 463 (1976), sustained a warrant which authorized seizure of a long list of specific documents relating to fraud with respect to certain realty, but also added the end phrase "together with other fruits, instrumentalities, and evidence of crime at this [time] unknown". Although acknowledging that the execution of a warrant "authorizing a search and seizure of a person's papers" presents "grave dangers" ordinarily not present in searches "for physical objects whose relevance is more easily ascertainable," the Court sustained this very general end phrase under the facts of the case. The needed content of the unknown items was sufficiently established by reference to the items and subject matter specified in the first portion of the paragraph, and no more was needed in light of the character of the particular investigation. The government here was looking at a "complex real estate scheme whose existence could be proved only by piecing together many bits of evidence" and "that complexity * * * could not be used as a shield to avoid detection when the State has demonstrated probable cause to believe that evidence of crimes is in the suspect's possession."

§ 21.05   THE *LEON* EXCEPTION

Ordinarily, evidence obtained through an unconstitutional search and seizure may not be used by the prosecution in its case-in-chief. *U.S. v. Leon,* 468 U.S. 897 (1984), however, created an exception to that "exclusionary rule" remedy as to certain unconstitutional searches made pursuant to a warrant. *Leon* held that "the Fourth Amendment exclusionary rule should be modified so as not to bar the use in the prosecution's case-in-chief of evidence obtained by officers acting in reasonable reliance on a search warrant issued by a detached and neutral magistrate but ultimately found to be unsupported by probable cause." *Leon* reasoned that the "exclusionary rule is designed to deter police misconduct rather than to punish the error of judges," and therefore it had no functional validity where the police officer acted in reasonable reliance upon the prior judgment of the magistrate. That was true in the case before the Court, as the search warrant affidavit here "provided evidence sufficient to create disagreement among thoughtful and competent judges as to existence of probable cause," producing an "officer reliance on the magistrate determination [that] was objectively reasonable." The Court added in this regard that what was "objectively reasonable" would be determined in light of what a "reasonably well-trained officer would have known"

Leon does not exempt from the exclusionary rule all searches based on invalid warrant. The Court identified four situations where warrant flaws would still result in the application of the exclusionary rule: (1) where the officer presented knowing or reckless falsehoods in the affidavit used to obtain the warrant; (2) "where the issuing magistrate wholly abandoned his judicial rule," as illustrated by a case in which the magistrate "allowed himself to become a member * * * of the search party"; (3) where the warrant was "so facially deficient—i.e., in failing to particularize the place to be searched or the things to be seized—that the executing officers cannot reasonably presume it to be valid"; and (4) where the warrant was issued on an "affidavit so lacking in indicia of probable cause as to render official belief in its existence entirely unreasonable."

Only the third and fourth exceptions have frequently been at issue in white collar cases. In applying both exceptions, but the fourth in particular, courts emphasize that the "reasonably well trained officer" is "not expected to be a legal technician." Thus, in *Diaz* (see § 21.03), the fourth *Leon* exception was held not to apply to a warrant error of including an earlier document starting date than supported by the probable-cause affidavit. The officer in fact had probable cause to believe the scheme extended back to that date and thought incorrectly that he had set forth enough information to encompass that date in the probable-cause affidavit. Consideration must be given, the court noted, to the "special problems for investigators attempting to draft warrants * * * [in] fraud investigations." On the other hand, *Diaz* held that *Leon* did not exempt that portion of the warrant which improperly authorized seizure of bank account records. Here, there was a "complete lack of justification" for including these items (as the prior fraud cited in the affidavit included only cash transactions) and the officer could not reasonably rely on the magistrate's conclusion that probable cause extended to those records.

Facial deficiency as to description particularity, sufficient to meet the third *Leon* exception, is especially difficult to establish where the character of the offense suggests that a wide variety of documents will provide evidence of the crime and the warrant therefore includes an extensive listing of categories of documents. Officers will not be expected to examine carefully each of the individual categories to determine whether a particular description might be overly broad. See *U.S. v. Travers*, 233 F.3d 1327 (11th Cir.2000). Of course, a quite different issue is presented if the description was overly broad because the officer intentionally deceived the magistrate by omitting details in the probable cause affidavit that would have led to a narrower description of the items to be seized. At that point, the first of the *Leon* exceptions comes into play.

Unconstitutional searches typically are challenged through a Rule 12 motion to suppress, which is made after the defendant has been charged. In white collar cases, there often is a considerable time gap between the search and the indictment, so the challenge to the search often is first presented in a Rule 41(g) motion for return of the seized property. That motion authorizes the return of property if it was obtained by an "unlawful search and seizure" or the moving party is "aggrieved * * * by the deprivation of the property." Since the issue before the court is not suppression, *Leon* does not apply in this proceeding. *Matter of the Search of the Kitty East*, 905 F.2d 1367 (10th Cir.1990). However, if the court concludes that the search was illegal, but that *Leon* might preclude suppression of the documents in a criminal proceeding, the court may require the government to return *copies* of the documents, with the government retaining the originals for possible use in a subsequent prosecution (where a motion to suppress may be made and the *Leon* issue resolved). *In re Search of Offices of Tylman*, 245 F.3d 978 (7th Cir.2001).

Where a *Leon* exception allows suppression, that remedy is available only to the defendant who has standing to contest the search. A defendant who is an entity employee may not have standing to contest the search of an entity's premises, as that defendant may not have a legitimate expectation of privacy in the precise location searched (e.g., it was not that person's office and the item seized was not his property or stored within "his immediate control.") Apart from a small family-owned business, managerial control does not in itself establish the necessary privacy expectation. *U.S. v. SDI Future Health*, 568 F.3d 684 (9th Cir.2009) ("personal connection" must be established, looking to a variety of factors, such as "whether the defendant took precautions on his own behalf to secure the place searched or things seized from any interference without his authorization").

§ 21.06 EXECUTION OF THE WARRANT

Leon applies only to reasonable reliance upon an invalid warrant. Fourth Amendment violations in the execution of the warrant, valid or invalid, continue to be subject to the exclusionary rule. With respect to document searches, claims of unconstitutional execution usually relate to the seizure of documents not specified in the warrant. In some instances, the claim is that the officer erred in treating a particular document as within a particular category adequately specified in the warrant, but more often the claim relates to the seizure of a document clearly not specified in the warrant, which the government justifies under the "plain view" doctrine.

Under the plain view doctrine, if an officer, in the proper course of executing the search, comes across other matter in plain view and has probable cause to believe that matter constitutes evidence of a crime, the officer may seize that matter even though it is not among the items specified in the warrant. A critical issue in plain view cases is whether the officer was acting in the proper execution of the warrant when he came across the seized item in plain view. As applied to documents, the resolution of this issue typically depends on whether the officer had reason to inspect the document even though it turned out not to be one of the documents specified in the warrant. The Supreme Court has recognized that, in the course of identifying those documents that fit within the warrant description, officers will be required to "examine at least cursorily" many documents that they will then determine not to be within that description. *Andresen v. Maryland* (§ 21.04). These documents then will be in plain view, and if their proper examination carries the officer to the point where the content of the document establishes probable cause as to a different crime, the Fourth Amendment permits immediate seizure of the document. That was exactly what happened in *Andresen*, where the warrant authorized a search for documents relating to false pretenses in the sale of real estate lot 13T, and the officers came across (and seized) documents evidencing an identical modus operandi as to another lot in the same subdivision.

In looking for documents specified in the warrant by reference to content or type, the executing officer is not restricted by the business' apparent filing system; where documents have incriminating content, they might well not be stored in the "obvious place". As a result, officers often must examine vast quantities of intermingled records to find the specified records. Indeed, the administrative burden of this task often justifies seizing a large batch of intermingled records and removing them to a place where the sorting out process would be less intrusive.

Lower courts have uniformly recognized that search warrant execution presents special difficulties in the search for data stored in a computer. The computer stores more information than the filing cabinet (the traditional repository for business records) and is far more likely to have personal data stored alongside business data (particularly in e-mails). Here, a thorough examination of contents can dramatically expand the consequences of the plain view doctrine and result in substantial invasions of privacy. Nonetheless, courts generally have rejected the contention that officers executing computer searches must limit their examination by reference to file labels or items identified through keyword or other search devices. Executing officers may take into account the target's capacity to mislabel and otherwise conceal or disguise data that reflects criminality, and therefore insist upon at least a cursory reading of a far broader range of files.

The Tenth circuit, in an unusual case, did hold improper the searching of a series of obviously related files after it was apparent that this group of files did not contain documents related to the subject of the search warrant (the sale of controlled substances) but did contain pornography. *U.S. v. Carey*, 172 F.3d 1268 (10th Cir.1999). Although the Supreme Court has rejected the position that plain-view requires a showing that the discovery was inadvertent, the Tenth Circuit apparently viewed the executing officers as having shifted from the execution of the warrant to looking for more pornography. The Tenth Circuit's analysis suggested the value of having the executing officers, once recognizing the need for a massive examination due to potential intermingling, shift back to the court or to a neutral computer expert the shaping of the procedure for further examination of the files. Some courts will attach execution protocols for screening computer data and through the protocol achieve such a shift or otherwise seek to respond to the inclination of executing officers to expand the examination in order to gain significant plain view discovery. See WCH § 21.8.

CHAPTER 22

ATTORNEY-CLIENT PRIVILEGE

§ 22.01 GROUNDING AND POLICY

The attorney-client privilege (also known as the lawyer-client privilege) is an evidentiary privilege that protects the confidentiality of communications made for the purpose of facilitating the rendition of professional legal services to the client. At its core, the privilege protects the confidentiality of communications between the client and the client's attorney, but as explained in § 22.03 and § 22.15, the privilege can provide protection of related communications of other persons whose functions bring them within the scope of the privilege. In the federal courts, the privilege is recognized pursuant to Rule 501 of the Federal Rules of Evidence. Rule 501 provides that, in proceedings relating to a federal-law cause of action (which includes the enforcement of federal criminal and regulatory law), evidentiary privileges "shall be governed by the principles of the common law as they may be interpreted by the courts of the United States [i.e., the federal courts] in light of reason and experience." The attorney-client privilege is a well-established part of the federal common law of privileges, although federal courts are divided on certain aspects of the privilege that bear particularly upon the investigation of white collar crime.

The objective of the attorney-client privilege, the Supreme Court has noted, is to "encourage full and frank communications between attorneys and their clients and thereby promote broader interests in the observance of law and administration of justice." *Upjohn Company v. U.S.*, 449 U.S. 383 (1981). The assumptions underlying this objective are: (1) ensured confidentiality of communication "encourages clients to make full disclosure to their attorneys," *Upjohn*; (2) such complete disclosure is needed for attorneys to render appropriate legal advice and provide proper legal services; and (3) "the social good derived from the proper performance of the functions of lawyers acting for their clients * * * [will] outweigh the harm that may come from the suppression of the evidence in specific cases," *U.S. v. United Shoe Machinery Corp.*, 89 F.Supp. 357 (D.Mass.1950).

Although the attorney-client privilege is grounded in facilitating the attorney's representation of the client, the privilege is created for the client, not the attorney. The client is given the right to assert the privilege by refusing to disclose protected communications and by preventing other persons (including the attorney) from disclosing such communications. So too, the client has the ultimate authority to waive that right. As discussed in § 22.08, when an attorney takes action that asserts or waives the privilege, the attorney does so as the agent of the client, not in the exercise of any authority belonging to the attorney.

Citing Wigmore's analysis of evidentiary privileges, federal lower court have frequently noted that, because the attorney-client privilege presents "an obstacle to the investigation of the truth," it should be "strictly confined within the narrowest possible limits consistent with the logic of its principle." A "strict" or "narrow" construction of this privilege is said to be particularly appropriate because, as Wigmore noted, "its benefits are all indirect and speculative [and] its obstruction [of the truth] is plain and concrete." However, the Supreme Court has stated that courts should not narrow a long established application of the privilege on the basis of no more than "thoughtful speculation" that the narrowing would be consistent with the underlying purpose of the privilege. See *Swidler & Berlin v. U.S.*, 524 U.S. 399 (1988) (government argument for an exception to the posthumous application of the privilege where the deceased client's communications are relevant to a criminal proceeding, with the government contending that such a limited exception was not likely to diminish a client's willingness to confide in an attorney, did not make the compelling case needed to "overturn the common law rule").

§ 22.02   BASIC ELEMENTS

The core protection of the privilege requires (1) a communication, (2) that was made by the client to a lawyer, (3) that was made in confidence, and (4) that was made for the purpose of obtaining professional legal advice (or services relating thereto). WCH §§ 22.1. These requirements combine to impose a broad range of limitations upon the scope of the privilege. Sections 22.04–22.07 discuss the aspects of those limitations that bear particularly upon the investigation of white collar crime. Initially, however, § 22.03 explores derivative protections that take the privilege beyond the core protection of client communications.

The privilege can be lost through a variety of actions by the client (or the attorney, acting on behalf of the client). Sections 22.08–22.11 consider those actions producing a waiver or forfeiture of the privilege that are most likely to be at issue in white collar investigations. Section 22.12 considers the crime-fraud exception which also makes the privilege inapplicable, here because of the client's improper purpose in making the communication.

Where the privilege does apply, it permits the client (or the attorney acting on behalf of the client) to block the disclosure of the protected communications notwithstanding an otherwise valid court order of disclosure (such as a grand jury or administrative subpoena). This protection extends both to documents or recordings that contain the communication, and to testimony, documents, or recordings that describe the content of the communication. Unlike the self-incrimination privilege, the attorney-client privilege cannot be replaced by a grant of immunity, and unlike the work-product doctrine, its protection cannot be overcome by a showing of compelling need for disclosure. However, there are exceptions that limit the protection afforded by the privilege. Sections

22.13 and 22.14 discuss two exceptions of particular significance in the white collar area (the "fiduciary exception" and the "government attorney" exception). Section 22.15 discusses a different type of "exception", the joint defense agreement which works to expand rather than limit the privilege.

§ 22.03   DERIVATIVE PROTECTIONS

Courts have long recognized that, to fulfill the function of the attorney-client privilege, its protection must extend beyond the communication of the client to the lawyer. In particular, it must recognize that: (1) the function of the privilege extends to statements made by a potential client in the course of seeking to retain an attorney; (2) the function of the privilege extends to the attorney's statement to the client as well as the client's statement to the attorney; (3) both the client and the attorney may utilize employees or other agents to convey their communications; and (4) where technical information is involved, there may be need to retain an expert to facilitate the attorney's understanding of the client's communication. The coverage provided in the implementation of these principles is sometimes described as the "derivative protection" of the privilege, although courts also have referred to at least certain aspects of this protection (in particular, the attorney's communication to the client) as an inherent element of the privilege.

Potential clients. Where a communication made in the course of seeking to retain a lawyer otherwise fits the prerequisite of a privileged communication of an actual client to the client's attorney, that communication will be privileged. The "fiduciary relationship existing between lawyer and client extends to preliminary consultation by a prospective client with a view to retention of the lawyer, [even though] actual employment does not result." *Westinghouse Elec. Corp. v. Kerr-McGee Corp.*, 580 F.2d 1311 (7th Cir.1978).

Lawyer communications. Federal courts uniformly agree that the privilege encompasses at least certain types of communications by the lawyer to the client, but are divided as to prerequisites for applying the privilege to such communications. The narrowest view requires that the lawyer's communication be directly responsive to a protected client communication and that it reveal, either explicitly or implicitly, some aspect of the content of the client's protected communication. A somewhat broader position accepts the underlying premise that the protection of the attorney's communication is derivative, arising from the need to avoid revealing the client's communication, but nonetheless protects all responsive communications by the attorney. A responsive communication, it is argued, will almost invariably reveal, at least by implication, some aspect of the client's communication, and the drawing of fine lines to exclude the rare exception only creates uncertainty that undermines the privilege. Thus, in contrast to the narrowest view, this position will extend the privilege to a memorandum providing a general update on legal developments relating to the subject of the representation. A still broader position views the privilege as aimed at protecting an attorney-client dialogue. Here it would extend to an attorney communication containing legal advice that is not responsive to a specific client request and not based on any confidential communication from the client (such as an attorney's self-initiated legal advice regarding activity that the attorney independently observed). See WCH § 22.2(B).

Communicating agents. Both the client and the attorney may use agents in their communications and retain the privilege. The key here is a reasonable expectation that the person will operate as a confidential conduit in preparing or conveying the communication. Those agents typically are regular employees of the client or attorney (e.g., secretaries or paralegals), but special circumstances can justify the use of a trusted non-employee (e.g., a relative acting as an interpreter). However, if it is later found that the third person was not an appropriate communicating agent, the consequence is a breach of confidentiality and loss of the privilege. See § 22.07.

Outside experts. Communications between the attorney and a retained expert, or between a client and a retained expert, even where designed to facilitate legal representation, ordinarily does not fall within the privilege. However, an exception has been recognized for situations in which the expert's assistance is deemed necessary to assist the attorney in understanding the information provided by the client. See *U.S. v. Kovel*, 296 F.2d 918 (2d

Cir.1961) (accountant's performance in such a role analogized to an interpreter, a position traditionally viewed as an acceptable communicating agent). The exception confines the retained expert to this limited role, and therefore does not encompass the expert who provides advice or general knowledge based on his or her expertise to the counsel or client. See e.g., *U.S. v. Ackert*, 159 F.3d 136 (1999) (privilege inapplicable since investment broker acted as a non-lawyer advisor, rather than as an interpreter of client's communication, in explaining tax ramification of a particular type of transaction). Nonetheless, courts have found a wide range of experts, typically retained by the attorney rather than the client, whose services were viewed as facilitating the attorney's understanding and evaluation of the information provided by the client—including accountants, psychiatrists, engineers, and even a public relations expert (where the attorney's objective was to avoid an indictment, expert assisted attorney in obtaining information from the target that could offset public pressure to indict). See WCH § 22.2(D).

§ 22.04   THE COMMUNICATION LIMITATION

The attorney-client privilege protects against the compelled disclosure of a protected confidential communication. It does not preclude disclosures that stand apart from describing the content of the communication. This limitation is reflected in rulings rejecting attempts to utilize the privilege to preclude: (1) compelling testimony as to the client's knowledge of factual information that may have been included in the communication; (2) compelling production of preexisting documents that were conveyed to the attorney as part of the communication; and (3) compelling attorneys to describe aspects of the attorney-client relationship deemed separate from the privileged communication.

Underlying facts. While the client cannot be compelled to testify about what he told the attorney about a certain event, the privilege has no bearing on compelling the client to testify about what he knows about the event (even though that is probably a good part of what he told the attorney). WCH § 22.2(B). Indeed, the client can even be required to disclose factual information gathered at the attorney's suggestion. See *In re Six Grand Jury Witnesses*, 979 F.2d 939 (2d Cir.1992) (where client had prepared a cost analysis at the request of counsel, client could be asked about how the analysis was conducted and what conclusions were drawn, but not questions about sharing the analysis with others, as the answers here might refer to communications to counsel).

Preexisting documents. In contrast to a document prepared specifically for submission to counsel, a preexisting document does not become exempt from disclosure because it was part of the information conveyed to counsel in seeking legal advice. Thus, the government may seek to obtain such a document by subpoena, provided it does not identify the document by reference to the client having included it in a communication to counsel. If the client conveyed the original copy to counsel, the document can be subpoenaed from the attorney. However, in conveying the document to the attorney for the purpose of obtaining legal advice, the client does not relinquish the protection against production that the client would have had if the document had remained in the client's possession. Thus, where the client could have raised a self-incrimination objection to his required production of the preexisting document, the attorney-client privilege will be viewed as having absorbed that protection, allowing the subpoena to the attorney to be challenged as violating the client's self-incrimination privilege, notwithstanding that the subpoena does not compel production by the client. See *Fisher v. U.S.*, 425 U.S. 391 (1976) (recognizing that a contrary position would undercut the function of the attorney-client privilege, as a client with a privilege against production "will be reluctant to transfer possession to the lawyer unless the documents are also privileged in the latter's hands").

Client information. Various aspects of the lawyer-client privilege ordinarily can be acknowledged without revealing the client communication. Consistent with the confinement of the privilege to the narrowest limits that suit its objective (see § 22.01), the privilege does not protect against compelling the attorney to reveal that information (although other concerns may impose restrictions upon subpoenaing attorneys, see § 16.07). Accordingly, absent "special circumstances," the existence of an attorney-client relationship, the identity of the client, and fee information are not privileged. Courts note that, "while consultation with an attorney and payment of a fee, may be necessary to obtain legal advice, their disclosure does not inhibit the ordinary communication necessary for an attorney to act effectively, justly, and expeditiously." Also, with respect to some of this "tangential information," the privilege is seen as inherently precluding protection since the person claiming the privilege must initially establish that an attorney-client relationship existed. WCH § 22.2(C).

Various federal circuits have recognized, however, exceptional situations in which revealing the identity of an unknown client or information relating to a third party payment of legal fees will be barred from disclosure by virtue of the privilege. See WCH § 22.2(C). One standard, having limited support, asks whether revealing the client identity or fee information will produce the "last link" in an evidentiary trail leading to a prosecution of the client as to the very matter for which the client sought legal assistance. Courts supporting this position acknowledge that information which stands apart from the client communication should not become privileged simply because it might incriminate the client in some wrongdoing. They argue, however, that an exception is needed where the evidence known to be available to the government already points to the client's liability and revealing the client's identity or third-party payment of a fee will constitute, in effect, the "last nail in the coffin", for that is the situation in which the client will certainly hesitate in seeking legal assistance for fear that his identity will be revealed. Courts rejecting this last link approach note that, while it "may promote concepts of fundamental fairness against self-incrimination, these concepts are not proper considerations to invoke the attorney-client privilege."

Another standard for extending the privilege to identity and fee information is sometimes described as the "legal advice" rule. Under this standard, which has broader judicial support, the privilege will apply where, in light of information already known to the government, revealing the client identity or the fee information will, in effect, reveal some significant aspect of the client's communication. Thus, where the government was aware that a defendant had unknown co-conspirators, and the circumstances surrounding the structure of defendant's representation indicated that the third-party payor would have been a person who consulted the attorney as to his own possible involvement in the conspiracy, the privilege barred compelling the attorney to identify that third-party payor. The key was not that disclosure would be incriminating, but that it would reveal the specifics of the client's consultation.

§ 22.05 COMMUNICATIONS OF CORPORATE CLIENTS

The attorney-client privilege does not protect third party communications to the client's lawyer, even where the third party speaks to the lawyer at the request of the client and conveys information which is critical to the attorney providing adequate legal advice. Where the client is an individual, third party communications and client communications are readily distinguished. Where the client is a corporation, however, the distinction presents additional complexity since the corporation can speak only through individuals and a variety of different persons might be viewed as its agent for this purpose. Prior to the Supreme Court's ruling in *Upjohn Co. v. U.S.*, 449 U.S. 383 (1981), most lower courts had held that the privilege extended only to communications to the attorney by those corporate employees that were within the corporate "control group" (i.e., those in a position to establish corporate policy in response to counsel's advice). The Court in *Upjohn* rejected the control group test, and though "declin[ing] to lay down a broad rule or series of rules" for determining who spoke for the corporation, provided guidance that pointed to protecting the communications of a much broader spectrum of corporate employees in most instances.

Upjohn sustained the application of the privilege to various documents reflecting the content of communications made to counsel in the course of counsel's internal investigation of questionable payments by various employees to foreign officials. The communications in question went well beyond the corporate control group, but the Supreme Court concluded that precluding protection on that ground would "frustrat[e] the very purpose of the privilege by discouraging the communication of relevant information by employees to attorneys seeking to render legal advice to the client corporation." "In the corporate context," the Court noted, "it will frequently be employees beyond the control group * * * who will possess the information needed by the corporate lawyer * * * [as] middle and, indeed, lower-level employees can, by actions within the scope of their employment, embroil the corporation in serious legal difficulties." Also, "the attorney's advice will * * * frequently be more significant to non-control group members than to those who officially sanction the advice."

Turning to the specific circumstances of the communications at issue, the *Upjohn* Court cited a variety of factors which combined to support privilege protection. The Court noted that: (1) the communications were made (and sought by counsel) in order to secure legal advice; (2) the employees were directed by their corporate superiors to provide information to counsel; (3) the employees were "sufficiently aware that they were being questioned in order that the corporation could obtain legal advice"; (4) "the communications concerned matters within the scope of the employees' corporate duties"; (5) the communications provided "information that [was]not available from upper echelon management" and "was needed to supply a basis for legal advice"; and (6) the employees were informed that the communications were considered "highly confidential" and the communications subsequently "had been kept confidential by the company."

The *Upjohn* ruling leaves open the question of whether all of these factors are central to bringing a communication within the privilege. Lower courts holding the privilege inapplicable to internal investigations have relied primarily on the failure to satisfy the first factor, finding that the investigation was not aimed at seeking legal advice. See § 22.06. Since internal investigations typically seek first-hand knowledge from lower-level employees, which is not available to "upper echelon management," lower courts have had no reason to address the importance of the fifth factor noted above. As to the second and third, lower courts have suggested that the employee must know that the communication is sought to assist in providing legal advice, but that knowledge can exist without the employee also being ordered to provide information to counsel.

Upjohn left open the question whether the privilege would extend to communications with former employees. Chief Justice Burger's concurring opinion indicated that the key factor was that the individual was asked by management to cooperate by providing information "regarding conduct or proposed conduct [then] within the scope of [the person's] employment," rather than employment status when cooperating. Most lower courts have accepted that standard, reasoning that the extension of the privilege to communications with employees rests on the attorney's need to be fully informed of the client's actions and that includes the conduct of all persons employed during the time period in questions. See WCH § 22.3. A contrary position would focus on the inability of the employer to force the former employer to participate, since a threat of termination is not available, but termination also may not be available as to current employees who nonetheless cooperate.

Internal investigations serve various interests of the corporation, including the acquisition of information that may be disclosed to governmental authorities as evidence of the corporation's willingness to cooperate in proceedings against wrongdoers (a factor that may lead to more lenient treatment of the corporation, see § 2.04). Since the corporation is the client and the holder of the privilege, the corporation may make such a disclosure notwithstanding the objection of the employee whose communication is revealed. Some corporate counsel, to avoid any confusion on this score, include "*Upjohn* warnings" in their interview protocol. Such warnings emphasize that the attorney represents the corporation, rather than the employee, and while the attorney-client privilege applies, the corporation, as the holder of the privilege, has the authority to waive the privilege. Absent such a warning, the employee may later argue that the corporate counsel was representing both the corporation and the employees, producing a joint defense arrangement as to the privilege. (as discussed below).

Where the employee is revealing matters that might expose him or her to personal liability, the employee may seek to obtain protection against a subsequent corporate decision to disclose by insisting that counsel represent the employee as an individual as well as the corporation. If the employee holds the privilege along with the corporation, the employee may be able to exercise the privilege to protect his or her communication, notwithstanding the corporation's desire to waive. (See § 22.15). Representation of both the employer and employee presents a potential conflict of interest, but that representation may be acceptable under the Rules of Professional Conduct. See WCH § 22.4.

A corporate employee claiming that corporate counsel also represented the employee as an individual bears the burden of establishing that relationship. Absent a clear documentation (such as a separate billing), that task will be difficult, as the standing presumption is that corporate counsel represents only the corporation, even when the employee is the chief executive. See *Matter of Bevill, Bresler & Shulman Asset Mgmt. Co.*, 896 F.2d 54 (3rd Cir.1986) (five-prong test must be met, including showing that corporate counsel was willing to disregard possible conflict arising from "communicating with the employee in the employee's individual capacity," and showing that the communication focused on the employee's rights and liabilities rather than the corporation's rights and responsibilities). Moreover, even if personal representation is established, it will give the employee control over waiver only "to the extent communications regarding [the employee's] individual acts and liabilities are segregable from discussions about the corporation." The corporation still retains the authority to "unilaterally waive the attorney-client privilege with respect to any communications made by a corporate officer in his corporate capacity." *In re Grand Jury Subpoena (Custodian of Records, Newparent, Inc.)*, 274 F.3d 563 (1st Cir.2001).

§ 22.06   THE LEGAL ADVICE LIMITATION

The privilege applies only where the client is communicating with the lawyer for the purpose of obtaining "legal advice" (which includes not only a lawyer's statement of advice, but also the providing of legal services based on the lawyer's legal analysis). Thus, the privilege does not apply where the lawyer is being asked to provide services typically offered by non-lawyers, such as detectives (e.g., a strictly factual investigation), political or labor consultants (e.g., election strategy), or accountants (e.g., tax return preparation). In interpreting the legal advice requirement, courts guard against allowing clients to substitute attorneys for other professionals and thereby create an evidentiary privilege where none would otherwise exist (as in the case of accountants, as the federal law does not recognize an accountant-client privilege). At the same time, courts also recognize that non-legal considerations can be integral to the framing of legal advice. Thus, a lawyer communication which is "primarily" legal in nature will not fall outside the privilege because it alludes to business considerations. *In re Kellogg, Brown, & Root, Inc.*, 756 F.3d 754 (D.C.Cir.2014) (communication can have more than one primary purpose, so issue is whether legal advice was "a primary purpose * * *, meaning one of the significant purposes"). So too, some courts have concluded that shaping public opinion as it relates to litigation may be part of the attorney's legal advice. See *In re Grand Jury Subpoenas Dated March 24, 2003*, 265 F.Supp.2d 321 (S.D.N.Y. 2003).

In determining whether a client's communication was for the purpose of obtaining legal advice, courts tend to apply greater scrutiny to communications made to in-house counsel (as opposed to outside counsel). Courts point to two factors in placing a greater burden on the claimant of the privilege in this setting. First, in-house counsel are often extensively involved in the business matters of a company (frequently holding a combined legal and executive position). Second, the proximity of in-house counsel often leads to keeping in-house counsel "informed" of every activity that may have potential legal consequences, and if the "legal advice" category is not carefully restricted to exclude such informational communications, the corporation will be able to shield against disclosure the bulk of its internal communications simply by routing those communications through the office of legal counsel. Accordingly, where a communication was to in-house counsel, the client/employer must clearly establish that the communication was aimed specifically at obtaining legal advice (typically by specifically requesting such advice). Limited participation by outside counsel cannot alter the character of an internal investigation that basically has a business goal. *U.S. v. ISS Marine Servs., Inc.*, 905 F.Supp.2d 121 (D.D.C. 2012) (internal investigation did not qualify where corporation rejected proposal to have outside counsel conduct the investigation, assigned the investigation to internal auditors, and then sent finished report to outside counsel for its views; " 'consultation lite' does not qualify").

§ 22.07   THE CONFIDENTIALITY LIMITATION

The confidentiality requirement has two prerequisites: (1) the client must have subjectively intended that the communication be kept confidential, and (2) reasonable precautions must have been taken to ensure confidentiality. If either prerequisite is not met, the communication does not fall under the privilege even though a breach of confidentiality did not actually occur. If the prerequisites are met at the time of communication, a subsequent breach of confidentiality may result in the loss of the privilege through a waiver (see § 22.10) (although very often a court will find that the privilege did not apply in the first instance because the subsequent breach was indicative of an original intent not to keep the communication confidential).

Where a client conveys information to a lawyer for the purpose of public disclosure or disclosure to a third party (such as to a government agency), courts find that the subjective intent prerequisite is lacking. Thus, the privilege does not apply to communications containing information to be included in a prospectus, a tax return, a filing with an agency, or a letter to be conveyed to an opposing party. Although the lawyer will be using legal skills in shaping the information for disclosure, the attorney is treated as basically a "conduit" for conveying the communication to the third party. See *U.S. v. Ruehle,* 583 F.3d 600 (9th Cir.2009) (even if outside counsel was representing the CFO as well as the corporation in the internal investigation, CFO could not clam privilege as to information that clearly would have to be disclosed to the corporation's outside auditors).

The second prerequisite of reasonable precautions has been found to be lacking in a variety of situations, including: (1) the participation of a third person in the communication (which often occurs where the client viewed the third person as an appropriate agent, see § 22.03, but the court held otherwise); (2) the communication was made in a public place under circumstance which could readily have permitted known bystanders to overhear the communication; (3) a written communication (or a document describing an oral communication) was handled in a manner that made it readily accessible to employees who had no "need to know" of the communication (e.g., indiscriminately mingled with routine documents); and (4) a written communication was distributed to appropriate persons but without seeking in any way to ensure against further disclosure by those persons (such as identifying the document as "privileged" or "confidential").

§ 22.08   FORMS OF WAIVER

In the context of the attorney-client privilege, the term "waiver" has been described as a "loose and misleading label for what is in fact a collection of different rules addressed to different problems." *U.S. v. M.I.T.*, 129 F.3d 681 (1st Cir.1997). Here, the traditional form of waiver (an "intentional relinquishment of a known right") is only one of various types of waiver. Indeed, in most cases involving an issue of waiver, the client quite clearly did not intend to relinquish the privilege, and is now arguing that it has not been waived. Sections 22.09–22.11 describe the three forms of "waiver" that have been the most frequent subject of litigation.

It commonly is stated that only the client can waive the attorney-client privilege. Nonetheless, attorneys, acting as the agent of the client, may readily take steps that produce a waiver even though the client has not been consulted. In particular, an intentional disclosure by the attorney will be binding absent the client having expressly forbidden the disclosure, and an inadvertent disclosure may result in a waiver even though it clearly would have been opposed by the client.

Where the corporation is the client, the current management acts on behalf of the corporation on the decision to waive. Thus, new management is free to waive the privilege as to an internal investigation of actions taken by the former management. So too, a trustee-in-bankruptcy may waive the privilege as the trustee becomes, in effect, the new management. *Commodity Futures Trading Comm'n v. Weinstraub*,

471 U.S. 343 (1985). Although management operates as the holder of the privilege, in placing corporate employees in a position where they have the authority to make disclosures that might reveal privileged communications, management assumes the risk that actions taken by those employees will produce a waiver of the privilege. Thus, where a corporate officer appears to be representing the corporation in giving grand jury testimony, that officer's disclosure of the privileged material may be attributed to the corporation. *Velsical Chemical Corp. v. Parsons*, 561 F.2d 671 (7th Cir.1997) (noting that the officer, in giving the grand jury testimony constituting a waiver, had been advised by corporation's outside counsel). On the other hand, where the corporate officer appeared to be testifying on his own behalf, and the corporation had previously stated that it would not waive the privilege, the officer's testimony was not attributed to the corporation in assessing whether a waiver had occurred. See *In re Grand Jury Proceedings (U.S. v. Doe)*, 219 F.3d 175 (2d Cir.2000).

§ 22.09 WAIVER BY INTENTIONAL DISCLOSURE

Purposeful disclosures of privileged communications produce waiver in a variety of situations, including disclosures to the public, disclosures to experts assisting the client (e.g., auditors), disclosures to opponents in the course of negotiation or litigation, disclosures to government agencies, and disclosures pursuant to a subpoena or court order where no objection is made (waiver does not occur where a court, over objection, erroneously orders disclosure). Such disclosures raise two issue concerning the scope of the waiver—whether it may be "partial" and whether it may be "selective" (i.e., applicable only to the party to whom disclosure was made). See WCH § 22.6(B).

The partial waiver issue arises where the disclosure encompasses only a portion of the privileged communications on a general subject (e.g., only a portion of an internal investigation). Federal courts traditionally held that the waiver consequence had to extend to all otherwise privileged communications concerning the same "subject matter." They showed some flexibility, however, in determining what constituted the same subject matter, considering a variety of factors. Federal Rule 502(a) altered that analysis for intentional disclosures made in a "federal proceeding" (which includes both judicial and administrative proceedings) and intentional disclosures made to a "federal office or agency." Rule 502(a) provides that an intentional disclosure which waives the attorney-client privilege extends to "disclosed and undisclosed communications or information [that] concern the same subject matter," but only if "they ought in fairness to be considered together." The "fairness" component provides greater flexibility, although it requires consideration of the same factors that previously led to narrow or broad assessments of whether the undisclosed communications concerned the same subject matter. A key consideration in assessing fairness is whether the partial disclosure was designed to achieve a tactical advantage (seeking, as one court noted, "to let a whisker out of the bag, but not the whole cat"). The primary concern here is to avoid distortion, but that concern may extend beyond inconsistent information in the undisclosed information, as where that information could furnish a lead to other relevant evidence. Even without distortion, fairness may recognize the need to combine the undisclosed and disclosed information to provide a complete picture. Cf. Fed.R.Evid. 106 (restricting introduction of only one portion of a written or recorded statement).

"Selective waiver" presents an issue that applies even to an acceptable partial disclosure; does the disclosure to one party extend to all others? The traditional rule was that a party cannot "pick and choose" among potential litigants. The Eighth Circuit at one time proposed an exception for voluntary disclosures to regulatory agencies, which would encourage waivers in agency investigations by allowing the target to refuse to disclose the same communications (e.g., an internal investigation) to private litigants. Various other circuits then considered and rejected that possible exception to the general rule (and the Eighth Circuit itself appeared to back away from it). The Eight Circuit position did receive support in a proposed revision of Federal Rule 502, but that proposal was withdrawn in light of strong opposition. See WCH § 22.6(B). However, Federal Rule 502(d) includes a provision authorizing "selective disclosure" agreements that conceivably could operate to effectuate selective waiver.

Rule 502(d) authorizes a court to issue an order holding that the privilege "is not waived by disclosure connected with the litigation before the court—in which event the disclosure is also not a waiver in any other Federal or State proceeding." A major objective of this provision is to permit the parties to agree to a process of pretrial discovery that would not require all the steps that might be demanded to ensure against waiver by inadvertent disclosure (see § 22.10) and to gain court approval of that agreement, which would then be binding on third parties as well as the litigants. See Rule 502(e). However, the Rule 502(d) provision is not so limited. It can also protect, with judicial approval, an agreement to disclose otherwise protected communications to the government for its confidential use (i.e., where the disclosed communications would not become part of the public record), so that subsequent litigants (should they become aware of the disclosure) cannot rely on the waiver doctrine to demand protection of those communications. Here, the "selective disclosure" authorized under Rule 502(d) produces, in effect, selective waiver. Since a Rule 502(d) order is available only for "disclosure connected with litigation pending before the court," its use in this fashion would be limited primarily to disclosures made in government enforcement proceedings (as opposed to disclosures made at the investigatory stage).

Another issue raised by intentional disclosures to the government is whether the disclosure constituted, in effect, a coerced waiver, rendering the waiver invalid. Corporate disclosures of internal investigations to government agencies often are made in the face of harsh consequences (including possible criminal prosecution) following from a failure to provide such "voluntary cooperation." The Second Circuit found a constitutional violation in the government's insistence that corporate cooperation include a refusal to pay the legal fees of indicted employees, see *U.S. v. Stein*, 541 F.3d 130 (2d Cir.2008), but that ruling involved the constitutional rights of the employees and the government's interference with a prior commitment of the employer. The relinquishment of the attorney-client privilege involves only a right of corporation, and is comparable to the relinquishment of rights made by guilty plea defendants in exchange for reduced sentences. Accordingly, even if the government should insist upon a waiver of the privilege as an absolute prerequisite to avoiding prosecution (a position rejected in DOJ internal guidelines, see § 2.04), that would not render the waiver involuntary.

§ 22.10 WAIVER BY INADVERTENT DISCLOSURE

Inadvertent disclosures commonly involve the accidental inclusion of documents containing privileged communication along with non-privileged communications sent to a third party in the course of negotiation or litigation. Inadvertent disclosure also occurs where a privileged communication is incorrectly addressed and received by a person outside of the "small circle of 'others' " with whom privileged information might be shared (see § 23.03). Of course, since the "cat is out of the bag," the unintended recipient now has knowledge of the content of the communication and that can hardly be erased. The critical questions are whether disclosure will now be required as to other parties and other privileged communications and whether what was disclosed can be used in evidence by the recipient and by others who become aware of it (such as government investigators).

The governing standard on inadvertent disclosures is set forth in Evidence Rule 502(b). It provides that disclosure of an otherwise protected communication, "when made in a federal proceeding or to a federal office or agency, * * * does not operate as a waiver in a federal or state proceeding" if three conditions are satisfied: (1) the disclosure is inadvertent; (2) the holder of the privilege took reasonable steps to prevent disclosure, and (3) the holder promptly took reasonable steps to rectify the error, including (if applicable) following Federal Rule of Civil Procedure 26(b)(5)(B). The latter provision applies to discovery in civil litigation and allows the party that made the inadvertent disclosure to impose various obligations on the receiving party (to preclude further disclosure) by informing the receiving party that certain information it recorded was inadvertently disclosed privileged material.

A key to avoiding waiver under Rule 502(b) is establishing that reasonable steps were taken to prevent disclosure. The Advisory Committee Notes to Rule 502(b) cited in this connection a pre-Rule 502 listing of factors to be considered in assessing whether the equities relating to inadvertent disclosure justified relieving the client of adverse consequences due to that disclosure. Those factors include: (1) the reasonableness of the precautions taken to prevent inadvertent disclosure, considering the scope of the discovery; (2) the number of inadvertent disclosures; (3) the extent of the disclosure; (4) measures taken to rectify the disclosure and the timing of those measures; and (5) whether the overriding interests of justice would or would not be served by relieving a party of its error. The Committee Notes added that the importance of these factors would "vary from case to case." In some respects, they also may vary from court to court as judges have different perspectives both on what constitutes extreme carelessness and the weighing of the carelessness against other considerations (the difficulties presented in precluding litigant use and further disclosures where an extensive body of material is involved, or the sensitive nature of the disclosed material). See WCH § 22.6(C).

§ 22.11 WAIVER BY AFFIRMATIVE RELIANCE

Courts commonly note that the attorney-client privilege is designed only to be used defensively as a "shield" and not "offensively" as a sword. Under this principle, where a client raises the "advice of counsel" as a defense to a civil or criminal action, that constitutes a waiver of all privileged communications on that issue. Similarly, a client may not testify as to some portion of a communication with the client's attorney and then refuse to permit full disclosure of the entire communication.

Application of this concept of waiver-by-affirmative-use becomes problematic where the client is the corporation and the affirmative use is made by an employee of the corporation. If the employee is acting on behalf of the corporation (or appears to be doing so, see § 22.08), the waiver clearly applies. In some instances, however, the employee (or former employee) may seek to use the advice of counsel as a personal defense, against the express wishes of the corporate client. Under standard doctrine, the privilege belongs to the corporation and it should control waiver, but without the waiver, the opposing litigant challenging the employee's "advice of counsel" defense will be deprived of discovery essential to that challenge. *In re Grand Jury Proceedings (U.S. v. Doe),* 219 F.3d 175 (2d Cir.2000), while not providing a dispositive answer on waiver in that situation, emphasized that the analysis of the waiver issue "should be guided primarily by fairness principles," as applied on a "case by case basis." Binding the corporation by the employee's affirmative use is most readily justified where the corporation basically is the alter ego of the employee (as in a closed corporation).

§ 22.12   CRIME-FRAUD EXCEPTION

Client communications made for the very purpose of furthering an ongoing or future crime or fraud (and, perhaps, other intentional torts as well) fall outside the attorney-client privilege because they rest on a misuse of the attorney-client relationship. Typical crime-fraud scenarios are the client who seeks legal advice for the purpose of structuring a transaction so as to make undetectable an underlying crime or fraud and the client who seeks a legal service that will further the crime or fraud (e.g., preparing a deceptive legal document that might later be used in a fraud). Since clients may appropriately seek an attorney's advice concerning past wrongdoings, communications relating to past behavior will only fall within the crime-fraud exception if the client's purpose is to facilitate continuing that activity or executing a cover-up. The key is the purpose of the client, not the knowledge of the lawyer, as the exception applies whether or not the lawyer is aware of the client's purpose. It also applies whether or not that purpose was actually achieved.

An extensive body of federal precedent addresses the crime-fraud exception. Most of the rulings arise out of efforts by federal prosecutors and federal regulators to use the crime-fraud exception to override privilege claims, with many of those cases involving grand jury investigations. The federal decisions focus primarily on three issues: (1) what elements establish the applicability of the crime-fraud exception; (2) what burden of proof does the government carry as to those elements; (3) when may or must the court ruling on the issue examine in camera the record of the protected communication as an aid in determining whether the crime-fraud exception applies.

Elements of the exception. The crime-fraud rests on a sufficient showing being made as to two elements; (1) at the time when the otherwise privileged communications were made, the client intended to commit a crime or fraud, either as the continuation of an ongoing activity or an activity to be initiated in the future; (2) the client's sought to achieve through the communication the "furtherance" of the planned crime or fraud. The two elements are shaped to clearly exclude from the exception two types of consultations that the privilege is aimed particularly at protecting. First, the exception recognizes that a person who has engaged in a completed transaction that might be illegal should not be discouraged from seeking the assistance of counsel with respect to that conduct. Where counsel's advice is sought after the wrongdoing has been completed, the first element affords protection by looking to the client's intent as to future behavior at the time of the consultation. However, the post-illegality consultation is not given absolute protection; depending upon the client's subsequent response with respect to the wrongdoing, there remains the possibility of viewing the consultation as aimed at the future crime of covering-up the past offense.

The two-pronged standard also is designed to ensure protection of the client who "innocently proposes an illegal course of conduct to explore with his counsel what he may or may not do." *U.S. v. Doe*, 429 F.3d 450 (3d Cir.2005). Such a person does not have the intent to engage in the conduct if is unlawful, and even if he should later change his mind and proceed with the action, the requisite timing for the two elements would not be met. Thus, courts have held that a mere showing that the client later engaged in illegal conduct does not, without more, establish the prerequisite intent at the time of the communication.

Although not always described as such, the second element, like the first, focuses on the client's purpose, insisting that the client intended to use the communication in furtherance of the commission of the crime or fraud. As with the commission of the wrongdoing, success in the use of communication is not needed. Moreover, the decisions reflect a broad view of what furthers the commission of a client's wrongdoing. Thus, a seemingly innocuous explanation of what information would be relevant to an investigation can serve to further a crime by indicating what records should be altered or destroyed to avoid detection. See *In re Grand Jury Investigation,* 445 F.3d 266 (3d Cir.2006).

Proof standards. Federal courts agree that the burden of proof is on the movant seeking to defeat the privilege. That burden takes into account the difficulties posed in characterizing a communication when its content is unknown. It may readily be established that an individual committed or attempted to commit a crime and that the individual previously consulted an attorney, but that does not necessarily establish as well the two requisite elements of the crime fraud exception. To some extent the standard of proof must accept a showing based on inference.

The common starting point in describing the requisite level of proof is that only a "prima facie" showing is needed as to both elements. The lower courts differ, however, in further explanations of what constitutes a prima facie showing. See WCH § 22.7. These explanations include, as to each of the elements; a "reasonable cause to believe"; a "reasonable basis to suspect"; "evidence which, if believed by the fact-finder would be sufficient to support a finding that the elements * * * were met"; evidence "such as will suffice until contradicted and overcome by other evidence"; and "evidence that, if believed by a trier of fact would establish the elements." The First Circuit has noted that " 'prima facie' is among the most rubbery of all legal phrases," and in this context means "little more than a showing of whatever is required to permit [the] inferential leap sufficient to * * * [pierce the privilege]" (which it also described as a "reasonable basis") *In re Grand Jury Proceedings*, 417 F.3d 18 (1st Cir.2005).

A prima facie showing does not necessarily defeat the client's claim of the privilege. The opinions hold open the possibility that client may respond by rebutting the government's showing. Clients face a significant hurdle, however, as they often are unaware of the specifics of the government's showing. The government commonly will be allowed to make its showing by ex parte affidavit to protect the secrecy of its investigation, and that may be required by Rule 6(e) secrecy requirements when the government relies on grand jury testimony. Very often, the best opportunity for rebuttal comes in the court's examination of documents setting forth the privileged communications, as the nature of the communication may clearly indicate that it could not have been used to further the client's alleged crime or fraud.

In camera review. Under *U.S. v. Zolin*, 491 U.S. 554 (1989), if there is a threshold showing of a "factual basis adequate to support a good faith belief by a reasonable person" that the communication itself "may reveal evidence to establish that the crime-fraud exception applies", the district court has discretion to examine the communication in camera and consider its contents in determining whether the necessary quantum of proof (which the *Zolin* Court declined to define) has been met. *Zolin* overruled earlier decisions which had held that the crime-fraud exception must be shown by evidence entirely independent of any inspection of the privileged communication. Where courts view the prima facie standard as simply requiring probable cause, they often refer to the prima facie standard as the prerequisite for inspecting the communication. Where the prima facie standard is read as requiring a greater level of proof, a distinction is drawn between that standard and the "good faith belief" standard of *Zolin*. Appellate opinions strongly suggest that, no matter what standard of proof is ultimately applied, a court should not hold the crime-fraud exception applicable without first conducting an in camera review of the privilege-protected evidence to determine what light it casts on the issue. Once the exception is held to apply, where a series of documents are subject to the privilege, courts commonly conduct a document-by-document review to determine which meet and which do not meet the "in furtherance" requirement.

§ 22.13   THE FIDUCIARY EXCEPTION

Chapter 18 explores many of the perils facing the target of a grand jury investigation when also subjected to a civil suit involving the same subject matter. Where the target is a corporation, the fiduciary exception to the attorney-client privilege may add to those perils in the context of a limited class of parallel civil actions. The fiduciary exception rests on the recognition that the true beneficiary of legal advice may not be the nominal client, but persons in a fiduciary relationship with that client. The prime example of such "ultimate clients" are the shareholders of the corporation. Since all corporate actions, including privileged communications, are undertaken on their behalf, shareholders have a strong claim for access to the privileged communication where they claim that it would show that management acted contrary to the fiduciary duty owed to them. The reality of shareholder litigation, however, is that actions supposedly brought on behalf of all shareholders may in fact have little shareholder support and have a grounding more strategic than substantive. If shareholder actions, such as stockholder derivative suits, automatically called for disclosure of privileged communications, that could well work to the disadvantage of shareholders in the long run by discouraging management from seeking legal advice on decisions likely to be second-guessed by dissatisfied shareholders (or, the lawyers who specialize in such actions).

Balancing these concerns, the leading ruling of *Garner v. Wolfinbarger*, 430 F.2d 1093 (5th Cir.1970) held that shareholders could gain access to privileged communications but only upon a showing of cause. In determining whether cause exists, *Garner* directed district courts to consider a variety of factors including: the number of shareholders pursuing the claim and the percentage of the shares they represent; the "bona fides of the shareholders"; the nature of the shareholder's claim (particularly whether it claims misconduct that would be criminal) and whether it is "obviously colorable"; the "apparent necessity or desirability of the shareholders having the information"; the possibility of obtaining that information from other sources; the extent to which the communication is identified (in contrast to the shareholders "blindly fishing"); and the alleged nature of the communication (in particular, whether it related to past or prospective actions, and whether it constituted advice concerning the litigation itself). Courts have extended the "good cause" approach of *Garner* to other fiduciary situations, such as a government action against former officials of a pension fund for violation of their fiduciary responsibilities and actions by union members against union officials. See WCH § 22.8

§ 22.14   THE GOVERNMENT ATTORNEY EXCEPTION

Although direct holdings are sparse, courts generally agree that government entities (such as regulatory agencies, executive departments, and local and state governments) can be treated as "clients" with respect to their communications with government lawyers in much the same way that corporations may be clients in their communications with in-house counsel. Thus, a government entity may exercise the attorney-client privilege in the context of civil and regulatory litigation to preclude compulsory disclosure of confidential, legal-advice communications between government officials and government lawyers.

Several circuits have held, however, that a claim of privilege cannot be advanced by federal government officials when their communications with government lawyers are sought by a federal grand jury. See WCH § 22.9. These courts emphasize two factors that distinguish the government lawyer from the private lawyer. First, the government lawyer's foremost obligation is not to protect a wrongdoer client within the limits of the law, but to ensure compliance with the law. This obligation "to uphold the public trust" carries with it a duty to report to appropriate authorities evidence of criminal conduct on the part of government officials. Indeed, in the federal system, an executive branch attorney has a statutory obligation under 28 U.S.C. § 535(6) to "expeditiously report to the Attorney General" any information received in the attorney's employment "relating to" criminal violations by government employees. The government attorney therefore is viewed as an attorney who owes "ultimate allegiance" not to the executive being advised, but to the public being served by the government, a body "represented by the grand jury." Second, the interests of the government entity as a client are quite different from the interests of a private entity, for the government entity does not face the potential of criminal liability, and it has an obligation to the public which includes "exposing wrongdoing by public officials."

In *In re Grand Jury Investigation of John Doe*, 399 F.3d 527 (2d Cir.2005), the Second Circuit distinguished such precedents in holding that a state governor's office could invoke the attorney-client privilege where a federal grand jury sought to compel disclosure of conversations between the office's chief legal counsel and the governor and various staff members. Although noting the distinguishing characteristics of the particular state's view of the role of its government attorneys, the court "broadly questioned" the rationale advanced in the cases involving attorney-client communications within the federal executive branch. It questioned, in particular, the conclusion that the public interest necessarily lies with the "disclosure and furtherance of the truth-seeking function of the grand jury" rather than encouraging government officials to freely communicate with government attorneys, particularly in the context of internal investigations.

§ 22.15   JOINT DEFENSE AGREEMENTS

A joint defense agreement is designed to extend the coverage of the attorney-client privilege through a "pooling arrangement" in the disclosure of lawyer-client communications. Under such an arrangement, participant clients may share communications to their lawyers (and the lawyers responsive communications) with the lawyers for the other participants, and may communicate directly with those lawyers. Communications that otherwise would not be protected because made in the presence of, or shared with, third parties, are now privileged because each counsel for each participant has become, in effect, a co-counsel for the other participants.

The term "joint defense agreement" comes from the common use of such agreements by codefendants in a criminal prosecution who are represented by separate attorneys and seek to present a common defense. However, the extension of the attorney-client privilege to include multiple clients is not limited to jointly charged criminal defendants. This concept can be used in various situations in which different clients have the requisite "common interest" (also described as a "community of interest"). Thus, many courts prefer to refer to the agreements as "common interest" agreements, or describe the agreements as resting on a "common legal interest privilege." The advantages offered by a common-interest extension of the attorney-client privilege include: (1) development of a common strategy; (2) pooling the information of the different participants as to the content of their common opponent's case; (3) division of case preparation responsibilities among different legal teams, with the results shared by the group; (4) avoiding the conflict of interest challenge that would be raised by an opponent if the different client-participants sought to achieve such advantages by all being represented by a single law firm.

The common interest needed to justify a joint defense agreement must be a legal (rather than business) interest. Where that interest lies in the possibility that each of the client-participants might have a legal liability arising from the same transaction, they also must reasonably anticipate a not-too-distant litigation brought to enforce that liability. A group of participants in questionable activities cannot take advantage of a joint defense agreement simply because they assume that their conduct "might some day result in litigation." *In re Santa Fe International Corp.*, 272 F.3d 705 (5th Cir.2001) ("palpable threat" needed). On the other hand, an anticipation of litigation that would be sufficient to make the work product doctrine applicable (see § 23.03) also is sufficient for a joint defense agreement. Thus, such agreements commonly are used in the context of internal investigations, with the corporation and individual officers participating, often with separate counsel, but sometimes with the same counsel. So too, such agreements are common among persons who are subjects or targets of the same grand jury investigation. If the common interest exists, a formal agreement is not essential. The participants can take advantage of the common interest privilege if they can show that they shared communications with an understanding that they were utilizing that privilege. Of course, they must also show that those communications met the other requirements for protected communications (e.g., aimed at obtaining legal advice and made in a setting designed to ensure confidentiality). See WCH § 22.5.

The joint defense arrangement allows any of the client-participants to invoke the privilege against a third party's attempt to compel disclosure of communications made within the protection of the joint defense agreement. This includes communications made by other clients to the objecting client's attorney and communications between that objecting client's attorney and the attorneys of other participating clients. A client-participant may intervene (even in a grand jury proceeding) to challenge such compelled disclosure, though the subpoena directing production is addressed to another client-participant or another participant's attorney. Such intervention permits one client-participant to preclude a subpoena compliance that would undercut the joint defense agreement, but it does not provide complete protection against adverse consequences when, as in white collar investigations, a participating-client decides to withdraw from the agreement and cooperate with the government.

Courts commonly note that a single participant cannot unilaterally waive the common interest privilege; a true waiver requires the consent of all the participating clients. At the same time, however, a participating client cannot be prohibited from testifying as to his communication to his lawyer or to the lawyers of other participating-clients. Also, while the cooperating witness who was a former client-participant cannot testify as to information learned from the privileged communications of others, the identification of that portion of his testimony derived from such communications is not an easy task. "Assuming that the government has not interfered with the attorney-client relationship deliberately, the defendant bears the burden of alleging specific facts that indicate communication of [common interest] privileged information to the prosecutor and prejudice resulting therefrom." *U.S. v. Aulicino*, 44 F.3d 1102 (2d Cir.1995).

Another possible adverse consequence of a participating-client becoming a government witness is the possible disqualification of the attorneys for the remaining client-participants should those attorneys be placed in a position of having to cross-examine the cooperating witness at a subsequent trial. The argument for disqualification rests on the conflict that arises due to those attorneys having received confidential information from the cooperating witness pursuant to the joint agreement. Joint defense agreements commonly seek to respond to that concern by including in the agreement a waiver provision that permits joint defense participants to cross-examine defecting members with their own confidential communications. See *U.S. v. Stepney*, 246 F.Supp.2d 1069 (N.D.Cal. 2003) (requiring such a waiver as condition for permitting multi-defendants to enter into a joint defense agreement).

CHAPTER 23

WORK PRODUCT PROTECTION

§ 23.01 CHARACTER AND PURPOSE

The work product doctrine grants protection against the compelled production of certain materials developed by an attorney in anticipation of litigation. The doctrine emanates from the Supreme Court's opinion in *Hickman v. Taylor*, 329 U.S. 495 (1947), holding that the "work product" of an attorney, developed in "anticipation of litigation," had a qualified exemption from pretrial discovery by the opposing party in a civil case. That exemption, the Court reasoned, would encourage lawyers to generate valuable trial preparation aids by removing the strong disincentive that would flow from those aids regularly being available to litigation opponents through pretrial discovery. An effective adversary system required "a zone of privacy in which a lawyer can prepare and develop legal theories and strategies, with an eye toward litigation, free from the intrusion of adversaries."

Courts sometimes describe work product protection as a "privilege" and sometimes describe it as an "immunity," although they acknowledge that neither characterization fits precisely. An evidentiary privilege (unless waived or otherwise lost) grants absolute protection against compelled production, while work-product protection is qualified, as it can be overcome (at least as to certain types of work product) by a sufficient showing of need. Also, an evidentiary privilege extends to all types of proceedings, but it is not clear that the work product protection has that range. See *U.S. v. Nobles*, 422 U.S. 225 (1975) (White, J., concurring) (questioning whether work product protection applied as a barrier to the evidentiary use at trial of non-opinion work product). Characterization of work product protection as an "immunity" is usually associated with its origin as an exemption from pretrial discovery (recognized in both civil and criminal cases). However, work product protection extends beyond that limited setting. It is available, for example, as an objection to a subpoena in the contexts most relevant to the investigation of white collar crime—grand jury and regulatory agency investigations. Indeed, the discussion that follows focuses on those work-product issues most likely to arise in white collar investigations.

§ 23.02 BASIC ELEMENTS: *HICKMAN* AND RULE 26(b)(3)

Although *Hickman v. Taylor*, 329 U.S. 495 (1947), and Rule 26(b)(3) of the Federal Rules of Civil Procedure both deal with pretrial discovery, courts look to these sources in determining the basic features of work product protection in other contexts as well. *Hickman* established three basic components of the exemption, and Rule 26(b)(3) repeated and added to those three components.

The *Hickman* Court initially provided a basic definition of work product, using as a point of reference the lawyer's function in the "proper preparation of a client's case" in "anticipation of litigation." Such preparation demands that the lawyer "assemble information, sift what he considers to be the relevant from the irrelevant, prepare his legal theories, and plan his strategy", and that work is "reflected . . . in interviews, statements, memoranda, correspondence, briefs, mental impressions, personal beliefs, and countless other tangible and intangible ways—aptly though roughly termed . . . the 'work product of the lawyer.' "

Second, *Hickman* established that, while "such materials [would not be] open to opposing counsel on mere demand," disclosure could be required where the party "who would invade that privacy [of work product materials] * * * establishes adequate reasons to justify production through a subpoena or court order." As an illustration of an adequate reason, it noted that, "where relevant and non-privileged fact remains hidden in an attorney's file and where production of these facts is essential to preparation of one's case, discovery may properly be had."

Third, *Hickman* identified one class of work product that would rarely, if ever, be subject to disclosure on a need basis. The most critical element of work product protection was ensuring that "an attorney's thoughts * * * [were] his own." Thus, work product that revealed an attorney's mental impressions, conclusions, evaluations, strategies, and theories required the greatest protection, and it would be a "rare situation", if any, in which disclosure of such work product (which came to be known as "opinion work product") would be ordered. This distinction between opinion work product and other work product has been carried forward in subsequent work product jurisprudence, with the non-opinion work product sometimes described as "fact work product".

Federal Rule 26(b)(3) is often described as having "substantially incorporated" the *Hickman* standards in identifying when matter otherwise discoverable under Rule 26 will require a special showing of need as a prerequisite for disclosure. Initially, Rule 26(b)(3) describes the material in this category as "documents and tangible things * * * prepared in anticipation of litigation or for trial by or for another party or by or for that other party's representative (including the other party's attorney, consultant, surety, indemnitor, insurer, or agent)." This provision differs from *Hickman* in two respects. First, it refers only to documents and tangible things, while the rationale of *Hickman* would certainly extend as well to requiring an attorney to testify as to work product matter (e.g., opinions) that were never recorded. Courts have concluded, however, that such work product coverage remains under the authority of the common law protection as set forth in *Hickman*.

Second, while *Hickman* focused on the personal work product of the attorney, Rule 26(b)(3) clearly extends work product protection to materials prepared by others. This provision, as noted in *U.S.*

v. Nobles, 422 U.S. 225 (1975), recognizes that "attorneys often must rely on the assistance of investigators and other agents in the compilation of materials in preparation for trial." Therefore federal courts uniformly accept as within work product protection materials developed by nonattorneys who are acting under the general supervision of the attorney. The language of Rule 26(b)(3) extends beyond that situation and also encompasses the work of nonattorneys assisting the client in anticipation of litigation without attorney supervision. However, a substantial line of cases reason that, where there has been no involvement of an attorney sufficient to suggest the "employment of an attorney's legal expertise," it should be presumed that the materials were not truly developed in anticipation of litigation.

Rule 26(b)(3) also sets forth a standard as to the showing needed to overcome work product protection. Discovery will be available "only upon a showing that the party seeking discovery has substantial need of the materials in the preparation of the party's case and that the party is unable without undue hardship to obtain the substantial equivalent of the materials by other means." This standard has replaced the more general "adequate reasons" standard of *Hickman*, and is applied in the context of investigatory subpoenas as well as pretrial discovery. Rule 26(b)(3) also recognizes, consistent with *Hickman*, that greater protection must be afforded "opinion" work product. It states that, "in ordering discovery * * * when the required showing has been made, the court shall protect against disclosure of the mental impressions, conclusions, opinions, or legal theories of an attorney or other representative of a party concerning the litigation."

Lower courts are divided in their reading of the Rule 26(b)(3) provision on opinion work product. One view is that it provides for absolute protection of opinion work product. The other is that such work product may be discoverable under rare circumstances, as suggested by *Hickman*, but good cause here requires a stronger showing of necessity than the "substantial-need-and-undue-hardship" standard. See *Upjohn v. U.S.*, 449 U.S. 383 (1981) (recognizing this lower courts split, but finding no need to resolve the issue). As a practical matter, in the investigation setting, work product protection is only overridden as to non-opinion work product and that is not easily achieved. Work product protection is available even though the work product is sought from a party that the government does not intend to proceed against, was developed in connection with anticipated litigation not involving the government, and would be produced in a setting (e.g., the grand jury) providing protection against disclosure to likely opponents in the anticipated litigation.

In the grand jury setting, the availability of alternatives often poses a stumbling block to overriding work product protection; the grand jury is not limited to consideration of evidence admissible at trial and therefore "substantial equivalents" include sources (e.g., hearsay testimony) that could not be used at trial. See *In re*

Grand Jury Subpoena Dated Oct. 22, 2001, 282 F.3d 156 (2d Cir.2002). That obstacle is most readily overcome as to the transcribed statements of a witness (an item not likely to contain opinion work product) where the witness is deceased or otherwise unavailable. The need standard also may be met where the actions of the attorney are under investigation, although disclosure in such cases is more likely to be ordered under the crime-fraud exception.

§ 23.03   ANTICIPATION OF LITIGATION

Although *Hickman* had in mind preparation for a lawsuit, the "litigation" that must have been anticipated as a prerequisite for the creation of work product can include any form of adversary process, including an investigatory subpoena from a grand jury or an administrative agency. Where the alleged work product was created before an adversary proceeding was actually initiated (e.g., before a complaint was filed or subpoena received), it often will be less than obvious that the material, though prepared at a lawyer's direction, was prepared "in anticipation of litigation." Courts frequently require either or both of two types of proof in such situations. One type is specific evidence indicating that the purpose behind the creation of the alleged work product was to assist in potential litigation. Relevant factors here include the content of documents (e.g., whether they refer to prospective litigation) and the usual role of counsel (particularly where only in-house counsel was involved). A question frequently asked is whether the same document most likely would have been prepared apart from any concern about potential litigation.

The second type of proof often required relates to the likelihood of litigation. Courts here insist on a showing that, at the time of the creation of the alleged work product, there was an identifiable prospect of the initiation of particular litigation in the near future. Courts requiring such proof note that almost every business activity carries a potential for litigation, and the routine use of counsel's input on that potential should not be sufficient to cloak otherwise routine business documents with work product protection. The potential conflict between this approach and one that focuses on motivational evidence is illustrated by the situation in which the alleged work product was clearly motivated by the prospect of litigation likely to flow from a proposed business transaction, but that litigation was obviously contingent upon a future business decision to enter that transaction (in contrast to *Hickman's* reference to preparation for possible litigation "after a claim has arisen"). Many circuits apply a "because of" test in assessing the "in anticipation" component. Under this test, the contingency is not critical if the document would not have been created but for the possibility of litigation. *U.S. v. Adlman*, 134 F.3d 1194 (1998).

The anticipation-of-litigation requirement has been the subject of particular attention in cases involving internal corporate investigations. Such investigations have an obvious business purpose (to determine if practices are inappropriate and, if so, to correct them) apart from responding to possible litigation. Also, in many industries, certain types of investigations are routine (e.g., accident reviews), and placing them all under the work-product shield is viewed as excessive. Here again, the prevailing "because of" test will overcome the business purpose if it can be shown that the internal investigation was shaped by concern for litigation—i.e., that it had a content that went beyond what would be present in an investigation designed simply for business purposes. This may require establishing many of the same features as were identified in *Upjohn* as bringing the employee-communications there within the attorney-client privilege (see § 22.05). Indeed, *Upjohn* concluded that internal investigation materials at issue there (which went beyond the employee interview reports) were protected work product.

The "because of" standard is not uniformly accepted in dealing with reports that may have dual functions. See WCH § 23.3. The Fifth Circuit has adopted an arguably narrower standard which looks to the "primary purpose" of the creation of a report, so reports commonly created for business purposes are less likely to be protected as work product. The First Circuit has looked to the remoteness of litigation, indicating that a report which serves a business purpose will not be deemed work product unless litigation was clearly anticipated. Under this view, anticipation means "done * * * in advance of litigation," not simply that the report takes into account that the "subject might conceivably be litigated."

Even if an internal investigative report is work product, some aspects of the investigation will not be protected. The work product protects documents prepared under the direction of counsel and the thoughts of counsel, but that does not preclude discovering from the persons interviewed by counsel the very same information that may have been given to counsel. Indeed, quite often, the identity of the persons interviewed must be disclosed. So too, preexisting documents examined as part of the investigation and left in the possession of counsel are not protected as work product, although the work product doctrine ordinarily protects against requiring disclosure of the attorney's selection and compilation of existing documents, as that reveals potential litigation strategy.

§ 23.04   WAIVER

The standards governing waiver of work product protection are in many respects similar to the standards governing waiver of the attorney-client privilege (see § 22.08–11), but they sometimes differ. Those differences are the product of two factors. First, unlike the attorney-client privilege, work product protection is not absolute. Since the protection can be overcome by a sufficient showing of need, waiver doctrine is not so heavily influenced by the concept of confining the disclosure prohibition to its narrowest limits (see § 22.01), resulting in work product protection not being as "easily waived" as the attorney-client privilege. *U.S. v. M.I.T.*, 129 F.3d 681 (1st Cir.1997). Second, the different grounding of the work product protection, tied to the protection of the adversary system rather than the attorney-client relationship, produces differences in the focus of waiver doctrine.

As in the case of the attorney-client privilege, a voluntary disclosure of work product materials to a third party may constitute a waiver. Here, however, a voluntary disclosure constitutes a waiver only where the disclosure is to an adversary or to some other third party under circumstances that substantially increase the possibility that the adversary will gain access to the materials. Thus, there is no need for a special rule (compare § 22.15) to avoid waiver where work product is disclosed to a third party with a common interest (e.g., another investigative target), since such a person also seeks to prevent disclosure to the adversary.

While it is true that a service provider may become an adversary if a dispute over performance later arises, that does not make its present position adversarial. Similarly, if that service provider is ordinarily subject to a duty of confidentiality, the disclosure does not pose a sufficient risk of disclosure to an adversary simply because a future litigant may force disclosure from that service provider. Hence, most cases find that disclosure to an independent auditor is not a waiver. A federal audit agency, on the other hand, serves a different function as it represents the government, a potential adversary. Here, the intentional disclosure does constitute a waiver. See WCH § 23.5.

Where work-product material is intentionally disclosed to an adversary, the consequences tend to be similar to the waiver of the attorney-client privilege by intentional waiver. Where only a portion of the work product has been disclosed, Federal Evidence Rule 502(a) applies the same "subject matter" standard for both work product and attorney-client waivers. See § 22.09. However, where fairness considerations lead to making available other work product involving the same subject matter, those considerations are unlikely to encompass opinion work product unless opinion work product was intentionally disclosed.

The possibility of selective waiver is the same as for attorney-client privilege, available, if at all, through the court order issued under Rule 502(d). See § 22.09. Federal Rule 502(b) governs inadvertent waivers, under a standard that applies to both work product and attorney-client privilege. See § 22.10.

As in the case of the attorney-client privilege, an implicit waiver will be recognized where the client seeks to make affirmative testimonial use of work product. See § 22.11. Thus, *U.S. v. Nobles*, 422 U.S. 225 (1975), held that where a party's investigator testified as to his recollection of work party interviews, the opposing party was entitled to the work product documents recounting that interview.

§ 23.05   CRIME-FRAUD

For largely the same reasons as apply to the lawyer-client privilege (see § 22.12), a crime-fraud exception also applies to work product protection. It applies to the client's use of the lawyer client relationship for the same wrongful purposes, and requires a similar relationship of the material at issue to that wrongful purpose (i.e., the work product material must relate to that aspect of the lawyer's performance that would further the client's wrongful purpose). Standards of proof also follow the standards developed in applying the crime-fraud exception to attorney-client material.

One major distinction separates the work-product exception for crime-fraud from the lawyer-client exception. Since the work product protection serves the interest of the attorney apart from the client, where the client has been involved in the ongoing or future crime or fraud, the "innocent attorney" still has a separate interest in not revealing his mental processes. Accordingly, client fraud eliminates the exemption of non-opinion work product, but the innocent attorney remains free to insist upon protection of opinion work product. If the attorney is complicit in the client's illicit purpose, then the attorney's opinion work product can also be obtained. See WCH § 23.6.

PART 4
PUNISHMENT

CHAPTER 24

SANCTIONS

§ 24.01   INTRODUCTION

An indeterminate sentencing system was the norm in the United States federal criminal system for nearly the past one hundred years. Although a judge had the outside restrictions of the maximum sentence specified in the statutory offense, coupled with basic Eighth Amendment prohibitions against cruel and unusual punishment, an enormous latitude was afforded to a judge in deciding a convicted defendant's term of imprisonment, fine, or imposition of probation. Discretion was also given to parole officers in making their parole determinations.

This indeterminate sentencing system was premised upon a goal of rehabilitation. By giving broad discretion to the court and parole officer, they were able "to make their respective sentencing and release decisions upon their own assessments of the offender's amenability to rehabilitation." *Mistretta v. U.S.*, 488 U.S. 361 (1989).

This "outmoded rehabilitation model" was designated a failure by a 1983 Senate Report. The report noted two significant consequences of the indeterminate sentencing model: judicial disparity in sentences and uncertainty in time to be served by a defendant. *Mistretta v. U.S.* To correct these perceived problems, Congress passed the Sentencing Reform Act of 1984.

This Act created a Sentencing Commission charged with the duty of establishing sentencing guidelines. The guidelines provide sentence ranges as computed via a grid system that considers the defendant's offense level in conjunction with the offender's criminal history. Initially the guidelines were seen as mandatory, although some judicial discretion remained. As a result of several rulings by the Supreme Court, the judiciary now serves an increased role in the sentencing process. Significant focus is now placed on sentencing factors that include consideration of the guidelines. 18 U.S.C. § 3553(a).

On November 1, 1991, the United States Sentencing Commission adopted guidelines for sentencing organizations. These guidelines provide fines, probation, and in some instances restitution. The sentencing guidelines for organizations permit reductions for self-reporting and for effective programs to prevent and detect violations.

Both individual and corporate sentences are often a result of a plea agreement. Typically following a conviction or entry of a plea, a presentence investigation report is prepared by the probation office. Both the government and defense may also file sentencing memorandums. WCH § 24.6.

In addition to sentences pursuant to federal sentencing guidelines, white collar criminals often are subject to collateral proceedings in the civil arena. One finds parallel proceedings in areas such a tax and securities. See chap. 18. Some white collar offenders have faced a loss of license or exclusion from participating in government contracts. For example, lawyers have found their convictions used as a basis for suspension and disbarment from the legal profession. Convicted defense contractors have in some cases been precluded from obtaining future government contracts.

§ 24.02 FEDERAL SENTENCING COMMISSION

The Sentencing Reform Act of 1984 creates a United States Sentencing Commission. This Commission "is established as an independent commission in the judicial branch of the United States. . . ." (28 U.S.C. § 991(a)). The Commission is composed of seven voting members appointed by the President, "with the advice and consent of the Senate," and two nonvoting ex-officio members. The Attorney General, or a designee of the Attorney General, is a non-voting ex-officio member of the Commission. Not more than three of the members of the Commission can be federal judges, and not more than four members of the Commission may be from the same political party. (28 U.S.C. § 991). The Sentencing Reform Act of 1984 directs the Commission to devise sentencing guidelines for the imposition of criminal sentences in federal court. (28 U.S.C. § 994). The Act also abolishes the Parole Commission.

Seven factors are set forth as considerations in imposing a sentence. These factors include, "the nature and circumstances of the offense and the history and characteristics of the defendant, . . . any

pertinent policy statement issued by the Sentencing
Commission . . ., and the need to avoid unwarranted
sentence disparities among defendants with similar
records who have been found guilty of similar
conduct." (18 U.S.C. § 3553(a)). A court is instructed
that a sentence shall be sufficient "but not greater
than necessary to comply with the [following]
purposes, . . . the need for the sentence imposed (A)
to reflect the seriousness of the offense, to promote
respect for the law, and to provide just punishment
for the offense; (B) to afford adequate deterrence to
criminal conduct; (C) to protect the public from
further crimes of the defendant; and (D) to provide
the defendant with needed educational or vocational
training, medical care, or other correctional
treatment in the most effective manner."

Congressional legislation instructs the
Commission to "insure that the guidelines reflect
the inappropriateness of imposing a sentence to a
term of imprisonment for the purpose of
rehabilitating the defendant . . ." (28 U.S.C.
§ 994(k)). The Commission is also instructed that
the guidelines should reflect sentences other than
imprisonment when the defendant is a first offender
engaging in non-violent and non-serious offenses.
Consideration for imprisonment should, however, be
given when the offender engages in a crime of
violence that results in serious bodily injury. (28
U.S.C. § 994(j)).

The Sentencing Commission is an ongoing body
charged with the duty to periodically "review and
revise" the guidelines. (28 U.S.C. § 994(o)). In some

cases Congress will direct the activity of the Commission. For example, in the Sarbanes Oxley Act of 2004, Congress requested the Commission to "review and amend" the sentencing laws related to fraud and obstruction of justice to reflect the new penalties added by the Act. Most recently, the Sentencing Commission is examining modifications to the fraud guideline—2B1.1.

The Commission is authorized to promulgate and submit to Congress amendments to the guidelines. "Such an amendment or modification shall be accompanied by a statement of the reasons therefor and shall take effect on a date specified by the Commission, which shall be no earlier than 180 days after being so submitted and no later than the first day of November of the calendar year in which the amendment or modification is submitted, except to the extent that the effective date is revised or the amendment is otherwise modified or disapproved by Act of Congress." (28 U.S.C. § 994(p)). Sentences are calculated by reference to the guidelines in effect at the time of the sentencing, but where the guidelines applicable at the time of the commission of the crime were more lenient, defendant may challenge application of the current guidelines on ex post facto grounds.

§ 24.03 FEDERAL SENTENCING GUIDELINES

The Sentencing Guidelines commence with a policy statement that includes an explanation of the methodology used in formulating the guidelines.

This policy statement notes the extensive study and use of existing empirical data in formulating the guidelines. It states that the guidelines are intended "toward the achievement of a more honest, uniform, equitable, proportional, and therefore effective sentencing system." (Chapter One, Part A, Guidelines).

The policy statement preceding the actual guidelines explains the Commission's struggle with deciding if a real offense or charge offense sentencing system was more appropriate. A real offense system looks to the actual conduct engaged in by the defendant, without regard to the charges brought. A charge offense system examines the conduct that forms the elements of the offense upon which the defendant is convicted. The Commission's guidelines compromises these two positions by commencing with a charge offense system, in initially determining the base level offense, and modifying this result to consider some of the actual conduct. For example, the defendant's role in the offense and quantitative amounts involved in the offense are used to adjust the base level.

Section 1B1.1 of the guidelines provides a general overview of how to use the guidelines. It offers a step-by-step approach to determining a defendant's sentence. Section 1B1.3 of the guidelines describes the relevant conduct that a court may consider in determining the applicable guideline range. This includes "all acts and omissions . . . caused by the defendant."

In computing a defendant's sentence under the sentencing guidelines, a grid is used. On the horizontal axis there are 43 offense levels. On the vertical axis there are six criminal history categories.

Computation of a sentence can be commenced by determination of the offense level. One starts by taking the conviction and matching it to the base offense levels as specified in the guidelines. For example, the crime of mail fraud (18 U.S.C. § 1341) is located in 2B1.1 of the guidelines and carries a base offense level of six or seven "if (A) the defendant was convicted of an offense referenced to this guideline; and (B) that offense of conviction has a statutory maximum term of imprisonment of 20 years or more." If the mail fraud pertains to a public official and involves the deprivation of the intangible right to honest services (18 U.S.C. § 1346) then the guideline is located in 2C1.1 and commences with a base level of fourteen if the defendant is a public official, otherwise it is a twelve. Courts use not only the conduct proven at trial or through a guilty plea, but the judge may also consider relevant conduct in determining the guideline sentence. WCH § 24.4(A)(2).

Within each guideline are adjustment factors that reflect the "real offense" as measured by all "relevant conduct." For example, in the fraud guideline found in 2B1.1, adjustments are made for the amount of loss involved. Thus, to the base level of six or seven, there is an increase in level by adding twelve when the loss is more than two hundred thousand dollars. With some exceptions, "loss is the greater of actual loss or intended loss," with definitions of these items provided in the Commentary. Courts have criticized the focus on loss and the fraud guidelines "fetish with abstract arithmetic." *U.S. v. Adelson*, 441 F.Supp.2d 506 (S.D.N.Y.2006).

Chapter three of the guidelines provides general adjustment factors used in determining the offense level (also with reference to all relevant conduct). The first three factors considered are victim-related adjustments, role in the offense adjustments, and obstructive conduct. For example, where the "defendant knew or should have known that a victim of the offense was a vulnerable victim," the guidelines authorize an increase by two levels. (3A1.1).

An aggravating role in the offense, as specified in the guidelines, can increase the offense level. (3B1.1). Likewise, a mitigating role serves to decrease the offense level. (3B1.2). "If the defendant abused a position of public or private trust, or used a special skill, in a manner that significantly facilitated the commission or concealment of the offense," there is an increase by two levels. (3B1.3). White collar cases can involve the abuse of trust when the defendant has professional or managerial discretion. An increase by two levels is also provided when a defendant "willfully obstructed or impeded, or attempted to obstruct or impede, the administration of justice during the course of the investigation, prosecution, or sentencing of the instant offense of conviction," (3C1.1) or "recklessly created a substantial risk of death or serious bodily injury to another person in the course of fleeing from a law enforcement officer." (3C1.2).

The Supreme Court held that it is constitutional for a court to enhance a defendant's sentence "if the court finds the defendant committed perjury at trial." This obstruction of justice enhancement, pursuant to 3C1.1, was found not to infringe on the defendant's constitutional right to testify. *U.S. v. Dunnigan*, 507 U.S. 87 (1993).

Also contained in chapter three of the guidelines is the method for applying multiple counts in factoring the base level. Base levels applicable to each count are not added together. Rather, the most serious count is examined and relevant-conduct increases in this level of offense are provided to reflect the increase in harm. Closely related counts are grouped together. (3D1.1). Thus, when a prosecutor uses separate charges for "conduct involving substantially the same harm," the counts will be grouped together for purposes of determining the base level. (3D1.2).

A final adjustment provided in chapter three of the guidelines offers a defendant a reduction for an acceptance of responsibility. "If the defendant clearly demonstrates acceptance of responsibility for his offense," the guidelines authorize a reduction by two levels. Additionally a defendant is permitted a one level decrease when the offense level is sixteen or greater prior to the initial two level decrease for acceptance of responsibility and the government files a motion stating that the "defendant has assisted authorities in the investigation or prosecution of his own misconduct by timely notifying authorities of his intention to enter a plea of guilty, thereby permitting the government to avoid preparing for trial and permitting the court to allocate its resources efficiently." (3E1.1).

The number ascertained after taking the initial base level and factoring in the applicable adjustments reflects the number on the vertical axis. It is next necessary to determine the numerical value of the defendant's criminal history. Chapter four of the guidelines pertains to a defendant's criminal history with points added in circumstances like when a defendant has a prior sentence of imprisonment. The greater the criminal history, the greater the points attributed to the defendant.

The point on the grid at which the offense level of a defendant meets the defendant's criminal history level is the sentencing range for that defendant. It defines the period of time of a defendant's sentence. For example, an offense level of 19 with a criminal history category II results in a sentencing range of 33 to 41 months.

Below a certain point on the grid, a court has the option for alternatives to prison. Chapter five of the sentencing guidelines specifies the rules for probation, supervised release, restitution, fines, assessments, forfeitures, and costs of prosecution. Sentencing options, such as community confinement or home detention, are also described in this chapter.

Once the grid point total is calculated, a departure—i.e., a sentence above or below that prescribed in the grid—can be considered. Noteworthy in subsection K is the permissibility of departure upon a motion of the government stating that defendant provided substantial assistance to authorities. (5K1.1). Upon the filing of a 5K1.1 motion by the prosecutor the court can reduce a sentence below a statutory minimum. A sentencing judge is not bound, however, to accept a government motion for departure premised upon substantial assistance. *U.S. v. Mariano*, 983 F.2d 1150 (1st Cir.1993).

The Supreme Court considered a defendant's right to challenge the failure of a prosecutor to file a 5K1.1 motion requesting the district court reduce a sentence for substantial assistance to the government. The Court viewed the discretion normally accorded to prosecutors in decisions as applicable to the decision of a prosecutor on whether to file a substantial assistance motion under 5K1.1. Thus, claims that the defendant provided substantial assistance which the government refused to recognize, or generalized claims of the prosecutor acting on improper motive in refusing to file a 5K1.1 motion, will not merit a remedy for the defendant. The Court did state, however, that "a defendant would be entitled to relief if a prosecutor refused to file a substantial-assistance motion say, because of the defendant's race or religion." *Wade v. U.S.*, 504 U.S. 181 (1992).

In *U.S. v. Alegria*, 192 F.3d 179 (1st Cir.1999), the First Circuit reviewed whether prosecutors violated a plea agreement when defendant cooperated and was not provided with a 5K1.1 substantial assistance motion, a motion that would have allowed for a downward departure below the guidelines. Although the court held that "the government must perform in good faith the discretionary obligations that it affirmatively undertakes in a plea agreement," no showing of bad faith was demonstrated in this case. In *Alegria*, the court stated that "[t]he government's good faith is only a burden of production, not of persuasion. As long as the government satisfies this modest burden, the trial court need go no further unless the defendant makes a substantial threshold showing that the government acted in bad faith."

Absent a government motion, departure from the guidelines is also permissible when "there exists an aggravating or mitigating circumstance of a kind, or to a degree, not adequately taken into consideration by the Sentencing Commission in formulating the guidelines that should result in a sentence different from that described." (18 U.S.C. § 3553(b)). Certain factors are considered encouraged while others are considered discouraged bases for departure. (5K2.0 et. seq.) In deciding whether to depart from the guidelines, courts need to consider the following four questions: "(1) What features of this case, potentially, take it outside the Guidelines' 'heartland' and make of it a special, or unusual, case? (2) Has the Commission forbidden departures based on those features? (3) If not, has the

Commission encouraged departures based on those features? (4) If not, has the Commission discouraged departures based on those features?" *Koon v. U.S.*, 518 U.S. 81 (1996) (*citing U.S. v. Rivera*, 994 F.2d 942 (1st Cir.1993)).

Forbidden factors (e.g., race or socio-economic status) cannot be used as a basis for departure under the guidelines. Encouraged factors (e.g., diminished capacity) can be used as a basis for departure if the applicable guidelines have not taken the factor into account. If the factor is a discouraged factor (e.g., family responsibilities), or an encouraged factor taken into account by a guideline, the court should depart only when "the factor is present to an exceptional degree or in some other way makes the case different from the ordinary case where the factor is present." Factors that are omitted from the guidelines can be a basis for departure if the court determines that the case is outside the "heartland" "after considering the 'structure and theory of both relevant individual guidelines and the Guidelines taken as a whole.'" *Koon v. U.S.*, 518 U.S. 81 (1996).

Section 5G1.1 provides that if Congress has specified a statutory minimum or maximum sentence for the applicable crime, then that minimum or maximum sentence authorized by Congress shall be used. When a defendant provides substantial assistance, the government has the option of filing a motion pursuant to 18 U.S.C. § 3553(e) requesting the court depart below the statutory minimum. The Supreme Court has held that a government motion pursuant to 5K1.1 does not authorize a court to depart below the statutory minimum absent a specific government request pursuant to 18 U.S.C. § 3553(e). *Melendez v. U.S.*, 518 U.S. 120 (1996).

In addition to providing the methodology for determining a sentence, the guidelines also provide procedural structure to the plea agreement and sentencing process. For example, the commentary to the guidelines provides that "[t]he Commission believes that use of a preponderance of the evidence standard is appropriate to meet due process requirements and policy concerns in resolving disputes regarding application of the guidelines to the facts of a case." (6A1.3, Commentary).

§ 24.04 CONSTITUTIONALITY OF THE GUIDELINES

The federal sentencing guidelines were initially met with many cases contesting their constitutionality. Lower courts resolving these issues ruled inconsistently with some finding the guidelines valid and others holding them unconstitutional. In 1988 the Supreme Court accepted on certiorari the case of *Mistretta v. U.S.*, to consider the constitutionality of the guidelines as promulgated by the United States Sentencing Commission. In granting the petition for certiorari the Court noted the " 'imperative public importance' of the issue" and the "disarray among the Federal District Courts."

The *Mistretta* case, in upholding the guidelines, resolved two key constitutional attacks on the guidelines. The first argument questioned the propriety of delegating the promulgation of guidelines for every federal offense to an independent sentencing commission. The second argument questioned the constitutionality of the Act in light of the separation of powers doctrine.

Justice Blackmun, writing the opinion for the majority, found Congress' delegation of authority to the Sentencing Commission to be "sufficiently specific and detailed to meet constitutional requirements." Although the Court admitted that the Commission was given significant discretion, it noted that "[d]eveloping proportionate penalties for hundreds of different crimes by a virtually limitless array of offenders is precisely the sort of intricate, labor-intensive task for which delegation to an expert body is especially appropriate."

The Court also rejected Mistretta's claim of a violation of separation of powers. Examined by the Court was the effect of the Sentencing Commission being placed in the judicial branch, having federal judges serve on the Commission, and the giving of the power to appoint and remove members of the Commission to the President. The Court found the Act's placement of the Commission within the judicial branch justified "since substantive judgment in the field of sentencing has been and remains appropriate to the Judicial Branch, and the methodology of rulemaking has been and remains appropriate to that Branch."

The Court also validated the Act's placement of federal judges on the Sentencing Commission. The Court held that the judges were not serving pursuant to their authority as Article III judges, but rather in an administrative capacity resulting from their Presidential appointment. The Court stated that, "the Constitution, at least as a *per se* matter, does not forbid judges from wearing two hats; it merely forbids them from wearing both hats at the same time." The mixed nature of the Commission did not violate the Constitution, since the Sentencing "Commission is not a court and exercises no judicial power . . . the Act does not vest Article III power in nonjudges or require Article III judges to share their power with nonjudges."

Mistretta also claimed that by having the President appoint and remove the members of the Commission, the Judicial Branch was being prevented from performing its constitutional functions. The Court found that the appointment power of the President would not corrupt the integrity of the Judiciary. Likewise the removal power, limited to good cause, would pose no risk of preventing "the Judicial branch from performing its constitutionally assigned function of fairly adjudicating cases and controversies."

§ 24.05 ROLE OF THE GUIDELINES

Prior to *U.S. v. Booker*, 543 U.S. 220 (2005), the federal sentencing guidelines operated as mandatory guidelines. Although courts had some discretion, such as determining which guidelines apply or computing the amount of loss caused by the defendant, the sentence received was usually a function of a guideline computation.

Booker changed this landscape finding a Sixth Amendment violation in the mandatory nature of the guidelines. Because the Sentencing Reform Act authorized fact finding to be done by judges as opposed to juries, the Court found it violated the Sixth Amendment right to a trial by jury. *Booker* "invalidated both the statutory provision, 18 U.S.C. § 3553(b)(1), which made the Sentencing Guidelines mandatory, and § 3742(e) which directed appellate courts to apply a de novo standard of review to departures from the Guidelines." *Gall v. U.S.*, 552 U.S. 38 (2007). Although the *Booker* decision rendered the guidelines advisory, courts were uncertain as to how much deference should be accorded to them.

Several later decisions clarified this issue, namely *Rita v. U.S.*, 551 U.S. 338 (2007), *Gall v. U.S.*, 552 U.S. 38 (2007), and *Kimbrough v. U.S.*, 552 U.S. 85 (2007). Although an appellate court can apply a presumption of reasonableness in the guidelines, an outside the guideline range should not be considered unreasonable. The Court in *Gall* rejected "an appellate rule that requires 'extraordinary' circumstances to justify a sentence outside the Guidelines range."

In contrast, a district court sentencing the defendant, cannot apply a presumption of reasonableness to the guidelines. The guidelines "should be the starting point and the initial benchmark." The district court should then give the parties the "opportunity to argue for whatever sentence they deem appropriate." The Court in *Gall* stated that the district court should then "consider all of the § 3553(a) factors to determine whether they support the sentence requested by the party." But in doing this, the Court made clear that the guidelines should not be given a presumption of being reasonable. There needs to be an "individualized assessment based on the facts presented." The district court needs to "adequately explain the chosen sentence to allow for meaningful appellate review and to promote the perception of fair sentencing."

Courts in white collar cases may issue a sentence closely aligned to the sentencing guidelines or far removed. Additionally, the sentence may be stiffer than white collar sentences seen in pre-guidelines days. For example, the former CEO of WorldCom received a sentence of 25 years, an unlikely sentence for a white collar offender prior to the enactment of the federal sentencing guidelines. In contrast, two defendants who faced guideline sentences of 360 months to life in a securities fraud prosecution, were sentenced to 60 months by a judge who stated "if not for the wisdom of the Supreme Court in recognizing the need to free district courts from the shackles of the mandatory guidelines regime, I would have been confronted with the prospect of having to impose what I believe any rational jurist would consider to be a draconian sentence." *U.S. v. Parris*, 573 F.Supp.2d 744 (E.D.N.Y. 2008).

In addition to prison sentences, there can also be sentences of probation or supervised release. The defendant may be placed in community corrections facility, halfway house or placed in home detention. There may also be restrictions on the use of assets as a part of the sentence. WCH § 24.2.

§ 24.06   CRIMINAL AND CIVIL FINES AND RESTITUTION

Statutory provisions set forth the factors a court should consider in imposing a fine. (18 U.S.C. § 3572) For example, a court should consider "the defendant's income, earning capacity, and financial resources," as well as the burden of the fine on the defendant and others associated with the defendant. 18 U.S.C. § 3571 specifies the maximum fines that can be imposed against individuals and organizations. For example, in determining an individual's maximum fine permitted upon conviction of a felony, one looks to not more than the greatest of the "amount specified in the law setting forth the offense," a fine based on gain or loss as computed under the statute, or an amount not to exceed $250,000.

Civil proceedings brought by the government, after completion of a criminal action, can raise issues of collateral estoppel when the issue being litigated in the civil proceeding has previously been litigated in the criminal action. Parallel civil and criminal actions by the government also raise questions of double jeopardy. In *U.S. v. Halper*, 490 U.S. 435 (1989), the Supreme Court accepted for review a case involving a civil action brought by the government that was premised upon the same conduct upon which the defendant had been criminally punished. The Supreme Court in reviewing this matter held that, "under the Double Jeopardy Clause a defendant who already has been punished in a criminal prosecution may not be subjected to an additional civil sanction to the extent that the second sanction may not fairly be characterized as remedial, but only as a deterrent or retribution." The Court in *Halper* remanded the case to permit the government the opportunity to show that "the District Court's assessment of its injuries was erroneous."

In *U.S. v. Ursery*, 518 U.S. 267 (1996), the Supreme Court held that civil forfeitures do not constitute "punishment" for purposes of the Double Jeopardy Clause without regard to whether the forfeiture is disproportionate to the harm suffered by the government. Civil forfeitures, the Court noted, serve a unique nonpunitive function of disgorgement. The fact that they may be limited by the Eighth Amendment prohibition against excessiveness does not mean that they also are so "punitive" as to constitute "punishment."

In 1997, the Supreme Court went even further and completely disavowed *Halper*. In *Hudson v. U.S.*, 522 U.S. 93 (1997) the "Government administratively imposed monetary penalties and occupational debarment on petitioners for violation of federal banking statutes, and later criminally indicted them, for essentially the same conduct" The

Court stated "that the Double Jeopardy Clause of the Fifth Amendment is not a bar to the later criminal prosecution because the administrative proceedings were civil, not criminal."

A court may also order restitution. The Victim and Witness Protection Act and the Mandatory Victims Restitution Act provide the basis and procedure for restitution orders. WCH § 24,2(D)(2).

§ 24.07 SENTENCING GUIDELINES FOR ORGANIZATIONS

Federal sentencing guidelines for organizations became effective on November 1, 1991. These guidelines provide the rules applicable for computing fines against organizations. These rules are applicable only to organizations. Thus, individual agents of an organization that are convicted for criminal conduct, are sentenced under the general federal sentencing guidelines for individuals.

An overview of the guidelines is provided in Part A. (8A1.2). Part B of the guidelines provides the sentencing requirements and options relating to restitution, remedial orders, and community service. For example, "community service may be ordered as a condition of probation where such community service is reasonably designed to repair the harm caused by the offense." (8B1.3).

Part C describes the considerations for determining a fine. When the organization operated for primarily a criminal purpose, or primarily by criminal means, the guidelines state that the fine should be sufficient to divest the organization of all its net assets. (8C1.1). Organizations that are not criminal in nature, that have committed offenses listed in the organization guidelines are subject to fines as computed under these rules. Inability to pay, however, can eliminate or reduce a fine. (8C2.2).

In computing the fine, one commences by taking the offense level as listed in the guidelines for individuals and adjusting that figure as designated in the applicable guideline for individuals (see § 24.03). Multiple counts use the combined offense level as designated in the individual guidelines. (8C2.3). The base fine is then calculated by taking the amount corresponding to the offense level on a table located in the organization guidelines. (8C2.4(d)). If, however, the pecuniary gain to the organization from the offense, or the "pecuniary loss from the offense caused by the organization, to the extent the loss was caused intentionally, knowingly, or recklessly," is greater, that figure becomes the base fine. If the calculation of the pecuniary gain or loss will unduly complicate the process, then that amount should not be used in computing the fine. Further, if special instructions exist in the individual guidelines that reflect consideration of organizational fines, that special instruction should be applied.

The organization's culpability score is next determined by starting with a level of five points and adding or subtracting points based upon actions that reflect upon the organization's culpability. The level of authority and size of the organization can increase the culpability score. Points are also added when the organization is involved in or tolerates criminal activity, has a history of criminal activity, violates a judicial order, or obstructs justice. In contrast, points are subtracted when the organization has an effective program to prevent and detect violations or self-reports, cooperates, or accepts responsibility for the criminal conduct. (8C2.5). These latter guidelines provide increased incentives for an organization to plead guilty and cooperate with the government. Organizations often conduct internal investigations to ascertain problems within the entity and then reveal this information to the government to minimize the entity's culpability. See § 2.04.

Guideline 8B2.1 discusses what constitutes an effective compliance and ethics program. An effective compliance and ethics program allows for a reduction in points in determining the culpability score. Civil corporate law provides added incentives to the Board of Directors of a corporation for making sure that an effective program is in place. *In re Caremark International Inc. Derivative Litigation*, 698 A.2d 959 (Ct. Chancery Del. 1996).

The ascertained culpability score corresponds to minimum and maximum multipliers found in a table in the organization guidelines. (8C2.6). To determine the applicable fine range, one multiplies the previously determined base fine by the minimum multiplier and the base fine by the maximum multiplier. This provides the minimum and maximum guideline range. The judge imposing the fine then has eleven factors to consider in determining where within the range the actual assessed fine should be. These factors include, "the need for the sentence to reflect the seriousness of the offense, promote respect for the law, provide just punishment, afford adequate deterrence, and protect the public from further crimes of the organization." The judge should consider the vulnerability of the victim, as well as the collateral civil consequences of a conviction. In addition to the eleven specified factors for consideration by the court in determining the fine within the range, the guidelines also permit the court to "consider the relative importance of any factor used to determine the range." (8C2.8).

The organization guidelines contain a disgorgement provision that instructs a court to add to the fine "any gain to the organization from the offense that has not and will not be paid as restitution or by way of other remedial measures." (8C2.9). As with the individual guidelines, the organization guidelines also provide for upward and downward departures. For example, upward departures may be warranted when there is a death or bodily injury, or foreseeable risk of death or bodily injury. (8C4.2). Other examples of instances that may warrant an upward departure are threats to the market, national security, or environment. Similarly, upward departures can be given if the mandatory program to prevent and detect violations of law was implemented in response to a court order. (8C4.10). Upon a motion of the government alleging substantial assistance to authorities, a court may depart downwards from the guidelines. (8C4.1).

The guidelines set forth situations in which probation is to be given (8D1.1), and the applicable terms (8D1.2), and conditions of the probation (8D1.3). Recommended conditions of probation are also specified (8D1.4). The guidelines also account for special assessments statutorily placed on organizations (8E1.1), forfeiture (8E1.2), and assessment of costs (8E1.3).

§ 24.08   LICENSES AND PROGRAM EXCLUSION

Professional licenses are usually issued by individual states. These jurisdictions often adopt rules for the acquisition and maintenance of the license. For example, in most states a lawyer must pass a bar examination and character and fitness review for admission into the bar. When the attorney later violates the provisions set forth in the ethical mandates of that state, the attorney is subjected to bar disciplinary action. This discipline can include punishments such as a reprimand, suspension, or disbarment.

Conviction of a felony offense usually has severe implications on a professional license. The American Bar Association Model Rules of Professional Conduct, explicitly state that it is professional misconduct for a lawyer to "commit a criminal act that reflects adversely on the lawyer's honesty, trustworthiness or fitness as a lawyer in other respects." (Rule 8.4 (b)). In the Comments to this Rule, it is noted that illegal conduct "such as offenses involving fraud and the offense of willful failure to file an income tax return," reflect adversely on one's fitness to practice law. Thus, white collar offenses committed by attorneys may subject the attorney to disciplinary action by the bar, court, or the state agency charged with the enforcement of the disciplinary rules.

Discipline for felony convictions is not limited to attorneys. Many states provide for disciplinary action in other professional codes. For example, in Georgia a doctor "convicted of a felony in state or any other state, . . . ," may be subject to discipline. According to the Georgia statute, conviction is not limited to a finding by a judge or jury of guilt or the defendant entering a guilty plea. Rather, it includes a plea of nolo contendere in a criminal proceeding. Ga.Code Ann. § 43–34–37 (1992).

Those practicing before the Securities Exchange Commission (SEC) have been disciplined, including temporary or permanent suspension to practice before the Commission, when they have violated a provision of federal securities law. In *Touche Ross & Co. v. Securities and Exchange Commission*, 609 F.2d 570 (2d Cir.1979), the right of the SEC to conduct administrative proceedings against an accounting firm, for the purpose of determining whether the accountants should be censured or suspended from practicing before the Commission, was questioned. The administrative proceeding in the *Touche Ross* case was commenced to determine whether the accountants had "engaged in unethical, unprofessional or fraudulent conduct in their audits" of the financial statements of two companies. The accounting firm brought this action to obtain an injunction stopping the SEC's administrative proceeding against them. The District Court granted the SEC's motion dismissing the complaint.

In affirming the right of the SEC to proceed administratively, the Second Circuit in *Touche Ross* noted that rules permitting these actions had existed for over forty years and had been the basis for disciplinary actions against professionals such as accountants and attorneys. The court noted that "Rule 2(e) thus represents an attempt by the SEC essentially to protect the integrity of its processes. If incompetent or unethical accountants should be permitted to certify financial statements, the reliability of the disclosure process would be impaired." The court found that the accounting firm would be required to exhaust its administrative remedies before the Commission prior to bringing a civil action in court.

In addition to discipline relating to a license, or discipline with respect to a right to practice before an agency, criminality can exclude an individual or company from continuing to participate in a government program. This has had significant ramifications for defense contractors convicted for fraud. Government regulation "specifically permits an agency to debar a contractor if it has been convicted of, or is subject to a civil judgment for, *inter alia*, fraud in connection with obtaining a government contract, a violation of the antitrust laws, or bribery, or for '[a]ny other cause of so serious or compelling a nature that it affects the present responsibility of a Government contractor . . .'" *Robinson v. Cheney*, 876 F.2d 152 (D.C.Cir.1989).

Health care providers may suffer collateral consequences when they engage in criminal acts. Specifically there is the possibility of exclusion from Medicare and Medicaid programs. "In 1977, Congress enacted the Medicare-Medicaid Antifraud and Abuse Amendments requiring the Secretary to suspend any physician or 'other individual practitioner' convicted 'of a criminal offense related to such physician's or practitioner's involvement' in the Medicare and Medicaid programs." *Greene v. Sullivan*, 731 F.Supp. 835 (E.D.Tenn.1990).

An attorney representing an individual charged with a white collar offense needs to be particularly aware of the collateral consequences to the individual. Considerations such as civil suits, license suspensions, program debarment, and benefit exclusions, may impact the course taken in the litigation.

INDEX

References are to Pages

EXTORTION
See Hobbs Act

EXTRATERRITORIALITY

FALSE CLAIMS STATUTE
See False statements

FALSE DECLARATIONS

FALSE STATEMENTS

GRATUITIES
See Bribery

HAZARDOUS WASTES
See Environmental Cases

HEALTH CARE FRAUD
See Mail Fraud

HIGH MANAGERIAL AGENT
See Corporate Criminal Liability

HOBBS ACT

OATHS
See False Declarations; Perjury

OBSTRUCTION OF JUSTICE
Generally, 351–373
Assault on process server, 109
Corruptly, 116–119
Due Administration of Justice, 121–123
Elements, 115–116, 121
Endeavors, 119–120
History, 109–116
Intent, 116–119
Materiality, 124
Nexis, 124–125
Penalties, 114
Pending proceeding, 121–123
Sarbanes-Oxley, 112–114
Victim and Witness Protection Act, 110–112, 115, 125–126

OCCUPATIONAL HEALTH & SAFETY ADMINISTRATION (OSHA)
See Corporate criminal liability

ORGANIZATIONS
See Corporate Criminal Liability; Sentencing

OUTRAGEOUS GOVERNMENT CONDUCT
See Entrapment

PARALLEL PROCEEDINGS
Generally, 351–373
Collateral estoppel, 371–373
Delaying parallel proceedings, 356–359
Grand jury matter, 363–365
Overview, 351–353
Particularized need, 368–371
Preliminary to, 366–368
Prosecution discovery, 353–355
Self-Incrimination, 360–363

PAROLE
See Sentencing